CURRENTS
OF THOUGHT IN
FRENCH LITERATURE

Essays in Memory of
G. T. Clapton

D1355652

BARNES & NOBLE

176004

First Published in the United States
in 1966
by Bains & Noble, Inc.
New York, N.Y.

CONTENTS

G. T. Clapton (1898–1964)

G. T. CLAPTON (1898–1964)

G. T. Clapton entered the University of Sheffield on his return from active service in the First World War. In 1921 he obtained a B.A. with First Class Honours in French and English and in 1922 an M.A. In the same year he was awarded the Diploma in Education (with Distinction in Theory) and the Diploma in Modern Language Teaching. From 1922 to 1925 he gained valuable experience of school and technical college teaching before returning to Sheffield in 1925 as a Lecturer in the Department of French.

His first major publication had been in English, an edition of selected Essays by Charles Lamb which appeared in 1925. But it was for his work on Baudelaire that Clapton became best known. This was done between 1930 and 1934, that is to say, largely during his first period at Sheffield, where he served under A. T. Baker. The text of his lecture, *Baudelaire the Tragic Sophist* (1934), is probably the most familiar of his writings, his brief monograph, *Baudelaire et De Quincey* (Paris 1931), probably the most admirable. Substantial and authoritative studies likewise appeared over his name in English and French periodicals: 'Balzac, Baudelaire and Maturin' in *The French Quarterly* (vol. XII, 1930), 'Baudelaire, Sénèque et saint Jean Chrysostome' in *Revue d'Histoire littéraire de la France* (1931), 'Lavater Gall et Baudelaire' in *Revue de Littérature comparée* (1933). 'Carlyle and Some Early English Critics of Baudelaire' appeared in the Kastner *Miscellany* (1932).

In 1933 he joined the staff of the French Department in Edinburgh, where he remained until 1937. In a remarkable department, every member of which was to distinguish himself, he quickly made his mark both as a scholar and as a teacher. As a scholar his reputation rested mainly on his work on Baudelaire; as a teacher he was already exhibiting some of that universality of interest and of competence that was to become his hallmark. Throughout his career he was militant in the cause of his subject, an exacting and inspiring teacher. He lectured frequently on the values and problems involved in the teaching of French and the organisation of French studies. He was part author, with W. McC. Stewart, at present Professor of French in the University of Bristol, of *Les Etudes françaises dans l'Enseignement en Grande-Bretagne*, which was published in Paris in 1929. *Modern Languages* contains the text of a few of his lectures (March, 1952; vol. 41, 1960 etc.) in which the vitality and scholarly good sense of their author are unmistakably apparent.

In 1937 he left Edinburgh for the Chair of French in Sheffield, where—particularly during the very difficult war years—he gave an inspiring example of zeal and selflessness.

In Sheffield, and again in Leeds, where he accepted the Chair of French in 1949, Clapton became a living legend. His wit was incisive, his learning encyclopaedic, his energy inexhaustible, and his humanity limitless. Among so many attractive characteristics two appeared to dominate: selflessness and helpfulness. No one was less concerned with promoting his own interests or with fostering his own reputation; and none was so helpful to so many people in so many ways. No task was too great and none too humble for him. He was as ready to correct proofs for his most junior Assistant Lecturer as he was to give a clear lead in important matters of university policy, locally, nationally or internationally. He sat on almost every important committee in the University and in many of them he took the chair. Outside the University he worked tirelessly to improve the teaching of French in schools (and the work of Sixth Forms in general) as well as presiding benevolently over the well-being of the many French Assistants in the West Riding. A convinced democrat—though with a limited capacity for suffering fools gladly—Clapton was a natural administrator; and it is perhaps as a Head of Department that he was seen at his best. The loyalty and affection that he inspired in his staff and in his students is perhaps his best memorial.

He was for many years a member of the Editorial Board of *French Studies* and also of *Archivum Linguisticum*.

Clapton's death occurred very shortly after his retirement in October, 1964. With his passing are lost the services of a great scholar, who had laboured unceasingly in the interests of learning and of educational standards. It is the hope of the Editors that the present volume of essays and studies, which was to have graced his retirement, will now fittingly honour his memory.

The Editorial Committee is grateful for the help given by the secretarial staff of the French Department of the University of Leeds and by Mr. F. J. Manning of the Registrar's department. It also wishes to express its thanks to Professor A. J. Steele of the University of Edinburgh, to Miss M. Blaess, Lecturer in French in the University of Sheffield, to Mrs. P. Drake and Miss M. Hemmings, members of the administrative and secretarial staff of that university.

The publication of the book has been made possible by the generous financial assistance of the University of Leeds. The Editors also wishto thank the publishers for help and understanding given at every stage.

Editorial Committee: T. V. BENN
G.W. IRELAND
J. C. IRESON
W. ROTHWELL
S. ULLMANN

STELE FOR PAUL VALERY

All that shone forth twixt void and pure event
Tree, Serpent, Fountain — mirror of your essence,
The drunkenness of acts, their iridescence:
All move to make your shimmering monument!

O diamond rigour, cryptic perseverance —
Flouting the flash that tore the terrible schism!
O crystal-gazer caught within your prism,
Weaving clear arabesques on incoherence!

Yet proud-leafed Plane, yet Patience of the Palm!
O whirl, O whorl, O flowering grace of feature,
Loving . . . scoffing at life, irked as a creature,
Stirred to acclaim the Gods' eternal calm:

Echo of the Divine that seized your sight —
You, dazzled by the mystery of light!

WILLIAM McCAUSLAND STEWART

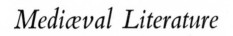

Mediæval Literature

MADELEINE BLAESS

Predestination in Some Thirteenth-Century Prose Romances

Is man really justified in asserting, with Henley, that:

> I am the Master of my Fate,
> I am the Captain of my Soul?

This is a problem which everyone must solve, consciously or not. As such, it is a question that has troubled philosopher and theologian alike.

The Roman Catholic Church teaches that God, who knows all things from eternity, has given each man the grace with which to achieve salvation. But man also has freedom of will to use this grace or not: Adam chose to disobey God, so his descendants are handicapped by original sin, which must be removed by baptism before they can profit — or not, as they will — by the grace necessary for salvation.

Not everyone has agreed with this doctrine; in the fifth century the Pelagians denied that man, since he depends on God's grace for salvation, had freedom of will; and it was largely owing to St Augustine that the Council of Carthage condemned this as a heresy in 418. But while defining his views, St Augustine shifted ground slightly in his various treatises, so that his interpretation of Christ's words to the disciples after the Last Supper: 'Without me, ye can do nothing'[1] gave grounds for arguing that God does indeed choose who will be saved.[2] The semi-Pelagians claimed the support of the Doctor for the belief that the great mass of souls was destined to suffer damnation in Hell; this was anathematized as a heresy by the Second Council of Orange in 529.[3]

Here the matter rested for three centuries until Gottschalk, a monk of Orbais, after many years' study of the teachings of St Augustine, came to the conclusion that:

> Omnes quos vult Deus salvos fieri sine dubitatione salvantur: nec

---

[1] John, xv, 5.

[2] For a brief survey of this question see Nigel Abercrombie, *The Origins of Jansenism* (Oxford, 1936), pp. 1–60.

[3] H. J. D. Denzinger, *Enchiridion symbolorum, definitionum et declarationum de rebus fidei et morum* . . . , 17th ed. (1928), no. 200.

possunt salvari, nisi quos Deus vult salvos fieri: nec est quisquam, quem Deus salvari velit, et non salvetur . . .[4]

This teaching attracted so many followers that the great Hrabanus Maurus was persuaded in 840 to write a treatise refuting it. But Gottschalk's greatest adversary was bishop Hincmar of Reims, whose views may be summarized as:

(1) God wills the final salvation of all souls, to be attained by the redemption offered to all by Christ in His Passion, and by the Divine gift of grace offered to all during their lives on earth.

(2) God has also given to all souls the gift of free will. He has known from all eternity what will be the final state of each in the life to come; but He compels none to co-operate with His grace. The soul that chooses to reject Him, God will not, and cannot, compel to accept Him, or that Vision of Himself which will be the joy of the life hereafter.[5]

With this Gottschalk did not agree, and after a momentary recantation, died unrepentant. Nor was Gottschalk the only one to disagree with Hincmar: the scholars connected with the Church at Lyons; Prudentius, bishop of Troyes; even the noted Lupus, abbot of Ferrières and adviser of Charles the Bald, considered that God has chosen certain men to be saved; while the Councils of Quierzy (849 and 853) and of Valence (855) did little to settle the question which persisted unresolved until late in the thirteenth century. Consequently

throughout the Middle Ages, the name and authority of Augustine dominated the literature of theology. Two points upon which he had laid the greatest possible emphasis were that Predestination is more than mere prescience, being the preparation of a gift to an unworthy, but elect, recipient; and that, under grace, and with the gift of perseverance, the elect man is borne 'insuperably' over all the obstacles which seem to hinder his salvation. A servile use of texts, and indifference to non-literary fact, will easily enable the student of Augustine to twist these doctrines into Predestinarianism. All that is needed is to establish an unreal parallelism between the elect and the damned, and to mechanize the moral efficacy of divine grace.[6]

The position of the Church on the subject was clarified by St Thomas

---

[4] Migne, *PL.*, CXXI, 366 c.

[5] See E. S. Duckett, *Carolingian Portraits* (Ann Arbor, 1962), pp. 258–9. For Hincmar's writings on predestination, see Migne, *PL.*, CXXV, 49a–474b.

[6] N. Abercrombie, op. cit., p. 59.

Aquinas, but the prose romances to be considered had already been composed before he started to teach.

The 'comédie humaine' to be discussed is the vast compilation known to modern scholars as the *Vulgate Cycle*. It comprises the *Estoire del Saint Graal*, the *Merlin*, the *Lancelot*, the *Queste del Saint Graal* and the *Mort le Roi Artu*,[7] and it deals with the arrival of the Grail in Britain, the reign of king Arthur, the finding of the Grail and the destruction of the realm. The main body of the work is generally thought to have been composed between 1215 and 1230, with the *Merlin* added a little later than 1230.[8]

If we take predestination in its lesser meaning of 'fate', then we are in full agreement with Professor Frappier[9] and other critics when they point out that the theme of predestination is dominant in the romances. Nor could it be otherwise. The author has a story to tell; he wants to make it clear that Joseph of Arimathea will bring the Grail to England, and in fact Joseph seems to have little choice in the matter. Since Galahad is to be the Grail hero, dreams, prophecies, inscriptions foretell and point to the event. But consistency may fail unless the author lives to complete his tale. For instance, Perceval was the hero chosen by Chrétien de Troyes, but since — unlike his thirteenth-century successors — Chrétien did not make it abundantly clear from the beginning exactly what was to be accomplished, it was Galahad who later became the Grail hero, curing the Roi Méhaigné and being crowned king whilst guardian of the Grail; when he dies a hand takes the Grail and the Holy Lance up to Heaven. Perceval is not entirely eliminated, but takes second place; he does not succeed Galahad as Grail king, and dies in a hermitage a year after Galahad.[10]

So in the story there can never be any doubt of the ultimate success of

---

[7] Ed. H. O. Sommer, *The Vulgate Version of the Arthurian Romances*, 7 vols. (Washington, 1909–13). However, we shall use A. Pauphilet's edition of *La Queste del Saint Graal* (Paris, 1949) and J. Frappier's 1954 edition of *La Mort le Roi Artu* (Geneva and Lille) as being the better editions. No use will be made of the incomplete *Livre d'Artus* (Sommer, op. cit., vol. VII) or the *Huth-Merlin* (ed. J. Paris, J. Ulrich [Paris, 1886], SATF) which are both intended to replace the Vulgate *Merlin*. We shall ignore the *Didot-Perceval* (ed. W. Roach [Philadelphia, 1941]), the *Perlesvaus* (ed. W. A. Nitze [Chicago, 1932–7]), as also the other great prose romances which do not belong to this cycle.

[8] See especially pp. 295 and 317 in J. Frappier, 'The Vulgate Cycle', pp. 295–318, and A. Micha, 'The Vulgate *Merlin*', p. 322, both in *Arthurian Literature in the Middle Ages*, ed. R. S. Loomis (Oxford, 1959).

[9] Op. cit., *passim*.

[10] Bohort, who like Galahad, does not seem to have been 'predestined' before the Vulgate Cycle, is the third and least expected of the Grail heroes. Little in his early life seems to destine him for this exalted position, and after the death of his two companions, he returns to king Arthur's court and leads a life distinguished more by common sense than by holiness.

the hero. But to what extent are the characters only puppets driven to their destinies by an inexorable Fate? The author is necessarily omniscient and allows his readers to share his knowledge, but do his characters feel that, in spite of all the omens, they have free will? And in the case of those whose success or otherwise in the quest is not essential to the story, are they predestined, or do they work out their own fate, and are any ultimately damned?

Though it is generally agreed that not all parts of the *Vulgate Cycle* are necessarily by the same author, and that the first two 'branches' (i.e. books) were added later,[11] yet it is a coherent whole, and the additions are not late enough for the introduction of Thomist doctrine. Consequently the obvious beginning is with the *Estoire del Saint Graal*.[12] This tells how Joseph of Arimathea collected some of Christ's blood in a 'vessel'; how he was imprisoned for years without food by the Jews, but was sustained by the 'vessel'; how he was delivered, and eventually founded the Grail Table and came to England with his family and followers to convert the land. This is essentially a religious story, and as such, relies heavily on predestination. In actual fact, there is a double strand in the story; one dealing with Joseph, his *maisnie* and his followers; the other with the trials and tribulations of the first converts, many of whom are to be numbered among the ancestors of the Grail hero.

In the first strand, Joseph himself, once he has collected Christ's blood, seems to have little free will. He undergoes his fate, and at no time seems to take the initiative. Nor can much be said of his immediate family, even of his son, confusingly enough named Josephe, made bishop by divine will. Indeed, if Josephe so much as hesitates, his hand is forced, as when, receiving Holy Communion and seeing a body instead of the host, he tries to draw back,

si ne pot. Ains le senti en sa bouce anchois qu'il le peust clore (I, p. 40).

The other members of the family are mostly puppets, and though indeed Joseph's youngest grandchild chooses the priesthood, the author does not allow us to judge whether this is through his own or God's choice.

The followers, however, present more 'humanity'. Some *do* choose to sin, and find themselves cut off from the food provided by the Grail. On repenting, they are once more fed. More particularly three of them appear to choose their own fate: Moses, Simeon and Chanaan. The Grail Table has been provided with an empty seat to be occupied by the Grail hero.

---

[11] See Frappier, op. cit., pp. 295 and 313–17.
[12] Ed. Sommer, op. cit., vol. I.

Several disbelieve Joseph's word about this, and Moses asks for permission to try. Although he has been a sinner, Joseph believes him to have repented, and accedes to his request, but warns him of the danger. No sooner has the presumptuous man seated himself than seven flaming hands set him on fire, and carry him off to a forest where he will burn until delivered by Galahad (I, pp. 247–9).

Chanaan too is a sinner, and has not repented. Because of this, like Simeon, Moses' father, he is deprived of the food of the Grail; yet both of them blame their kindred for their own shortcomings; and from there it is a short step to despair and murder. Chanaan slays his twelve brothers in their sleep; Simeon, through the intervention of God, only wounds his cousin Peter. When condemned to be buried alive, a heavenly voice announces that God's vengeance is ready. Indeed, before judgment can be carried out on Simeon (who had suggested the crimes) two fiery men sweep him off none knows where. Chanaan repents at the eleventh hour, and asks for prayers. Is he saved? Because of his previous sin he was without grace to withstand despair and the temptation to murder; yet he has the grace to repent at the last. Is this repentance acceptable, or is it only a natural reaction to the fate of Simeon and the imminence of his own death? The sole clue given by the author is that Chanaan remains alive in a burning tomb. The fact that no priest is brought to hear his confession and give absolution is not here significant, since confession seems to be seldom practised in Joseph's entourage. The author cannot forget he is dealing with Jews (now Christians, of course), and seems mostly to consider them still under the Old Law. Simeon and his son Moses (who sat in the Siege Perillous) will be delivered by Galahad, just as the Old Testament Moses was delivered by Christ. They need to be delivered by the best and most religious character of the *Cycle*, since they did not repent, though the more merciful author of the *Lancelot* tells us they would have been damned had not Joseph prayed for them.[13] Chanaan, who did repent, is to be delivered by Lancelot, the best knight in the world were it not for his adultery. It is striking that these three sinners are not each delivered by one of the three Grail heroes, or by Galahad alone, but the author of the *Estoire* has a weakness for the world of chivalry. The author of the *Queste*, however, appears to have had second thoughts, and though Simeon is in fact delivered[14] (perhaps because he did not kill anyone), Moses is nowhere mentioned; though it would have been poetic justice for the owner of the Siege Perillous to deliver the usurper. F. Lot[15] suggests that the omission is

[13] Sommer, op. cit., vol. IV, pp. 176–7.
[14] Ed. Pauphilet, pp. 264–5.
[15] *Etude sur le Lancelot en prose*, 2nd ed. (Paris, 1954), pp. 253–6.

deliberate because the author felt unhappy about the whole Moses episode.

As regards the liberation of Chanaan, also predicted in the *Lancelot*,[16] according to Lot: 'On voit en effet dans la Quête, Lancelot délivrer Chanaan.' [17] But 'en effet' one sees nothing of the sort. On his way home after his Quest, Lancelot dismounts to look at the tombs of the slain brothers, then rides away to Arthur's court.[18] Thus are the two greatest criminals in the eyes of the *Queste* author ultimately not delivered on earth, and he is silent as to their eternal salvation.

When we turn to the converts made by Joseph, we find a more carefully defined doctrine. The first of these converts is Evalac, king of Sarras, converted ostensibly by Joseph, but in reality by dreams, Joseph's knowledge of his real parentage, and by impending defeat in a battle which only turns to his advantage when he prays to the God of the Christians. This sequence of events makes it clear that Evalac's conversion is fore-ordained; he is brought to it by proof piling on proof, is baptized, taking the name of Mordrain, and is followed by his brother-in-law who takes that of Nascien. As for his wife, Sarracinte, sister to Nascien, she has secretly been a Christian for twenty-five years. The author describes at length the trials undergone by Mordrain and Nascien with temptation and consolation alternating, and in which they triumph, more by doing nothing, praying, and waiting for the trials to end, than by active choice. If one of them unwittingly transgresses he is immediately punished by Heaven, so leaving no doubt in his mind as to what the correct religion is.

The most remarkable episode, however, is that of King Label. After numerous adventures, Nascien's son, Celidoine, finds refuge at King Label's court. He is welcomed with kindness, as befits the son of an old friend, and though Label is distressed to hear that Nascien and Celidoine are Christians, he insists on treating the young man with honour. While arranging to reconvert him so that he may marry his daughter, Label is troubled by a dream, which can be interpreted only by Celidoine. Its meaning is that Label must become a Christian and repent of his sins, for he is to die within four days. As proof of the correctness of the interpretation, Celidoine reminds the king of an act he had thought entirely secret: the recent murder of his own sister as she was resisting his efforts to rape her. This so alarms Label that he takes to his bed, where he has another dream in which he sees his sister in Paradise (she was a Christian, unknown to him), whilst he is seized by robbers and thrust into a dread dark house. This second dream, which means he will go to Hell unless he repents, con-

---

[16] Op. cit., pp. 340–1.
[17] Op. cit., p. 252.
[18] Pauphilet, op. cit., p. 262.

vinces Label, who is instructed by a hermit, baptized, and the following day dies, as predicted, in the odour of sanctity, since

> fist puis Nostres Sires maint bel miracle por lui! (Sommer, I, p. 158).

This extraordinary episode can only reflect the author's own difficulty over the problem of why some people are given the grace of baptism whilst others are not. So far as we can see, there is no reason why Label should be elevated to the sainthood. No conversions among his own people follow his death, so that it seems to serve no immediate purpose. It is emphasized that he has been a sinner in his past life; we know that he tried to commit incest and did commit murder, nor does he undergo any penance for this. Indeed, the whole affair is so arbitrary that later in the story when we meet Label's daughter in distress, she tells her rescuers that her father (still a pagan) was killed in battle (I, p. 166).

As concerns the newly converted knights of lower rank, justice is harsh and immediate. Nabor pursues his master Nascien who is going secretly to his son, and tries to persuade him to return. On his refusal, Nabor decides to kill him, but is struck dead as he raises his sword. This upsets Nascien

> quar bien pense que l'ame est perdue uraiement (I, p. 199).

He is still pondering this when liegemen of his ride up. One of them, Karabel, declares that Nabor has deserved his fate. Thereupon a voice from Heaven reproves him for passing judgment, he who had killed his own father to seize his land; and forthwith Karabel is struck by lightning and burnt to death. This is God's vengeance, states a passing white monk, and he does not allow the two reprobates to be buried in hallowed ground (I, pp. 200–1). At the crossing to Britain on Josephe's miraculous shirt, only the pure can be drawn across the sea on it. Since the remainder would otherwise drown, God will provide them with ships, for

> Nostre Sires ne ueut pas la mort del pecheour, ains veut qu'il s'amende et reuiegne a la uoie de uerite (I, p. 210).

This merciful staying of the divine hand of retribution certainly does not apply to Nascien's unfortunate knights.

Thus it is obvious that throughout the *Estoire*, its author was convinced of the arbitrary nature of predestination. This is a mainly religious work, containing a good many edifying digressions, but the author deals directly with predestination only when giving the history of the three spindles in Solomon's ship (which is to convey Solomon's descendant Galahad on his way to the Grail). These are made from the wood of the fated apple tree in

Eden, a twig of which Eve had planted in exile. Under this tree God orders Adam and Eve to assemble,

> et Sa uolentes estoit teile que de ces .ij. uoloit restablir l'umaine lignie et la disime legion des angeles qui du ciel auoint este trebuchie par orguel.[19]

So the author not only believes in the predestination of the elect, but in the idea, current in some quarters during the Middle Ages, that only a limited number (that of the fallen angels) are to be saved.

When we turn to the *Merlin*[20] we find little to our purpose. This, again, is later than the *Lancelot* proper, and is an account of Arthur's immediate ancestors and of the early years of his reign. It opens with a Miltonic scene of demons plotting an Antichrist,[21] a plot that comes to naught. The girl destined to be the Antichrist's mother remains steadfast in spite of all temptations, and it is only because she heeds not the injunction:

> sol non occidat super iracundiam vestram. Nolite locum dare diabolo,[22]

that the incubus can have his will of her; but both she and her child Merlin are saved by her repentance.

The remainder mostly derives from Geoffrey of Monmouth's *Historia Regum Britanniae*, and after Arthur's conception, though the author abandons Geoffrey, the chronicle form still prevails. Consequently there is little opportunity to determine the author's opinion on the subject under discussion. The secondary meaning of predestination, 'fate,' is, however, strongly emphasized. Utherpendragon does not publicly acknowledge Arthur to be his son, and so there is the floating stone and the sword no man can draw but the heir to the throne; the enchanter and prophet Merlin to foretell the future and to guide Arthur in all his doings, even in the seemingly trivial matter of when to kiss his betrothed; dreams and prophecies to point to future events.

However, there are isolated cases where free will is apparently allowed, though in actual fact it is either overridden, or is part of predestined fate. In one case, king Ban is staying the night at the castle of Agravadain des Mares. Ban, married to a young wife, has a spell cast over him by Merlin, causing him to fall in love with the young daughter of his host. In spite of this spell-induced love, Ban is determined not to commit adultery and so

---

[19] Ibid., p. 127. This is repeated almost verbatim in the *Queste*, p. 215.

[20] Sommer, op. cit., vol. II.

[21] This follows an earlier verse redaction written by Robert de Boron, ed. W. A. Nitze (Paris, 1927), CFMA, which is wholly religious in tone.

[22] Ephesians, iv, 26–7.

shame his host. Merlin has to bring the enchanted maiden to Ban before his resolve is finally overcome by the strength of the spell.

Another instance is Merlin's knowledge that he will find his destruction through a woman, though the time and person are hidden from his prophetic eyes. He falls in love with Viviane, a young girl of 12, oblivious of the fact that she may be his destroyer. Later, when he realises who she is, his love for her sweeps aside any instinct of self-preservation, and he lapses into a fatalistic acquiescence.

The *Lancelot*[23] proper deals with the story of Lancelot from infancy until the advent of his son as Grail hero. Here, the author is not handicapped by the necessity of following a definite source, except in one or two cases, or even of supplying antecedents to known characters and events. He is not fundamentally a religious man, and so is not concerned essentially with the question of free will and predestination. He has a tale of chivalry to tell, and he has advantages over the authors of the *Estoire* and the *Merlin* in that he is a better writer and interested in psychology. So, though the *Lancelot* treats of fights and quests, it is not a mere chronicle of events or a manual of strategy, but in general a psychological study of the principal characters.

Very often the author is careful to give at some point a detailed physical description of the person involved, as well as a moral appreciation. Thus, Claudas de la Deserte, who takes king Ban's lands by treachery, is described as

> moult boins cheualiers et moult sages, mais moult estoit traitres (III, p. 3).

Later (III, pp. 26–7), he is described as exacting and miserly; preferring his knights to be poor and valiant; hating men stronger and richer than he, and putting his trust in those who were dependent on him. He loved going to church, but hated almsgiving; rose early and loved his food, but cared neither for chess nor other games, and preferred sport on the river to hunting. He was slow to keep his word and inclined to fraud and deception though he never betrayed a confidence. He had loved only once in his life, but had given up his lady rather than risk his life in deeds of prowess for her sake. He hesitated to dub his fifteen-year-old son knight, fearing he might be attacked by him, but was indulgent towards his disorderly conduct. All Claudas' actions flow naturally from this character study: his attack on the more powerful king Ban; the capture of Ban's castle by treachery and his pleasure at being rid of the traitor-tool who might have had a hold upon him; his annoyance at the firing of the rich quarters of

---

[23] Sommer, op. cit., vols. III–V.

Ban's city, which deprives him of coveted wealth; the seizure of the defenceless lands of Ban's dead brother; his desire to attack Arthur, but first his careful reconnaissance of Arthur's court; and his love for his son expressed in the funeral oration once death has removed the threat of rebellion. All Claudas' acts are a logical outcome of his character; and we are given a physical description which is symbolic of this.[24] So his hair is a mixture of red and black — showing a mixture of the principle of good with treachery, though his wholly red beard shows treachery predominant. His black eyes denote cunning; his small nose fine feelings, though since it is tip-tilted it also reveals an overbearing nature; while his wide mouth indicates his assertiveness and love of food. Thus his physiognomy symbolically bears out the thumb-nail sketch of his character, and concords with his actions.

It would be tedious to consider all the descriptions of physique and character, but Lancelot's is particularly *soignée*, so that we may expect of him deeds of nobility and chivalry, as well as the determined singlemindedness with which he pursues his desires. Where we are not given a careful description, the characters behave as would be expected under the circumstances. The children Lionel and Bohort show great courage at king Claudas' court, as is to be expected of princes and descendants of king David. The various knights in the adventures, when confronted by death or dishonour, choose death rather than break a promise or face dishonour, but surrender when their defeat is of no great moment. As for the host of minor characters, they are too briefly seen to throw any light on the subject under consideration.

But what of the major characters? Lancelot has been described as a naturally 'royal' child, much loved by his foster-mother, the Lady of the Lake, fond of the hunt and of his own way, brooking no restraint; perfect in form, liberal, but with little control over his temper or desires. He goes to be knighted at king Arthur's court from a domain dominated by women, with the recent unnerving knowledge that he is not the true son of the Lady of the Lake. So he will be very unsure of himself in this totally different environment.

The day after his arrival at court, Lancelot meets the Queen, and for him it is the *coup de foudre*. Though almost thirty years older than he, her beauty impresses him, for she is 'la dame des dames, et la fontaine de biaute' (III, p. 125). Sitting on the ground at her feet, he can only glance surreptitiously at her, too troubled to understand what she says, and he shudders like a

---

[24] See G. Jobes, *Dictionary of Mythology, Folklore and Symbols*, 2 vols. (New York, 1961), under the appropriate headings; also W. C. Curry, *Chaucer and the Medieval Sciences*, 2nd ed. (London, 1960), pp. 55–90 especially.

man roused from sleep when she takes his hand to give him confidence. From that moment, Lancelot decides to do great deeds, and on the day he is dubbed knight undertakes two difficult enterprises. There has been no opportunity for him to speak to the Queen, so he engineers a meeting to say goodbye in private and ask to be considered her special knight; he has also seen to it that Arthur has not girded him with his sword, so that he may be only the Queen's knight. From now on, Lancelot's one thought is of being the best knight for the Queen's sake; the Lady of Malehaut may love him, king Galehot may become a member of Arthur's court to honour Lancelot and do everything in his power to please him, yet nothing can turn him away from his single-minded love.

And what of the Queen? At first, she is merely curious about the new arrival, and having met him, well-bred enough to try to cover up his seeming bad manners, breaking short the interview when she suspects that the youth is love-smitten. She does not try to see him again, and is merely courteous when Lancelot takes his leave. When he sends prisoners to the Queen and requests a sword from her, she can but comply. The reports of Lancelot's prowess flatter her, but had she known of it, she would have been more flattered by Lancelot's ecstatic trance whenever he happens to set eyes on her. Yet the Queen refuses to beg help for the king from him and it is only after a good deal of persuasion that she consents to ask a favour of Lancelot. Finally, his prowess is such that Guenevere is curious to see again the brave knight who, she is sure, is in love with her. And so king Galehot secretly engineers a meeting one evening. There, the Queen, flattered and amused, extracts a full confession from the trembling Lancelot, but she tries to convey that she herself is not in love with him, though taking malicious pleasure in teasing him. However, since Lancelot is too tongue-tied to press his suit, Galehot persuades the Queen to reward her hero; whereupon Guenevere kisses him and promises her love according to courtly convention, at the same time asking him, in accordance with the convention, to keep this a secret. But if, at the first leave-taking from the Queen, Lancelot had read so much into her conventional 'Biax dous amis' (III, p. 131) — and so would have earned Chrétien's jeer:

> Et çaus puet l'an nices clamer,
> Qui cuident, que les vuelle amer,
> Quant une dame est si cortoise,
> Qu'a un maleüreus adoise,
> Si li fet joie et si l'acole.
> Fos est liez de bele parole (*Yvain*, vv. 2459–64),[25]

[25] Ed. T. B. W. Reid (MUP, 1948), p. 69.

what could he read now into her declaration? Especially since each evening there is a courtly amorous meeting, with Galehot and the Dame de Malehaut nearby whispering sweet nothings together in order to console themselves and each other for Lancelot's single-minded love of the Queen. But so far the courtly code has not been transgressed; and after a few days Galehot and Lancelot depart for a lengthy stay far from the court, until eventually a search is made for Lancelot. After an absence of nine months, Lancelot is unable to eat or sleep, so great is his desire to see the Queen; at last Gawain finds him, and brings him back to the court, but Lancelot does not speak to the Queen until he has again performed wonderful deeds before the castle. When Lancelot is wounded, the Queen whispers to him that she will heal him before the next day unless his wound be mortal, and that very night they become lovers. Granted that this had all been foretold by various signs; but was this fulfilment as arbitrary as might appear from a bald summary? Decidedly not; at first the Queen treats this love more as a game, flattered by the passion of such a brave, young, and handsome knight, but each evening there are secret meetings and kisses. Each night Guenevere and the Dame de Malehaut whisper the hours away about their lovers, adding a little excitement to a dull court routine and a marriage over twenty years old. Like Madame Bovary six centuries later, Guenevere finds herself imperceptibly snared in the gossamer meshes of love, while Lancelot's return comes at a critical moment in her emotional life. He has been absent for nearly a year, has been dreamt about, and been discussed with the Dame de Malehaut. He appears in a blaze of triumph, still full of love, at a time when king Arthur is in the process of ardently wooing Camille, the Lady of Arestuel where the court is encamped. On the very night of Lancelot's return, Arthur tells his wife not to expect him, so she finds consolation in Lancelot's arms. About midnight she rises, and feels the split shield, now whole, which was only to become so when she and Lancelot were truly lovers,

> si le trueue tout entier sans fendure, si en est moult lie. Car ore seit ele bien que ele est la miex amee de nule autre amie (III, p. 411).

So Arthur's infidelity is avenged.

The first secret meeting arranged by the Queen seems an act of free will, but that act once taken, the whole affair is implicit in it, helped on by a long absence and by the 'chance' of a husband's defection. After this Guenevere will become as ravaged by passion as Lancelot, urged on by Arthur's light-hearted and swift desertion of her for the false Guenevere, and inflamed by Lancelot's absences and by the false claims of Morgain. The fact that she can inspire love in this perfect youth, who is the bravest knight in the world, this passion, in short, is Guenevere's natural defence against age and an unfaithful husband.

Can one speak here of predestination, when the whole story seems so natural? It is much more like the determinism of the philosophers, where heredity, environment, upbringing, cause a person to act in one way and not in another. This determinism seems the dominant note of the *Lancelot*. We have briefly mentioned Claudas, and dealt at some length with the coming together of Lancelot and Guenevere, but a consideration of Galehot's love and life, and of the actions of the various knights leads to the same conclusion. Prophetic dreams and warning inscriptions there are, as well as enchantments; this is part of the literary *genre*, but they are far less abundant than in the *Merlin*, and the author makes the story spring from the natural reactions of his characters rather than from too naked direction from above.

When we turn to the *Queste del Saint Graal*[26] we find a different author and a completely different atmosphere. This is a profoundly religious work with a Cistercian slant, and so we can expect to find orthodox Christian teachings. As regards the hero of the tale, it is made clear that Galahad is predestined from the very start, since the Siege Perillous at the Round Table is found to bear his name. And he passes triumphantly through the whole of his Quest; there is never any doubt of the outcome either in his own mind or in that of the reader. Perceval, the second Grail hero, has more of a fight, for, among other things, he is tempted by the flesh, going so far as to lie down in bed beside the lady — but he sees the cruciform pommel of his sword, and immediately repents before the sin is accomplished (pp. 105–10). Bohort too is sometimes tempted, the strongest temptations being the urge to sin in order to save others. But when he remains steadfast, all is shown to be an illusion conjured up by the devil. Throughout their various temptations, the heroes are saved by constant prayer and the grace it brings.

The other knights of the Round Table are, as Pauphilet remarks (Introduction, pp. x–xi):

> jugés du point de vue religieux et échelonnés depuis l'impiété jusqu'à la sainteté. Les uns sont des réprouvés: Lyonel, Hector, Yvain, Gahieret, Gauvain surtout: les grands noms de la Table Ronde.

And a little further on:

> Lancelot représente ici le pécheur repentant. . . . Vertu trébuchante et chancelante, pénitent ballotté du repentir à la rechute, véritable

---

[26] The Pauphilet edition.

'âme du Purgatoire'. Cette étude pénétrante, ingénieuse, d'un caractère où le bien et le mal se mêlent en nuances subtiles, fait de Lancelot, sinon le héros, du moins le personnage le plus vivant de la *Queste*.

One would like to develop *in extenso* Pauphilet's pertinent judgment. Against all the other characters who move inexorably to their fate and are little more than allegorical religious arguments, Lancelot stands out in the pathetic struggle of his will-power against his destiny. He goes on the Quest very much against Guenevere's will. He is struck down by Galahad, and spends the night in a trance from which he is unable to rise even when he sees a knight cured by the Grail. For this a voice from Heaven reproves him; his unaccustomed defeat, the whole of the adventure, so shake Lancelot that at length he confesses and repents. He endures bitter words from a squire he meets, he who could brook no master or disapproval; he puts on a hair-shirt, he who was so proud of his body; and he abstains from meat and wine. After many confessions, and much penitence, he is brought to the Grail castle, where he sees the object of his desire, but is struck down when he tries to enter the Grail chamber which is forbidden him, and lies insensible for twenty-four days — he had been in the sin of adultery for twenty-four years. But his Quest is over. He has twice seen the Grail: once when in mortal sin, and he lay like one dead as it passed him; once in a state of grace, and awake, but not allowed to draw near. So he returns to Arthur's court.

But why did Lancelot repent? Was this through free will, or was it predestined? His repentance seems more to stem from Lancelot's character. He has been the Queen's lover for twenty-four years, the fine edge is worn off, so that he goes on a quest without her permission; and since he has always been single-minded in what he wanted, he realises that only repentance will allow him to succeed; while psychologically the unwonted defeat at Galahad's hands[27] and the Grail vision apply the final spur. He mortifies the flesh so that there is no room for desire for the Queen,[28] as there was twenty-four years ago in the first flush of his love. This is a quest he could not have achieved at an earlier age, he who never had any control over his passions, so that his actions seem rather to rise from his own inner character than stem from predestination.

Gawain, however, is not psychologically ready for penitence, since to

---

[27] Could it also happen that having been for so long the best knight in the world, subconsciously and despite all the evidence to the contrary, Lancelot cannot accept the fact that he is displaced, and believes that repentance will automatically restore him to first place?

[28] As F. Lot, op. cit., p. 106, poin s out, the hair shirt is a talisman against mortal sin. When his quest is over Lancelot must be deprived of it, though against his will, to allow his predestined relapse into sin to take place. Here, Lancelot's free will is overruled.

him a quest means merely the piling up of adventures. He refuses confession (p. 55), and later, when he is told that he cannot find adventures because he is in mortal sin, he again refuses (p. 161), and places a waiting companion above the state of his soul. He is a brave man, but 'la grâce lui a manqué'.

Though at one point a priest tells Bohort (p. 165) that the heart of man governs his whole body, by grace to do good, by the Devil to do evil — so that presumably everyone has free will — in actual fact it is pre-election that dominates this work. As J. C. Payen remarks:

> Il est abusif de prétendre que la *Queste* soit un roman janséniste: elle montre cependant qu'il y a comme des degrés dans l'élection divine . . .[29]

And it is this 'élection divine' which is so clearly shown in the *Queste*.

Finally, the *Mort le roi Artu*,[30] the conclusion of the whole structure. Again, the main story is secular, it is the winding up of king Arthur's court, earthly punishments and heavenly rewards. Judging the work, Professor Frappier remarks: 'les fatalités intérieures des héros collaborent avec l'action de la Fortune' (p. XXIII). This is precisely the spirit that we found in the *Lancelot*. The characters act as they do because by their own natures they cannot act otherwise; they could avoid their fate by other action, but 'l'alternative n'offre que l'illusion du choix et de la liberté' (p. XX). For one thing, Lancelot at court, without his hair shirt, and daily in the presence of the Queen (who has *not* renounced him) cannot maintain his good resolutions of the *Queste*, and before a month is over he relapses into sin. But long custom has made the lovers careless, and their passion is soon brought to king Arthur's notice. Guenevere is still the 'fountain of beauty', and time is standing still, for the author here says she is fifty, forgetting that she met Lancelot in her middle forties . . . more than twenty-five years previously! It is this discovered love which is one of the forces of destruction of the kingdom, since it divides the court, and causes Gawain to hate Lancelot mortally when three of his brothers are killed by Lancelot as he delivers Guenevere from being burnt as an adulteress. Arthur no longer has the support of his whole court in his fight against the Romans; and he has to leave his queen and kingdom in the keeping of his nephew Mordred. But Mordred is also king Arthur's incestuous son, born as a result of that night long ago when as a squire chance gave him the opportunity to commit adultery with his own half-sister unknown to all but

---

[29] 'Le sens du péché dans la littérature cistercienne en langue d'oïl,' *Commentarii Cistercienses*, XIII (1962), p. 293.

[30] Ed. J. Frappier.

himself.[31] So Nemesis overtakes the king, as it overtakes all the characters. The whole of the *Mort le roi Artu* is full of prophetic warnings, dreams and inscriptions, but as in Greek tragedy, the persons in it seem to go inevitably to their destruction, not heeding the portents; because of their own characters, no other alternative is possible to them. Gawain cannot let the blood feud lapse, so dies eventually of a wound inflicted by Lancelot. Lancelot is too much dominated by passion to renounce the Queen, even for the good of the kingdom; the Queen cannot renounce Lancelot. So to the final battle, the deaths of Arthur and Mordred, the defeat of Mordred's sons by Lancelot. But Guenevere and Lancelot are still alive. Will they now legalize their union and end their lives in wedded bliss since they are both free to do so? But no; Guenevere has fled to a convent to escape from the sons of Mordred, and appalled by the destruction her love has brought, renounces the throne and even sends Lancelot away. Lancelot retires to a hermitage. Never content with half-measures, he takes holy orders, and after penance and prayer dies some years after the Queen, like her in the odour of sanctity. Moreover, in a dream before the final battle, Arthur had seen the dead Gawain in Paradise.

So there is salvation for all. Is this a conventional 'happy ending', an arbitrary predestined salvation? Professor Frappier is unhappy about this, and takes refuge (pp. XXVII–XXVIII) in Alfred Adler's exposition of medieval Aristotelianism whereby the imperfections of man do not destroy the merit of his perfections.[32] But there is little need for this. The author(s) of the *Lancelot* and the *Mort le roi Artu* are determinists 'avant la lettre'. The figures in their stories are driven by character, environment, heredity, upbringing; for them, especially in the *Mort le roi Artu*, the choices apparent to other eyes do not exist. Since they are not responsible for their actions, they cannot be punished for them, and consequently the final grace of repentance and salvation is vouchsafed to them. The more religious authors of the *Estoire* and the *Queste* see things differently. For them, man has sufficient grace to choose his salvation, at least in theory. But the authors cannot forget the manual of the Christian faith, the *Elucidarium*,[33] in which they learnt that God has predestined a certain number of elect to Paradise (p. 365); that man depends entirely on God's grace (p. 407) (which is orthodox, but could be interpreted in a narrow sense); and that chance does not exist (pp. 413–4).

---

[31] See Sommer, vol. II, pp. 128–9.

[32] 'Problems of Aesthetic versus Historical Criticism in *La Mort le Roi Artu*,' *PMLA*, LXV (1950), pp. 930–43.

[33] See Y. Lefèvre, *L'Elucidarium et les Lucidaires* (Paris, 1954), who establishes that the *Elucidarium* was certainly very well known from the twelfth century onwards (p. 101).

The author of the *Estoire*, like the author of the *Queste*, believes in establishing a certain order in those to be predestined. First and foremost come Joseph and his descendants, who are definitely elect and can do no wrong except unwittingly. Still elect, but in a lesser order, are Joseph's tribe and followers, who often sin, but nevertheless will all be saved. Those of their number who are swept from their midst in sin will have to wait years in torment before being delivered by the Grail hero, the Christ-figure. Then come the converted kings and nobles, not of Jewish race. These, with the exception of Label, undergo great trials for their new faith but will also be saved; and those who are not converted will be damned. Neither category has any say in the matter. Finally come the ordinary rank of Christians who are struck dead and damned if they sin. For them time is not offered for repentance, as it is for the followers of Joseph.

The author of the *Queste* is concerned rather with allegory and with the condemnation of the ideals of chivalry; but here again the idea of the pre-destined elect is dominant. However, he is not as indulgent towards the erring Chanaan and Moses as are the authors of the *Estoire* and the *Lancelot*, condemning them by his silence. Yet he does have some pity for the mighty fallen, as we see in his treatment of Lancelot.

There is little opportunity to judge the philosophy of the author of the *Merlin*, but it would seem that he too believes in predestination, since whenever some character chooses to exert his free will he is overruled by fate or some enchantment.

On the other hand, though the author(s) of the *Lancelot* and of the *Mort le roi Artu* share the belief that one is not master of one's fate, that is not because of some arbitrary decision on God's part, but by the compulsion of character, environment, upbringing and heredity, though chance also has its part to play.

Perhaps free will in its technical sense can rarely be successfully portray-ed, and in the *Vulgate Cycle* it is noteworthy that if the author has strong religious leanings, he inclines to predestination in a narrow, almost Jansen-ist sense. But the more secular-minded author tends to explain the actions of his *dramatis personae* by their inner urges and character, a way of thinking later called determinism. It is this determinism, with its accent placed more on character, less on the decrees of fate, which marks an important stage in the development of the psychological novel.

W. H. LYONS

Doctrinal logic and poetic justice in the twelfth century: the case of Herman de Valenciennes, Solomon and Henry II

I

MEDIEVAL commentators who unhesitatingly accepted as the height of judicial wisdom Solomon's judgment in the case of the two harlots were understandably embarrassed by the problem of judging Solomon himself. Perhaps only the accused could have adequately dealt with the case. In the *Estoire del saint Graal* this actually happens. For after building the ship that was to bear his descendant triumphantly on his quest, Solomon was warned that only one whose faith was entire should enter it. He realised that he was unworthy, so did not embark.[1] The story shows Solomon as supreme artificer (a rôle also attested, incidentally, by the common use in Old French literature of the phrase 'uevre Salomon'[2]), sage or even magician, but at this point touches upon the fact that he was also the centre of a controversy that embarrassed religious thinkers for centuries. The lineaments of this controversy are clearly visible in Hainaut in the twelfth century. The well known passage in the first (or third, if the alternative system of numbering is followed) book of Kings, chapter xi, verses 4–9, poses the problem:

> Cumque jam esset senex, depravatum est cor ejus per mulieres, ut sequeretur deos alienos: nec erat cor ejus perfectum cum Domino Deo suo, sicut cor David patris ejus. Sed colebat Salomon Astarthen deam Sidoniorum, et Moloch idolum Ammonitarum. Fecitque quod non placuerat coram Domino, et non adimplevit ut sequeretur Dominum, sicut David pater ejus. Tunc aedificavit Salomon fanum

---

[1] *Vulgate Version of the Arthurian Romances*, ed. Sommer, vol. I, *Lestoire del saint Graal*, Washington, 1909, n. 136. I am indebted to my colleague, Miss M. Blaess, for this reference. See also *La queste del saint graal*, ed. A Pauphilet, Paris, 1949, p. 225.

[2] See G. D. West, *Modern Language Review*, XLIX (1954), pp. 176–82, and H. W. Lawton, *Modern Language Review*, L (1955), pp. 50–2.

Chamos, idolo Moab, in monte qui est contra Jerusalem, et Moloch idolo filiorum Ammon. Atque in hunc modum fecit universis uxoribus suis alienigenis, quae adolebant thura, et immolabant diis suis. Igitur iratus est Dominus Salomoni, quod aversa esset mens ejus a Domino Deo Israel, qui apparuerat ei secundo.

The exegis on this passage has been summarized by M. Bloch's article, 'La vie d'outretombe du roi Salemon' (*Revue belge de philologie et d'histoire*, IV (1925), pp. 349–77). Not only was there a conflict between this passage and other Biblical references to Solomon but even Judaic opinion was far from unanimous as to the place he should be accorded.[3] The question was relatively simple if reward and punishment were considered merely in the context of earthly existence, for the answer was provided by verses 11–14 of the same chapter of Kings:

> Dixit itaque Dominus Salomoni: Quia habuisti hoc apud te, et non custodisti pactum meum, et praecepta mea, quae mandavi tibi, disrumpens scindam regnum tuum, et dabo illud servo tuo. Verumtamen in diebus tuis non faciam propter David patrem tuum: de manu filii tui scindam illud. Nec totum regnum auferam, sed tribum unum dabo filio tuo propter David servum meum, et Jerusalem quam elegi. Suscitavit autem Dominus adversarium Salomoni Adad Idumaeum de semine regio, qui erat in Edom.

But when life in the next world began to preoccupy Jewish thinkers, the problem became more serious: 'quel avait été, dans l'autre monde, le sort de Salomon?'[4] It is said that the Great Synagogue wished to add his name to those of the three other kings denied eternal life and was deterred neither by a vision of David pleading for his son, nor by fire sent from heaven. Only a heavenly voice intervening in the debate vetoed the proposal.[5] But if a heavenly voice had settled the matter for Jewish (and apparently Islamic) polemicists, 'chez les chrétiens, en particulier dans l'Eglise d'Occident, la discussion se poursuivit bien plus longtemps. Elle avait pour eux quelque chose de singulièrement plus angoissant. La pensée de l'autre monde avait sur leurs esprits une force bien plus grande que chez le commun des Juifs; ils imaginaient par delà la mort un système de récompenses et de châtiments infiniment plus exact et plus minutieux. Comment eussent-ils sans hésitation cru au salut de celui dont la Bible disait qu'il avait détourné son cœur de Dieu, sans que rien par ailleurs dans

[3] Bloch, loc. cit., p. 359.
[4] Ibid.
[5] Ibid., p. 360. See also M. Sel, 'Solomon in Rabbinical literature and legend,' in *Jewish Encyclopedia*, XI, pp. 438–44.

le texte sacré indiquât que le coupable avait fait pénitence?'[6] And Solomon's offence was particularly abominable. He was 'idolâtre, certes, mais plus encore luxurieux'.[7] The root of his transgression lay in the sin of the flesh. This might be overlooked by rabbis and devout Moslems, but 'inspirait au contraire à un prêtre et surtout à un moine nourris dans l'ascétisme catholique une insurmontable horreur'.[8]

Yet Solomon was not only the divinely inspired author of four books of the Scripture (*Proverbia, Ecclesiastes, Cantica Canticorum, Sapientia*). In St Matthew's genealogy he is an ancestor of Christ[9] and in Christian exegesis he had become a prefiguration of Christ.[10] It is not surprising, therefore, that the condemnation of Solomon did not win universal support. In the *Dictionnaire de la Bible* of F. Vigouroux,[11] St Jerome, St Cyril of Jerusalem and St Hilarius are numbered among those who affirmed his salvation. St Iraeneus, however, did not commit himself and St Ambrose seems ambiguous. On the other hand, Tertullian and St Cyprian 'ne sont pas favorables au repentir de Salomon'. St Augustine exclaims in apparent distress 'Jam de Salomone quid dicam, quem vehementer arguit sancta Scriptura atque condemnat (III Reg. 11), nihilque de pœnitentia ejus vel in eum indulgentia Dei omnino commemorat?'[12] The author of the article himself concludes: 'L'impression dernière reste donc défavorable et la conversion douteuse; les dons divins avaient été si magnifiques et la chute si profonde!'[13]

As Bloch points out,[14] Solomon fares rather better in literature and art than he does at the hands of the theologians. 'Dante ne connaît pas le doute ... c'est dans une demeure paradisiaque qu'il rencontre Salomon.'[15] In medieval iconography, the king seated on his throne symbolises the God-Child — Eternal Wisdom — on Mary's knee. His meeting with the queen of Sheba represents either the Saviour's meeting with his Church or the Adoration of the Magi.[16] His judgment in the case of the two women

---

[6] Bloch, loc. cit., p. 362.
[7] Ibid.
[8] Ibid.
[9] Matt., i, 6–7.
[10] See *A Catholic Commentary on Holy Scripture*, ed. B. Orchard *et alii*, London, 1953, 270f, 352d, 934a. Even Philip of Harvengt, who condemns Solomon, says: 'Quod Salomon in multis actibus suis Christum figuraverit, neminem aestimo dubitare,' though he adds 'quod in omnibus eum figuraverit nullus praesumat affirmare' (Migne, *PL*, col. 623B).
[11] Under the entry 'Salomon', t. V (cols. 1382–96), H. Lesêtre, 'La mort de Salomon' (col. 1395).
[12] *Contra Faustum*, Book 22, ch. LXXXVIII (*PL*, XLII, col. 459).
[13] H. Lesêtre, loc. cit.
[14] Bloch, loc. cit., p. 367.
[15] *Paradiso*, X, 109–11, and XIII, 46–8.
[16] E. Mâle, *L'Art religieux du XIIIe siècle en France*, 8e édn., Paris, 1948, p. 158.

claiming the one child is sometimes taken as an allegory of the Old and the New Law, sometimes as a prefiguration of the Last Judgment. In Byzantine art, representations of the Descent into Hell, from the end of the eleventh century at the latest, show, at the side of the Redeemer, two crowned figures, identified as David and Solomon.[17] In the west, at a later date, although David is often in evidence, he is usually unaccompanied by his controversial son.

The dispute about Solomon's fate in the hereafter flared up again in the verbal warfare between Calvinists and defenders of the Roman Church.[18] Finally, Dom Ursmer Berlière notes in his series of articles on Philip of Harvengt in the Revue bénédictine (t. IX, 1892, p. 197, n. 1) that a little work, Salomon pœnitens, was published at Mons in 1727 by Père Gilles Martin, religieux de Bonne Espérance.

II

Whatever conclusions Martin may have reached, his subject had been exhaustively treated at a much earlier date in his own community. The second abbot of Bonne Espérance, Philip of Harvengt, joined the abbey soon after its foundation in 1126 or 1127 and was already prior about 1130.[19] He became involved in a dispute with St Bernard of Clairvaux over the latter's 'poaching' of talent in accepting a deserter from Bonne Espérance, was banished from his community as the result of an intrigue in some way connected with this and later returned in triumph, eventually succeeding Odo, the first abbot, between 1156 and 1158. Philip was,

---

[17] Bloch, loc. cit., p. 367: 'Près du Rédempteur, on aperçoit deux personnages couronnés et nimbés, qui d'ailleurs ont l'air d'assister à l'action plutôt qu'ils n'y participent vraiment; dans ces deux rois, les archéologues ont unanimement reconnu David et Salomon.' Mâle, L'Art religieux du XIIe siècle en France, 5e édn., Paris, 1947, p. 104, refers to the mosaic at Torcello. In this elaborate composition, the two kings are prominent on the extreme left, raised slightly above all the other figures except Christ (E. W. Anthony, A History of Mosaics, Boston, 1935, plate LVIII). They occupy the same position in the simpler and probably earlier mosaic at Daphni (ibid., plate XLIV). They can be seen on the extreme right with St John the Baptist in St Mark's at Venice (ibid, plate LV) and in the twelfth century MS (Harley 1810) at the British Museum (O. M. Dalton, Byzantine Art and Archaeology, New York, 1961, p. 254). In the mural at Boyana, near Sofia, there are three figures in this position, two of whom may be kings (G. Stoykov, Boyanskata tsŭrkva, Sofia, 1954, plate 16). This was executed in 1259 (N. Mavrodinov, Starobŭlgarskata zhivopis, Sofia, 1947, pp. 89 ff). In a fifteenth century ikon the royal personages are again on the extreme left (D. Talbot Rice, Russian Icons, London, (1947, plate 8). Bloch, speaking of this theme, comments: 'En affirmant ainsi leur foi dans le salut non seulement de David mais encore de son fils, les peintres, émailleurs ou mosaïstes de Byzance ne se mettaient pas en contradiction avec l'opinion de leur Eglise; car il semble bien que, au moyen âge, les théologiens grecs aient été, en règ le générale, beaucoup mieux disposé pour Salomon que leurs confrères latins' (loc. cit., pp. 367–8).

[18] Bloch, loc. cit., p. 372.

[19] Berlière, Revue bénédictine, IX (1892), pp. 24 ff.

therefore, a figure of some stature in the monastic life of his time, but to later ages he is known as the author of a considerable body of theological writings occupying an entire volume of the *Patrologia*.[20] These works include the *Commentarius in Cantica, Moralitates in Cantica, De somnio Nabuchodonosor, Responsio de salute primi hominis* and, of greater relevance to the present discussion, the *Responsio de damnatione Salomonis*.

For Philip of Harvengt, as for the Church in general, the fundamental prerequisite for the sinner's salvation is 'pœnitentia' and in the teaching of the Roman Church repentance includes penance.[21] The *Responsio de salute primi hominis* begins: 'Quaeritis, fratres, utrum primus Adam salvus habeatur, cum eum damnabiliter pecasse Genesis liquido fateatur; penituisse vero eum aperte non legatur.'[22] In the *Responsio de damnatione Salomonis*, Philip searches in vain for evidence of the 'pœnitentia' of Solomon. Commenting on the phrase 'et non adimplevit ut sequeretur Dominum, sicut pater ejus', he writes: 'Quid est enim adimplevit? Nihil aliud esse videtur, quam: Non perfecit, non consummavit, ad finem usque non perduxit. Si vero pœnitentiam egisse affirmaretur, profecto adimplevit ut Dominum sequeretur.'[23] Again he comments: 'Sequitur: "Igitur iratus est Dominus Salomoni, quod aversa esset mens ejus a Domino Deo Israel. . ." Post haec verba nihil in Scriptura canonica legitur de Salomone unde pœnitentia ejus possit vel evidenter approbari, vel saltem aliquatenus aestimari.'[24]

Philip had, however, other material besides the Scriptures to consider. 'Inveni quippe quaedam foliola in quibus ad testimonium pœnitentiae ejus quaedam conscripta erant, quae de sanctorum opusculis Patrum excerpta erant.'[25] After disposing of a number of points in these excerpts, he continues: 'Sequitur in foliolis: "Aiunt libri Hebraei Salomonem quinquies tractum fuisse per plateas civitatis, pœnitentiae causa. Item aiunt eum venisse in templum quod aedificaverat cum quinque virgis, et dedit eas legisperitis ut verbaretur ab illis. Qui communi accepto consilio dixerunt, quod in unctum Domini non mitterent manum. Inde frustratus ab

---

[20] Migne, *Patrologia Latina*, CCIII.
[21] The article 'Penance' in *Catholic Encyclopedia*, XI, p. 618, says: '*Necessity*. The Council of Trent expressly declares (Sess. xiv, c. 1) that penance was at all times necessary for the remission of grievous sin ... theologians state that in the present order of Divine Providence God Himself cannot forgive sins, if there be no real repentance. . . . Christ restates the doctrine of the Old Testament, saying (Luke, xiii, 5): "except you do penance, you shall all likewise perish". In the New Law therefore repentance is as necessary as it was in the Old, repentance that includes reformation of life, grief for sin, and willingness to perform satisfaction.'
[22] *PL*, CCIII, col. 594A.
[23] Ibid., col. 635D.
[24] Ibid., col. 637B.
[25] Ibid., col. 644B.

illis, a se ipso est depositus de regno." '[26] Philip can find no authority for this apparently otherwise unrecorded account of Solomon's 'pœnitentia'. It will be observed that, according to this story, (1) the king was paraded through the town, (2) that he asked to be beaten in the temple, (3) that the 'legisperiti' refused to lay hands upon the Lord's anointed, and (4) that Solomon, seeing his request for corporal punishment refused, abdicated, 'a se ipso est depositus de regno'.

III

Was this part of Philip of Harvengt's exposition known to Herman of Valenciennes? Friedrich Mehne, without actually describing it as a source, quotes it in a note on a passage from the work of this French author.[27] The poem in question, preserved in whole or in part in over thirty manuscripts but as yet unpublished in full,[28] is in fact a versified paraphrase of what doubtless appeared to the author to be the most significant parts of the Old and New Testaments, together with a certain amount of apocryphal material. Of the author we know nothing except what he himself has told us. He says (Bibliothèque nationale, ms. français 20039, fo. 95r):

> Je sui nez de Hainnaut et toz mes parantez,
> A Valenciennes fui batisiez et levez.
> Li bons quens Baudüins, sachiez i fu mandez
> Et o lui Yolans, la contesse, a ses lez,
> Et des autres barons i avoit il assez,
> Et Dudars li evesques fu cel jor confermez.
> D'icel mëisme evesque fui je puis coronnez.
> Mes pere ot non Robers, uns hom molt renomez,
> Et Erambors ma mere, granz fu ses parantez.
> En ceste vie furent, mais or en sont alez.

Again (fo. 35r):

> Clers sui povres de sens si sui .i. jones hom,

---

[26] Ibid., col. 658D–659A.

[27] Friedrich Mehne, *Inhalt und Quellen der Bible des Herman de Valenciennes nach der Maihingen Handschrift und den Ms BN. fr.* 2162, Halle, 1900, pp. 40–41. The actual words are 'Philipp der Harveng . . . widmet der Frage ob Salomo vor seinem Tode noch Busse gethan habe, und sich von der ewigen Verdammnis befreit habe, eine besondere Abhandlung; er verneint jene Frage unter Berufung auf die Schrift und viele Kirchenväter. Doch weiss er auch von anders Denkenden: procliniores (sic) ad credendum quod famam loquacem Judaeis garrientibus ventilare quam quod ecclesiastici doctores inveniuntur in suis litteris affirmare. Besonders erwähnt er quaedam filiola (sic) auf denen Zeugnisse der Kirchenväter und manches de libello cuiusdam Bachiarii sich finden. Harveng sagt dann (S. 658): sequitur in filiolis . . .' Mehne adds that what follows is not taken from Bachiarius, which is of course clear from Philip's text.

[28] An edition is in preparation by the present writer.

Nez sui de Valenciennes, Hermant m'apele l'on . . .
Chanoines sui et prestres, faiz par election.

From this it is apparent that Herman belonged to a family of some note in Hainaut, that he was born in Valenciennes and that, at the time of writing, he was a canon. According to Paul Meyer (*Notices et extraits des manuscrits français*, t. XXXIV, Ière partie, pp. 202 ff.), the 'quens Baudüins' must have been Baudouin IV, Count of Hainaut (1120–71). The 'contesse' was the count's mother Yolande (d. 1167), who, in 1127, had taken as her second husband Godefroi de Bouchain, Seigneur de Valenciennes. So Herman was born before 1167 (the statement in a recent publication[29] that he was born 'à la fin du XIe siècle' is, of course, incorrect like a number of others in the article, which is based on Dinaux and other outdated sources). However, as we shall see (page 32 below), his poem was composed in 1189 at the earliest and at that time he was still, apparently, a 'jones hom', so his birth cannot be placed earlier than the fifties or sixties of the twelfth century. The identity of the bishop Dudars, a name which appears in differing forms in the various MSS, is unknown, so he cannot help us to date the baptism.

Herman concludes his account of the life and deeds of Solomon in the following words (MS BN.fr. 20039, fo. 45r–fo. 46r):

Signor, or m'escoutez, je vos dirai ja voir,
Onques hom fors Adam n'en ot si grant savoir,
Ne en cest mortel siecle n'ot onques tant avoir.
Molt par fu redoutez et fu de grant pöoir,
A ceaus de la contrée molt se par fist cremoir.
Mais en vie mortel ne pot nus hom menoir
Qui ne pechast, fors Deu, ice sai je de voir.
 Signor, ce sachiez vos, Salemons i pecha,
Si sages com il ere, Damerdeu ne douta,
Que une damoisele por sa biauté ama.
Diex! que devint ses sens qant Deu en renoia?
Lui ne vost aörer, cele si l'angingna,

45v Que ele estoit paiene et ses diex li livra,
Por amor de la dame et il les aöra.
Mais qant de li ot fait son bon si la lessa.
Malëoite soit cele qui ce li conseilla.
Qant sot qu'il ot mesfait dolans fu si plora,

[29] H. Platelle, 'Hermann de Valenciennes' in *Catholicisme, hier, aujourd'hui, demain*, Encyclopédie . . . dirigée par S. Jacquemet, fasc. 19, Paris, 1958, p. 622, col. 1.

Manda le patriarche, profetes äuna.
  Qant ot le patriarche tres devant lui mandé,
A ses piez est chëuz, merci li a crié:
'Aiez merci de moi, que molt ai meserré.
J'ai mon signor guerpi et si l'ai degeté,
Le dëable requis et si l'ai äoré.'
'Por qoi?' 'Por une dame, n'est pas en cest regné.'
'Fu ele donc paiene?' 'Oïl, par verité.
J'ai fait de li mon bon si m'en sui retorné.
Sire, par Dieu, de moi si vos praingne pité.'
  Ce dient li profete: 'Sire, vos estes hom.
Dites que volez dire et nos l'escouterom.'
'Ostez moi la corone, ou nos l'en osterom,
Et toz ces dras roiaus, avoir ne les devom.'
Et respondent trestuit: 'Taisiez, rois Salemons,
N'est nostre pöestez, ne faire ne l'osom,
Ice que Diex a fait pas ne desferiom,
Ne nos mains desor toi metre n'oserion.
Diex te doint bon conseil, que nos nos en irom.'
'Comment,' dist Salemons, 'conseil ne me donrez?'
'Nos qel?' 'Jel vos dirai, que me descoronez.
J'ai perdu mon signor si voil estre acordez.
Mes roiaus dras ostez si me deceplinez.'
'Ja fu tes peres rois, voirs est, bien le savez,
Et fu esliz de Deu enoinz et coronez,
46r Si estes ausimant.' 'Ha! las, com mar fui nez!'
'Ne vos pöons desfaire, n'i serez desposez.
Et que devint tes sens?' 'Il fu toz oubliez.'
'As tu ancor les ydres?' 'Toz les ai deboutez.'
'Or pran ta penitance.' 'Et vos le me donez.'
  La fu la penitance de lui bien esgardée,
Ne fu de patriarche mais de lui porpensée,
La fu toute la genz do païs assamblée,
La faisance q'ot faite lor a a toz mostrée
Signor, cel jor i fu mainte larme plorée,
Molt en furent dolant la gent de la contrée.
Li rois osta ses dras si a la char lavée,
A .iiii. de ses homes fu sa chars dessirée.
Par toute la cité qui tant est longue et lée
Ont mené Salemon a icele assamblée.
Onques mais chars de roi ne fu si malmenée,

Por le pechié q'ot fait ot itel destinée.
Signor, tel penitance Salemons esgarda
Que sa char a .iiii. homes a martire livra.
Ne cela som pechié, a toz le raconta.
Apres itel pechié molt longuement regna

. . . .

Tozjors durront ses œuvres tant com cist mons durra.
Ice nos dist li livres, nus mar ce doutera,
Que il ne soit a Deu et toz jorz i sera,
Mais ançois qu'il fust morz Roböan engendra,
Apres la mort celui icil bons rois rainna.

The resemblances between Herman's account and that examined and rejected by Philip of Harvengt are obvious. Solomon is paraded through the town and demands that he should be beaten as an act of penance for his offence. But in Herman's poem this demand is granted, whereas in the 'foliola' it is refused. In both versions the question of abdication or deposition arises, but in the French story Solomon, having obtained satisfaction in the matter of public chastisement, does not persist in his desire to be deposed; on the contrary, 'molt longuement regna'. In the account quoted by Philip, his proposed penance having been rejected, 'a se ipso est depositus de regno'. If Herman was using either Philip's résumé or its original, are the differences to be explained by a deliberate transposition of certain elements dictated by his own partisanship, which finds passionate expression in his declaration: 'Ice nos dist li livres, nus ce mar doutera, Que il ne soit a Deu et toz jorz i sera?' Certainly, if 'li livres' refers to some other source, this must have been unknown, not only to the theologian of Bonne Espérance, but to all other commentators.

In the absence of any more precise quotation of authority by Herman, it is perhaps worth considering whether he was likely to have known either the writings of Philip or his 'foliola'. Dom Ursmer Berlière in the articles already referred to can find no evidence for dating the *Responsio de damnatione Salomonis*, but it must, of course, have been written between about 1130 (the beginning of Philip's career) and 1183 (the year of his death). So Herman, born early in the second half of the century and writing in 1189 or later, could easily have been acquainted with it. The abbey of Bonne Espérance at Binche was at no great distance from Valenciennes, so geography presents no greater obstacle than chronology to Philip's account having come to the knowledge of Herman. Finally, Bonne Espérance belonged to the Premonstratensians, that vigorous and expanding order of regular canons. And Herman describes himself as a canon. Had he perhaps at some period been a member of that same community?[30] If so, it would have been natural for him to see some or all of the documents or at least to hear echoes of the controversy which Philip's *Responsio* suggests may have existed there concerning Solomon's fate and to become emotionally involved in it.

It seems probable, therefore, that the 'foliola' were Herman's ultimate source for this part of his poem. We can only speculate as to the reasons that may have led him to transform the story so significantly. If he was passionately convinced, as his words seem to imply, of the necessity, in any reasonable scheme of things, of Solomon's salvation, he was bound to believe in the reality of that sinner's repentance. To this rather simple-minded priest, 'povres de sens', repentance probably implied a definite, visible penance, not merely a proffered gesture. And for so great a sin, 'itel pechié', the penance must surely have been dramatic. What more fitting than public chastisement? Yet it was an audacious act to represent, without authority or precedent, the laying of hands upon the Lord's anointed, the king.

IV

One is tempted to wonder whether any event in Herman's experience could have provided such a precedent. The parallel in real life to Solomon's supposed penance that immediately springs to mind is Henry II's gesture at Canterbury in July 1174, in Herman's own lifetime.

King Henry's final act of atonement for any responsibility for the murder of Thomas à Becket is briefly described by Roger of Hoveden[31] and related with an abundance of detail by Edward Grim, who had witnessed the crime itself.[32] This author describes how Henry made his way from the church of St Dunstan 'ad ecclesiam majorem ubi beati martyris corpus quiescit, nudis pedibus et veste communi incedens et flens, ubicunque asperior apparuit via, per medium civitatis ascendit, non itineris inclementiam, non pedum teneritudinem, non vulgi hinc inde spectaculum, sed animae consideravit periculum. . . . Dicta autem confessione astantibus episcopis, cum tremore multo ac reverentia ad tumbam accessit.'[33] The Bishop of London made a statement on the king's behalf, then: 'Post haec autem exteriori exutus veste, scapulis et capite inclinato in unam

---

[30] Berlière, loc. cit., p. 131, observes: 'Les seigneurs du Hainaut se firent un honnur d'être comptés au nombre des bienfaiteurs de l'abbaye.' The greatest of these seigneurs was the principal guest at Herman's baptism.

[31] *Chronica Magistri Rogeri de Hovedene*, ed. Stubbs (Rolls Series), vol. II, p. 61

[32] *Vita Sancta Thomae, Cantuarensis Archiepiscopi et Martyris, auctore Edwardo Grim* in *Materials for the History of Thomas Becket*, ed. J. C. Robertson (Rolls Series), vol. II, pp. 445–7.

[33] P. 445.

fenestrarum tumuli humili prorsus devotione, adeo ut in luctum conver-
teret universos, primo quinquies caesus a prelatis, postmodum a monachis
octoginta et eo amplius ter a singulis caesus, et sic solenniter absolutus
est ... Neque facile reperitur in aliqua historia Christiani temporis aut
humilior isto principe in pœnitentia aut devotior aliquis extitisse.'[34] In
spite of the differences in detail reflecting the differences in circumstances,
we find here the same general features as in Herman's description of
Solomon's penance: the assembled crowds, the procession through the
town, the public confession, the stripping off of the royal robes and the
chastisement at different hands. And the final sentence is roughly paralleled
in Herman's 'Onques mais chars de roi ne fu si malmenée'.[35]

There is nothing improbable in the supposition that Herman knew of
Henry's penance, although the parallel between it and his account of
Solomon's atonement does not seem to have been previously noted. The
possibility that Herman emigrated to England might lend it support. Lois
Borland has shown that the author of the *Cursor Mundi* adapted considerable parts of Herman's poem, including the episode with which we are
here concerned, observing that 'The assumption of L'Abbé De la Rue and
of Arthur Dinaux that Herman lived and wrote in England is neither
accepted nor disproved. In its favour, at least, are two obvious facts: the
poet reiterates that he is *from* Valenciennes;[36] and a great number of the
manuscripts show evidence of having been copied in England.'[37] This
statement is perhaps unjustifiably strengthened later to: 'Herman's *Bible* is
highly interesting for its intrinsic literary value; its wide popularity is
attested by the number of extant MSS; it is probable that the author lived
and worked in England.'[38]

At least it is clear that Herman was interested in Henry and impressed by
his fate, if only as an example of the favourite medieval *vanitas vanitatum*
theme. Here is what he has to say of the English king (BN. fr. 20039, fo.
95v):

> Signor, molt par est feble iceste mortex vie.
> Sitost com li hom naist a premiers plore et crie,
> Ja dou liu ne movroit se il n'avoit aïe.
> Molt vient de povre chose, ne sai en quoi se fie.
> Gardez au roi Henri et a sa menantie.
> Il fu rois d'Angleterre et quons de Normendie,

---

[34] P. 447.
[35] Is there any significance in the use by Herman of *dessirée* (déchirée) where Grim uses
caesus in contrast to Philip's *verbaretur*?
[36] Which does not necessarily mean that he has come *to* England.
[37] 'Herman's Bible and the Cursor Mundi,' *Studies in Philology*, XXX (1933), p. 428, n. 4.
[38] Ibid., p. 443.

Gale et Escoce tint trestout en sa baillie,
Fiers fu com uns lions, molt ot grant signorie,
Princes ot et barons et grant chevalerie.
Ou est or li prodom, ou est sa menantie?
Or li prest Diex son regne, que de cest n'a il mie.
Mar i menons orgueil, por quoi portons anvie?[39]

Herman de Valenciennes had a certain gift for dramatic description and possessed a simple eloquence, but he was certainly not a profound thinker. Yet one of the controversies that occupied religious thinkers of his own and preceding ages finds an echo in his narrative. In the absence of any reason for thinking that he possessed evidence not known to Philip of Harvengt, we may probably conclude that in his imaginative distortion of his source he was influenced by contemporary events and was guided less by his intellect than his feelings. Like Dante, that much greater poet of a century later, he is on the side of mercy. Perhaps he took a more compassionate view than more learned churchmen of Solomon's fundamental weakness, for, earlier in his poem, having described the destruction of Gomorrha, he exclaims: 'Au naturel pechié des femes vos tenez!' (BN. fr. of 20039, fo. 8r).

---

[39] This passage shows that Herman was writing after Henry's death, which took place in 1189.

3

W. ROTHWELL

The Mystic's Way in Medieval French and Provençal

IT is hard not to be carried along, perhaps unconsciously, by the current of contemporary thought, and there is a tendency among modern scholars to look for systems everywhere in language. They seem reluctant to envisage the possibility of a language having at any time a structure so fluid, so poorly disciplined that it could be recalcitrant to any firm, clear systematization. They seem also to overlook the possibility that some types of experience may be so personal as to call forth responses so individualistic as to make them unlikely to fit into any arbitrary system. It is, therefore, not difficult to understand why ideas which seem to derive ultimately from the structuralist school of linguistics should make their appearance in some rather unexpected places in linguistic research.

A case in point is the language used by certain mystical writers in medieval French. Being the vehicle for the innermost yearnings of the individual soul, this, one might have thought, could be expected to show considerable variation from one writer to the next. Yet apparently it is not so. It would seem that, for those who have eyes to see, even in medieval France the mystic's way was a clear, well sign-posted one. In a recent thesis, *The French Expressions for Spirituality and Devotion*,[1] Sister L. Tinsley writes:

> The tendency to analyze and clarify, characteristic of French thought and language, is very evident in the domain of spirituality, especially where the development of a system is involved, ... It is particularly noticeable in the greatest language-making epochs, that is, among the XIth to XIIIth century mystics ... (p. 6).

Sister Tinsley's director, Professor Hatzfeld, writes in similar vein about these same mystical texts in the vernacular. In an article entitled 'Linguistic Investigation of Old French High Spirituality',[2] although he states first that:

> The popular mystical texts are vague and not as well organized as

---

[1] The Catholic University of America Press, 1953.

[2] *PMLA*, LXI (1946), pp. 331–78.

the texts of the Schoolmen, whose clear terminology generally contains a more precise expression of the Ineffable (p. 331),

he then proceeds to explain how he proposes to find in these popular texts
'an adequately recognizable *system*'[3] (p. 331). His method is this:

> It will be possible to make all these texts reveal systematically the
> Old French vocabulary and phraseology of higher spiritual ex-
> periences, if we approach them equally with an onomatological
> questionnaire taken from the later classical mystical system of the
> Spaniards. This *anachronic* procedure to illustrate earlier *words and
> things* by later ones, . . . , is one of the soundest methods of modern
> mystical theology itself (p. 333).[3]

Using this procedure, he is able to draw up a detailed table of the
successive steps in the mystic's ascent to God, each with its Old French
vocabulary paralleled by equivalent expressions in medieval Latin, sixteenth-century Spanish, and, on occasion, in German, Dutch or some other
vernacular (pp. 370-8).

Whilst it might be considered improper for someone not trained in
theology to hazard an opinion as to the soundness or otherwise of this
particular line of investigation into mystical theology, it may perhaps be
permitted to treat the matter from a purely practical linguistic angle. By
looking carefully at certain mystical texts in Old French and Provençal we
may be able to see whether the assumptions made by Professor Hatzfeld
are justified. For assumptions there are, and they are of cardinal importance
in determining the results of the investigation.

His first assumption seems to be that a mystic will always follow the
same path of development as other mystics, experiencing the same mystical states in the same order and arriving eventually at the same goal. The
second, that such mystical states will always present themselves clothed in
the same linguistic material of images, comparisons and the like. These
two assumptions imply that the fundamental religious experience is para-
mount and so uniform that differences between a man's reaction and a
woman's, between the intellect of the Victorines and that of an anonymous
Beguine, between the passionate outpourings of St Bernard or the often
monstrous visions of St Hildegarde[4] on the one hand and the scholastic
turn of mind of St Bonaventura or the cold, dispassionate exposition of

---

[3] Author's own italics.

[4] P. Pourrat, *La Spiritualité chrétienne*, t.II: *Le Moyen Age* (Paris, 1924), pp. 122-3, quotes a
remarkable vision in which Hildegarde sees the Church as a monstrous woman without arms
or legs, her belly a net into which are taken hordes of black children from the air, to be
cleansed by a man bright as flame.

Eckhart on the other, between the thirteenth century in France and the sixteenth century in Spain — these differences are as nothing. That these are, indeed, the assumptions which underlie Professor Hatzfeld's reasoning is borne out by his statement in the conclusion to his article that:

> since the same psychological conditions are bound to produce similar terms, in all languages, the Old French expressions are ... compared to later, particularly Spanish, coinages which represent a generally recognized standard for mystic language (p. 369).

To speak of 'the same psychological conditions' is to assume not only that mystics are all of one kind, but that they think, feel and write in a vacuum, quite untouched by the life of the world in which they live. Yet modern scholarship has for years past been revealing the intimate connection between all manner of artistic production and the social and economic environment in which it was created.[5] It would be odd, to say the least, if even a subject so unwordly as mysticism were to be uninfluenced by its surroundings.

That it should be felt necessary to look for a clear system in the writings of the medieval French mystics would seem to be due to the fact that French during the Middle Ages is not considered to be a fully developed language, being rather like the speech of a child unable to express any but the most immediate and concrete of thoughts. Professor Hatzfeld contrasts the clarity of Santa Teresa and the limpidity of San Juan de la Cruz with 'the stammerings of the awkward medieval mystics' (p. 333). He reads these latter as though they were bound to follow the same lines of development as the later Spaniards and finds their writings in conformity with the more clearly expounded ideas of their great successors, for at the very outset of his work he is at pains to state that the six stages of mystical experience drawn up by modern scholars are to be found in all the texts he handles (p. 333).

Given the rigid assumptions mentioned above, it is hardly surprising to find that not all the medieval French expressions dealt with in the article fit easily into the pattern laid down for them.[6] A more constructive approach

---

[5] E.g. F. Antal, *Florentine Painting and its Social Background* (London, 1947); E. Panofsky, *Gothic Architecture and Scholasticism* (New York, 1957); M. Schlauch, *English Medieval Literature and its Social Foundations* (Warsaw, 1956), etc., reaching as far back as Henry Adams, *Mont-Saint-Michel and Chartres* (New York, 1913).

[6] E.g. (i) *passemens* (p. 333) are not 'the mystical stages', equivalent to the *gras* < *gradus* in Provençal or the *rains* of the mystical palm-tree; the word is clearly translated in the very next line of the text as *visettement*, God passing to visit, to call upon the soul. (ii) *acorer le cuer* does not mean *arracher* (p. 357) or *mourir* (p. 364); it simply means 'pierce' as on p. 356. (iii) *radaiche d'orison* seems to lend but little support to the statement that: 'Those who are familiar with

to their understanding might be to consider them on their own terms, set against the backcloth of their times. For the thirteenth and fourteenth centuries, when these texts were written, the age of the great scholastics, was also a time of great popular ferment, especially in northern France.[7] An age of brilliant orthodox teachers, it was also one of bitter controversy, to which the massive condemnations of 1277 and the attacks of a Gerson on his fellow-mystic Ruysbroeck bear ample witness. It is against this background of living people — the saints and the Averroists, Saint Louis and the *Pastoureaux*, the Flagellant movements and the Brethren of the Free Spirit — that the vernacular mystical texts must be read. If read in this light, they will be seen to be the work not of people to be pitied and 'explained', because the linguistic tool they used was a rough, crude, inadequate one,[8] people to be fitted into a particular mould only by reference to later writers of another land, but of living individuals, each expressing to the best of his ability his own most intimate relationship with his God. Perhaps if we look at these writers as perfectly articulate individuals, with a right to be judged on their own merits, then in so doing we may arrive at a better understanding both of what they were saying and of the language in which they said it.

It does not need much study to realize that the mystical texts surviving in old French fall into two widely differing categories. There are, on the one hand, the truly popular, deeply personal writings of the Beguines, and on the other hand the more systematized tracts going back to the Victorines' theory of contemplation. These two groups are so different in character that any lumping of them together can lead only to vitiated conclusions. The first group consists of the highly lyrical outpourings of people who have known from personal experience a state of rapture; the second contains largely academic accounts, using scholastic methods of exposition, of the stages through which a soul may progress towards mystical union with God.

This latter category is by far the easier to handle, both from the point of

mystical texts certainly are struck by the beauty, exactness and originality of the expression *radece d'orison* for the concept of *prayer of quiet*' (p. 339). Taken in its context — the soul wrestling with God as Jacob did with the angel — this phrase means 'torrent of prayer', a torrent welling up from the depths of ardent desire and sweeping God off His feet. (iv) *orisons faite en bondie* is not 'an echo-prayer, a boomerang prayer' (p. 339), but a resounding prayer ringing out like battle-trumpets.

[7] For a most illuminating account of this ferment, see N. Cohn, *The Pursuit of the Millenium* (London, 1962).

[8] 'There seem to be no simple, amorphous, or imperfect languages, . . . People who have not invented textiles, . . . need no privacy and mind no filth and roast their enemies for dinner, will yet converse over their bestial feasts in a tongue as grammatical as Greek, and as fluent as French!' (Susanne K. Langer, *Philosophy in a New Key* [Cambridge, Mass., 1960], p. 103.)

view of language and subject-matter, and is excellently illustrated by *Le Livre du Paumier*.[9] This late thirteenth-century comparison of the mystic's ascent to God with a seven-branched palm tree is steeped in medieval learning.[10] The palm tree, narrow at the base (closed to earthly things), is wide at the top (opening out to the love of God), and each of its seven branches holds a bird and a flower to which is attributed a symbolic meaning, a procedure taking us back straightaway into the world of the medieval Church.[11]

The first branch represents the examination of conscience and contains a peacock and a violet, the connection being that just as the peacock is supposed to wake up and cry out in the night, thinking that he has lost his beauty, so the soul, in its examination of conscience (the first step in mysticism), is fearful of losing its beauty in the night of the world. The violet, of course, is the sign of humility. After recognizing its own state and applying to it the virtue of humility, the soul then moves on to the next branch, which is compassion for its neighbour. This is symbolized by the owl and the sword-flag: the bird haunts the dying and the tombs of the dead, just as the compassionate soul dwells among sinners dead through sin and attempts to bring them back to salvation, whilst the sword-flag, growing beside water, represents the soul dwelling beside those slipping away on the waters of sin. On the third branch the soul suffers without complaint all manner of temporal affliction: the swan sings at the moment of its death, representing the soul's joy in tribulation, and the lily gives off sweet perfume in the midst of thorns, showing that the soul is to return good for evil. On the fourth branch, compunction, are the harpy and the rose. By now the soul is so immersed in the sufferings of Christ that it is oblivious of its own afflictions, just as the harpy, a bird of human appearance, having killed the first man it sees, then gazes into water and, seeing that it has killed something akin to itself, breaks into lamentation. The rose is the symbol of martyrdom. The fifth branch of the palm tree is expectation, containing a nightingale and the saffron or crocus, the nightingale because it sings all night and almost bursts with joy at the rising of the sun, the crocus perhaps because the soul in expectation of God's visit is only too

---

[9] Ed. K. Christ in *Mittelalterliche Handschriften: Festgabe Degering* (Leipzig, 1926), pp. 57–81.

[10] 'Wortschatz und Ausdrucksform liefern keine Stütze für die These eines vulgären Ursprungs' (p. 67).

[11] E.g. Hugo of St Victor's Tree of the Old Adam, with each of its seven branches being a particular vice, and his Tree of the New Adam, where the branches are the seven virtues. See also 'The Tree of Jesse Window of Chartres: *Laudes Regiae*,' by J. R. Johnson, in *Speculum*, XXXVI (1961), 1–22. The most searching and wide-ranging treatment of this whole theme is to be found in the remarkable article by Spitzer, 'Er hat einen Sparren,' in *Essays in Historical Semantics* (New York, 1948), pp. 67–134.

conscious of not being pure white.[12] The sixth branch is visitation: God takes pity on the waiting soul and visits it. The bird on this branch is the swallow and the flower the marigold. The swallow is placed here firstly because it eats on the wing, being so little interested in the things of this world, and secondly because it is supposed to be disconsolate in the absence of its mother. The marigold follows the sun around in its course, opening in sunlight and closing when the sun does not shine, just as the contemplative soul opens to God's presence and closes when grace is withdrawn. The highest branch of the palm tree is ecstasy. The bird found on this branch is, inevitably, the phœnix, the symbol of Christ, and Christ is the flower too. Such, in bare outline, is the content of Le Livre du Paumier. It is a typically didactic medieval treatment of the theoretical stages of the soul's mystical development. Nowhere does it contain anything to suggest the passionate outbursts of a soul that has known rapture.

To move from the Paumier to the Beguine texts is to pass from one world to another, so completely different are they in content and style, for these texts begin where the Paumier ends: they are the product of practising mystics who have attained, at least momentarily, to a degree of union with God such as marks the highest branch of the Paumier, where 'les fuelles de cest rain sont li cri, li pasmement, li soupir, li segloutement'. Yet it is dangerous to treat these texts as a group: they must be handled individually,[13] for the Beguine movement was in essence individualistic. Subjected to no close and uniform discipline, living no uniform pattern of life, the Beguines were largely untrammelled by restrictions of orthodoxy, so that they were condemned by the official Church as early as the middle of the thirteenth century.[14] It is hardly to be expected that the writings of such people (where they have been allowed to survive) would lend themselves to neat and tidy categorization.

If we examine first the three poems written in Picardy in the thirteenth century and published by Bechmann,[15] it will be seen that each is different from the others in both spirit and language, and that all are poles removed from the Paumier. The first of these is a highly personal, lyrical invocation

[12] We are given here a quotation from the Song of Songs: 'Ne me regardés mie pour ce que je suis noire, car li solaus m'a descoulouree.' St Bernard comments upon this at length in his Sermon XXX.

[13] Cf. '... the divisions of the life of grace and the spirit, though resting upon real psychological and theological entities and powers, are in their external manifestations refracted and clouded by all the differing circumstances, qualities and graces of the individual soul.' (Dom David Knowles, The English Mystical Tradition [London, 1961], p. 91.)

[14] Cohn, op. cit., p. 167.

[15] 'Drei Dits de l'Ame' in Zeitschrift für romanische Philologie, XIII (1889), pp. 35-84.

of Christ the lover of the soul, very reminiscent of the *Jesu dulcis memoria*, with the passionate *O douls amis* recurring time and again. Here is no trace of any stages, any ascent of the soul to God. All the emphasis is on the pleading desire for union with the crucified Christ, union on the highest level. Yet, if there is no systematized ascent of the soul outlined, it would be a gross error to see in this poem nothing but 'stammerings of the awkward medieval mystics'. Linguistically, this is a well turned-out poem with a regular metrical pattern and a fairly sophisticated rhyme scheme, a poem written by someone with a keen sense of semantic oppositions:

> O douls boutés, o douls sachiés!
> O sages com fols buffiés!
> O grans rikecche despoullie!
> O tous poissans entre les piés!
> O tres honnestes vieutiiés!
> O tous sens tenus a sotie!
> O benignes contre estoutie!
> O tres douls contre felonnie!
> O tres grans pris, trop pau prisiés   (v. 4).

> Fai me toi cognoistre en sentant,
> et si sentir en cognissant,
> que li miens coers l'a desiré   (v. 9).

To say, as does Professor Hatzfeld, that in this second extract 'there is made a clear distinction between a desired feeling (longing) and a granted feeling (quietude)' (p. 338) seems to miss the point that the writer is deliberately juxtaposing the feeling and the intellect in semantic opposition, not in order to make any clear distinction, but to intensify the force of her desire for knowledge of God. Again later, the sharply contrasting ideas of burning and drowning are deliberately juxtaposed:

> Amis, mech en m'affection
> un sentement de tel boichon,
> qui m'arge et noye de tous les[16]   (v. 16).

Of greater interest here than any attempt to find ascending stages or the obvious states of alternating ecstasy and depression caused by the mystic's sense of now attaining to a union with God and now being deprived of His

---

[16] See also the short poem printed after the *Drei Dits*, where prayer is likened to a crossbow: Les cordes sont *coiement cri* en orison pour son ami . . . (p. 79).
For the abundant use of this technique by courtly poets, see R. Dragonetti, *La Technique poétique des trouvères dans la chanson courtoise* (Bruges, 1960), pp. 55 ff.

presence is the exclusive concentration of the female writer on one aspect
of the Trinity, namely Christ. It is not merely that she threatens to com-
plain to her lover's Father (God) and Mother (Mary) if she is not speedily
taken from this life to join Him (v. 23), or that she posits a brother and
sister relationship with Him (ibid.). The whole poem, in complete contrast
to the didactic *Paumier*, is based on feeling, a feeling of immense love, a
woman's feeling at that. The verbs used to describe her means of knowing
Christ are time and again *sentir* and *gouster*:

> Douls amis, je ne puis durer
> sans toi sentir et savourer . . .   (v. 10).

> Quant daigniés que vous puis gouster . . .   (v. 15).

> Amis, t'amour me fai gouster
> et si sentir et savourer, . . .   (v. 18) etc.

This reality of feeling, not some unexplained deficiency in Old French,
is the reason for the lack of any clear, logical progression in the poem; this
is the reason for the occasional difficult phrase, and it is with this reality in
mind that the poem must be interpreted.

The second of Bechmann's texts, although written in the same form as
the poem just examined, differs from it basically in being not a personal
lyrical outburst addressed to Christ, but a description of the perfect life.
Consequently, it contains more historical references — to Jacob's struggle,
to the clothing of the poor and so on — and also a more analytical account
of what the mystic experiences. Yet here again there is little doubt that we
are in the presence of one who has actually passed through the stages
described, the images used being far stronger than any found in the
Paumier and also more familiar. We meet again the Bernardine concept of
Christ as the lover in this very bold image of God being pulled about,
scalded and ducked until the soul makes Him a prisoner, getting from Him
a ransom:

> Aultre chose n'est chils luitiers
> fors que par ardans desiriers
> en le radaiche d'orison
> soit dieus et boutés et sachiés
> et si escaudés et baigniés,
> que li coers l'ait en sa prison.
> He dieus, com douche raenchon
> li coers en a de cest prison!   (v. 9).

Dwelling upon the thought of God's goodness, beauty and *poissanche humeliie* (semantic oppositions again), the soul is so filled with tenderness, sweetness and love that it is rendered dumb:

> Mais li desiriers pour li prie
> ardanment et dieu magnefie
> en decourant de se douchour   (v. 10).

We are here close to the inexpressible, not by reason of any defect in medieval French, but because the writer is moving beyond the realm of thought to that of feeling.[17] Another case of this occurs in v. 11, where this almost wordless prayer of desire is to be 'roasted in the fire of love' *en l'espoi de desir diervé*, that is, 'on the spit of mad desire' (for union with God).

As in the previous poem, the writer has recourse to the juxtaposition of semantic opposites to render the inexpressible:

> Tels feus font l'ame en ses desirs
> de chou que n'est ens ou païs
> chelui qui en solant l'afame   (v. 14).

> Amours saole sans mengier,
> et si enivre de legier
> le coer, sans boire vin qui flaire.
> Plorer fait et esleechier
> et mener doel sans courechier . . .   (v. 15).

The writer of the *Paumier* apparently did not feel the need to use this kind of image simply because he had not personally experienced the state it attempts to describe.

The third of Bechmann's texts is no less personal in its descriptions of the way in which the questing soul may reach God. To pass over the more usual images which one might expect to find — the soul burning with love or melting, and so on — what strikes the reader most is the violence and familiarity of the writer's approach to God. Here is no reverent awe of the majesty of God, but rather a lover's intimacy. Its home is not the carefully ordered, integrated, intellectual world of Thomism, but the turbulent, violent everyday life of the northern French towns. God is to be hunted and ensnared by the soul; when He is captured, the soul dare not even sigh

---

[17] Cf. 'Thus burning and vehement love . . . , takes no heed of the order nor connection of the words it employs, nor even of their fewness, provided that it suffers no diminution of its vigour. Sometimes it does not seek for words, not even for articulate language at all, but is content with the wordless aspirations of the spirit alone' (St Bernard, *Sermon* LXVII/3, transl. S. J. Eales).

for fear He might escape (v. 17); the soul clings so tightly to God that it 'goes to school' in His side, learning there the love of God (v. 16); nails of love are to fix the soul to God, nails fashioned by the hammer of jubilation against the anvil of failure and disappointment, nails which prick the soul with an ointment of Paradise, sweeter than honey (vv. 13–4). At times the imagery passes over into what for us is the tasteless,[18] as when the soul is described as being so fat that it melts in the fire of love (v. 17), or when prayer is said to send up sweet smells to God, these smells being ropes by which God pulls up the sweet desires to which the soul is attached (v. 19). In similar vein is the image of prayer as a tournament, where the soul is seen tilting at the quintain of the Cross, with pennants of desire flying at its lance (v. 20).

As an illustration of the diversity of expression used in medieval French to render these highly personal mystical experiences, it would be hard to better the poem published by Tanquerey under the title of *Exhortation à l'Amour divin*.[19] Again a thirteenth-century product from north-eastern France, this is so typically medieval in style and content that to attempt to understand it through sixteenth-century Spanish texts is to attempt to understand one civilisation simply by reference to another. Although many footnotes list the literary sources upon which the writer has drawn, the liveliness of the poem lies in its completely uninhibited approach to God. There is no trace of analysis here, no ordered ascent to God, but simply an almost random succession of forceful images taken from everyday medieval life to express the intimate relationship of the soul to God — the soul sitting down to a hearty meal of the Lamb of God, pulling it about at will and saying *Par ici le me taille* (ll. 16–20); God, after being subdued and brought into subjection, being used as a poultice to keep out the cold (ll. 176–83). Images again show the nature of love: love as a gibbet, with the holy soul hanging from it, a living gibbet able to bend down to the writer's heart and lift it up to God (ll. 232 ff.); love as a ladder down which God climbs to visit His beloved in her cell (ll. 251 ff.); love as a clock ensuring that the soul gets up early in the morning in spite of the slothful flesh (ll. 277 ff.); love slitting God's side in order to give His heart to the writer (l. 263). Prayer here is not just a rope as in the Bechmann text, but a well-rope; it lets the soul (= bucket) down into the well from which is drawn the water of life, but lacking the stone with a hole in it (= Christ)

---

[18] We must beware of transferring this twentieth-century value judgment uncritically to the thirteenth and fourteenth centuries, using this tastelessness as an argument for the immaturity of the medieval French writer: St Bernard himself talks about the soul grinding psalms between the teeth of his intelligence (*Sermon* VII/5).

[19] *Romania*, LXVI (1940), pp. 322–54.

to weight it down, the soul is too light and floats aimlessly on the surface (ll. 158 ff.).[20]

Other features of this text give fairly broad hints that the writer may have been pretty close to the brink of heresy in the individualism of her approach to God. She is far from St Bernard's perfect selflessness with regard to the reasons for loving God: *Causa diligendi Deum, Deus est*,[21] and asks:

> Quel avantage a dont cuers qui a toy s'atire,
> Qui d'aimer coralment se desront et descire
> S'un po plus no li fais de ce que il desire?   (ll. 65–7);

she is delighted at the prospect of her enemies bursting with envy at the sight of God's pennants flying from her window (ll. 217 ff.); moreover, she sees the Virgin as founder and fount of the Beguine movement and rejects the value of the Church's offices as a means of knowing God:

> Jhesus, livres de vie, sapïence divine,
> Livres que Dex escrit en la pel pure et fine,
> En la pel qui no fu ne grasse ne verrine;
> La fut escriz li vers a la sainte raïne
> Que elle versilloit sovent sor la cortine.
> Jhesus, tu fus li livres ou la sainte beguine,
> Qui de saint beguinage fut fontaigne et orine,
> Lisoit et relisoit en la quaste gesine.
> Quant elle te baisoit la face et la poitrine,
> Ne queroit autre messe, n'oïr autre matine   (ll. 80–9).

Again, on reading lines such as these:

> Cueil grant planté de verges, dame maistresse, cueil;
> De lïece et de joie devant toy me despuel.
> Bat ton malvés deciple et a toy le recueil   (ll. 123–5),

one is reminded of the heretical flagellant movements which broke out in various parts of Europe in the thirteenth century.

There is one other text which must find a place here in view of its typically medieval manner of describing the mystic's ascent. It is a long,

---

[20] Cf. 'Leurs (= des prédicateurs) comparaisons, prises dans la vie journalière, choquent presque toujours par leur trivialité. . . . Un autre compare le crucifix à un beau miroir qu'une femme a placé dans sa chambre, devant lequel elle s'habille et se lave, et qu'elle nettoie, quand il n'est pas bien net, en crachant dessus . . .; le crucifix, qui est le miroir du monde, a été si bien lavé par les crachats des Juifs qu'il est de la plus parfaite pureté . . . Un troisième compare Notre Seigneur à un médecin qui examine l'urine des malades et ordonne des saignées . . .' (Petit de Julleville, *Histoire de la langue et de la littérature française* [Paris, 1896–9], II, p. 245.)

[21] *De Diligendo Deo* I, ed. E. G. Gardner (London, 1916).

rambling work of some 670 lines, with verses of widely varying length. Its content is of a banal religious character until the last verse (comprising 450 lines!), a strange, allegorical account of a soul's visit to Heaven.[22] In brief, this last section treats the substance of the *Jesu dulcis memoria* and develops it after the manner of the *Roman de la Rose*:

> L'autrier passai par un boscaige.
> La vois oï d'une dame sage
> Qui aprés amours languissoit   (ll. 216–8).

The lady's lament turns out to be a fairly close translation of the *Jesu dulcis memoria*:

> Mout seis bien grans joie donneir
> A ceus qui te veulent amer.
> Tu es confors as repentans,
> Et qu'es tu donc a toi trouvans?
> Ihesus, dou cuer toute douçours
> Fontaine, lumiere et savours,
> Langue ne porroit raconteir,
> Nule escripture deviser
> Le preu qui est en toi amer!   (ll. 228–36).

Yet once her supplication for union with Christ is ended (v. 289), we are switched abruptly over to the cold, artificial world of allegory. A talking bird promises her that if she believes in him she will soon be taken up to Paradise. He then flies off to Heaven, leaving the lady disconsolate. She enters into a state of contemplation, sleeping on a bed of Poverty, with Charity for a pillow, Virginity a sheet and so on. These virtues make their way up to Heaven, riding on the charger of Faith along the path of Purity until they reach Paradise, where Pity opens the gates for them. Having made their plea before God, they prevail upon Him to leave His throne and descend to the devout lady in the form of the child Jesus, surrounded by the whole Heavenly Host. The lady invites the child to supper, and upon His accepting, we are launched into allegory again, Pity setting up the table, Prudence putting on the cloth, Confession serving water and Discretion the towel. The food likewise is allegorical — laughter, sighs, jubilation and so forth. After the wine, served by Devotion, Discretion serves fruit in an orchard, suitably described. The joyful feast is brought to a fitting end with song and dance provided by the Heavenly Host, then

---

[22] Ed. Hilka, 'Altfranzösische Mystik und Beginentum' in *Zeitschrift für romanische Philologie*, XLVII (1927), pp. 126–42. Two further texts published with this need not detain us, the one dealing only with the qualities necessary to the true Beguine and the other being too short (28 ll.) to have much development.

the child is put to bed after the various attendant virtues have each had a share in preparing bed and bath. The poem continues in this vein until the lady is taken up to Heaven, escorted by the Heavenly Host, to be united with God.

The texts examined above have shown how great can be the differences between mystical works of the same period, written in the same language, depending upon whether the writer is giving an account of his innermost feelings and experiences or setting out a more didactic and theoretical scheme of mystical progress. Examples have been adduced of the purely subjective union of the individual soul with Christ the lover, of the more precious, allegorical handling of the mystic's way to communion with God, and also of the didactic treatment of the mystic's ascent as represented by the palm tree. The strangest approaches to mysticism have, however, been reserved till last. One of these is to be found in the Provençal text, *Scala Divini Amoris*,[23] a fourteenth-century scholastic demonstration, by means of medieval science, of the possibility of the soul's attaining to the love of God.

The *Scala* is, above all else, an excellent example of the mystic's way seen from outside and set down by one who has definitely not reached any useful degree of mystical knowledge.[24] It is in no sense the recollected experience of a man whose soul has known God. Here, for instance, is part of the writer's proof that his soul is capable of loving God:

> ... doussors es bona per asaborar, e suavetat es bona per tocar, e odor es bona per sentir, e cantars es bos per ausir, e beutat e nedeza es bona per vezer. [Therefore] ... per so car Dieus es la mager doussor que puesca esser cossirada, e la plus doussa suavetat el plus plazent cant e la plus suaus odors e la plus delechabla beutat que sia, cove per forsa que tota doussors e tota suavetat e tot cant e tota odor e tota beutat, que es en creatura, sia dins Dieu (p. 1).

He then goes on to say that since the soul is capable of loving all these qualities in creatures, then it ought to be capable of loving them in the Creator. This theme is developed, the argument being that all created things are made up of the four elements, earth, water, air and fire, each of which contains *doussor e suavetat e odor e melodi de cant e beutat e nedessa*, the task of the soul in search of God being to recognize these qualities in created nature and then in God, the Creator. Here, stripped of the wealth

---

[23] Ed. V. Motte, Diss. Halle, 1902.
[24] After describing the first step in mystical progress he says: *Certas la mia arma non a pas puiat aquest escalo* (p. 4).

of medieval science adduced to prove the case, are the steps as the writer sees them:

(1) ... que dedins la doussor de totas las creaturas sapia trobar e sentir la granda doussor de Dieu (p. 4).

(2) ... cant en tota suavetad que es en creatura sento la suavetat de Dieu ... (p. 5).

(3) ... cant en la odor de las creaturas sab sentir la doussa odor de Dieu ... (p. 6).

(4) ... cant arma per la granda doussor que au del so que fan totas las creaturas que totas lauzan Dieu e la pregan d'amar ve en tan gran descenamen, que no ve ni au ni no sent, car oblidat s'a si mezeissa ... (p. 10).

(5) So es cant hom en tota beutat & en tota netessa qui es en creatura, sab conoisser e vezer la cara resplandent de Jhesu Crist qui resplandis e ri ins la beutat de las creaturas (p. 14).

The names attached to the above five steps are as follows: first, *Gaug*, the joy of the soul on experiencing the sweetness of God through all creation; second, *Familiaritat*, when the soul feels the hand of God touching it in the touch of every created thing; third, *Noeleza*,[25] the soul being given a new lease of life as the smell of earthly things brings a new smell of spiritual things; fourth, *Descenamen*, the earth is now filled with the sound of all creation praising God, and the soul is transported in complete self-forgetfulness; fifth, the culminating *Certanetat*, when the soul sees the face of Christ in all creation.

Now the importance of the *Scala* for any study of the way of thought of the medieval French mystics is not merely that it has only five steps as against the *Paumier's* seven branches;[26] the real distinctiveness of the *Scala* lies deeper, in its basic approach to the question of man's higher spiritual development. Whilst the Beguine texts are characterized by a movement of exclusion, the soul becoming ever more detached from all that surrounds it, until finally it is absorbed in Christ, the *Scala* leads the soul to perfection precisely through an expanding awareness of God's creation, the human senses being increasingly refined to a heightened perception of God present in His created world. For the enraptured Beguine there might well be no world at all: for the writer of the *Scala* the created world is the essential means of communication with God the Creator.

[25] Professor Hatzfeld puts *Noeleza* into the fifth of his six stages of mystical ascent (op. cit., p. 375).

[26] St Bonaventura and modern scholars establish six stages, but cf. Ruysbroeck's *Seven Steps of the Ladder of Spiritual Love*.

The fact is that the texts we have been discussing have their roots in two widely differing traditions. Just as the kinship of the Beguine texts with the writings of St Bernard becomes obvious on reading the *De Diligendo Deo* or the sermons *In Cantica*, similarly one cannot read the *Scala* without being reminded of the Victorines' approach to the reality of God through the world of sensible objects considered as symbols of that reality, and, perhaps more specifically, of St Bonaventure's *Itinerarium mentis in Deum*, where we read, for example:

> For, inasmuch as ... this universe of things is a ladder whereby we may ascend to God, since among these things some are God's footprints, some God's image, ... it follows that if we are to attain to the contemplation of the First Principle and Source of all things, ... we must begin with God's footprints which are corporeal, temporal, and outside us and so enter on the Way that leads to God.[27]

The danger of attempting to reduce medieval mystical writings to any particular system will be apparent from a glance at the texts copied down in the same manuscript as the *Scala*.[28] Leaving aside several short works of conventional piety, there is a Provençal version of the *Jesu dulcis memoria* and also a most strange *Liber Divini Amoris*[29] in which the experienced teacher instructs his pupil in the love of God by means of question and answer. Moreover, for a considerable part of the work the vehicle of instruction is the detailed conjugation of the Latin verb *amare*. When the pupil begs *que tu m'en metas al Donat*, the teacher launches into an exhaustive exposition of all the forms of *amare*, using not only the Latin verbforms themselves but also grammatical terms such as 'infinitive', 'optative', etc. to expound the love of God.[30] This is the epitome of the scholastic method at its dullest and most artificial, yet from the very outset the master makes it clear that God is to be found not by studying the created world, as in the *Scala*, but by complete immersion in Him. He goes so far away from the Victorine approach as to advise his pupil to close his senses and even his intelligence to the world of sensible things, nothing mattering apart from the direct personal experience of God.

Any comprehensive study of mysticism in French must treat the medieval vernacular texts not as imperfect attempts at some blue-print ideal, to be explained and interpreted by reference to texts produced centuries later in

---

[27] Transl. R. C. Petry, *Late Medieval Mysticism* (London, 1957), p. 133.

[28] British Museum, Egerton, 945.

[29] I hope to publish this in the near future.

[30] For the reverse of the coin, the use of grammatical terminology in the service of eroticism, see P. Lehmann, *Die Parodie im Mittelalter* (Munich, 1922).

a different intellectual and social climate: they must be understood in the light of the language and society of their own day.[31] Efforts to reduce human activities and human experience to some particular system call to mind the conclusion to Gilson's *Héloïse and Abélard*: 'Before reality, perceived in all its ordered complexity, who will stop to worry about formulas?'[32] In this particular case the last word may safely be left with St Bernard:

> For, according as the desires of a soul vary, so the delight felt in the Divine Presence must needs vary also; and that heavenly sweetness strikes in divers ways upon the palate of the soul, according to the variation of its desires and longings.[33]

[31] For a penetrating analysis of the reciprocal and constantly changing influence exerted by Christianity and the social order, see E. Troeltsch, *The Social Teaching of the Christian Churches*, transl. Olive Wyon (London, 1931).

[32] Transl. L. K. Shook (London, 1953).

[33] *Sermon*, XXXI/7, transl. J. S. Eales (London, 1895).

Poetry

4

L. C. SYKES

'Il y a une grandeur, dans La Fontaine . . .'

'Il y a une grandeur, dans La Fontaine, dont nos académiciens ne peuvent trouver la mesure.'[1] Provocative as always, Alain seems to challenge the student of La Fontaine to say precisely where the greatness in him lies — if, indeed, there is greatness in him. 'La Fontaine paraît insipide aux étrangers,' observed Valéry.[2] For Macaulay (as Taine noted) he was no more than 'a trifler', and in England at least that opinion is not altogether dead. A week-end critic referred to him not long ago as 'a worldly dancing-master', and an estimable *Introduction to the French Poets* damns the *Fables* with faint praise.[3] Can we reasonably look for greatness in a poet judged fit to be learned by heart — 'Il ouvre un archevêque et laiss' tomber sa croix' — by little children? Whatever may be his reputation elsewhere, in France the greatness of La Fontaine is unquestioned; and if, when Alain delivered his verdict in 1921, the critics had not yet succeeded in defining it to his satisfaction, it was certainly not for want of trying. The last decade has seen a marked renewal of interest in La Fontaine on the part of academics. Professor Philip A. Wadsworth's *Young La Fontaine* (1952) has been followed by Monsieur G. Couton's *La Poétique de La Fontaine* (1957) and *La Politique de La Fontaine* (1959), Madame Simone Blavier-Paquot's *La Fontaine: Vues sur l'Art du Moraliste dans les Fables de 1668* (1961), Mrs Margaret Guiton's *La Fontaine Poet and Counterpoet* (1961) and Professor Renée Kohn's *Le Goût de la Fontaine* (1962).[4] Monsieur P. Clarac has brought out revisions both of his Pléiade edition of the *Œuvres diverses* (1958) and of his *La Fontaine* (1959), as well as an attractive *La Fontaine par lui-même* in the series 'Écrivains de toujours' (1961). Finally, at the end of 1962, came *O Muse, fuyante proie . . . Essai*

---

[1] *Propos*, Bibliothèque de la Pléiade, Gallimard, Paris, 1956, p. 247. The date of Alain's *propos* on La Fontaine is 17 July 1921, so that he is no doubt thinking especially, in the sentence I quote, of the official tributes paid to the poet to mark the tercentenary of his birth.

[2] *Variété II*, Paris, 1929, p. 130.

[3] G. Brereton, op. cit., London, 1956, pp. 80–83.

[4] Professor Wadsworth's book was published by the Northwestern University Press, Evanston, Illinois, Mrs Guiton's by the Rutgers University Press, New Brunswick, New Jersey.

sur la poésie de La Fontaine, in which Madame Odette de Mourgues satisfied appetites whetted two years earlier by the excellence of her succinct discussion of the *Fables* in 'Studies in French Literature'.[5] The *Essai* is a masterpiece of scholarly criticism in which Alain, had he lived long enough to read it, could well have found what his 'académiciens' had failed to give him; and certainly the pages that follow, though their theme has long been in my mind, will owe much to it. To seek a definition of the greatness of La Fontaine is in any case no very original undertaking: its fascination remains. Precisely what are the essential elements of that definition? How do they cohere?

Where to look for the greatness in La Fontaine, there will be no doubt. Did ever writer attempt so many genres, and achieve immortality only in one? His thousands of lines of miscellaneous verse exhibit an astonishing diversity: madrigals and sonnets, ballads and odes, epistles and epitaphs, elegies and epigrams; indecent *chansons*, and paraphrases of a psalm and of the *Dies irae*; a comedy that is a comedy (*L'Eunuque*) and one that is not (*Clymène*), a ballet (*Les Rieurs du Beau-Richard*), three libretti — two of them complete (*Daphné* and *Astrée*), one unfinished (*Galatée*) — and two acts of a tragedy (*Achille*); *Adonis, Le Poème du Quinquina* and *Le Poème de Saint-Malc.* . . . The pious curiosity of scholars can discover here material for a biography, and the revelation of a personality — not always an attractive one, it may be remarked in passing: that the sage fabulist should have applauded the persecution of the protestants—

> Louis a banni de la France
> L'hérétique et très sotte engeance,[6]

—may serve as a sharp reminder that poet and person are not necessarily the same thing. More interestingly, the miscellaneous verse affords evidence of La Fontaine's sedulous cultivation of poetic craft, includes experiments and exercises that help to explain the mastery displayed in the *Fables*. But all this verse is scarcely ever more than verse, and the general consensus of opinion that consigns it to near-oblivion is not mistaken. Valéry may have persuaded us to recognise great poetry in the Racinian lament of Vénus at the close of *Adonis;* whether, sharing his enthusiasm for the poem as a whole, we can read it 'presque tout avec délice'[7] seems to me very doubtful. The *Relation d'un Voyage de Paris en Limousin* is entertaining, but no more than mildly. Among all the *œuvres*

---

    [5] *La Fontaine: Fables*, London, 1960.
    [6] 'A son Altesse Monseigneur le Duc de Vendôme,' *Œuvres diverses*, Bibliothèque de la Pléiade, Gallimard, Paris, 1942, p. 701.
    [7] 'Au sujet d'Adonis,' *Variété*, Paris, 1924, pp. 59–97 (p. 95).

diverses, Les Amours de Psyché et de Cupidon alone deserve better recognition
— and the honour of a separate scholarly edition, to be undertaken by
someone less interested in identifying the famous four friends than in
resolving doubts about the meaning La Fontaine intended to give to the
myth. If only for the marvellously sustained elegance of its prose, *Psyché*
deserves to rank as a *classique du second rayon*: it lacks the authority and
the unity of the authentic masterpiece.

And the *Contes?* They form the major coherent part of La Fontaine's
writings, a considerably greater part than the *Fables*. He took pleasure in
writing them, we may suppose. The first appeared in 1665, and he
continued to write them notwithstanding the success of the *Fables* of
1668. As a candidate for election to the Academy he prudently promised
to abandon a genre that had brought him ill repute in high places; yet in
1685, little more than a year after his reception, he allowed five new tales
to be published. Valéry's admiration for *Adonis* is accompanied by frank
detestation of 'ces Contes assommants'.[8] Can we appeal from this judgement to that of Musset, temperamentally a more sympathetic reader of
such frivolities?

> Que ne demandez-vous un conte à La Fontaine?
> C'est avec celui-là qu'il est bon de veiller;
> Ouvrez-le sur votre oreiller,
> Vous verrez se lever l'aurore.
>
> *(Silvia)*

The commendation would be more persuasive if it promised less. The
Contes have a piquancy that can please, if they are merely sampled: try to
prolong the pleasure, and their monotonous conventionality soon palls.

Uncertainty of intention, insignificance of theme, unevenness of
achievement, facile diffuseness, jejune virtuosity — these are the defects
that variously mar all that La Fontaine wrote, save only the *Fables*. It is in
these alone that his greatness is to be looked for; and it would therefore
appear that something in the nature of the genre to which they belong
must offer at least a first and partial explanation of their manifest superiority. Scores of critics and hundreds of pedagogues have set side by side a
text of Æsop and a text of La Fontaine, expatiated on the mediocrity of
the former, and exhibited infallibly and irrefutably the latter's excellence.
But whatever profit is to be derived from such exercises, it may well be
that understanding of La Fontaine's greatness should begin with reflection
on the truism that without the fables of Æsop, his own could not have
been written. For the fables of Æsop were surely his aesthetic salvation:

[8] Op. cit., p. 94.

5

they led him to what I like to call 'the deep sources' — a deep source of
meditation, and a deep source of imagery.

We smile at the childishness of the fable; yet we cannot but respect a
genre so ancient, so universally cultivated, and so serious in its purpose.
The fable is a practical guide to that most important of preoccupations,
the conduct of life. It has no concern with ethical principles, which are
infinitely debatable: the lessons it offers are derived from the permanent
and common fund of ordinary human experience, which perpetually
confirms their soundness. These lessons, our sophistication pronounces,
are excessively simple; but the complexity of a statement is no measure of
its truth, any more than its novelty is a measure of its importance. A
condition of greatness in poetry is, it seems, the recognition (whether
explicit or implied) of simple, fundamental truths. In the Æsopic fable,
La Fontaine discovered such truths. Whatever conventional professions he
thought it politic to make in his *Préface* of 1668 and elsewhere, nothing
that we know of his personality allows us to credit him with any serious
didactic vocation or intention. Nor was his mind in any strict sense
philosophical: when, in the *Discours à Madame de La Sablière*, he tries to
adopt the philosopher's manner, he immediately loses his sureness of
touch. But his mind was receptive, and reflective. Capable of interesting
himself in the lewdness of Boccaccio and in what seem to us the intermin-
able insipidities of *L'Astrée*, he was capable also of graver cogitations, and
in particular of attending to the unpretentious wisdom of the fable. The
themes of the *œuvres diverses* are — characteristically if not always —
trivial: the very nature of the genre ensures that the themes of the *Fables*
are immeasurably more substantial.

As the lessons of the fable are basic truths of experience, so its animal
fictions rely on basic inventions of imagination; for they are scarcely more
than simple, natural developments of those images which, seeking to
interpret man by reference to animals and animals by reference to man,
are surely among the most spontaneous of all metaphors, and almost as
old, one guesses, as language itself. More readily than anything else in
man's natural environment, animals — that so closely resemble him in
their instincts and passions, and often in their posture, their movements
and the cast of their features also — lend themselves to every exigence and
caprice of anthropomorphic fancy. 'Now the serpent was more subtil
than any of the beasts of the field.' Is the serpent indeed 'subtil'? The
question is as reasonable as, in relation to poetic truth, it is impertinent.
Nor is it very useful to make explicit the relationship between the serpent's
sinuous movements and the insinuation of temptation: what is important

is our unhesitating recognition of the rightness of the choice of the serpent as Eve's tempter. Nobody doubts that Jaguar cars are well named, even if reflection suggests some connotations presumably not intended by the manufacturers. The novel metaphor achieves its effect by surprise, Animal metaphors are familiar — scarcely less elemental than those which associate darkness with death and guilt, light with life and innocence. height with aspiration, water with purity. They work in the same way, finding confirmation of their veracity in intuitions more certain and more intimate than the conclusions of reason, and experienced with something approaching universal unanimity. Such were the metaphors the fable offered to La Fontaine — potent metaphors indeed, by contrast, for example, with those merely ingenious metaphors, so characteristic of the *Contes*, which speak of love in the language of war:

> Le galant donc près de la forteresse
> Assied son camp, vous investit Lucrèce
>
> *(La Mandragore)*
>
> je ne veux de plein saut
> Prendre la ville, aimant mieux l'escalade.
>
> *(Féronde)*

In other respects also, the fable was a genre salutary for La Fontaine to cultivate. It encouraged him to be brief; and outside the *Fables*, prolixity is his besetting sin. In his *Préface* of 1668 he shows himself very well aware that 'un des Maîtres de notre Éloquence' — Patru — prized 'la brèveté' as an essential quality of the fable; and for his own part he professes admiration for 'l'extrême brèveté' of Phædrus, whilst modestly recognizing that he is incapable of imitating it. That he has in fact no intention of trying to imitate it, even in the *premier recueil*, is clear. Against the judgement of Patru and the practice of Phædrus, it suits him to invoke the authority of Quintilian: 'on ne saurait trop égayer les narrations'. Nevertheless, the example of brevity set by the Æsopic fable was far from losing all its force: it restrained La Fontaine the fabulist from lapsing into the complacent discursiveness of *Psyché* and the garrulity of the *Contes*.

Moreover, the Æsopic fable provided him with material at the same time fragmented yet homogeneous. 'Les longs Ouvrages me font peur'[9] is one at least of his confessions that we can take at its face-value. Each separate fable was by no means a 'long Ouvrage'; and though much patient craftsmanship was required to perfect it, the satisfaction of accomplishment could not be over-long delayed. Each fable was complete in itself, and no two were alike: the admirable range of their themes and

---

[9] *Fables VI, Épilogue.*

the variety of their manner are indeed among the most obvious and are
not the least compelling of their charms. Yet when a hundred-odd pieces
had been composed over the years and at last neatly arranged in their six
books, there could be no doubt that, simply because all save a handful of
them were fables, the diversity of the *premier recueil* was unified by the
homogeneity of the genre. In the *second recueil* there is a larger number of
poems that are not fables; and the fables themselves are often much more
than fables, for La Fontaine had, in Sainte-Beuve's well-known phrase,
'fini ... par y voir surtout [?] un cadre commode à pensées, à sentiments,
à causerie'.[10] One may indeed, venturing to dissent from the prevalent
opinion, prefer the first six books, on the grounds that the art of the fable
proper is there displayed in greater purity.[11] But in any case the *second
recueil* and the *douzième livre* — and it was, we may imagine, with peculiar
satisfaction that La Fontaine rounded out the number to the epic twelve[12]
— are unquestionably, like the collection of 1668, very different from
mere poetic miscellanies. They too remain, essentially if not with strict
consistency, collections of fables, and it is to this that they owe both their
diversity and their unity.

The fable, then, offered La Fontaine models of conciseness, the occasion
for poetic creation on the scale most appropriate to his temperament, the
attraction of variety in the units, and the guarantee of wholeness in the
sum of them. Above all, it offered him a deep source of meaning and a
deep source of symbolism. Here was a virtuality of greatness. To explain
its realization in the *Fables*, two complementary propositions suggest
themselves: La Fontaine accepted what the fable offered him; and he
brought to its enrichment nothing that was not wholly consonant with
its nature.

Consider, for instance, the explicitly stated morals of the *Fables*. They are,
as to their substance, either those of the traditional fable, or variations of
them that seem no less trite. Sometimes a deliberate flatness of style
emphasizes their banality:

> Nous n'écoutons d'instincts que ceux qui sont les nôtres
> (*L'Hirondelle et les Petits Oiseaux*)

[10] 'La Fontaine,' 20 September 1829 (*Portraits Littéraires, I*).
[11] Cf. Gide, *Journal, 1942–1949*, Paris, 1950, p. 180: 'Je ne suis point du tout de ceux qui
dédaignent un peu ces premières fables de La Fontaine. Les suivantes, plus étendues, ont de
tout autres qualités; mais celles du début gardent une densité, un poids, une épaisseur à la
Breughel, qui me ravissent.'
[12] This is admittedly pure speculation. Surprisingly and inaccurately, the twelfth book was
in fact published as the 'livre septième de la 2e partie'.

Certainly no attempt is made to conceal it:

> Ne t'attends qu'à toi seul, c'est un commun Proverbe.
>
> (*L'Alouette et ses Petits* . . .)

The proverb, precisely, is the epitome of banality; and in the expression of the moral, La Fontaine's most consistent effort seems to be to achieve the proverb's tough mnemonic simplicity:

> Rien ne sert de courir; il faut partir à point.
>
> (*Le Lièvre et la Tortue*)
>
> La raison du plus fort est toujours la meilleure.
>
> (*Le Loup et l'Agneau*)

(That such lines have long since passed into proverbial use is testimony to the eminent success of the effort.) Everyman's style is the perfect vehicle for everyman's wisdom; and to deplore the limitations of that unambitious, prudential wisdom is as futile as to challenge its authority. It is certain that the function of the moral in a fable of La Fontaine is very far from being as naïvely didactic as it had been traditionally. No longer the fable's *raison d'être*, it has to be understood and savoured in its subtle — and sometimes ironical — relationship with the whole.[13] Considered in itself, the moral nevertheless remains in La Fontaine what it was in Æsop: a grave truism, perhaps not lacking a certain austere beauty, and without doubt deep-rooted in the perennial experience of mankind.

It is the same with the stories as with the morals: they are everyman's, 'ces Fables étant sues de tout le monde,' as La Fontaine blandly recognizes in his *Préface*. Only a very few of them are of his own invention. An invented fable implies, indeed, something like a contradiction in terms. Our attitude towards fables is conditioned by our respect for their antiquity, which justifies their naïveté, and enriches them with a venerable patina. It is conditioned also by our familiarity with them, which is why the fables La Fontaine takes from the Æsopic tradition command a readier and fuller response than those he takes from the oriental. (It is, of course, from the Æsopic tradition that — through various intermediaries — he borrows most often.) Had he chosen to invent, rather than to imitate, the robust impersonal generality that commonly characterizes his themes would surely have been lacking. A recent critic[14] has expressed surprise that the amorous La Fontaine — amorous if all his 'confidences' are authentic — should have allowed love so small a place in the *Fables*. But

---

[13] See for example Madame de Mourgues' excellent analysis of the role of the moral in *Le Rat et l'Huître, O Muse, fuyante proie* . . . , p. 182.
[14] R. Kohn, *Le Goût de La Fontaine*, Paris, 1962, pp. 168 and 224.

love — 'an invention of the thirteenth century, deceased in the twentieth'[15] — is a luxury: the fable is concerned with relationships that exist of necessity, and are more significant than the ephemeral preoccupations of any particular society or age. It is true that the colours of the poet's own day and place are by no means absent from the *Fables* — and true also that they are particularly apparent in some pieces that are by common consent among the weakest, such as *La Ligue des Rats*, and the second version of *Le Soleil et les Grenouilles*, both of which La Fontaine excluded from the collected editions. In general, these colours are discreet.[16] La Fontaine had doubtless seen Perrette, 'légère et court vêtue', with her 'cotillon simple et souliers plats'. But nothing in his picture requires us to situate her either in France or in the seventeenth century, and it is only by a singular constraint of the imagination that the court and the courtiers in the *Fables* can be seen as necessarily and uniquely those of Louis XIV. The world of animals with human voices is of all centuries because it is of none.

Just as La Fontaine respects the extemporality of the fable, so he is content to believe what it relates and to endorse the judgements it passes. The cruelty of the wolf and the fate of the innocent lamb are data he wisely accepts without question — wisely, or perhaps rather with the double indifference of an artist whose theme was no more than a pretext for the exercise of his craft, and of a reflective man who, lacking strong convictions of his own, could nevertheless (as I have suggested) recognize truth in the thoughts of others. For Alain,[17]

> Le génie propre de La Fontaine fut sans doute en ceci qu'il était comme absent de lui-même, et sans aucun mélange de sa pensée avec ses actions; ce qui fit qu'Ésope l'éveilla seul, et prit forme de nouveau par cette main inoccupée. Ce qui donnerait à croire que nonchalance est presque tout en cette grandeur.

For 'nonchalance' explains the impeccable moral realism of the *Fables*, that 'longue frise des choses humaines, où chacun, de la nuque au talon circonscrit, trouve sa place éternelle ... où toutes choses sont fixées en leur vérité ... sans rien à reprendre'. And Alain is surely right to suggest that

---

[15] Many a French humorist of the 1930s and 1940s, notes H. Peyre (*The Contemporary French Novel*, New York, 1955, p. 286) 'proposed [this] mournful epitaph to inscribe on the grave of the theme that once enraptured poet and novelist'.

[16] 'Accenni alla vita moderna, all'età, al paese dell'Autore, hanno quasi sempre il solo fine di togliere gli animali di Esopo dalla vaga antichità, immergendoli in un'epoca certa, senza che perdano il carattere immutabile e come fuore del tempo.' (V. Lugli, *Il Prodigio di La Fontaine*, Messina and Milan, 1939, p. 227.)

[17] Op. cit., p. 249.

this realism derives directly from the Æsopic fable. The epic fosters illusions of grandeur, the fairy-tale consoles with the magic of wish-fulfilment; but the fable would fail of its didactic purpose if it did not tell the prosaic truth. 'Toutes nos pensées, ou presque, sont plaidoyers,' observes Alain. Even among the greatest works of the classical century, the *Fables* are altogether exceptional in their impartiality. 'Plaidoyers' are the rule, not only and most obviously in Descartes and Pascal, in La Rochefoucauld and La Bruyère, but in Corneille, and in Molière also, and even in Racine. 'Le mensonge héroïque,'[18] the corrosive scepticism of comedy of intellect, the cathartic and seductive poetry of tragic destinies, all, admirable in their manner and beyond doubt salutary, have a ten-dentiousness that can never be imputed to the *Fables*. There, the action follows simply and exactly the course prescribed for it by the common-place order of things human, which it was the business of the traditional fable to observe and interpret; and the actors are judged surely and sanely — 'en leur vérité' — by the fable's strict empiricism.

No less than lion, bear and monkey, La Fontaine's fox, crow and ass are creatures not of his native *pays de Brie*, but of the genre. In this, the critics like to insist, they had lost everything of their animality except their names; and La Fontaine restored it to them. The truth is perhaps less dramatic. He preserves in every animal the character traditionally ascribed to it. But to present the fox as cunning and the lion as kingly is not to treat them as animals (whose 'character', if they have one, must forever remain enigmatic): it is to exploit the suggestions immediately conveyed by the fox's pointed mask, and the puissant frame and 'majestic' head of the lion. It would be preposterous to suggest that it was easy to exploit them as happily as La Fontaine does. Yet even while we admire his sureness in the choice of words and rhythms that make his animals spring so vividly to the mind's eye, we may also observe the discrepancy between the little he gives us, and the much our imagination makes of it — thanks to the rich associations with which these creatures of the fable (and not of the fable only) are endowed. 'Peintre animalier incomparable,'[19] we have been taught. No doubt: yet the characteristic picture of an animal in the *Fables* is no more than the most rapid and incomplete of sketches —

> Un Loup n'avait que les os et la peau.
> (Le Loup et le Chien)

[18] The expression will be recognized as having been borrowed from the title of A. Rous-seaux's essay, 'Corneille ou le mensonge héroïque' (*Le Monde classique* (première série), Paris, 1941, pp. 37–68).

[19] G. Lanson, as quoted with approbation (and a trifle incorrectly) by G. Michaut, *La Fontaine*, Paris, 1913–14, I, p. 279.

Described rather than evoked, La Fontaine's animals could not have served as the symbols the genre requires them to be. Nor, refining on the simple analogies used in the traditional fable, could he have made of them more than symbols, fascinating personages whose ambiguity is often indicated by their nomenclature — Sire Rat, Maître Baudet, Dame Belette, Dom Pourceau — and who are now animal, now human, now both at the same time. La Fontaine himself invites us to suppose that this ambiguity has a philosophical implication, affirming in his *Préface* that men and animals have a common nature ('puisque nous sommes l'abrégé de ce qu'il y a de bon et de mauvais dans les créatures irraisonnables'), and calling into question, in *L'Homme et la Couleuvre, Le Loup et les Bergers* and *Les Compagnons d'Ulysse*, our supposed superiority. Commentators have not been slow to underline the lesson: 'Es gibt kein besseres Mittel, den Menschen aus seinem Grössenwahn herunterzuholen, als dadurch, dass man ihm seine Animalität erinnert.'[20] This may well be: but in the *Fables* as a whole such severity is less striking than a predominant 'gaieté'. Whatever philosophical sense the animal metaphor may have is clearly limited, for if men and animals alike have instincts, the crucial distinction remains that, unlike animals, men are held responsible for the control of theirs. It is more important to recognize that the animal metaphor is an illusion, a game; and that, because it is a game, it is conducive precisely to that predominant 'gaieté', as well as to the lucidity of detachment. 'Les animaux . . . sont étrangers à l'homme, qui y prend un léger intérêt et s'émeut moins des catastrophes qui leur arrivent; de plus, ils nous sont inférieurs et excitent de notre part un sourire d'ironie bienveillante, comme le fait [*sic*] l'homme à la vue d'enfants jouant entre eux et offrant une miniature de la société.'[21]

The traditional fable is enacted on a stage bare of all but indispensable and featureless properties. Yet the genre is rustic, and its actors — often countryfolk when they are not animals — perform mostly out-of-doors. Nature, then, offers a décor so appropriate that its presence in the *Fables* seems spontaneous. Like the ambiguity of the animal-human characters, this presence can be understood as implying a philosophical intention, as the expression of a comprehensive view of the Universe in which all things obey the same laws; and this interpretation finds support in La Fontaine's reference in his *Préface* to the idea of man as microcosm. But does he make the reference in all seriousness? And is his thought so rigorously systematic? It seems more plausible to suppose that he valued evocations of the natural scene chiefly as one way of giving to the *Fables*

[20] T. Spoerri, 'Der Aufstand der Fabel,' *Trivium*, I (1943), pp. 31–63 (p. 52).
[21] P. Soullié, *La Fontaine et ses devanciers*, Paris and Angers, 1861, pp. 18–19.

that 'certain charme', that 'air agréable' of which he also speaks in his *Préface*, a way all the more congenial because it enabled him to draw on a rich and well-loved store of literary reminiscences. There is in fact a curious contradiction between the acerbity prevalent in the human relationships he depicts, and the amenity of the background: the *Fables* invite us to contemplate pleasant pastures, but not the unfamiliar and unfriendly landscapes that are the natural haunts of the great beasts of prey. If the contradiction passes unnoticed, it is because the familiarity of the décor assorts so perfectly with that banality of behaviour which is the concern of the genre. Indeed, Nature in the *Fables* is scarcely more than the countryside, scenes of man's labour or recreation, the commonplaces of a vaguely pastoral tradition. Is it (as editors commonly suggest) Virgil that he imitates in the last two lines of *Le Chêne et le Roseau*? But in Racan, the oak's 'tronc vénérable'

> Attache dans l'enfer ses fécondes racines,
> Et de ses larges bras touche le firmament.[22]

Lucretius (editors likewise suggest) prompted the celebrated evocation of

> le temps
> Que tout aime et que tout pullule dans le monde:
> Monstres marins au fond de l'onde,
> Tigres dans les Forêts, Alouettes aux champs.
> (*L'Alouette et ses Petits* . . .)

But in *L'Astrée*, which was La Fontaine's chief source of 'images champêtres' according to d'Olivet, he could have read:

> Ainsi je vois qu'en l'air, sur la terre, et dans l'onde
> Les oyseaux, les poissons, et le reste du monde
> Tirent quelque plaisir d'un si doux changement.[23]

Such themes, however distinctive his handling of them, are no more his own than the morals, the stories and the animals of his *Fables*; and they come from the same 'deep sources'. How else can their extraordinary power of suggestion be accounted for? It is significant that the attention

[22] *Ode pour Monseigneur le duc de Bellegarde.* Cf. Scarron, *Le Virgile travesti*:
  'Si sa tête est des cieux voisine,
  Ses pieds qu'on nomme sa racine
  Sont proches des pays d'enfer.'
[23] Op. cit., ed. H. Vaganay, Lyons, 1925–28, t.V, p. 185. Cf. Mathurin Régnier, *Satyre XV*:
  'Mais aux jours les plus beaux de la saison nouvelle
  Que Zephire en ses rets surprend Flore la belle;
  Que dans l'air les oyseaux, les poissons en la mer,
  Se pleignent doucement du mal qui vient d'aymer . . .'

critics of La Fontaine almost invariably give to his rustic sketches is quite disproportionate to their number and their dimensions. It is significant, too, and curious, that these sketches should move Sainte-Beuve to write:

> Ces plaines immenses de blés où se promène de grand matin le maître, et où l'alouette cache son nid; ces bruyères et ces buissons où fourmille tout un petit monde; ces jolies garennes, dont les hôtes étourdis font la cour à l'aurore dans la rosée et parfument de thym leur banquet, c'est la Beauce, la Sologne, la Champagne, la Picardie; j'en reconnais les fermes avec leurs mares, avec les basses-cours et les colombiers.[24]

The difference is great, yet perfectly comprehensible to any reader of the *Fables*, between Sainte-Beuve's confident localizations, and the unparticularity of the texts themselves. The water that flows or mirrors in the *Fables* is simply 'une onde pure', 'transparente', 'le cristal d'une fontaine' — the same, no doubt, as that of the 'crystal rivulets' at the mouth of Calypso's cave, as the 'clear water'[25] where Nausicaa washed the clothes, as the 'fons inlimis, nitidis argenteus undis',[26] where Narcissus fell in love with his reflection. The rest of the landscape is scarcely more precise, is equally ideal, quickens the same poetic feeling.

One more 'deep source' on which La Fontaine habitually draws remains to be noted: the legacy of Greece and Rome. The Æsopic fable itself is indeed part of that legacy. But an air of the primitive clings to it. To give warmth to its austere tones, without disturbing their harmony, there could be no more appropriate resource than the colours of the classical past, still bright with the lustre of spiritual ancestry; and by a fortunate conjuncture, La Fontaine's education and the accepted literary theory of his age encouraged him to respect and cultivate ancient literature. Recognition of their origin in Virgil, Horace or Lucretius enhances the resonance of many a line and turn of phrase in the *Fables*, especially in the *second recueil*: 'L'ombre et le frais' raises the echo 'frigus opacum'; 'les Parques blêmes', 'pallida mors'; and in

> Je voudrais qu'à cet âge
> On sortît de la vie ainsi que d'un banquet

an older wisdom can be heard:

> Cur non, ut plenus vitae conviva, recedis?[27]

[24] Op. cit., n.10 *supra*.
[25] *The Odyssey*, tr. by E. V. Rieu, London, 1946, pp. 89, 104.
[26] Ovid, *Metamorphoses III*, l.407.
[27] *Le Songe d'un Habitant du Mogol, Ecloga I*, l. 53; *Le Vieillard et les trois jeunes Hommes, Carmina I*, iv, l. 13; *La Mort et le Mourant, De rerum natura III*, l. 951.

Occasionally Roman history casts an ironic gleam:

> Ce Monseigneur du Lion-là
> Fut parent de Caligula.

> *(La Cour du Lion)*

More often, the light that plays delicately over the *Fables* is the perennially fresh light of Homeric epic and, above all, of the Greek myths. When, as happens from time to time, the gods of Olympus appear in the Æsopic fable, they seem ill at ease on that cramped didactic stage. La Fontaine's wider scene accommodates them without difficulty. They are introduced necessarily, and frankly, as fictions. If they are not mocked, neither can there be the slightest question of believing in them. Thus they serve, paradoxically, to confirm the realism of La Fontaine's picture of humanity. The supernatural, they seem to confess, has no more reality than men choose to give to it, and to look there for succour is to deceive oneself. The resolute paganism of the *Fables* is not the least important aspect of their permanent truth.[28] Morally impotent, the gods nevertheless retain, like the legendary heroes, their poetic power. They bring to the *Fables* the prestige of the cosmic and of the immortal. Their fleeting presence suffices to touch the familiar with the splendour of their fame: the simplicity of 'l'écharpe d'Iris' and of

> Le blé, riche présent de la blonde Cérès

conveys intimations of pristine wonder at the world's strange beauty.

'Un jour' . . . : it was a long time ago, surely; but precisely when we cannot say, any more than we can hope (or would wish) to identify 'une Tortue' or — equally indefinite — 'la Bique' that we meet in opening lines of the *Fables*. The world these creatures inhabit is correspondingly imprecise: a hare muses 'en son gîte', a cock stands sentinel 'sur la branche d'un arbre', The rare adjectives usually serve either to supply a minimum of essential definition ('un arbre creux'), or a simple affective nuance ('la pauvre haie'). The verb in the moral is in a tense whose present is not that of now, but of all time. Archaisms are used, sparingly, not to differentiate past from present, but to merge them. The delicately stylized speech of the actors, scarcely marked by the imprint of the poet's century, produces, like the studied *négligences*, an effect of naturalness that sometimes becomes, thanks to the introduction of colloquial, plebeian and dialectal terms,

---

[28] Anyone who supposes that *Le Gland et la Citrouille* supplies evidence that the *Fables* are not altogether pagan should ponder Voltaire's comment: ' . . . dans l'Inde, . . . les cocos sont fort élevés' (*Dictionnaire philosophique, s.v.* CALEBASSE).

an effect of naïveté. These are some of the stylistic features that express
La Fontaine's respect for the fable as a genre primitive and rustic, ex-
temporal and universal. It is *de rigueur* to pay tribute to the richness of the
vocabulary by which he enhanced it. But the flowers of his 'amateur de
jardinage' —

> De quoi faire à Margot pour sa fête un bouquet,
> Peu de jasmin d'Espagne, et force serpolet
> > *(Le Jardinier et son Seigneur)*

— are very different from the *Orientale*, the *Veuve*, the *Drap d'or*, the
Agathe and the *Solitaire* 'nuancée, bordée, huilée, à pièces emportées' that
especially holds the enraptured gaze of La Bruyère's tulip-fancier. If,
against the prevalent linguistic trend of his age, La Fontaine resorts to
concrete particularity, it is in order to suggest rather than to define. Rich
his vocabulary may be; but more through variety than through rarity.
In Racine's line

> Et du temple déjà l'aube blanchit le faîte
> > *(Athalie*, I, 1, l. 160)

the poetic current could not pass if the word 'temple' had no religious
connotations, and if 'l'aube', designating merely an astronomical phenomenon, told nothing of the poignancy of the first light of a new day.[29]
In the *Fables* similarly, the poetic current passes thanks to abundant
associations of common ideas, quickened for the most part by references
to familiar animals, a familiar countryside, and familiar gods and heroes.[30]

Whatever their 'sorcellerie évocatoire', isolated words do not constitute
a poem. Besides, the more a word is inherently poetic and charged with
affective associations, the greater the risk that its banality will prevent its
poetry from being felt. This was the fate, precisely, of the animal metaphors of the traditional fable. It is, then, no more than a partial explanation
of the poetic force of the *Fables* to say that their language draws copiously
on the 'deep sources'. A complete explanation is, in the nature of the case,
scarcely to be looked for: we can at least add a little. If, as Tristan Derème
observed, 'c'est à manier [un] langage tout chargé de souvenirs qui
luisent faiblement et qui frémissent comme d'une vie ralentie, que La

---

[29] Analysis easily reveals, of course, other secrets of the line's power: the correlation, for
example, of the idea of purity in 'temple', 'aube' (<alba), 'blanchit', and of this idea with
that of aspiration suggested by the high-poised 'faîte' — to say nothing of effects of stress and
harmony.

[30] 'Das Geheimnis der La Fontaineschen Sprachkunst ist, der Sprache so wenig wie möglich
zuzumuten und sich soviel wie möglich von ihr suggerieren zu lassen.' — K. Vossler, *La
Fontaine und sein Fabelwerk*, Heidelberg, 1919, p. 97.

Fontaine triomphe',[31] it seems that the triumph and the secret of the handling lie in the exquisite sensitivity with which he adjusted the *relationships* between the words that carry the poetic charge. The importance of these relationships was hinted at by a few earlier critics:[32] it has been left to Madame de Mourgues to establish it, in her *Essai*, as the very principle of La Fontaine's exploitation of language, and to demonstrate its application in the *Fables* with a precise and persuasive lucidity that confers on her remarks the force of a revelation. Thus, analysing the first nine lines of *Le Chat, la Belette et le petit Lapin*,[33] she comments:

> Le terme familier et badin 'Dame Belette' s'ennoblit par le voisinage du mot 'palais'. Les 'souterrains séjours' pourraient aisément se charger de résonances caverneuses, nous suggérer le monde noir de Pluton. Mais cette image traditionnelle se volatilise dans le parfum d'un terroir bien français que dégage l'appellation 'Janot Lapin'; inversement, Janot Lapin, effleuré après coup par cette noble tradition qui vient de s'évanouir, quitte sa blouse de paysan et ses gros sabots et devient une stylisation élégante et littéraire du folklore français. 'Pénates' délaisse la mythologie romaine pour n'être plus qu'un symbole du geste solennel et définitif par lequel la belette prend possession de son nouveau logis . . .[34]

— But, as Alain says of La Fontaine in his *propos*, 'il faudrait citer tout'.[35] Might just a slight change of emphasis be suggested, however? Is it quite certain that ' "Pénates" délaisse la mythologie romaine'? Does it not remain, must it not remain attached, if only tenuously, to Roman mythology? Just as 'souterrains séjours' — 'sedes infernae' — cannot but evoke 'le monde noir de Pluton'? However discreet the reverberations,

[31] 'Autour de La Fontaine et de ses élégies,' *Revue Universelle*, XXX (juillet-sept. 1927), pp. 385–403 (p. 388).

[32] Cf. for example some of the observations of G. Rudler and F. Strowski on the opening lines of *Le Chat, la Belette et le petit Lapin* (*L'Explication française*, Paris, 1902, pp. 71–78; 'La Fontaine et ses *Fables*' II, *Revue des Cours et Conférences*, XL (1938–9), pp. 401–17 (pp. 405–6)).

[33] It may be useful to recall them:

> Du palais d'un jeune Lapin
> Dame Belette, un beau matin,
> S'empara: c'est une rusée.
> Le maître étant absent, ce lui fut chose aisée.
> Elle porta chez lui ses pénates, un jour
> Qu'il était allé faire à l'Aurore sa cour
> Parmi le thym et la rosée.
> Après qu'il eut brouté, trotté, fait tous ses tours,
> Janot Lapin retourne aux souterrains séjours.

[34] Op. cit., p. 159.

[35] See in particular pp. 126–30 and 155–60.

they are still (as I am sure Madame de Mourgues agrees) perceptible — as they could not be, if 'pénates' and 'souterrains séjours' were not the expressions they are.

I leave to the *lecteur averti* (as the flattering French formula has it) the satisfaction of making such adjustments as my argument requires: 'mon siège est fait'. Yet in conclusion it is perhaps worth while to recall that there is in La Fontaine another wisdom besides that of the fable: a certain epicureanism, as it is commonly called, that finds expression especially in the *second recueil*, and notably softens the asperities of the fable's pessimism. How correctly it is called 'epicureanism' need not concern us here: what is thus designated is obviously enough another powerful complex of commonplaces, another 'deep source' — as is also the great and ancient theme of solitude as the means to self-knowledge, which is developed in *Le Juge arbitre, l'Hospitalier et le Solitaire*, the last of all the *Fables*.

It must in any case be confessed that the notion of greatness has about it something too monumental to suit the most supple and subtle of poets. But the portrait I have tried to sketch is only one among many possible portraits of La Fontaine — a left profile, let us say, the left side of the face being (as physiognomists used to declare) the one that exhibits inherited characteristics, the contribution of the past. In the *Fables* that contribution was, I have suggested, singularly substantial and precious. At the end of an essay in a volume dedicated to the memory of a great teacher of literature, I reflect that an important function of the profession to which he devoted himself is surely to affirm, against the insistent fatuities of the vociferous champions of modernity, that a civilization is first of all a heritage of values. No poet, I think, better epitomizes these values than La Fontaine; and that all the wisdom of the *Fables*, and their beauty, should be presented to us with a smile, is perhaps the ultimate confirmation of the greatness in him.

J. C. IRESON

Leconte de Lisle and the Ideal in External Nature

La contemplation constante de la beauté visible et invisible dans la nature (. . .) développe dans l'âme d'immenses désirs irréalisables (. . .).[1]

BETWEEN the contemplative disposition and the world exists, then, an inevitable and complex relationship. There is the range of sensuous experience which the objects and events of Nature offer to us. But, along with this 'visible beauty' and distinct from it, is an 'invisible beauty'. The commentary, thus begun by Leconte de Lisle in this early text (1846), could progress along many paths, theological or metaphysical. We have here no development but the involvement of two great principles in the studied or instinctive attitude of the observer. *Contemplation* is used in its exact sense. It concerns inward as well as outward attention. From this involvement, from this nexus, rises an intuitive and aspiring force whose movement eddies into undefined and undifferentiated longings. Such longings no doubt cling to the visible and invisible causes, but being activated, rise towards satisfactions which, if they can at all be adumbrated, are seen to be perpetually out of range.

Yet such contemplation is, for Leconte de Lisle, itself productive of great satisfaction, of happiness:

J'ai cherché ma plus grande somme de bonheur dans la contemplation interne et externe du beau infini, de l'âme universelle du monde, de Dieu (. . .).[2]

Nothing in the subsequent consideration of the sombre aspects of our

(References to Leconte de Lisle's works, except where specified, are to the Lemerre edition in 4 volumes, small octavo (in–18).)

[1] *Contes en Prose (Impressions de Jeunesse)*, Société Normande du Livre Illustré, 1910, p. 291. Quoted by Irving Putter: *The Pessimism of Leconte de Lisle*, University of California Publications in Modern Philology, 1961, vol. 42, no. 2, p. 291, n. 155.

[2] From a letter dated 18th January, 1845. Quoted by Marius-Ary Leblond: *Leconte de Lisle d'après des documents nouveaux*, Mercure de France, 1933, p. 158.

planetary condition will invalidate or modify this premise. Leconte de Lisle will abandon the use of terms suggesting the reality of a personal God. We see him, in the text just quoted, already (1845) groping through other formulations — aesthetic (*beau infini*), pantheistic (*âme universelle du monde*) — before using the conventional Christian term. We see as well that the satisfaction referred to derives not so much from aspirations or desires, powerful as they may be, as from the intuition of a universal principle transcending or informing the natural world.

Contemplation has thus, for Leconte de Lisle, a triple function. It rests on the natural world. It favours, in the individual consciousness, an upward trajectory, a movement of aspiration which remains vague as to its immediate object. It encourages the intuition of a principle which the author calls beauty and which he associates with the universal and the ultimate. Its power of conviction is found in the components of our consciousness rather than in external evidence. It cannot preclude doubt, but can overwhelm it by the states it induces:

> Quoi? La Beauté n'est-elle donc pas? Ces aspirations qui m'entraînent vers elle, cette admiration filiale du globe où je suis né, tout cela n'est-il donc point?[3]

It is easy to forecast, from such formulations, a movement towards a position analogous to that of the German Idealist philosophers. Individual pronouncements, significant though few in number, late as well as early in Leconte de Lisle's life, can be found to corroborate such a forecast.[4] The relative paucity of general formulations is interesting. It indicates how, for Leconte de Lisle, speculative thought has no other function than to end in art. Art is what, in the field of human activity, most nearly corresponds to a model of the forces and intuitions released by contemplation:

> (. . .) toutes les vertus imaginables sont impuissantes à mettre en relief le côté pittoresque, idéal et réel, mystérieux et saisissant des choses extérieures, de la grandeur et de la misère humaines. L'art est donc l'unique révélateur du beau, et il le révèle uniquement.[5]

The scope of art is clearly delineated in these lines. It is both exclusive and vast. We are to observe that detachment from preoccupations of an

---

[3] *Le Songe d'Hermann.* Quoted by J. Dornis: *Essai sur Leconte de Lisle*, 1909, p. 84.

[4] See, for example, *Discours sur Victor Hugo, Derniers Poèmes*, p. 294: (. . .) les choses n'existent et ne valent que par le cerveau qui les conçoit et par les yeux qui les contemplent. See also the extracts from Leconte de Lisle's notebook published in *Le Figaro, Supplément littéraire*, April 28 and May 5, 1928 by Jacques Patin: *Un cahier de Leconte de Lisle.*

[5] *Derniers Poèmes*, p. 279.

ethical or social character neither detracts in principle from the concern of art with human life nor impoverishes the interpretation of the natural world. Two things are here brought into the sharpest focus by Leconte de Lisle, the relationship of the artistic process to external reality and the uniqueness of art. It might appear that the relationship thus indicated allows a choice to the artist, since the objects and beings of the natural world can be considered in their banality, in their unremarkable and evident aspects as well as in their mystery, their impressive and evocative aspects. But this would conflict with the notion of the uniqueness of art closing the artist in a sole and inimitable function. Such a choice is not, moreover, characteristic of Leconte de Lisle's thought. Of the complex interchange between individual consciousness and the world he considers only the reward of contemplation, that is to say, the privilege of penetrating to a spiritual principle which is all-embracing or potentially all-explanatory. A structure results in which sense perception and the abstractions or intuitions it affords are tensely combined. We see this tension implied in the vocabulary of the extract we are considering: *pittoresque, idéal et réel, mystérieux et saisissant.*

Idéal et réel. It is comparatively rare that Leconte de Lisle opposes, without the intervention of the notion of the individual consciousness in which they combine, these two categories.[6] He does not conceive the real and the ideal as two realms each having an objective existence. For him there is what is given in the natural world, the here and now. There is also an indefinite number of possibilities of conceiving the existence of things in heightened or more perfect forms.[7] Such possibilities reach out, of course, towards the notion of an infinite and ultimate perfection, the *beau infini* which, as we have seen, may at times be identified with a universal and creative consciousness.

Again the unique importance of art must be underlined. The ideal is not necessarily beauty. Beauty is a unifying principle which arises out of the complexity of forms, 'ideal and real'. To present it in human terms and structures demands what Leconte de Lisle calls a revelation, not in the sense of a divine disclosure to the poet, but, in the literal sense of the French term, the showing, by the artist to other men, of what is hidden or unknown.

---

[6] Cf. *Derniers Poèmes*, p. 219: (. . .) donner la vie idéale à ce qui n'a plus la vie réelle n'est pas se complaire stérilement dans la mort. Cf., also, ibid., p. 230: (. . .) et, certes, il n'en est pas ainsi de l'Hélène d'Homère, à la fois si vivante et si idéale.

[7] This is the general sense in which *idéal* is used by Leconte de Lisle. It refers to qualities. Its existence is in the mind, in the realm of ideas. The qualities predicated draw it towards the notion of a typifying perfection. Cf. Littré's 3rd definition of the word: Terme de philosophie. Type, modèle éternel des choses.

The same sense is found in the definition of poetry in the preface to the *Poèmes antiques* (1852):

> (. . .) la révélation primitive de l'idéal contenu dans la nature extérieure.[8]

This is the most categorical of Leconte de Lisle's statements on poetry and we may look to it for light on his own verse.

We have seen that contemplation, with its undelineated rewards and its undirected aspirations, finds in art a control and a purposeful redirection back to the minds of other men. The fact that its immediate and apparently exclusive subject is the natural world does not presumably detract from the human value of art, because the ideal represents, as we have indicated, an extended range of human consciousness. Yet the ideal is involved, contained in the natural world. It is therefore inseparable, in the first instance, from the forms of things as they offer themselves immediately to our consciousness.

The formula is meant to cover poetry at its greatest, in its generality as well as in specific periods of antiquity considered by Leconte de Lisle to be the greatest in history.[9] The revelation of the outside world in such a way as to suggest the spiritual penetration or interpretation that informs it was, as Leconte de Lisle's definition suggests, intuitive or primitive in earlier times. The personification of natural forces and the peopling of nature with individual divinities are without doubt implied in the term *primitive*. In the case of later poetry, Leconte de Lisle supposes a more consciously intellectual process:

> La pensée surabonde nécessairement dans l'œuvre d'un vrai poète, maître de sa langue et de son instrument. Il voit du premier coup d'œil plus loin, plus haut, plus profondément que tous, parce qu'il contemple l'idéal à travers la beauté visible, et qu'il le concentre et l'enchâsse dans l'expression propre, précise, unique.[10]

Transposition, revelation. The action of the artist appears therefore as a visionary and interpretative action. For Leconte de Lisle it is more; it is a creative act:

> Le poète, le créateur d'idées, c'est-à-dire de formes visibles ou

---

[8] *Derniers Poèmes*, p. 222.

[9] Cf. ibid., p. 227: En général, tout ce qui constitue l'art, la morale et la science était mort avec le Polythéisme. It is important to note that Leconte de Lisle considers the demise of polytheism as having no irrevocable character. He refers, in this same preface (*Poèmes antiques*), to its 'renaissance' in sixteenth-century Italy (*Derniers Poèmes*, pp. 227–8). It is to be presumed that the value and 'truth' of this system, being 'eternal', will, cyclically at any rate, ensure its survival.

[10] Ibid., p. 241 (*Les Poètes contemporains. Avant-Propos*).

invisibles, d'images vivantes ou conçues, doit réaliser le Beau, dans la mesure de ses forces et de sa vision interne, par la combinaison complexe, savante, harmonique des lignes, des couleurs et des sons, non moins que par toutes les ressources de la passion, de la réflexion, de la science et de la fantaisie (. . .).[11]

The word *créateur* and its allied forms does not appear to be a central term in Leconte de Lisle's writings; it has a less primary function than *révélation*. It concerns the effort of the imagination which bears upon the choice of the expressive elements of poetry. This is the force which combines the elements of the 'visible' and 'invisible beauty' that we have already noted. These exist in the mind as ideas, which we see Leconte de Lisle define exactly as 'forms' or 'images'. The fact that these ideas can derive from the actual forms of things or from mental conceptions remote from immediate reality implies the presence and action of a factor not mentioned by Leconte de Lisle, that of time. The process of expression is rigorously delineated. The human handling of the substance of art, the product of the 'revelation' achieved by the artist, subject to the vagaries of memory and the pressure of personal choice, is left unmentioned.

Viewed theoretically, the work of a poet stands, for Leconte de Lisle, in no particular relationship to time. Will, intellectual control, plenitude of thought and perception, the mastery of artistic processes are universals. The author suspends his dichotomic theory of the history of poetry when, in *Les Poètes contemporains* or the *Discours sur Victor Hugo*, he attempts to define great poetry or the characteristic action of great poets:

Aussi le grand Poète saisit-il d'un œil infaillible le détail infini et l'ensemble des formes, des jeux d'ombre et de lumière (. . .) Ces perceptions diverses, qui affluent incessamment en lui, s'animent et jaillissent en images vivantes, toujours précises dans leur abondance sonore, et qui constatent la communion profonde de l'homme et de la nature.[12]

The poetic act, which Leconte de Lisle sees in its initial stages as invariable and universal, can, from what this text shows, be called creative

[11] Ibid., p. 240.
[12] Ibid., pp. 296–7 (*Discours sur Victor Hugo*). See also p. 307: Car toute vraie et haute poésie contient en effet une philosophie (. . .) and p. 241: J'étudierai dans cet esprit l'œuvre des poètes contemporains. Je demanderai avant tout à chacun d'eux ses titres d'artiste, certain de rencontrer un penseur et une haute nature morale, mais non comme l'entend la plèbe intellectuelle, là où j'admirerai la puissance, la passion, la grâce, la fantaisie, le sentiment de la nature et la compréhension métaphysique et historique, le tout réalisé par une facture parfaite, sans laquelle il n'y a rien.

only in an instinctive and reflex manner. The unvarying or unerring quality of the poet (*infaillible*) is a matter of perception and control of perceptions. His creative force as an artist depends upon the vigour of his reactions to the afflux of 'forms' from the outside world[13] and the vigour and precision with which these can be projected into an expressive medium. This action or reaction, universal in itself, is, we may presume, infinitely variable in its sources and substance. It is also the accompaniment of a psychological process, the mystery of which Leconte de Lisle does not try to probe in his theoretical and critical writings, but upon which his poetry throws much light.

In the first place, of course, the intellectual formulation of ideas is almost entirely absent from Leconte de Lisle's verse which, in its treatment of nature, may be considered at the outset as attempting an illustration of the author's theories. In one text at least (*Khirôn*),[14] he shows the process of poetic inspiration and utterance. The Centaur here undergoes the experiences of the poet seeking to pass from contemplation to expression. In this case it is the 'ancient glory' of past ages which inspires the penetration of immediate reality towards an 'invisible world' and a consequent inarticulate ecstasy which recalls the 'immense desires' and the 'profound communion of man and nature' of the theoretical passages. There is a pain-pleasure motif involved in the act of utterance by the Centaur which is never expressed in the theories but which may be implied from the author's insistence on the role of will and effort as prerequisites of noble or great works. Elsewhere, the significance of nature is left to be inferred from his handling of it.

Superficially, as has been pointed out by Bourget and others, the evocation of landscape in Leconte de Lisle's poetry can be said to have a documentary or ethnological purpose.[15] Races and civilizations, moulded by factors of history and climate, base their mythology as well as their social and religious customs on the scenery and natural forces by which they are conditioned. This gives a scientific aspect to his poetry, which was certainly one of Leconte de Lisle's intentions and which has received more than its due share of attention from commentators. Superficially too, it can be said that the great majority of poems by this author are composed according to an order which, whatever the erudition or documentation involved, owes infinitely more to art than to science. First a place is evoked, vague or closely delineated, sometimes barren,

---

[13] The examples given in Leconte de Lisle's text include auditory as well as visual images.
[14] *Poèmes antiques*. See p. 195.
[15] P. Bourget: *Nouveaux Essais de psychologie contemporaine*, 1886, pp. 99–118. Brunetière, Estève, Vianey, Flottes, Jobit develop the same idea.

sometimes teeming with life. This is the stage of an action which plays itself out, often with violence. This action may be a vision or the recreation of a myth, a historical or quasi-historical episode, an event based on natural history or, occasionally, on the poet's personal experience. The action, brought to its conclusion, motivates the dispersal of its own elements and a return either to silence or to the normality of the setting seen in its stylized aspects, but usually simplified, invested with a heightened significance.

We see here already how far Leconte de Lisle's creative works, as distinct from his theoretical writings, are conditioned by the idea of time. This cyclic structure, presenting enduring or, more often, transient phases of experience, reproduces an intuitive perception of the time process, both on the cosmic and the human scale. *La Joie de Siva*,[16] for example, represents the two principles, infinite time and finite time and the forces they embody. Siva is the personification of a divine consciousness governing an eternal process of change and disappearance. Maya, in the same poem, personifies the illusion of the external world which is part of cosmic time, vast in extent but finite. Elsewhere, the antithesis rests on the separated notions of human time and infinite time:

Par delà l'heure humaine et le temps infini.[17]

The human mind is thus able, at privileged moments, to reach out beyond even the unending continuum to an absolute, the notion of which derives purely from psychological urges of the type which we have already seen.

The perspectives of Leconte de Lisle's poetry are thus twofold. There is on the one hand the attempt on the part of the poet to consider the universe from a point of view which, strictly speaking, is only possible to some form of universal consciousness; on the other, there is the scrutiny and penetration of the 'heure humaine'. It is interesting to observe that these two perspectives correspond closely to those noted by Vigny in his *Journal d'un Poète* when he attempts to specify the two fundamentally opposed attitudes to philosophical or theological problems.[18] In the first analysis, this dual perspective appears to form part of the 'tragic dilemma' of Leconte de Lisle brought out by A. R. Chisholm in a fine chapter devoted to this poet.[19] But the characteristic movement of the mind in contemplation, piercing the 'forms' and 'images' sent to us

[16] *Derniers Poèmes*, p. 10.
[17] *Poèmes tragiques*, p. 71.
[18] See op. cit., '1843. Croyance ou Religion.'
[19] *Towards 'Hérodiade'*, Melbourne U.P., 1934, p. 35.

by the natural world, tends to a transcendence both of the human and the cosmic:

> Soleils, Mondes, Amour, illusions sublimes,
> Désirs, splendeurs! si tout est éphémère et vain
> Dans nos cœurs aussi bien qu'en vos profonds abîmes,
> Votre instant est sacré, votre rêve est divin,
> Soleils, Mondes, Amour, illusions sublimes![20]

Even within the limits of individual experience, a sense of supernatural plenitude is possible. The theological vocabulary used here to characterize this state (*sacré, divin*) is interesting, given that the text is a late one, because these two adjectives, common and unremarkable in themselves in the work of Leconte de Lisle, are used here to mark the brevity of life and the unreality of its texture as having a preternatural quality.[21]

In the lines just quoted, the experience representing the human scale is sexual love which, though too unstable in its effects and action to procure a true transcendence, is able to create an illusion of eternity within the moments of human time:

> Ils ne savent plus rien du vol de l'heure brève,
> Le charme et la Beauté de la terre et des cieux
> Leur rendent éternel l'instant délicieux,
> Et, dans l'enchantement de ce rêve d'un rêve,
> Ils ne savent plus rien du vol de l'heure brève.[22]

It is not difficult to find formulations of this kind in Leconte de Lisle's poetry.[23] What is remarkable about this is not that the poet, despite the somewhat artificial order of his three principal volumes, should allow the sentimental or sensual chord to be struck at repeated intervals, but that he should allow such a privileged status to an experience which is merely part of the work of Maya, part of the ephemeral flux. Such an experience can not only suspend the motion of time; in its deepest moments it can exercise an enchantment that brings it into line with the state induced by contemplation. The absorption of lovers is made meaningful, in the passage we have just seen, by the action and influence of the natural world. It is the 'beauty of earth and sky' which produces the transmutation of the moment of time into the timeless moment.

Otherwise, such calls as there are in Leconte de Lisle's work to a magical

---

[20] *Derniers Poèmes*, p. 79.

[21] See also, *infra*, p. 86.

[22] *Poèmes tragiques*, p. 18 (*Dans le ciel clair*).

[23] See also *Parfum impérissable* (*Poèmes tragiques*), *Çunacépa* (section VII) (*Poèmes antiques*), *Les Étoiles mortelles* (*Poèmes antiques*), *Le Baiser suprême* (*Derniers Poèmes*).

suspension of human time derive from the frustrations of experience, round which a number of pessimistic poems may be grouped. There is, for example, the call to Sélène in the *Hymnes Orphiques* of the *Derniers Poèmes*:

> Et guéris-nous, pour un instant délicieux,
> Des maux dont notre vie est faite.[24]

But all desires to find or create an enclave in time suppose the aid of a supernatural or, at any rate, extra-human, agent. In this respect the poems of despair as well as those adducing a privileged or enlightened moment may be said to be controlled by the poet's notion of the ideal.

It is, as one might expect, through the theme of human time that Leconte de Lisle most often reaches an intuition of the ideal. Cosmic time furnishes the themes of creation myths as well as visions of terrestrial or universal change inspired by contemporary scientific theory. Occasionally the perspectives interact, as when, in *La Forêt vierge*, the poet imagines the formation of the continents,[25] or in *La Tristesse du Diable*, where he evokes, within the context of remote space and time, the strictly human tedium and despair of Satan's damnation.[26] But generally it is by evoking real or imagined experiences within a terrestrial context that he is able, not always consciously or deliberately, to illustrate some of his own dicta on poetry and the ideal.

Leconte de Lisle is not fundamentally a descriptive artist. The evocations of the natural world which prepare events, out of which events arise, are not intended ultimately to represent places where one might have been or where one might go. Behind the famous 'objectivity' and the so-called 'painterly' talent is the eye of an artist concerned to isolate and depict scenes according to climatic variation, without fantasy, as symbols of the conditions of life on the globe, each representing an individual moment of perception and each charged with an individual significance well beyond its descriptive value. Let us consider the following lines:

> L'Orient se dilate et pleut en gerbes roses,
> La tourelle pétille et le dôme reluit,
> L'aile du vent joyeux porte l'odeur des roses
> Au vieux Liban trempé des larmes de la nuit.[27]

By this time (1878-9)[28] habits of synthesis and greater stylization have

---

[24] Op. cit., p. 17.
[25] *Poèmes barbares*, p. 186.
[26] Ibid., pp. 297-9.
[27] *Poèmes tragiques*, p. 1.
[28] *L'Apothéose de Mouça-al-Kébyr*, from which this verse is taken, first appeared in the *Nouvelle Revue*, October 15, 1879.

taken the place of the detailed elaborations of the outside world found in
the earlier poems. Underneath the conventional elements employed here
by Leconte de Lisle, possibly to Europeanize the exotic subject and *décor*,
runs the theme of light, in particular the theme of Oriental sunlight as a
vital and inspiriting force. The descriptive elements of the stanza are the
projection of this force, the prosodic and verbal structure its harmonic
accompaniment. We see therefore, in a stanza quite unremarkable in the
work of Leconte de Lisle, a manifestation of a process which characterizes
his whole production, the ordering of a description by the apprehension
of an agent or principle transcending phenomena but acting through them.
A more striking example is found in *La Mort de Valmiki*:

> La lumière sacrée envahit terre et cieux;
> Du zénith au brin d'herbe et du gouffre à la nue,
> Elle vole, palpite, et nage et s'insinue,
> Dorant d'un seul baiser clair, subtil, frais et doux,
> Les oiseaux dans la mousse, et, sous les noirs bambous,
> Les éléphants pensifs qui font frémir leurs rides
> Au vol strident et vif des vertes cantharides,
> Les radjahs et les chiens, Richis et Parias,
> Et l'insecte invisible et les Himalayas.
> Un rire éblouissant illumine le monde.
> L'arome de la Vie inépuisable inonde
> L'immensité du rêve énergique où Brahma
> Se vit, se reconnut, resplendit et s'aima.[29]

The detail in this passage is controlled by two factors, neither of which has
anything to do with the representation of a scene in terms of space and
mass: an inclusive vision of the hierarchy of living creatures and natural
objects; the action of light upon a landscape for which light is the equivalent of the life force. The perspective is, in the first instance, the universal
or cosmic perspective to which reference has already been made. The
theme, as can be seen from the last four lines, is close to the creation
theme. The attitude of the poet, however, approaches that of the contemplative, discerning in and beyond the prospects of nature a beauty that
is not finite and the presence of a universal spirit, a state which we have
already seen formulated in Leconte de Lisle's prose and which he
describes as productive of great happiness. In the text from *La Mort de
Valmiki*, the state of the observer is suggested by movement, sensation,
the sense of immense energy and plenitude. Light (*lumière sacrée*) is
represented as the manifestation of a divine entity (Brahma) which we

---

[29] *Poèmes antiques*, p. 27. *La Mort de Valmiki* was published in the 3rd edition, 1881.

also see personified as the intelligence governing Nature. Brahma, as we know from *La Vision de Brahma*,[30] corresponds to the second principle in Leconte de Lisle's cosmology, the eternal creative force, set in being by the prime undifferentiated principle for which the creation is a specific act of will or cognition and for which, presumably, many creations might be possible.

The attitude of the observer, that is, the poet, is not of course always the same as that of the personages he evokes in the context of the natural scenes and forces that inspire him. The three brahmins who at first practice a form of meditation which can hardly be that of the poet, ultimately penetrate as far as the presence of Bhagavat:

> Bhagavat! Bhagavat! Essence des Essences,
> Source de la beauté, fleuve des Renaissances,
> Lumière qui fais vivre et mourir à la fois![31]

The god appears to be, despite the abstract formulation of the lines just quoted, a Pan figure whose evocation recalls the dionysian Pan of Hugo's *Le Satyre*, that is to say, a symbol of the natural world seen in heightened forms of beauty and energy. But Bhagavat is for the poet, in his conclusion, this 'Essence', this 'Source', this 'Light' to which his mind is always drawn by contemplation of external nature.

Can we then say that the objects of the natural world represent for Leconte de Lisle signs or symbols of the ideal? The answer appears to be that, when these objects are viewed in their variety and harmony and particularly when they carry deep associations, they do in fact represent what the poet calls, in *L'Aurore*, 'formes de l'idéal'.[32] In *L'Aurore* itself, these forms are the great aspects and forces of the natural world that have always moved or inspired poets: sky, sea, mountains, woods, winds.[33] These large aspects can sometimes, when the process of memory is actively engaged, suggest an idealized past, that is, a personal Eden.[34] Indeed, there is running through Leconte de Lisle's poetry the theme of a privileged past age, when men lived in a familiarity and harmony with the forms and forces of Nature which urban and industrial civilizations have long since lost. Such harmony between certain fortunate races and

---

[30] *Poèmes antiques*, pp. 56–64. *La Vision de Brahma* appeared for the first time in 1857, in the *Revue contemporaine*.

[31] *Poèmes antiques*, p. 24.

[32] *Poèmes barbares*, p. 202.

[33] See ibid., eod. loc.:

> Mais, ô nature, ô ciel, flots sacrés, monts sublimes,
> Bois dont les vents amis font murmurer les cimes, (. . .)

[34] For example, *La Fontaine aux lianes*. See *Poèmes barbares*, p. 168.

the planetary and universal forces produces, as we can see, for example, in certain passages of *Le Massacre de Mona*, a dilation of experience that is made to appear supernatural or magical.[35]

This magical or supernatural quality is, in fact, always present in Leconte de Lisle's evocations of nature, whether or not any attempt is made to define the accompanying spiritual state in the observer. The great majority of the descriptions of nature are presented without any developed comment or analysis.

Mais l'âme s'en pénètre; elle se plonge, entière,
Dans l'heureuse beauté de ce monde charmant;
Elle se sent oiseau, fleur, eau vive et lumière;
Elle revêt ta robe, ô pureté première!
Et se repose en Dieu silencieusement.[36]

Thus the concluding verse of *Le Bernica*. It is one of relatively few passages describing the processes of the individual consciousness under the domination of scenes of particular grandeur or beauty. We find here the transcription of a complex action. The mind and the scene it contemplates are interfused and yet the individual consciousness is able to transcend the scene, not fortuitously, by reference to analogous or suggested scenes, but by exhausting the significance of the individual phenomena through identity with them. These phenomena (*oiseau, fleur, eau vive, lumière*) are at once stylized components of the beauty of the landscape and elements of the force that determines it. Yet the mind is driven beyond this identity, which must be a source of vigour and elation, towards a soundless and passionless communion with what is felt to be the ultimate source or principle. It is an almost perfect example, in Leconte de Lisle's poetry, of the process which we have been able to envisage from the prose texts quoted earlier. But we also see that memory enters here. When the mind becomes invested with an essential simplicity and serenity (*pureté première*), it is through the recollection of a primitive untroubled state. Memory is of extreme importance in the creation of Leconte de Lisle's landscapes. It is the lens through which most scenes are viewed. Although it may be the 'supreme illusion',[37] it tinges the recollected landscape with a sense of the divine. *In extremis*, the mind, as we see in the case of Valmiki and of Mouça-al-Kébyr, reaches back to absorb itself in the 'splendides années'.[38] It is possible to discern, in the poetry itself, some hesitation over the value

35 See *Poèmes barbares*, p. 120.
36 *Poèmes barbares*, p. 207.
37 See *Poèmes tragiques*, p. 36.
38 See *Poèmes antiques*, pp. 26–29; *Poèmes tragiques*, p. 10.

and function of memory and there is at least one letter in which Leconte de Lisle gives an almost Pascalian gloss to the problem of the use of time past and the anticipation of the future:

> (. . .) cette vie intérieure que je garde embaumée dans ma mémoire! Il se pourrait bien que cette habitude de concentration dans le passé ou dans l'avenir et presque jamais dans le présent, nuisît à l'expansion de mes sentiments (. . .).[39]

In a broad sense, retrospection and anticipation may be said to dominate Leconte de Lisle's poetry, despite the dramatic present in which many of the descriptions of natural events are set. The following two passages may be recognized as typical in many respects:

> La lumière, en un frais et vif pétillement,
> Croît, s'élance par jet, s'échappe par fusée,
> Et l'orbe du soleil émerge au firmament.[40]

> L'orbe d'or du soleil tombé des cieux sans bornes
> S'enfonce avec lenteur dans l'immobile mer
> Et pour suprême adieu baigne d'un rose éclair
> Le givre qui pétille à la cime des mornes.[41]

Both deal with the solar cycle, at moments seen by the poet as philosophically as well as artistically meaningful. Both subordinate the visual elements of the scene evoked to the play of an essential force and the vivid sense of the alternation of light and dark. What is less immediately apparent is that the two scenes, like so many others, are recollected, drawn from the store of images gathered in the poet's early years spent on an island (Bourbon) in the Indian Ocean. Elsewhere, the snowscapes of Le Runoïa and the harsh settings of the series of poems placed in north-western Europe are drawn from a collective past in the sense that they are reconstituted from legends and possibly from erudite descriptive works. Finally, the two scenes, while being, like all descriptions of nature in Leconte de Lisle, symbolical entities, prepare occurrences and conclusions that are at once part of a universal pattern and a unique moment of experience. The first is the prelude to the eagle's hunt for prey, the second motivates a movement towards contemplation, the results of which are negative or pessimistic.

We have not so far seen the negative accompaniment of contemplation, that is to say the reaction of the mind which, in the presence of the great

---

[39] From a letter quoted by Marius-Ary Leblond, op. cit., p. 163.
[40] La Chasse de l'aigle (Poèmes tragiques, p. 54).
[41] L'Orbe d'or (Poèmes tragiques, p. 61).

spectacles of nature, is impressed by a sense of the inconclusiveness and
vanity of its own perceptions. The last verse of *L'Orbe d'or* furnishes an
example:

> Et l'âme, qui contemple et soi-même s'oublie
> Dans la splendide paix du silence divin,
> Sans regrets ni désirs, sachant que tout est vain,
> En un rêve éternel s'abîme ensevelie.

This is the reverse of the theme of cosmic energy, the failure of the
empathy which elsewhere leads the poet towards the ambitious wording
of creation myths and the apprehension of universal forces and principles.
It must also be remarked that, in this case, the poet's consciousness, which
is able to envisage beyond itself only a prolongation of its indeterminate
state, is conditioned by the decline and disappearance of the dynamic
elements normally associated with life. In any case we find, in this poem,
the author reaching out towards the theme of cosmic time which, as we
have said, can only be envisaged from a perspective which accentuates the
brevity of the human span and the unimportance of individual being.

There are, of course, occasions when the theme of illusion is envisaged
pessimistically, as in the much-quoted verse from *La Ravine Saint-Gilles:*

> Pour qui sait pénétrer, Nature, dans tes voies,
> L'illusion t'enserre et ta surface ment:
> Au fond de tes fureurs, comme au fond de tes joies,
> Ta force est sans ivresse et sans emportement.[42]

It is doubtful, however, whether the idea expressed here is fundamentally
very different from the notion of *maya* expressed in *La Vision de Brahma.*
The gaze of the poet stops here at the surface manifestations of the
appearances and forces of Nature. The point of his judgement is to
separate the human and the natural order. The negative elements he lists
belong entirely to the realm of human passions (*fureur, joies, ivresse,
emportement*) which find no equivalent in the spectacle of the outside
world. It is also very doubtful whether Leconte de Lisle wishes to convey
the idea attributed to him in this context by A. R. Chisholm, that 'Nature
in itself has no real energy',[43] implying as this would the contradiction of
one of the most important lines of *La Vision de Brahma*:

> J'ai mis mon Énergie au sein des Apparences, (...)[44]

[42] *Poèmes barbares*, p. 176.
[43] *Towards 'Hérodiade'*, p. 38.
[44] *Poèmes antiques*, p. 62.

where the words are addressed by Hâri to Brahma:

La voix de l'Incréé parlant à l'Éternel.

Where Leconte de Lisle tends to pessimism is over human ephemerality, human perverseness, the limitations of human perception, the absence of guarantees of survival and, ultimately, of progress. Nature may send back images of an implacable planetary condition as often as, or more often than, signs of a transcendent order that can inspire and elevate individual human beings. But the overwhelming evidence of the texts is, none the less, of a poetic universe where a vigorous beauty, derived from uncompromising universal forces, is delineated in such a way as to suggest experiences and situations beyond itself.

It is in this way that the sense of the supernatural and the magical is present in all Leconte de Lisle's evocations of the outside world and not only in those in which contact with the infinite or ideal is consciously exploited.

> Le mâle orgueil de vivre emplissait ma poitrine,
> Et, sans m'inquiéter du fugitif instant,
> Je sentais s'élargir dans mon cœur palpitant
> Le ciel immense avec l'immensité marine.[45]

These lines, for instance, represent a midway state. The contact with the world is physical, but the euphoria so induced clings to intuitions of space and time, both of which are controlled and contained physically. At this stage we see a Rimbaldian fusion of sensation and intuition which discipline and erudition usually conceal.

Wherever descriptive preparations are used in Leconte de Lisle's poetry, they are imbued with anticipation or foreboding. The earth, 'marvellous' in its immensity and fecundity, hangs upon the meditation of Djihan-Guir in *Nurmahal*.[46] Night is evoked as an agent of magical suspense, metaphysical in *Villanelle*,[47] sentimental in *Le Sommeil de Leïlah*,[48] maleficent in *L'Incantation du Loup*,[49] sinister and pessimistic in *Sacra Fames*.[50] The sun has also the virtue of a magical force: life-giver at its dawn, devourer of energies at its zenith, liberator of the predatory forces and symbol of the inevitable return at its setting. These four sectors, dawn, zenith, sunset, darkness, motivate severally the individual poems of

[45] *Derniers Poèmes*, p. 62.
[46] *Poèmes barbares*, p. 137.
[47] *Poèmes tragiques*, p. 40.
[48] *Poèmes barbares*, p. 162.
[49] *Poèmes tragiques*, pp. 68–9.
[50] Ibid., p. 72.

Leconte de Lisle. Each phase of the solar cycle is evoked as a privileged or significant moment, meaningful philosophically, episodically and artistically. Thus, in *Le frais matin dorait*, the brief and stylized notations of dawn are presented as a symbol of the freshness of the poet's early life and also of man's first innocence in the years of Eden;[51] certain long works, like *Çunacépa*, trace the progress of the sun from dawn through the heat of the meridian to night, sometimes over several days, the descriptions underlining a ritual of quest or the several phases of a decreasing span of time that will settle the destinies of the characters;[52] the setting of the sun and the advance of twilight are traced, in a score or so of couplets, as a prelude to the meeting of Khirôn and Orphée; the moment of transition between night and dawn is used to motivate the departure of Orphée.[53]

The insistence on transitional phases or moments is profoundly characteristic of Leconte de Lisle's descriptive technique. The landscape dominated by the sleep and the waking hunger of the tiger is remarkable, in *Les Jungles*,[54] not so much for the multiplicity of life forms evoked, which gives it its superficial aspect, as for the suggestion of certain rhythms conditioning the natural world and the beast itself, which is a symbol and a projection of the forces contained by that world. The same is true of *L'Aboma*,[55] where the waves of life set in motion by the mounting sun break against the silence and the waking movements of the reptile which the poet presents in rich and heroic terms and which he elevates beyond the human plane, again as a symbol of Nature. This subordination of the pictorial aspects of landscape to the diurnal rhythms, transition, alternation, cycle, sequence, is to a large degree imitated from the natural world. But the elements of which individual settings are composed are themselves disposed according to a rhythm or an order which is artificial and artistic and which is varied from poem to poem, alternate, chiasmic, involuted, as the case may be.[56]

The evocation of a landscape subject to a force or forces is part of

---

[51] Ibid., p. 143–4.
[52] *Poèmes antiques*, pp. 36–55.
[53] Ibid., pp. 184–6, p. 216.
[54] *Poèmes barbares*, pp. 203–4.
[55] *Poèmes tragiques*, pp. 102–4.
[56] The opening description of sunrise in *Çunacépa* (*Poèmes antiques*, pp. 36–7) is an example of a setting constructed according to an alternating rhythm. The two elements involved are (a) images of dawn and (b) accompanying effects. The order is then the fourfold sequence of (a), (b) with (b) growing in length and significance as the passage progresses. The evocation of night in *Bhagavat* (*Poèmes antiques*, pp. 13–14) is composed of three elements: (a) the grief of the brahmins, (b) nightfall, (c) the movement of unseen life. These are repeated and disposed in an enclosed pattern: a,b,c,b,c,a. In *Le Rêve du Jaguar* (*Poèmes barbares*, pp. 216–17) the two main motifs, the tropical setting and the beast of prey, are presented in an interesting involuted pattern, corresponding to the divisions indicated by a complex rhyme structure.

Leconte de Lisle's descriptive procedure. This force can emanate from the percipient as well as from the outside world, while there are, of course, many areas of interaction between the two. We find, in the settings presented by the poet, frequent notations of effluvia which have the value of an emanation. There is not only the 'effluve invincible'[57] with its erotic and sentimental associations, more familiar to readers of Baudelaire than to those of Leconte de Lisle. There are perfumes in Nature which favour spiritual liberation, as those brought by the night wind, in *Ultra Caelos*,

(. . .) chargé du parfum des hautes solitudes.[58]

There are the special qualities of the wind that blows across individual landscapes, conditioning the creatures that inhabit them, as the slow, disturbing breath of the savanna or the odourless, raging wind of the polar regions.[59]

The descriptions of Leconte de Lisle are composed largely of events. These events mark, in many cases, an interchange between macrocosm and microcosm, a microcosm which remains, despite a number of serious attempts to reconstitute the experiences and perspectives of the more imposing of the lower animals, steadfastly human. Thus, *Sacra Fames*,[60] so far from being an effort, as one critic would have it, to 'reflect the universe through the eye of the shark',[61] is a profoundly human evocation of the duality of a universe that dwarfs the mind by its majesty and rouses fear and despair by the sinister laws imposed on all forms of life. The sense of reciprocation between the earth and the objects and cosmic forces about it produces an almost visionary awareness of other consciousnesses, near and remote, watchful and indifferent or hostile. A similar process may be observed in *L'Incantation de Loup*,[62] where the admirable firmness of line by which the artist depicts his wolf from the outside tends to be blurred by the effort to penetrate the animal's consciousness, an effort which steadily diminishes the distance between the artist and his subject and finishes by imposing human sensibilities on the animal. The visionary force of this poem, which is perhaps its finest quality, is nevertheless enhanced by such a procedure, for the implied admiration of the spectacle of the full winter moon lending a lunar aspect to the mountain setting, together with the implied comment upon the terrestrial condition and upon the nature of man, derive exclusively from the field of human awareness. These two examples illustrate the negative or pessimistic sense

---

[57] See *Poèmes barbares*, p. 135 (*La Vérandah*).
[58] Ibid., p. 219.
[59] See ibid., pp. 214–15 (*Les Taureaux*) and p. 261 (*Paysage polaire*).
[60] *Poèmes tragiques*, p. 72.
[61] See Irving Putter, op. cit., p. 305.
[62] *Poèmes tragiques*, pp. 68–69.

of correspondences, the moments at which the mind, faced with certain aspects of the 'visible beauty' that at other times may elate and transport it, remains fixed at the notion of individuation. There is, however, never any lack of intelligence between the individual and the world. If the extra-human forces are so often represented as converging maleficently upon man, it is because this poet idealizes man, for such bitter strictures on human degeneracy as those we find in the *Poèmes barbares* and the *Poèmes tragiques* themselves argue a nobler conception of man, a conception defeated or frustrated by the author's experiences or the evidence of history. Leconte de Lisle, fixed in the nineteenth century, cannot resolve, through the pantheism to which he inclines by instinct, problems which, he feels, an adherence to polytheism, no longer possible, could have rendered innocuous.

The strongest notes of pessimism are sounded in some of the least visionary poems. They are also often present in poems where the preliminary evocation of setting is, for one reason or another, at its feeblest. Thus, the anthology piece *Le vent froid de la nuit*[63] is placed in a vague winter scene, macabre in a banal Romantic way. *Fiat nox* is based on an image of the 'flux marin'[64] so generalized as to become a symbol. Notations of visions, at their most ferocious, rejoin the pseudo-scientific predictions of the running down of the solar system. Thus, there is little difference between the conjured eclipse in *Le Barde de Temrah*,[65] the prophecy made by the Child in *Le Runoïa*,[66] the symbol of Sahil in *L'Astre Rouge*[67] and the conclusion of *Solvet seclum*.[68] The implacable anticipations of doom, which are to be found sprinkled among the poems published in the decade following 1859, are not equal in imaginative force to the more purely artistic preparations for narrative or speculation. The most successful visionary landscapes are those worked by forces of destruction. They have their own depth and resonance, but are the inverse of the landscapes presenting the 'visible' and 'invisible beauty' which invests or manifests the ideal.

Is there then, in Leconte de Lisle, a Baudelairian equipoise of 'paradisal' and 'infernal' time?[69] The answer is surely no. As in every human consciousness there exists, in Leconte de Lisle, a desire to triumph over the irrevocable and the transitory. Art, recollection in the service of art,

---

[63] *Poèmes barbares*, pp. 63–64.
[64] Ibid., see p. 237.
[65] Ibid., see p. 64.
[66] Ibid., see p. 90.
[67] *Poèmes tragiques*, pp. 24–25.
[68] *Poèmes barbares*, see p. 362.
[69] See G. Poulet, *Étude sur le temps humain*, Edinburgh, 1949, pp. 334–53.

contemplation, are means towards this end. They are envisaged in terms of human time. But the infernal time he discovers is a remote condition. It is not experienced in terms of human time. It represents a suspension of the normal processes of life, an obliteration, imminent or accomplished, of human life. It demands the conscious exercise of the imagination, which is to say that the forms by which it is represented are to a considerable degree invented; and yet these inventions seem artificial and limited, whether the poet is evoking the pit of flames in *Le Massacre de Mona*,[70] or the preternatural sunrise afforded to Dom Guy,[71] or the two closed worlds, reality and dream, of the Bedouin in *Le Désert*.[72] Such notations do not arise from the intimate experience of the artist. They are really intellectual formulations of his destruction fantasies or his ethnographical ideas.

Leconte de Lisle's inspiration therefore runs in two principal cycles. The first traces the instinctive movement of the mental gaze outwards towards the ideal, the second fixes the attention upon the terrestrial condition which leads it towards closed images and closed structures. Typically, in the case of the artist or the sage, the physical eye and the mind's eye embrace the natural world and enclose superhuman perceptions in the form of suggested images. There are interesting variations. Occasionally, a purely religious inspiration is evoked, as in the following verse of *Le Barde de Temrah*:

> Il laisse l'aiguillon échapper de sa main,
> Et, les yeux clos, il ouvre aux ailes de son âme
> Le monde intérieur et l'horizon divin.[73]

Here the personal world of mental images and the world of sensible appearances are subordinated to an inspiring and obsessive force which turns inward, closing the mind to outside data. The dilatation of the mind thus induced seems to suggest an individual flight from the earth. When such flights are more clearly envisaged, they do not appear to be, in themselves, profitable either artistically or metaphysically. The mental faculties cannot ultimately sustain such a journey which finishes inevitably, for Leconte de Lisle, with

> (. . .) l'inerrable et pleine cécité.[74]

Inevitably, therefore, the intellect intervenes, trying, at the height of its

---

[70] *Poèmes barbares,* see p. 128.
[71] Ibid., see pp. 339–40.
[72] Ibid., see pp. 143–4.
[73] Ibid., see p. 62.
[74] Ibid., p. 238 (*In Excelsis*).

powers, to represent enumeratively the structures of the universe which can never be, for this artist, those of a machine, however complex, showing or refusing to show evidence of the controlling hand above it. The material world escapes always into an ambiguity behind which is an impenetrable darkness. But this very ambiguity, which causes Leconte de Lisle intellectually to despair over the range and nature of human perception and the value of human activity, permits intuitive flashes of a spiritual principle informing the physical world. We should do well to observe, in the passage which we have quoted from *Le Barde de Temrah*, the use of the word *divin*. This term, though it is used frequently enough by the poet to appear almost as a habit of style,[75] is in fact never used in the poems of the main collections without regard to its strict sense, which refers to qualities possessed or inspired by a superhuman being. Applied to the natural world, it indicates a transcendence. It is one of the elements which show the involvement of image and idea and the natural effort to penetrate beyond the image towards its source.

There is no doubt that Leconte de Lisle considered the interchange between Nature and the individual, particularly where such interchange is integral, involving the physical as well as the spiritual faculties, as the most rewarding of experiences. Nothing in his work suggests that his views changed much here, despite the abandonment of successive religious positions and despite the voluptuous distaste with which he regarded the life of his European contemporaries and their Christian forbears. We know, from *La Recherche de Dieu*, which dates from 1846,[76] of his sense of dilemma at finding no conclusive evidence of a divine presence. The theme of such a divine presence persists none the less throughout his work. From Bhagavat 'créateur des formes', through Brahma and the Greek personifications of natural forces, through representations of a sublime and purposeful but humanly empty Cosmos, he returns, in the *Derniers Poèmes*, to Pan. Forerunner, in the *Poèmes antiques* of 1852, of Mallarmé's Faun, the Pan of Leconte de Lisle becomes, in *Parfum de Pan*, the poet's final and finest evocation of an eternal Being constantly present in the universe it creates, source of the ideal as well as of the real:

> Ton souffle immense emplit la Syrinx éternelle!
> Tout soupire, tout chante ou se lamente en elle;
> Et le vaste Univers qui dormait dans tes yeux,
> Circulaire et changeant, sinistre ou radieux,

---

[75] Irving Putter notes its frequency, particularly in the verses of Leconte de Lisle's early years. See op. cit., p. 321.

[76] *La Phalange*, t. III, p. 60.

Avec ses monts, ses bois, ses flots, l'homme et les Dieux,
En se multipliant jaillit de ta prunelle,
Inépuisable Pan, vieux et toujours nouveau,
Toi qui fais luire au loin, pour des races meilleures,
Comme un pâle reflet de quelque vain flambeau,
L'Espérance stérile, hélas! dont tu nous leurres,
Et qui roules, marqués d'un implacable sceau,
Les siècles de ton rêve aussi prompts que tes heures,
Salut ô Dieu terrible, Origine et Tombeau![77]

[77] *Derniers Poèmes,* pp. 29–30.

6

AUSTIN GILL

Mallarmé on Baudelaire

IT is generally agreed that from 1862 to (say) 1867, the influence of Baudelaire on Mallarmé was strong. Opinions differ, however, as to how deep it went and how decisive or abiding it proved, and recent discussions have made it apparent that to assess it accurately is not a simple matter. In an article published in 1953 Adile Ayda compiled a long list of Mallarmé's borrowings from Victor Hugo, and claimed that they were so abundant as to place Hugo by the side of Baudelaire as a major influence.[1] Lloyd Austin expressed doubts about the extent of these borrowings, and objected that in any case the essential fact was that Mallarmé's poetic is founded on concentration and condensation, like Baudelaire's, whereas Hugo relies on the opposite principles, of enumeration and expansion.[2] To this Léon Cellier retorted that Mallarmé does indeed practise a Baudelairian concentration, but that what is concentrated in his poems is often Victor Hugo.[3] Thus the different questions that need to be answered are beginning to shake themselves clear of each other, *tant bien que mal*. The one that will be asked and in some measure answered in this article does not directly concern Baudelaire's influence on Mallarmé's poetry,[4] but his

---

[1] 'L'Influence de Victor Hugo sur Stéphane Mallarmé,' *Dialogues*, Istanbul, Cahier 3 (juillet 1953).

[2] 'Les "Années d'apprentissage" de Stéphane Mallarmé,' *Revue d'Histoire Littéraire de la France*, LVI (janvier-mars 1956).

[3] *Mallarmé et la Morte qui parle*, 1959, p. 61.

[4] I know of only one substantial study of Baudelaire's influence on Mallarmé's early writings, an unpublished thesis by Madeleine Marion Smith, entitled *Mallarmé's Grimoire* (Yale Ph.D. thesis, 1952). I am grateful to the author and the librarian of Yale University for allowing me to see this work, and to the librarian of the Taylor Institution for making the arrangements. On a very cursory examination (which in view of the undertakings one is required to give on such occasions is all one has the heart for) it seemed to me that the first part, a really methodical study, was more valuable than the more ambitious and speculative part that follows, and the appendix on Mallarmé's 'Tombeau de Baudelaire'. I was glad to be able to make sure that the subject I wished to choose for my contribution to this volume had not already been dealt with by Dr Smith. It is a pity that the first part of her thesis has not been made accessible, for instance in the form of articles, for the study of Mallarmé's sources helps enormously in the elucidation of his poems. This is shown very clearly in (for instance) Léon Cellier's book on *Mallarmé et la Morte qui parle* (1959); again and again a line or passage in Gautier or Hugo clarifies a difficult line in Mallarmé. For a particularly clear example of the usefulness of this kind of enquiry, I make bold to refer to a detail Professor Cellier seems to

impact on his thought. What can be learned of this impact, as far as the period 1862–7 is concerned?

They were years during which Mallarmé was resolutely engaged in the hazardous venture of making a poet out of a man, while he had still not completely emerged from another ordeal that has its perils too though it is part of the common lot, that of making a man out of a boy. Mallarmé's reflexions on Baudelaire had their effect on both processes and helped to co-ordinate them; they therefore provide some insight into the deeper organization of his moral and intellectual experience during this all-important phase in his development. Since our knowledge of this development is vaguer than is perhaps (in view of the vast literature on Mallarmé) usually supposed, I must acknowledge explicitly that the account of it presented here will be very restricted in scope. It will also be uncritical, even within these narrow limits, in the sense that I shall not attempt to do more than pick out the general tenor of Mallarmé's reflexions on Baudelaire, without enquiring how fair or unfair they are, or how far they rest on legitimate criticism and how far on the young poet's need to dis-cover and affirm his own originality. Already in those early years (I shall suggest) Mallarmé had his secrets and was a master at keeping them to himself. To see through the starry-eyed idealism of some of the early poems and the seeming artlessness of some of the letters and get at the private argufying (to use Empson's term) requires wary and inquisitive reading. Until more exploratory searching has been done to bring the thought out, theme by theme, it would be unwise to try to assess its scope and quality.

It appears to have been understood among Mallarmé's friends, and accepted almost as axiomatic, that he was Baudelaire's disciple. When they wanted to praise his poems they likened them to Baudelaire's. Thus Armand Renaud assured him, after reading 'L'Azur', that it was a poem 'de la famille de Poe et de Baudelaire, mais avec plus de spiritualisme.'[5] Even Des Essarts was moved to write of one of the early sonnets (probably the one entitled by Mallarmé 'A une putain', and by Des Essarts euphem-

---

have overlooked. When it is noticed that the general idea of the poem 'Sur les bois oubliés' is suggested by Hugo's 'A Celle qui est restée en France' (in *Les Contemplations*, 'Guernesey, 2 novembre, 1855, jour des Morts'), the byzantine discussions carried on by exegetists about there being or not being flowers on the tomb become unnecessary. The friend for whom Mallarmé is writing the poem is in the same position as Hugo; he cannot place flowers on the tomb because it is too far away:

Si je pouvais couvrir de fleurs mon ange pâle!
Hélas! du manque seul de lourds bouquets s'encombre.

[5] 12th February, 1864 (Stéphane Mallarmé, *Correspondance 1862–71*, ed. Mondor and Richard, 1959, p. 108, n. 2).

istically 'A une Dame d'honneur de la reine de Naples' or 'de la reine Victoria'[6]):

> Le sonnet que tu m'envoies est splendide d'exécution, profonde de pensée, et d'une clarté parfaite ce dont je te félicite. Vois Baudelaire comme il est suggestif et lucide à la fois, profond comme un puits où en se penchant on revoit le ciel et les étoiles.[7]

In a brief friendly notice which is the first published comment on Mallarmé's work, Charles Coligny wrote:

> Stéphane Mallarmé est un lyrique forcené et sera toujours un hyper-lyrique; Shakspeare et Edgard Poë sont ses dieux, et il dit que ses dieux le conduisent à M. Charles Baudelaire.[8]

Cazalis called Baudelaire 'ton dieu Baudelaire', and Mallarmé's devotion to him 'la religion, le culte pur de son croyant le plus fidèle.'[9] 'Baudelaire, s'il rajeunissait, pourrait signer vos sonnets' wrote Lefébure, as early as June 1862,[10] referring probably to 'Le Sonneur' and 'Spleen printanier'; and when in later letters he analysed his friend's poetic talent a comparison with Baudelaire was usually implied:

> Ce qui me frappe surtout, dans vos vers éclatants et sombres, c'est une singulière puissance de concentration. Il est probable que les causes en remontent très loin dans votre vie, et qu'elles ont abouti comme corollaire au spleen qui fait votre force comme poète et votre malheur comme homme.
>
> Comme on ne peut servir deux maîtres à la fois, les poètes du spleen idéalisé ne peuvent guère sentir ni rendre l'amour. Aussi E. Poe

---

[6] See *Correspondance*, p. 114, n. 2, and Mondor, *Vie de Mallarmé*, p. 117. It seems clear that it is to 'A une putain' that Des Essarts referred by these titles and not (as Mondor says) an unknown poem.

[7] 3rd March 1864 (*Correspondance*, p. 110, n. 1).

[8] *L'Artiste*, 15 juin 1865; the passage is quoted in Bandy and Pichois, *Baudelaire devant ses contemporains*, 1957, p. 199. That Mallarmé was Baudelaire's disciple seems to have been even more glaringly apparent to his contemporaries than it is to us. Catulle Mendès warned him that he would be criticized for imitating Baudelaire: 'Il y a certainement [en votre poésie] quelque chose qu'on ne retrouve pas ailleurs, pas même dans Baudelaire. A propos des *Fleurs du mal*, on vous reprochera de les avoir lues, pour moi, je n'y vois aucun inconvénient . . .' Mendès was right, Barbey d'Aurevilly's criticism of the *Parnasse contemporain* poems, in *Le Nain jaune*, reads: [Mallarmé] a évidemment pour générateur M. Baudelaire, mais l'effréné Baudelaire n'est qu'une perruque d'académicien, correcte, peignée, ratissée, en comparaison de ce poulain sauvage, à tous crins, échevelé, emmêlé' (quoted by Mondor, *Vie de Mallarmé*, p. 231). Mondor quotes (*Vie*, p. 238, n. 2) a remark which Mendès attributed to Charles Cros: 'Mallarmé est un Baudelaire cassé en morceaux, qui essaie en vain de se recoller.'

[9] December 1864 (?) (*Correspondance*, p. 146, n. 1).

[10] 25 juin 1862 (Mondor, *Eugène Lefébure*, 1951, p. 171).

exclut-il de l'Art la Passion, comme trop familière. . . . Pourtant, si j'aime les poètes qui s'efforcent vers la sensation travaillée, je ne déteste pas ceux qui ne sortent point du fond purement humain, et dont la bouche parle de l'abondance du cœur.[11]

That there is a reference in these passages to the qualities Mallarmé most admired in Baudelaire is confirmed by the terms used by the poet himself when in his turn he compared the writings of one of his friends to Baudelaire's — a rare occurrence so far as one can see from the correspondence. Wishing to compliment Cazalis on some of his poems he wrote (not altogether sincerely to judge by later comments,[12] but Cazalis had given him the lead by telling him he was a great poet[13]):

> Car tu es un fier poète, mon ami. Tu ne saurais croire quelle profonde impression m'ont causée les vers que tu m'as donnés. Toi seul, Edgar Poe et Baudelaire étiez capables de ce poème qui, comme certains regards de femme, contient des mondes de pensée et de sensations. . . . Tout y est merveilleusement disposé pour l'effet à produire. Je suis fou de ces vers parce qu'ils résument toute mon esthétique, et jamais je ne suis arrivé à un tel effet.[14]

Writing to Lefébure a little later about *Elën*, the prose drama which had just been published by a literary hero of his own generation, 'mon ami Villiers de l'Isle-Adam', Mallarmé praised the play lavishly, amongst other things for its style:

> Vous ressentirez une sensation à chacun des mots, comme en lisant Baudelaire. Il n'y a pas là une syllabe qui n'ait été pesée pendant une nuit de rêverie. Depuis trois ans, du reste, Villiers préparait cette œuvre.[15]

Poems that contain worlds of thought and sensation. A style that gives the reader a thrill with every word. It is indeed the concentration he admires in Baudelaire, as contrasted for instance with the looseness and slackness of Des Essarts's verse:

> *Les Élévations* me semblent détestables: la pensée lâche, se distend en lieux communs et, quant à la forme, je vois des mots, des mots, mis

[11] Mondor, *Eugène Lefébure*, p. 176 and pp. 189–90. The two letters quoted from are dated respectively 15th April 1864 and 2nd March 1865.
[12] See *Correspondance*, pp. 105, 118 and 157.
[13] See *Correspondance*, p. 112, n. 1.
[14] July 1864 (*Correspondance* pp. 122–3).
[15] February 1865 (*Correspondance*, p. 154).

souvent au hasard, sinistre s'y pouvant remplacer par lugubre, et
lugubre par tragique, sans que le sens du vers change. On ne ressent à
cette lecture aucune sensation neuve.[16]

To Baudelaire's rhythms there is one isolated tribute in Mallarmé's letters,
and it is interesting to note how subtly modern is the music that
delighted his ear. The song of a cricket had reminded him of the first
tercet in the sonnet 'Bohémiens en voyage' and he wrote to Lefébure:

> Du fond de son réduit sablonneux, le grillon,
> Les regardant passer, redouble sa chanson.

Jusqu'ici le grillon m'avait étonné, il me semblait maigre, comme
introduction au vers magnifique, et large comme l'autre cité:

> Cybèle, qui les aime, augmente ses verdures.[17]

Beyond fragments such as these, scattered in the correspondence, we
possess no precise statement of Mallarmé's opinion of Baudelaire's qualities
as an artist. As to his poetic theory, Mallarmé obstinately attributes it to
Poe. 'Plus j'irai,' he wrote, 'plus je serai fidèle à ces sévères idées que m'a
léguées mon grand maître Edgar Poe.'[18] It would no doubt be possible, by
studying the relevant passages in the letters, to see how much Mallarmé's
thinking about poetry was in fact nourished by Baudelaire rather than Poe.
His understanding of Poe may itself have been influenced by the bias of
Baudelaire's paraphrase or translation ('une impression ou un effet à produire' for 'an impression, or effect, to be conveyed', 'la sensation d'identité,
de répétition' for 'the sense of identity — of repetition', and suchlike
details). Again, it may be that the interest in the musicality of poetry
(which was already intense during the months when 'Sainte' and the
'Ouverture musicale' to Hérodiade were composed) was stimulated more
by certain sentences in Baudelaire's article on Wagner than by anything in
Poe. But the delicate task of sorting out the respective contributions has
not yet been carried out nor so far as I know attempted, and it will not be
attempted here.

[16] February 1865 (Correspondance, p. 153).
[17] 17th May 1867 (Correspondance, p. 250).
[18] Letter to Cazalis, January 1864 (Correspondance, p. 104). That Mallarmé used Baudelaire's
translations of Poe (and of course he could hardly do otherwise) is as it happens proved by a
letter from the Chevalier de Chatelain to Baudelaire, published by E. Crépet, Charles Baudelaire (1906), pp. 342–3. It was written from London on 26th March 1863 and contains the
sentence: 'Grâce à un jeune ami — M. Stéphane Mallarmé — je viens de lire votre belle
traduction des contes de Poe.'

We should know more of these things if Mallarmé had fulfilled the
intention, about which he wrote to Collignon, of publishing an article
'sur le spleen à Paris et sur l'œuvre de ce maître'.[19] One wonders why he
did not. It is true that he might be disappointed at Baudelaire's failure to
express interest in the poems Des Essarts read to him ('Les Fenêtres' and
'L'Azur'),[20] or even in 'Symphonie littéraire' when it appeared, while the
story passed on by Cazalis, 'Il paraît que ton dieu Baudelaire te hait', must
have given a twist to the knife.[21] But seeming indifference and alleged dislike would not prevent a zealous disciple from writing about his master's
work. They did not prevent Mallarmé from expressing extreme conster-
nation on hearing of Baudelaire's death,[22] and his continued admiration
whenever the occasion offered, as when he published his translation of

[19] The letter to Collignon is dated 11th April 1864 (*Correspondance*, p. 113). Mallarmé
hoped to publish 'Symphonie littéraire' in Collignon's magazine, *La Revue nouvelle*, and
tentatively offered also an article on Baudelaire. Neither the one nor the other was published
in the review, which ceased publication that summer. There is no proof, up to the present,
that the article was written. In his review of poems by Des Essarts (*Le Sénonais*, 22nd March
1862) Mallarmé quoted *Les Fleurs du mal*, and Banville's *Odes funambulesques* as 'les derniers
chefs-d'œuvre du siècle. His admiration for Baudelaire is expressed also in the article published in September 1862 by *L'Artiste*, 'Hérésies artistiques: l'Art pour tous'; *Les Fleurs du mal*
is chosen as the type of work that should be surrounded with mystery, and Baudelaire's
assertion that 'injurier la foule, c'est s'encanailler soi-même' is quoted with approval.

[20] This was at the end of March or beginning of April 1864; see *Correspondance*, p. 114,
notes 2 and 3.

[21] November or December 1864 (*Correspondance*, p. 146, n. 1). Mendès may have had the
same gossip in mind when he wrote of Mallarmé, in 1869: 'Edgar Poe eût aimé ce poète qui
étonna Charles Baudelaire' (quoted by Mondor in *Vie de Mallarmé*, pp. 279–80). On 30th
December 1864 Cazalis wrote to Mallarmé and commented on 'Le Phénomène futur,'
which Mallarmé had sent him 'l'autre jour'. It may have been about that time that Baudelaire
read the poem in manuscript, or had it read to him at the house of Cazalis's cousin Mme
Lejosne. His brief comment on it is published by Jacques Crépet in *Propos sur Baudelaire*
(1957), pp. 66–9. The comment suggests ill-humour; Baudelaire disagrees with a statement
about the beauties of bygone days which is very much akin to what he himself says in 'J'aime
le souvenir de ces époques nues.' Mallarmé told Ernest Raynaud that he never met Baudelaire
except once in the street; see Raynaud's *En Marge de la Mêlée symboliste* (second edition,
1936, pp. 41–2). On the other hand Des Essarts, in an article frequently mentioned in bibliographies but apparently seldom read (*Revue de France*, 15th July 1899) says they met at Mme
Lejosne's; he may very well be misremembering, thirty years after.

[22] In April 1866 he wrote to Cazalis (*Correspondance*, p. 209): 'Ne t'afflige pas non plus de ma
tristesse, qui vient peut-être de la douleur que me cause la santé de Baudelaire, que deux jours
j'ai cru mort (Oh! quels deux jours! je suis encore atterré du malheur présent)., After
Baudelaire's death, writing to Villiers on 24th September 1867, he expresses a filial piety:
'Vraiment j'ai bien peur de *commencer* . . . par où notre pauvre et sacré Baudelaire a fini'
(*Correspondance*, p. 259). Lefébure had written to him on 9th September to say: 'Je suis content d'avoir appris par vous la mort de Baudelaire et non par la voie banale des journaux: il
me semble qu'entre nous c'est resté en famille' (Mondor, *Eugène Lefébure*, pp. 266–7). Writing
to Catulle Mendès a few years later (in 1870), Mallarmé announced his intention of writing
'pour la Sorbonne, une thèse dédiée à la mémoire de Baudelaire et à celle de Poe' (Mondor,
Vie de Mallarmé, 1941, pp. 295–296.)

Poe's poems,[23] or when in his article on the Impressionists he referred to Baudelaire's championing of Manet:

> There was also at that time, alas! that it should have to be written in the past tense, an enlightened amateur, one who loved all arts and lived for one of them. . . . That amateur was our last great poet, Charles Baudelaire.[24]

In 1894 and 1895 we find him presiding over the committee set up to erect a monument in memory of Baudelaire, 'cet extraordinaire et pur génie',[25] and his 'Hommage' figured at the head of the 1896 volume *Le Tombeau de Charles Baudelaire*. There is a more significant reason than wounded pride for reticence about his master's work, after the year 1864 or thereabouts. In the following pages I shall try to show that it was to a deeper, more secret estrangement that he was referring when in a letter to Cazalis dated 14th May 1867 he made the often-quoted remark:

> Le livre de Dierx est un beau développement de Leconte de Lisle. S'en séparera-t-il comme moi de Baudelaire?[26]

The first explicit recognition of a serious divergence is found in a letter addressed to Cazalis, from Brompton Square, London, on 3rd June 1863. The occasion for it was Mallarmé's criticism of their friend and fellow-poet Emmanuel des Essarts. He wrote:

> [Emmanuel] confond trop l'Idéal avec le Réel. La sottise d'un poète moderne a été jusqu'à se désoler que 'l'Action ne fût pas la sœur du Rêve'. Emmanuel est de ceux qui regrettent cela. Mon Dieu, s'il en était autrement, si le Rêve était ainsi défloré et abaissé, où donc nous sauverions-nous, nous autres malheureux que la terre dégoûte et qui n'avons que le Rêve pour refuge? O mon Henri, abreuve-toi d'Idéal. Le bonheur d'ici-bas est ignoble — il faut avoir les mains bien calleuses pour le ramasser. Dire: 'Je suis heureux!' c'est dire: 'Je suis un lâche' — et plus souvent: 'Je suis un niais.' Car il ne faut pas voir au-dessus de ce plafond de bonheur le ciel de l'Idéal, ou fermer les yeux exprès . . . Adieu, mon Henri: oui, ici-bas a une odeur de cuisine.[27]

---

[23] See *Oc* (i.e. *Œuvres complètes de Stéphane Mallarmé*, 1945), pp. 229 and 241–2.

[24] *The Art Monthly Review*, vol. 1, no. 9 (13th September 1867).

[25] These are the terms he used (though in a cryptic sentence) when he wrote to thank Léon Deschamps for asking him to be chairman of the committee; see Mondor, *Propos sur la poésie*, second edition, 1953, p. 179.

[26] *Correspondance*, p. 244.

[27] *Correspondance*, pp. 90–1. There is a striking resemblance between Mallarmé's expressions here and those used by Flaubert, another artist who sought salvation in a purely aesthetic idealism: 'C'est étrange comme je suis né avec peu de foi au bonheur. J'ai eu, tout jeune, un

The line 'D'un monde où l'action n'est pas la sœur du rêve' occurs in Baudelaire's poem 'Le Reniement de saint Pierre', and there is no doubt whatever that Baudelaire is the modern poet referred to. There is no doubt, either, that the reference is very disrespectful. If the 'foolish' opinion imputed to the older poet by his disciple were one of little importance, the disrespect might be passed over as of no consequence. But the whole passage in which it occurs stresses the seriousness of Baudelaire's error, or in other words the radical nature of Mallarmé's disagreement with him. Baudelaire is accused of the same heresy as Des Essarts, his opposite in poetry as we have seen, and Mallarmé's 1862 articles on Des Essarts's poems will tell us, more precisely than the letter to Cazalis, what the heresy is:

> Dans les *Poésies Parisiennes*, ce n'est plus cet idéal étincelant et moqueur et harcelant la réalité de sa flèche d'or, qui vous enivre dans les vers exquis de ce divin maître [Banville]: c'est un idéal sincère s'élevant au-dessus du réel et le prenant au sérieux.

> [Banville], qui décoche contre la Réalité la flèche d'or de son arc divin, l'Idéal, fait juste le contraire d'Em. des Essarts, lequel prend le Réel au sérieux et le *lyrise*.[28]

The error lies not in starting from the real to rise towards the ideal; Mallarmé knew — Banville notwithstanding — that 'la divine transposition va du fait à l'idéal'. It lies in 'taking reality seriously', in its own right. That is what Baudelaire is accused of doing when he regrets that we live in a world where the real and the ideal do not dwell in harmony together. That is what constitutes 'la sottise d'un poète moderne', and the letter to

pressentiment complet de la vie. C'était comme une odeur de cuisine nauséabonde qui s'échappe par un soupirail' (letter to Maxime du Camp, 7th April 1846); 'au-dessus de la vie, au-dessus du bonheur, il y a quelque chose de bleu et d'incandescent, un grand ciel immuable et subtil dont les rayons qui nous arrivent suffisent à ranimer des mondes. La splendeur du génie n'est que le reflet de ce Verbe caché' (letter to Louise Colet, 29th November 1853). No doubt Mallarmé remembered that Baudelaire himself had written in the preface ('A J.G.F.') to *Les Paradis artificiels*: 'Le bon sens nous dit que les choses de la terre n'existent que bien peu, et que la vraie réalité n'est que dans les rêves. Pour digérer le bonheur naturel, comme l'artificiel, il faut d'abord avoir le courage de l'avaler; et ceux qui mériteraient peut-être le bonheur sont justement ceux-là à qui la félicité, telle que la conçoivent les mortels, a toujours fait l'effet d'un vomitif.' A sentence in Mallarmé's letter to Cazalis of 24th July 1863 (*Correspondance*, p. 92), 'les Anglaises, ces anges de cuisine qui rêvent aux rayons de leurs casseroles, sans se douter de l'étoile Astarté,' probably echoes a passage in Vacquerie's *Profils et Grimaces* (1856), ch. XXXVIII, 'L'Utilité de la beauté': 'Et cependant, c'est vrai, il y a des artistes qui croient que l'art se suffit à lui-même . . . Le beau, c'est le ciel entr'ouvert, c'est la face de Dieu entrevue. Ils ont horreur de retomber du ciel à la cuisine, de l'astre à la casserole.'

[28] *Oc*, pp. 251 and 255.

Cazalis tells us where to look for further reflexions on this important theme:

> J'ai fait sur ces idées un petit poème *Les Fenêtres,* je te l'envoie: et un autre *L'Assaut* qui est vague et frêle comme une rêverie.

So indeed it turns out to be. When the two poems named are examined in the light of the remarks in the letter, they are seen to express, in their very Baudelairian language, anti-Baudelairian thoughts. They symbolize a dual evaluation of Baudelaire by his disciple. Admiration for his poetry is asserted by obvious imitation, even while his ideas as Mallarmé understands them are opposed. This can best be shown by comparing the two poems with those Baudelaire compositions from which they borrow most.

'L'Assaut' is the short poem, never published in Mallarmé's lifetime, which now appears in the collected poems under the title 'Le Château de l'Espérance'. In sending it to Cazalis, Mallarmé judged it wise to send also this explanation:

> D'une chevelure qui a fait naître en mon cerveau l'idée d'un drapeau, mon cœur, pris d'une ardeur militaire, s'élance à travers d'affreux paysages et va assiéger le Château fort de l'Espérance pour y planter cet étendard d'or fin. Mais, l'insensé, après ce court moment de folie, aperçoit l'Espérance qui n'est qu'une sorte de spectre voilé et stérile.[29]

No doubt it was Marie Gerhard's hair that had suggested thus to his imagination the idea of a flag, but it had done so with the help of a poem in *Les Fleurs du mal,* 'La Chevelure'. It seems likely, at least, that an image in the opening stanza of this poem,

> Je la veux agiter dans l'air comme un mouchoir!

prompted, as a romantic or heroic variant, the comparison with a banner streaming in the wind. Further suggestions were offered by lines in another stanza:

> Cheveux bleus, pavillon de ténèbres tendues,
> Vous me rendez l'azur du ciel immense et rond;

In *pavillon de ténèbres tendues* there was some support for the idea of a flag, if only in the associations of the word *pavillon,* but what is more important is that this 'tent of darkness drawn' symbolizes the very conception of

---

[29] *Correspondance,* p. 91. In view of the connection which will be shown later between these poems and ' Le Guignon,' it may be remarked that the hero of ' L'Assaut' shows some resemblance to the 'mendieurs d'azur' in the earlier poem, who also have their banner.

happiness that Mallarmé condemns in his letter; it may indeed be the very *plafond de bonheur* that prompted him to write:

> Car il ne faut pas voir au-dessus de ce plafond de bonheur le ciel de l'Idéal, ou fermer les yeux exprès.

So the *chevelure-drapeau* is not simply an offshoot of Baudelaire's poem, but a reply to it. Love, to be worthy of a poet, must bring more than sensuous pleasures and what men call happiness. A few months before when Marie left him, for ever as it seemed, Mallarmé had written to Cazalis lamenting his state: 'pauvre enfant abandonné par tout ce qui fut ma vie et mon idéal';[30] and in all that wretched winter and spring he had done his best to persuade himself that Marie did represent for him an ideal. Poor Marie! The only ideal she could symbolize was one he had already outlived, a 'white celestial thought' lingering on as a ghost from his angel-infancy:

> Oui, elle est noble (he wrote), oui, elle est pure, oui, elle est vertueuse: elle est plus qu'un ange, elle est une sainte. La pauvre âme exilée a tout donné à celui qui l'a aimée. . . . Je la respecte, comme je respecte ma sœur morte.[31]

How far this vision of a 'divine et angélique enfant'[32] was from embodying any of the poet's present aspirations is what 'Le Château de l'Espérance' tells, or hides under the veil of allegory. The hope to which love has led him is 'une sorte de spectre voilé et stérile':

> larmoyant de nonchaloir,
> L'Espérance rebrousse et lisse
> Sans qu'un astre pâle jaillisse
> La Nuit noire comme un chat noir.

For this final image also, Mallarmé is indebted to Baudelaire. A year before, he had quoted to Cazalis the hemistich in 'Les Litanies de Satan' of which his allegorical figure of Hope is an imaginative elaboration:

> Oh! Espérance, 'une folle charmante', comme dit mélancoliquement ce grand Baudelaire.[33]

---

[30] 14th January 1863 (*Correspondance*, p. 70). [31] December 1862 (*Correspondance*, pp. 64–5). [32] 5th March 1863 (*Correspondance*, p. 83).

[33] 7th July 1862 (*Correspondance*, p. 42). 'Emparadise-toi dans ta folie,' he wrote to Cazalis, sighing after his Sperata. Earlier, with an exclamation which is also near the source of 'L'Assaut', he wrote: 'Ah! que l'amour est fort qui fait regarder l'avenir en souriant' (*Correspondance*, pp. 29 and 35). Nothing will be said here of The poem 'Apparition,' important as it is in the story of Mallarmé's *amour idéal – amour séel* debate. Its literary connections are with Hugo (particularly *Les Misérables*) rather than Baudelaire.

That he should use Baudelaire the sardonic blasphemer to answer Baudelaire the hedonistic lover is characteristic of Mallarmé's method in this
debate. In a disputation with the Tragic Sophist, no method could be
better if the aim were simply to prove Baudelaire wrong; but Mallarmé
had also to found and affirm his own beliefs, and to this side of his task
'L'Assaut' makes no positive contribution. His experience of love, as it is
told in this poem (and also in 'Le Pitre châtié' and a late insertion in 'Le
Guignon'[34]), had taught him, alas, not the pleasant lesson of the platonists,
that love is not mere happiness but a way to the ideal, but that from both
points of view, the real and the ideal, love is an illusion.[35] This is a gloomy
conclusion for a man to come to on the eve of his marriage, at twenty-one.
It is, however, not a conclusion about the ideal but only about love.
About the ideal, he did have positive things to say, in 'Les Fenêtres'. This
is one of Mallarmé's best-known poems, and its general import needs no
explaining. It will be instructive to relate it in its turn, however, on the one
hand to the author's London experience and on the other to his reflexions on
Baudelaire.

Of the reappraisal of his own aspirations which the experience of young
manhood led to, two other letters written to Cazalis from the lodgings in
Brompton Square give interesting news. They are dated respectively 27th
April and 24th July, and they reveal two facts which have an important
bearing on 'Les Fenêtres'. First, love was not the only banner for which
the poet was losing his enthusiasm at this time; secondly, he had already
embraced the faith which was henceforth to be his sole spiritual inspiration.
He wrote on 27th April:

> Si j'épousais Marie pour faire mon bonheur, je serais un fou.
> D'ailleurs, le bonheur existe-t-il sur cette terre? Et faut-il le chercher,
> *sérieusement*, autre part que dans le rêve? C'est le faux but de la vie:
> le vrai est le Devoir, qu'il s'appelle l'art, la lutte ou comme on
> veut.[36]

[34] In the eleventh stanza of the final version it is a *blanc couple nageur* (in place of *un superbe nageur*) that is plunged in the mire.

[35] '*Tous les baisers se valent*,' he wrote to the love-lorn Cazalis, underlining the words, and: 'Le mariage sérieux est trop primitif, tu as mille fois raison, mais pourquoi ne pas le considérer comme une façon d'avoir un intérieur, c'est-à-dire un peu de paix, et une "faiseuse de thé", ainsi que disait de Quincey?' (*Correspondance*, pp. 130 and 217). Which seems to relegate both Marie and Ettie to somewhere near the kitchen, *ici-bas*. De Quincey was kinder to his 'fair tea-maker.'

[36] *Correspondance*, pp. 87–8. It is only because Mallarmé's political views have been system-atically ignored by his admirers that this reference to 'the struggle' may seem surprising. The article by Des Essarts, mentioned in note 21 above, contains some interesting details about Mallarmé's attitude towards the civic authorities, which very likely cost him his post at Tournon in 1866.

Then, on 24th July, much more resolutely as regards the choice between art and 'the struggle':

> Tu sais que toutes mes illusions politiques se sont effacées une par une, et que si j'arbore un drapeau rouge c'est uniquement parce que je hais les gredins et déteste la force.
> Henri, tu le verras, il n'y a de vrai, d'immuable, de grand et de sacré que l'Art.[37]

Such is the direction of Mallarmé's thought on this topic at the time of writing 'Les Fenêtres', and the poem points decidedly in the same direction. What is not immediately clear is that it is an anti-Baudelairian direction.[38] To show this, an examination of the poem's Baudelaire connections is required, more detailed and more searching than was called for in the case of 'L'Assaut'.

'La sottise d'un poète moderne a été jusqu'à se désoler que "l'Action ne fût pas la sœur du Rêve" . . . J'ai fait sur ces idées un petit poème *Les Fenêtres.*' It has already been pointed out that the foolishness imputed to Baudelaire lies not in his proclaiming that the real and the ideal are alien to each other, but in his regretting it; if reference is made to 'le Reniement de Saint Pierre', it appears that the foolishness lies, more precisely, in despairing of the ideal in this world because it is not realised in our material life:

> — Certes, je sortirai, quant à moi, satisfait
> D'un monde où l'action n'est pas la sœur du rêve;
> Puissé-je user du glaive et périr par le glaive!
> Saint Pierre a renié Jésus . . . Il a bien fait!

As the terms he used to Cazalis implied, Mallarmé's poem 'Les Fenêtres' is his reply to this particular statement. That the ideal is alien to the real is no reason why idealists should despair and die, or, on the other hand, embrace material values, *glaive* or *pavillon*, power or voluptuous pleasures. It is indeed part of the artist's difficult task to keep the ideal free from contamination by the real. This proposition was to be a corner-stone of Mallarmé's aesthetic doctrine. To express it in 'Les Fenêtres', in answer to

---

[37] *Correspondance*, pp. 93–4.
[38] It has already been pointed out (in note 26 above) that the indigestibility of human happiness is itself a Baudelairian theme. It may be noted too that the impossibility of finding the ideal in the real, which is the leit-motif of Mallarmé's letter, is the subject of the poem 'L'Idéal', in *Les Fleurs du mal*. He was no doubt thinking of this poem when in a letter to Cazalis dated 23rd March 1864 (*Correspondance*, p. 111) he wrote: 'Marie pleure quand je pleure et s'ennuie quand j'ai le spleen. C'est mon ombre angélique, paradisiaque, mais sa douce nature ne saurait faire d'elle ma Lady Macbeth.' (His Lady Macbeth, his *rouge idéal*, was to be the dream-heroine, Hérodiade.)

Baudelaire, he once more has recourse to images taken from the same Baudelaire. The borrowings are numerous. The beginning contains reminiscences, for instance, of 'Réversibilité', 'Les Phares', and 'Le Tasse en prison'. The disconcerting[39] ending ('Au risque de tomber . . .') owes something to 'Hymne à la Beauté' and perhaps even more to the prose poem 'Le Mauvais vitrier', while the sick man's sunset reminds one of a passage in the Preface to the translations of Poe's *Histoires extraordinaires*.[40] What is more significant from the present point of view is the delicate relationship between the core of the poem (that is, the seventh and eighth stanzas) and several of Baudelaire's works. The prose poem of 1862, 'Le Mauvais vitrier', tells like 'Les Fenêtres' of magic casements. These do not, however, look out of life like those of Mallarmé (and Keats), but into life, beautifying it, 'lyricising reality' as Mallarmé had said Des Essarts's poetry did:

Comment! vous n'avez pas de verres de couleur? Des verres roses, rouges, bleus, des vitres magiques, des vitres de Paradis? Impudent que vous êtes! vous osez vous promener dans les quartiers pauvres, et vous n'avez même pas de vitres qui fassent voir la vie en beau![41]

Nearer to Mallarmé's 'croisées d'où l'on tourne l'épaule à la vie' are the 'magic mirrors' in the first section of *Le Poëme du Haschisch* (the section entitled'L'Idéal artificiel', then 'Le Goût de l'infini'). The passage is so well-known that it is unnecessary to quote it at length. In it is described an ideal state, a condition of the mind and senses such as to constitute as it were:

un miroir magique où l'homme est invité à se voir en beau, c'est-à-dire tel qu'il devrait et pourrait être; une espèce d'excitation angé-lique, un rappel à l'ordre sous une forme complimenteuse.

A condition so felicitous and at the same time so rare that man has striven,

---

[39] At least so far as the melodramatic and vaguely blasphemous tone, which seems pointless, is concerned. The last stanza is probably more germane to the subject than it at first appears, however. It seems to refer to Quinet's proposition: 'Si [l'artiste] abandonne le réel pour se livrer sans réserve à l'idéal, il tombe dans le vide' (*Le Génie des religions*, in *Œuvres complètes*, 1857, t. I, p. 92). The reference is given a Baudelairian ring of blasphemy by means of a reminis-cence of 'Le Mauvais vitrier': 'Mais qu'importe l'éternité de la damnation à qui a trouvé dans une seconde l'infini de la jouissance?'

[40] 'Quelquefois, des échappées magnifiques, gorgées de lumière et de couleur, s'ouvrent sou-dainement dans ses paysages, et l'on voit apparaître au fond de leurs horizons des villes orientales et des architectures vaporisées par la distance, où le soleil jette des pluies d'or.'

[41] In Baudelaire's prose poem itself entitled 'Les Fenêtres', which was only published in December 1863, the windows again look into life, not out of it. Mallarmé seeks out windows looking into 'le matin chaste de l'infini', but it is in anguish that Baudelaire exclaims (in 'Le Gouffre'): 'Je ne vois qu'infini par toutes les fenêtres.'

at all times and in all countries, to induce it artificially with the help of drugs, liquor and perfumes, and so 'fuir, ne fût-ce que pour quelques heures, son habitacle de fange.' How like Mallarmé's windows this magic mirror is, and yet how distant still, can be seen by considering another Baudelaire model, in a stanza of the poem 'Les Phares':

> Léonard de Vinci, miroir profond et sombre,
> Où des anges charmants, avec un doux souris
> Tout chargé de mystère, apparaissent à l'ombre
> Des glaciers et des pins qui ferment leur pays;

Here is Mallarmé's own window, the window of art.[42] For him, it is superior to all chance states of grace, and the experience it opens to us is as far above the 'artificial ideal' opened by drugs or wine as 'le ciel de l'Idéal' is above any 'plafond de bonheur'. 'Les Phares', if we except its conclusion, is one long gallery of casements opening out on worlds created by artists, but it is the Leonardo stanza that most clearly makes the work of art reflect 'l'homme tel qu'il devrait ou pourrait être', as in 'Les Fenêtres'. This stanza may well be one of the principal sources of Mallarmé's poem.

It is puzzling that despite his emphatic assertion, 'Henri, tu verras, il n'y a de vrai, d'immuable, de grand et de sacré que l'Art', the poet should seem in 'Les Fenêtres' to give equal importance to art and religion as escapes from the real, and that the glimpse of the ideal afforded by either window should be nearer to a child's dream of heaven (suggested, perhaps, by the last two stanzas of 'Bénédiction') than to a vision of artistic perfection:

> Je me mire et me vois ange! et je songe, et j'aime
> — Que la vitre soit l'art, soit la mysticité —
> A renaître, portant mon rêve en diadème,
> Au ciel antérieur où fleurit la Beauté!

The explanation may be that in 'Les Fenêtres' Mallarmé is no longer speaking as the creator of art but as its consumer, not as the poet with his vision of a poetry to be but as the reader of the poetry that is, 'Bénédiction' for instance. Perhaps also Mallarmé was finding that whereas Art had triumphed without much difficulty over Love and over the Struggle, those earthly passions, the final victory over religion was less easy to achieve. However that may be, he has figured in 'Les Fenêtres', very artfully, a lingering interference between Art and Religion, even while declaring them to be separate from each other. By so doing, he has blunted any

[42] Je me mire et me vois ange' is probably linked also with Baudelaire's 'L' Aube spirituelle': 'Dans la brute assoupie, un ange se réveille'. For the persistence of this image in Mallarmé's aesthetic, see A. Gill, 'Le Symbole du miroir dans l'œuvre de Mallarmé,' in *Cahiers de l'Association Internationale des Etudes Françaises*, 1958.

criticism he may wish to imply of that same interference in *Les Fleurs du mal*, for instance in the perverse and splendid conclusion of 'Les Phares':

> Ces malédictions, ces blasphèmes, ces plaintes,
> Ces extases, ces cris, ces pleurs, ces *Te Deum*,
> Sont un écho redit par mille labyrinthes:
> C'est pour les cœurs mortels un divin opium!...
>
> Car c'est vraiment, Seigneur, le meilleur témoignage
> Que nous puissions donner de notre dignité
> Que cet ardent sanglot qui roule d'âge en âge
> Et vient mourir au bord de votre éternité!

Baudelaire was certainly open to criticism on this count, for his practice was decidedly at variance with his preaching. He had told his disciples that 'la poésie ... n'a pas d'autre but qu'elle-même'[43] and made bold to suggest to Victor Hugo himself that perhaps 'l'art ne doit exprimer d'adoration que pour lui-même.'[44] Mallarmé had adopted this principle unreservedly, and from it was advancing to the firm belief that art was the one remaining alternative to religion, was indeed the last and only true religion, as Renan taught. Still more precisely, the belief that for modern man, brought up on literature, 'l'Idéal' and poetry were one;[45] as he was to put it later, 'que le monde est fait pour aboutir à un beau livre'. The part of prayer and sacrilege, 'godism and satanism', in *Les Fleurs du mal* could not but be condemned by the young poet who was soon to proclaim proudly the need to choose between poetry and religion:

> L'âme, tacite et qui ne se suspend pas aux paroles de l'élu familier, le poëte, est, à moins qu'elle ne sacrifie à Dieu l'ensemble impuissant de ses aspirations, vouée irrémédiablement au Néant.[46]

In the summer of his eighteenth year Mallarmé had written Hugo-inspired poems ('Pan' for instance, and 'Sa fosse est creusée'[47]) in which with more than Hugo's candour he had renounced the Christian worship of a God

[43] 'Notes nouvelles sur Edgar Poe,' by which Baudelaire prefaced his translation of Poe's *Nouvelles histoires extraordinaires*.

[44] '*Les Misérables* par Victor Hugo,' published in *Le Boulevard*, 20th April 1862, then incorporated in *L'Art romantique*. Mallarmé had read this article eagerly when it first appeared; see *Correspondance*, p. 25.

[45] For this interpretation of Mallarmé's well-known assertion, 'après avoir trouvé le néant, j'ai trouvé le beau', see A. Gill, 'Esquisse d'une explication de la "Vie d'Igitur",' in *Saggi e ricerche di letteratura francese*, vol. II, Feltrinelli, Milan, 1961.

[46] The sentence concludes the article on Léon Dierx, written in 1872; see *Oc*, p. 694.

[47] 'Sa fosse est creusée' is included in *Oc*, p. 4; 'Pan' was published by Mondor in 1954, in *Mallarmé lycéen*, pp. 181–3.

who, if he existed, was indifferent to human ills. From that time to the day when he wrote to Cazalis, in April 1866, 'nous ne sommes que de vaines formes de la matière, mais bien sublimes pour avoir inventé Dieu et notre âme',[48] he went on gradually extirpating from his mind (if not altogether from his heart) the religious beliefs he had been brought up in. Baudelaire, on the other hand, had perversely and paradoxically held on to them and given them a commanding place in his poetry, where according to his own teaching they had no right to be.

Criticism of the religious aspect of *Les Fleurs du mal* is certainly present in the next work that claims our attention, the one substantial statement on Baudelaire's poetry that Mallarmé is known to have written, one of the three prose poems published under the title 'Symphonie littéraire', nearly a year after 'L'Assaut' and 'Les Fenêtres' were composed. Of the three 'movements' which (with an introductory invocation which perhaps brings the number to four) make up this so-called symphony, it is the second that is devoted to *Les Fleurs du mal*. The first is in praise of Gautier and the third of Banville. The whole composition is packed with reminiscences of Baudelaire, however, and the two other poets are presented very much as he had presented them, with the qualities he had attributed to them described in terms partly borrowed from him. The device is ingenious. It allows Mallarmé to draw a contrast between Baudelaire as he sees him and Gautier and Banville as Baudelaire sees them, and so once more to measure Baudelaire by his own standards. The result — if we are careful to read what Mallarmé actually wrote and not what a known disciple of Baudelaire might be supposed to think — is unexpected. Judged by the result he produces on the reader (and therefore from a good Baudelairian standpoint) Baudelaire comes out of the contrast badly. Mallarmé contrives, in fact, to give in this seeming act of homage a firmer though still deceptive formulation to the criticism which had been behind the London poems. The continuity of the critical thought is apparent. The basic image in the 'Symphonie' is the same as in 'Les Fenêtres', the work of each of the three poets being criticized in its capacity as a mirror, in which the reader should see himself 'en beau'.

The argument begins with a reminder of its Baudelairian premises, a reference to the primary source of the mirror image in 'Le Poëme du Haschisch'. This is in the opening sentences of the Gautier section. The moment of exceptional happiness which Mallarmé describes there, and to prolong which, he says, he has recourse to Gautier's poems, is easily recognizable as that rare and fortuitous state of grace which acts, according to Baudelaire, 'comme un miroir magique où l'homme est invité à se voir en

<hr>

[48] *Correspondance*, p. 207.

beau'. Gautier is thus submitted to a test out of which he comes with the
highest honour. No other earthly adjuvant, says his grateful reader
(whom we must understand as meaning, no doubt, no other poet and also
none of those 'artificial ideals' that Baudelaire had written of), could have
kept him in such felicity:

> Bientôt une insensible transfiguration s'opère en moi, et la sensation
> de légèreté se fond peu à peu en une de perfection.[49] Tout mon être
> spirituel, — le trésor profond des correspondances, l'accord intime
> des couleurs, le souvenir du rythme antérieur, et la science mystérieuse
> du Verbe, — est requis, et tout entier s'émeut, sous l'action de la rare
> poésie que j'invoque, avec un ensemble d'une si merveilleuse justesse
> que de ses jeux combinés résulte la seule lucidité.
>
> Maintenant qu'écrire? Qu'écrire, puisque je n'ai pas voulu l'ivresse,
> qui m'apparaît grossière et comme une injure à ma béatitude?
> (Qu'on s'en souvienne, je ne jouis pas, mais je vis dans la beauté.) Je ne
> saurais même louer ma lecture salvatrice, bien qu'à la vérité un grand
> hymne sorte de cet aveu, que sans elle j'eusse été incapable de garder
> un instant l'harmonie surnaturelle où je m'attarde: et quel autre
> adjuvant terrestre ... ne détruirait pas un ineffable équilibre par
> lequel je me perds en la divinité? ... à la faveur de cette poésie, née
> d'elle-même et qui exista dans le répertoire éternel de l'Idéal de tout
> temps, avant sa moderne émersion du cerveau de l'impeccable artiste,
> une âme dédaigneuse du banal coup d'aile d'un enthousiasme humain
> peut atteindre *la plus haute cime de sérénité où nous ravisse la beauté*.

Banville's poetry too is a mirror which enables his poet-reader to experience something like his own apotheosis, but this time he is reflected not as
the perfect artist but as the lyric poet:

> Et quand je ferme le livre, ce n'est plus serein ou hagard, mais fou
> d'amour, et débordant, et les yeux pleins de grandes larmes de ten-
> dresse, avec un nouvel orgueil d'être homme. Tout ce qu'il y a
> d'enthousiasme ambrosien en moi et de bonté musicale, de noble et de
> pareil aux dieux, chante, et j'ai l'extase radieuse de la Muse! J'aime
> les roses, j'aime l'or du soleil, j'aime l'harmonieux sanglot des femmes
> aux longs cheveux, *et je voudrais tout confondre dans un poétique baiser*!

---

[49] There may be here an echo of Schiller's *Über naive und sentimentalische Dichtung*: 'Aber
wenn du über das verlorene Glück der Natur getröstet bist, so lass ihre Vollkommenheit
deinem Herzen zum Muster dienen.' There is a similar echo of the same sentence, perhaps, in
very much the same connection, in a letter to Cazalis of 25th April 1864: 'La *phrase* ... de
Théophile Gautier ... a une justesse de touche qui est de la justice, et offre le modèle parfait
d'une âme qui vit dans la beauté' (*Correspondance*, p. 119).

The obvious analogy between this passage and 'Le Phénomène futur' (written in November 1864) is significant. Banville affects his poet-reader very much as 'le montreur de choses passées' affects the poets of his day, renewing their faith and their hope in poetry:

> tandis que les poètes de ce temps, sentant se rallumer leurs yeux éteints, s'achemineront vers leur lampe, le cerveau ivre un instant d'une gloire confuse, hantés du Rythme et dans l'oubli d'exister à une époque qui survit à la beauté.

The contrast between this reaction and Mallarmé's reaction to *Les Fleurs du mal*, as expressed in 'Symphonie littéraire', is extreme:

> Enfin, des ténèbres d'encre ont tout envahi où l'on n'entend voleter que le crime, le remords, et la Mort. Alors je me voile la face, et des sanglots, arrachés à mon âme moins par ce cauchemar que par une amère sensation d'exil, traversent le noir silence. Qu'est-ce donc que la patrie?

To the disciple who cries out thus, what answer does the master give? None but the Christian answer of a hope on the other side of death. In the words of Baudelaire's 'Bénédiction':

> — Soyez béni, mon Dieu, qui donnez la souffrance
> Comme un divin remède à nos impuretés
> Et comme la meilleure et la plus pure essence
> Qui prépare les forts aux saintes voluptés!
>
> Je sais que vous gardez une place au Poëte
> Dans les rangs bienheureux des saintes Légions,
> Et que vous l'invitez à l'éternelle fête
> Des Trônes, des Vertus, des Dominations.

And in the words of 'Symphonie littéraire':

> J'ai fermé le livre et les yeux, et je cherche la patrie. Devant moi se dresse l'apparition du poète savant qui me l'indique en un hymne élancé mystiquement comme un lis. Le rythme de ce chant ressemble à la rosace d'une ancienne église: parmi l'ornementation de vieille pierre, souriant dans un séraphique outremer qui semble être la prière sortant de leurs yeux bleus plutôt que notre vulgaire azur, des anges blancs comme des hosties chantent leur extase en s'accompagnant de harpes imitant leurs ailes, de cymbales d'or natif, de rayons purs contournés en trompettes, et de tambourins où résonne la virginité des jeunes tonnerres: les saintes ont des palmes, — et je ne puis regarder

plus haut que les vertus théologales, tant la sainteté est ineffable; mais
j'entends éclater cette parole d'une façon éternelle: *Alleluia*!

The heaven here described is too close to the 'painters' paradise' ridiculed
by contemporary writers to be anything but satirical.[50] Any doubt that
it is a parody of Baudelaire's *de profundis* vein, and a sardonic comment on
the part played by religion in his poetry will probably be dispelled by a
careful examination of another of Mallarmé's compositions, 'Les Fleurs',
which is exactly contemporary with 'Symphonie littéraire' and contains
a hint that its theme is the same, in the shape of a glimpse of the same
holy-picture paradise. In this song of seeming innocence and angelic
sweetness, no note of mockery is usually detected by the reader of the
final version. It is very audible, however, in the earlier version, which
ends with the stanzas:

> Hosannah sur le cistre et dans les encensoirs,
> O mon Père, hosannah du profond de nos limbes!
> A jamais hosannah dans l'or des jours sans soirs,
> Par l'azur du rayon et le frisson des nimbes!

> Car, n'oubliant personne dans ton charmant effort,
> Tu donnas, lui montrant son devoir sans mensonge,
> De fortes fleurs versant comme un parfum la mort
> Au poëte ennuyé que l'impuissance ronge.

The bitterness here is undisguised, and confirms the ironical intention in
the concluding paragraph of the prose poem, which is so clearly parallel to
it. Out of the depths of limbo, the exiled poet echoes the praises of the
angels and saints in heaven. Glory to the God who has driven him from
Eden. Glory to God on high, not for the glimpses of paradise still vouchsafed us, in the laurel and the hyacinth, the rose and the lily. Like the azure
sky, 'bel indolemment comme les fleurs', their beauty is torment for the
sterile poet. No. Hosannah to the provider of sleepy poppies for the weary
poet, in love with easeful death.[51] 'Ce pays nous ennuie, ô Mort!
Appareillons!'

---

[50] For instance Jean Reynaud in *Terre et Ciel* and Mme de Gasparin in *Les Horizons célestes*;
see E. Caro, *L'Idée de Dieu et ses nouveaux critiques*, 1864, pp. 427–428. Emma Bovary's heaven
is not very different.

[51] That the flowers referred to in the last stanza are poppies is pointed out by Antoine Adam
in his notes 'Pour l'interprétation de Mallarmé,' in *Mélanges . . . Mornet* (1951): 'Ces vers de
Mallarmé sont très simplement une périphrase pour désigner la fleur du pavot. La Nature, qui
a créé les roses, les lys, l'hyacinthe et le glaieul fauve, a créé aussi le pavot, d'où l'homme tire
l'opium qui délivre de la vie.' It is of course the final version of the poem that is referred to.

'Les Fleurs' is so near to the prose poem on *Les Fleurs du mal*, in 'Symphonie littéraire', that its irony must be understood as having the same object, as being directed not simply at Christian worship, but also at the Christian pessimism, the de-profundism, of Baudelaire's poetry. If this is granted, the poem becomes an instructive document from our point of view. It confirms the shape into which Mallarmé's criticism has crystallized. Baudelaire is judged not so much as a poet for the general, but as a poet for poets.

It is as a master, judged by his disciple, that he is found wanting. In the name of God he promises poets a place 'dans les rangs bienheureux des saintes Légions', but he denies them the place that Mallarmé claims for them and will go on claiming for them, in the name of humanity, not hereafter but now. It would seem that Mallarmé was already beginning to entertain the idea to which his life was to be dedicated, of a poetry which would open up a paradise for the living, not the dead. He may have been helped to shape this notion by Baudelaire's thoughts on artificial heavens (and in 'Les Phares' on art as such a heaven: 'C'est pour les cœurs mortels un divin opium!') as well as by the uncongenial defeatism of Poe's *Poetic Principle:*

> Inspired by an ecstatic prescience of the glories beyond the grave, we struggle by multiform combinations among the things and thoughts of Time to attain a portion of that Loveliness whose very elements, perhaps, appertain to eternity alone. And thus when by Poetry — or when by Music, the most entrancing of the Poetic moods — we find ourselves melted into tears, not as the Abbate Gravia supposes through excess of pleasure, but through a certain petulant, impatient sorrow at our inability to grasp now, wholly, here on earth, at once and forever, those divine and rapturous joys, of which *through* the poem, or *through* the music, we attain to but brief and indeterminate glimpses.

But, however great the contribution of Baudelaire and Poe to Mallarmé's ambitious claim for poetry, this claim went beyond theirs and was directed against them. According to the interpretation of 'Symphonie littéraire' and 'Les Fleurs' suggested above it was not to *Les Fleurs du mal* that the poet of the future work must look for courage and inspiration. Baudelaire had joined forces with the avenging angel, against mankind; in plainer language, he had sided with the bourgeois against the poet. This statement may seem preposterous in the light of the literary history we have all been taught, but literary history is often wrong, or only superficially right. The fact is that Mallarmé had already charged Baudelaire with precisely that crime. This was in an early poem, 'Le Guignon'. It takes us to the beginnings of the quarrel.

'Le Guignon' is a poem in praise of the 'azure-beggars', the star-crossed dreamers whom no trials or disappointments can turn aside from the search for their ideal. It is partly imitated from Gautier and contains also several echoes of Baudelaire, and it faces the student of Mallarmé with two problems. The first concerns the circumstances of its publication. Although the original version was written in its entirety in 1862, as a dated manuscript proves, the greater part of it was not published till 1883. Only a fragment, consisting of the first five tercets, appeared in *L'Artiste* in March 1862. Why was this? Mallarmé's editors have left the question unanswered. The second problem concerns the identity of 'les vaincus' and 'les poètes savants', from whose lack of understanding and sympathy their luckless brethren suffer. Except for one tercet, the description of these unsympathetic elders is entirely contained in the part of the poem which was withheld for so long from publication.

If I am right in believing that these elders are, in effect, Baudelaire, this is the answer to both our questions. Either Mallarmé or (more likely) the editor of *L'Artiste* was unwilling to publish what in 1862 the more discerning readers would recognise as an attack on Baudelaire, accused of betraying his followers and going over to the enemy. The fifth tercet was the last that could be included in the published fragment; it describes, but only in general terms, the despairers who have gratefully accepted defeat at the hands of the angel guarding the gates of paradise:

> S'ils sont vaincus, c'est par un Ange très puissant
> Qui rougit l'horizon des éclairs de son glaive;
> L'orgueil fait éclater leur cœur reconnaissant.

If one more stanza had been printed, the identity of the chief of the vanquished would have been divulged, for the poem went on:

> Ils tettent la Douleur comme ils tétaient le Rêve,
> Et quand ils vont rythmant leurs pleurs voluptueux
> Le peuple s'agenouille et leur mère se lève.

The hostile character of these allusions (put down today to imitation) would be clear to the editor of *L'Artiste*. A reference, first, to the most voluptously sorrowing of Baudelaire's poems, 'Le Cygne', published in 1860 and included the following year in the second edition of *Les Fleurs du mal*, fresh therefore in the memory of Baudelaire's readers:

A quiconque a perdu ce qui ne se retrouve
Jamais, jamais! à ceux qui s'abreuvent de pleurs
Et tettent la Douleur comme une bonne louve.

Then a reference to the first stanza of 'Bénédiction':

Lorsque, par un décret des puissances suprêmes,
Le poëte apparaît en ce monde ennuyé,
Sa mère épouvantée et pleine de blasphèmes
Crispe ses poings vers Dieu qui la prend en pitié.

In this opening poem of *Les Fleurs du mal* Baudelaire had been the champion, had seemed in fact to present himself as the very type, of the 'mendieur d'azur' or 'téteur de rêve.' Hence another echo of it in Mallarmé's poem:

Dans le pain et le vin destinés à sa bouche
Ils mêlent de la cendre avec d'impurs crachats.
('Bénédiction')
Ils mangent de la cendre avec le même amour.
('Le Guignon')

The opposition between what Baudelaire had become and the followers he had deserted is completed in a later tercet of 'Le Guignon' by means of a sarcastic allusion to a line in 'Les Petites vieilles' (published in *L'Artiste* only a year before). Mallarmé describes his heroes as:

Malheureux sans l'orgueil d'une austère infortune.

Without the pride, that is (what else could this line mean?) with which Baudelaire describes himself in 'Les Petites vieilles':

Ces yeux mystérieux ont d'invincibles charmes
Pour *celui que l'austère Infortune allaita*!

Baudelaire, then, has become the type of the idealist who has accepted defeat. Why Mallarmé holds this so bitterly against him is not far to seek in the circumstances of the time. On 4th June 1862 he wrote to Cazalis:

Oui, vraiment heureux sont ceux qui peuvent souffrir pour quelque chose de grand!
Tu te rappelles ma pièce sur *Le Guignon*: je suis, hélas! parmi les seconds.[52]

The reference is to the seventh tercet (which Cazalis knew, it will be noted, though it was not in the published fragment):

Ceux-là sont consolés étant majestueux,

[52] *Correspondence*, p. 31.

Mais ils ont sous leurs pieds leurs frères qu'on bafoue,
Dérisoires martyrs d'un hasard tortueux.

The last of these three lines contains the clue to the deeper grievance against Baudelaire, who had not only deserted his luckless brethren but (like the woman in his poem 'La Béatrice') joined in mocking them. Baudelaire had published in *La Revue Fantaisiste*, in October 1861 (on the eve, that is, of his bid for membership of the Académie Française) his faithless preface to Léon Cladel's satire on Bohemian youth, *Les Martyrs ridicules*. In it Mallarmé had read passages like the following:

Alpinien, le *martyr* en premier de cette cohorte de *martyrs ridicules* (il faut toujours en revenir au titre), s'avise un jour, pour se distraire des chagrins intolérables que lui ont faits ses mauvaises mœurs, sa fainéantise et sa rêverie vagabonde, d'entreprendre le plus étrange pèlerinage dont il puisse être fait mention dans les folles religions inventées par les solitaires oisifs et impuissants. L'amour, c'est-à-dire le libertinage, la débauche élevée à l'état de contre-religion, ne lui ayant pas payé les récompenses espérées, Alpinien court la gloire, et, errant dans les cimetières, il implore les images des grands hommes défunts; il baise leurs bustes, les suppliant de lui livrer leur secret: 'Comment faire pour devenir aussi grand que vous?' Les statues, si elles étaient bonnes conseillères, pourraient répondre: 'Il faut rester chez toi, méditer et barbouiller beaucoup de papier!' Mais ce moyen si simple n'est pas à la portée d'un rêveur hystérique. La superstition lui semble plus naturelle. En vérité, cette invention si tristement gaie fait penser au nouveau calendrier des saints de l'école *positiviste*.

La superstition! ai-je dit. Elle joue un grand rôle dans la tragédie solitaire et interne du pauvre Alpinien, et ce n'est pas sans un délicieux et douloureux attendrissement qu'on voit par instant son pauvre esprit, — où la superstition la plus puérile, symbolisant obscurément, comme dans le cerveau des nations, l'universelle vérité, s'amalgame avec les sentiments religieux les plus purs, — se retourner vers les salutaires impressions de l'enfance, vers la Vierge Marie, vers le chant fortifiant des cloches, vers le crépuscule consolant de l'Eglise, vers la famille, vers sa mère; — la mère, ce giron toujours ouvert pour les *fruits-secs*, les prodigues et les ambitieux maladroits! on peut espérer qu'à partir de ce moment Alpinien est à moitié sauvé; il ne lui manque plus que de devenir un homme d'action, un homme de devoir, au jour le jour.

What Baudelaire does not say is that Alpinien, as well as seeking inspiration from Balzac's tomb, seeks it also in *Les Fleurs du mal*, reciting 'Les Petites vieilles' to himself as he follows the old and the maimed through the streets of Paris, in Baudelaire's footsteps.[53] In 'Le Guignon' Mallarmé avenges 'les martyrs ridicules' on their betrayer. Even if one did not remember that in 'Symphonie littéraire' Baudelaire is called 'le poète savant', there would be no doubt now that 'les poètes savants' of 'Le Guignon' are — again notwithstanding the plural — Baudelaire. At least they include Baudelaire, as the author not only of the preface but of an equally disloyal article on the *enguignonné* Pétrus Borel (ce baladin) and an outrageously flattering article on Victor Hugo (le Fort), published by *La Revue Fantaisiste* in the same series, during the summer of 1861.

Les poètes savants leur prêchent la vengeance,
Et ne voyant leur mal et les sachant brisés,
Les disent impuissants et sans intelligence.

'Ils peuvent, sans quêter quelques soupirs gueusés,
'Comme un buffle se cabre aspirant la tempête
'Savourer âprement leurs maux éternisés!

'Nous soûlerons d'encens les Forts qui tiennent tête
'Aux fauves séraphins du mal! — ces baladins
'N'ont pas mis d'habit rouge et veulent qu'on s'arrête!'

Quand chacun a sur eux craché tous ses dédains,
Nus, assoiffés de grand, et priant le tonnerre,
Ces Hamlet abreuvés de malaises badins

Vont ridiculement se pendre au réverbère.

The last line sends us back to 'Les Fleurs', and strengthens our conviction that this poem too, written two years after 'Le Guignon', expresses an anti-Baudelairian bitterness. The most obvious link between the two poems is the similarity of their endings, and the similarity reveals another scene in the Mallarmé–Baudelaire drama. The poet who hangs himself from a lamp-post, in the earlier poem, is presumably Nerval. The other, who poisons himself with opium, is Vigny's Chatterton. 'Despair and die', says society to the young poet, in Vigny's play. 'Despair and die' is the

---

[53] The publication date of *Les Martyrs ridicules* is given as 1862, but it appeared in fact, with Baudelaire's preface, in 1861: see Judith Cladel, *Maître et disciple: Charles Baudelaire et Léon Cladel*, 1951, p. 33. Mallarmé may very well have read the work as well as the preface before writing 'Le Guignon'. Baudelaire's preface, and also his articles on Pétrus Borel and Victor Hugo also mentioned here are included in *L'Art romantique*.

message of God's poppies, teaching the young poet his duty 'sans mensonge'. 'Despair and die' is Baudelaire's message to his disciple:

> Alors je me voile la face, et des sanglots, arrachés à mon âme moins par ce cauchemar que par une amère sensation d'exil, traversent le noir silence. Qu'est-ce donc que la patrie? J'ai fermé le livre et les yeux, et je cherche la patrie . . .

'Quels métiers notre société inflige à ses Poètes!' wrote Mallarmé to Coppée, and there are other echoes of *Chatterton* in his correspondence. In 'Symphonie littéraire' too there is a suggestion that he compared his situation with that of Vigny's hero. Chatterton's malady, says the understanding Quaker, 'c'est la haine de la vie et l'amour de la mort'. In more elaborate language, the poet of the 'Symphonie' offers his Muse 'ces quelques lignes de ma vie écrites dans les heures clémentes où tu ne m'inspiras pas la haine de la création et le stérile amour du néant.' In 'Les Fleurs', the poet's sickness is the same, and in the final version it is still Chatterton who is commemorated:

> O Mère qui créas en ton sein juste et fort,
> Calices balançant la future fiole,
> De grandes fleurs avec la balsamique Mort
> Pour le poëte las que la vie étiole.

There is a good reason why Chatterton should be associated with the criticism of Baudelaire. The preface to *Les Martyrs ridicules* had made 'Vigny versus Baudelaire' a theme for Mallarmé's thought and feeling. Vigny too had written a preface on the luckless poets, in terms that make Baudelaire's seem worthy of the Lord Mayor, offering Chatterton a place as head footman in his house:

> L'infirmité de l'inspiration est peut-être ridicule et malséante: je le veux. Mais on pourrait ne pas laisser mourir cette sorte de malades. Ils sont toujours peu nombreux, et je ne puis me refuser à croire qu'ils ont quelque valeur, puisque l'humanité est unanime sur leur grandeur, et les déclare immortels sur quelques vers: quand ils sont morts, il est vrai.
>
> Je sais bien que la rareté même de ces hommes inspirés et malheureux semblera prouver contre ce que j'ai écrit. — Sans doute, l'ébauche imparfaite que j'ai tentée de ces natures divines ne peut retracer que quelques traits des grandes figures du passé. On dirait que les symptômes du génie se montrent sans enfantement ou ne produisent que des œuvres avortées; que tout homme jeune et rêveur

n'est pas Poète pour cela; que des essais ne sont pas des preuves; que quelques vers ne donnent pas des droits. — Et qu'en savons-nous? Qui donc nous donne à nous-même le droit d'étouffer le gland, en disant qu'il ne sera pas chêne?[54]

Traced back to their origins, then, Mallarmé's thoughts on Baudelaire are those of a young poet on a lost leader. He had not taken his master's name in vain when in June 1863 he wrote the letter to Cazalis defending the uncompromising idealists, 'nous autres malheureux que la terre dégoûte et qui n'avons que le Rêve pour refuge'. The thoughts would lose their bitterness as they gradually became directed towards what he himself intended rather than what Baudelaire had failed to do, but the issues that had been raised were not forgotten. This is illustrated in a characteristic way in the very letter of 14th May 1867 which ends with the question: 'S'en séparera-t-il comme moi de Baudelaire?' With a condescending tolerance for Cazalis, a compromiser but his friend, the poet expresses a calm disdain for realist and Christian alike, *plafond de bonheur* and heaven hereafter, as he proclaims again his own faith:

> Puisque tu es assez heureux pour pouvoir, outre la Poésie, avoir l'amour, aime: en toi l'Être et l'Idée auront trouvé ce paradis que la pauvre humanité n'espère qu'en sa mort, par ignorance et par paresse, et, quand tu songeras au Néant futur, ces deux bonheurs accomplis, tu ne seras pas triste et le trouveras même très naturel. Pour moi, la Poésie me tient lieu de l'amour parce qu'elle est éprise d'elle-même et que sa volupté d'elle retombe délicieusement en mon âme; mais j'avoue que la Science que j'ai acquise, ou retrouvée au fond de l'homme que je fus, ne me suffirait pas, et que ce ne serait pas sans un serrement de cœur réel que j'entrerais dans la Disparition suprême, si je n'avais pas fini mon œuvre, qui est l'Œuvre, le Grand'Œuvre, comme disaient les alchimistes, nos ancêtres.[55]

---

[54] Preface to *Chatterton*. There are echoes of this preface still in Mallarmé's later plea for *les enguignonnés*, in his lecture or memorial oration on Villiers de l'Isle-Adam, delivered in 1890. The 'Vigny versus Baudelaire' theme can be traced in other poems than the ones mentioned. In the original version of *Tristesse d'été* for instance, probably composed in 1863 in London, Chatterton's sickness as diagnosed by the Quaker is found in association with a spleenetic version of *la chevelure-plafond de bonheur*.

[55] *Correspondance*, pp. 243-4. For a subsequent episode in Mallarmé's reflexion on Baudelaire, see A. Gill, 'Les vrais bosquets de la "Prose pour des Esseintes",' in *Cahiers de l'Association Internationale des Études Françaises*, No. 15 (March 1963).

Drama and Novel

7

JOHN HAMPTON

Beaumarchais 'Moraliste'

A PART from the obvious social criticism so often brought to our attention in the plays of Beaumarchais, the subject I have chosen for this article would seem to promise little. Indeed, one might question the propriety of including this author in a volume devoted to French thought. But in the history of ideas the disciples count as well as the leaders. Beaumarchais no doubt received much from the philosophical atmosphere of his day, yet he passed it on, vitalized and enriched with the flavour of his inimitable self. I do not wish to enumerate his sources, nor to set him up as an important initiator, but to observe him reflecting seriously on one of the tantalizing problems of his age, that of conceiving an ethic within the framework of a naturalistic philosophy. This will, I hope, serve to emphasize a neglected aspect of his work, and help to add depth to the portrait of the wit, the reformer and the dramatist.

The question has often been touched upon by Beaumarchais's many biographers, but largely on the basis of the plays and the correspondence. Lintilhac[1] on the other hand had access to the family archives, and was able to devote some five pages to this issue in his study of Beaumarchais. He tells us that he collected about four hundred reflexions and maxims in Beaumarchais's hand, all scribbled down at random on loose sheets of paper, as experience or reading suggested them, no doubt for use on future occasions. This indeed was the case, for, as Lintilhac already points out, many of them reappear in the plays, sometimes in modified form. Here we have, as it were, the artist's sketch book, a mine of information for later use in the studio. But there is far more than in fact reappears in the plays, and that is why these reflexions call for a separate study. True, Lintilhac has given us a brief survey of them, indicating the sources, with some observations on the breadth of interest and the liveliness of mind which they reveal. I am not here concerned, as he was, with the whole range of these disparate thoughts, but, as I have said above, with those which are directed towards the elucidation of the basic presuppositions of morality. And since, as will be seen, I wish to consider *la morale* in the broader context of *le moral*, I have chosen to keep to the French, and refer to the author as a *moraliste*.

[1] E. Lintilhac, *Beaumarchais et ses Œuvres*, Paris, 1887, pp. 329–33.

Without access to the manuscript material used by Lintilhac, little could have been added, but all this has recently been published under the editorship of Monsieur Gérard Bauër under the title *Notes et Réflexions*.[2] We have here an invaluable contribution to our texts, upon which I wish to draw copiously for illustration. Monsieur Bauër makes many cross-references to the plays, the *Mémoires* and the correspondence, and I shall not elaborate on that aspect of the work. I wish simply to make a preliminary attempt to co-ordinate what Beaumarchais wrote on the problem under discussion, with the hope of discovering some inner coherence characteristic of the author's mind.

Is there not, however, some difficulty in the fact that it is practically impossible to date these reflexions, and thus to trace any evolution in Beaumarchais's thought? What reappears in a particular play is of course prior to that play, but that is of little help, since the notebook, being always open, embraces everything. Fortunately or unfortunately Beaumarchais was a person whose inner life was turbulent without being tormented. There were turning points in his life, but were there any in his attitude to life? I doubt it. Was it not he who triumphantly sang of himself:

> Toujours, toujours, il est toujours le même. . . .?[3]

True, as he grew older he grew sadder. But such was the initial gaiety that he had a long way to go before he could claim to be melancholic, and in fact he never qualified. What he says of his change of attitude is relative only:

> 'En vieillissant, l'esprit s'attriste, le caractère rembrunit. J'ai beau faire, je ne ris plus quand un méchant ou un fripon insulte à ma personne, à l'occasion de mes ouvrages: on n'est pas maître de cela.'[4]

If the tone has altered, the will remains unchanged, even in those words. Surely Monsieur Bauër is right to observe that, in spite of everything, 'Il n'y a pas un mot de lassitude dans toute l'œuvre de Beaumarchais.'[5] It is this indomitable faith in life which constitutes the irresistible appeal of Beaumarchais, and this permanence of the will which makes the problem of the evolution of his thought of secondary importance.

Although Beaumarchais did not himself approach our question in a

---

[2] Hachette, 1961.

[3] Gudin de la Brenellerie, *Histoire de Beaumarchais*, publié par Maurice Tourneux, Paris, 1888, p. 145.

[4] *Un Mot sur 'La Mère Coupable'*, p. 462. References to all Beaumarchais's works, apart from the *Notes et Réflexions*, are from the *Théâtre Complet, Lettres relatives à son Théâtre*, Pléiade, 1957 edition.

[5] *Notes et Réflexions*, p. 1?. Further references to this work will be abbreviated: NR.

systematic way, it will be useful for our purpose to divide it into four parts, at the risk of imposing a pedantic framework on the least pedantic of writers. Firstly, what was, for Beaumarchais, the relationship between morality and general human nature: was it, for example, a form of fulfilment or of frustration? Secondly, what current moral attitudes or concepts did he reject, if any? Thirdly, what was the nature of his own affirmations, and lastly, where did he place the limits of human development?

On the first issue Beaumarchais would seem to have pessimistic views, based on the theoretical primitivism of the later eighteenth century. It is curious how this sophisticated, socially adapted man can on occasion speak like the Rousseau of the *Discours sur l'Inégalité* or the Diderot of the *Supplément au Voyage de Bougainville*. Society, and hence morality, is, as it were, the next best thing to an anarchy which is no longer viable, but we must not deceive ourselves into thinking that the resultant constraints are anything but painful. Whatever man is, it is obvious that he is not *integrally* moral, and so, to be moral at all, he must be divided. This division is incompatible with happiness. Man's intelligence surrenders the freedom of the body for its security, and the body is unimpressed. To the end of time it will bedevil the harmony of man's inner life with its proletarian impertinence, however much he may try to avert his eyes from its grimaces. The social analogy I would draw here is, I believe, appropriate. Beaumarchais's defence of the body has the same flavour as his pleas for the oppressed. Paradoxically enough, it is a moral condemnation of morality: 'Pour suivre l'ordre moral, on fait partout violence à l'ordre physique, partout les penchants les plus naturels sont en contradiction avec les devoirs. Dans ce combat perpétuel, les hommes ne sont plus qu'un assemblage de malheureux qui passent leur vie à se tourmenter tour à tour en se plaignant de la nature, qui les eût tous rendus heureux si leurs institutions ne l'avaient pas sans cesse outragée.'[6]

Such views were of course part of the intellectual furniture of most cultivated eighteenth century minds, and we should not give too much weight to them, at least to the particular form which they took. More important is the attitude of mind which led to the acceptance of such views. In the case of Beaumarchais, as with Rousseau too, the primitivist theory is a weapon to attack, not so much society as such, but the particular society of his day. This seems to be suggested by the following passage, which refers more precisely to political and social establishments, rather than to the vaguer notion of society as such: 'Celui qui considère le monde moral et qui en paraît satisfait, n'est selon moi guère moins insensible que

[6] NR, p. 40.

celui qui irait visiter les galères, les prisons, les inquisitions, les hôpitaux, et qui en sortirait tout content et réjoui. J'entends par monde moral, tout ce qui n'a pas été donné par la nature et qui est de sa pure institution, comme les diverses législations, la politique, les lois coutumières qu'on a fort bien imaginées pour contenir les hommes.'[7]

The most cherished ideal of Beaumarchais would seem to be, from such passages as these, liberty rather than goodness. But we must hasten to add that this is not a form of cynicism — we shall see later that this is far from the truth. Goodness is a necessary quality of the life which has lost its primitive or absolute liberty, whether the latter has in fact ever been manifest or not, like that of the child born into a modern society, who never actually exercises this liberty in reality, though it is there in the form of impulses checked at source. I am not concerned here with the issue of the real existence of any such neo-Rousseauist 'homme naturel'. What is important in this context is to uncover the deeper allegiances of Beaumarchais. We seem to be led to the assumption that he was the passionate defender of that aspect of human nature which lies below the moral level — the *id* of the Freudian as distinct from the *super-ego*, the existential value of life as distinct from its formal or ideal value. Such an attitude tallies perfectly with Beaumarchais's life-long hatred of, and rebellion against — la morgue!

We have seen that the picture is pessimistic. But there are two kinds of pessimist: there is the man who is glad to be a pessimist, and the man who is sorry to hold this position. Beaumarchais obviously is never tempted to gloat over the human condition, he never once shows pleasure in gloom. This is one reason why he opens his mouth so rarely on this basic issue, and prefers to make the best of life, in which, for all the evidence to the contrary, he cannot lose faith: 'La réflexion nous rend malheureux sans nous rendre plus sages ni meilleurs.'[8] The attitude is the same as that expressed in the famous words of Figaro: 'Je me presse de rire de tout, de peur d'être obligé d'en pleurer.'[9] Away with demonstrations of man's misery, salvation lies in action: 'Il faut voir. Non! Il faut faire!'[10] It is as though the truth were not something to be discovered, but created.

Let us not, however, slur over the difficulties too easily. Beaumarchais has more to say on this question of the general human situation, and we must see to what extent he is able to bring the latter into focus and describe it in concrete terms. For instance, in terms of money, power and

[7] NR, p. 115.
[8] NR, p. 35.
[9] *Barbier*, I, 2, p. 175.
[10] NR, p. 75.

prestige, the pain of temptation — and of resisting it! — is a permanent one, since it will always be more profitable to exploit one's neighbour than to treat him as a person: 'Il n'y a point de profit légitime qui ne soit surpassé par celui qu'on pourrait faire illégitimement dans le même cas. Le tort fait au prochain est plus lucratif que les services. Il ne s'agit que de s'assurer l'impunité, et c'est à quoi les puissants emploient toutes leurs forces, et les faibles leurs ruses.'[11]

So much for economic relationships. What of our more personal affairs — can we hope to be rational in the face of pressure of one sort or another? The answer is a firm negative: passion comes like a superior assailant who floors us in spite of all our bravado: 'Le philosophe aux prises avec ses passions ressemble au fanfaron qui se vante sans cesse de plus qu'il ne peut faire et qui, après avoir bravé et insulté tout le monde, se laisse battre à la première rencontre.'[12]

Society has, in fact, done nothing to abolish the evils which, according to the social contract theorist, it was meant to abolish. Beaumarchais is at his most sarcastic on this point: 'Ils étaient trop méchants et trop malheureux sous le loi de nature. Mais depuis ces divins établissements politiques, les princes souverains ne se font plus la guerre, on ne voit plus les particuliers se manger en procès, l'orgueil et l'ambition sont anéanties, l'avarice est écrasée, les cabales font de vains efforts, la calomnie, la malignité, l'hypocrisie ont perdu tout crédit, le mensonge n'ose plus se montrer, le luxe est sans force, le mal a disparu de dessus la terre; en un mot, tout est au mieux depuis que la raison nous a fait sortir de la liberté naturelle! O misérables raisonneurs!'[13]

Such a passage is hardly compatible with the view that society is the source of all goodness, though it is in harmony with a Rousseauistic attitude towards society. Of similar inspiration could be the way out of this dilemma which Beaumarchais finds — if man is amoral outside society, and wicked in it, how can he ever become good? With Rousseau, Beaumarchais sidesteps this issue by attributing to natural man the same *potentiality* for goodness which the Citizen of Geneva had done — pity: 'La pitié est la première vertu que la nature ait donnée à l'homme. D'elle seule découlent toutes les vertus sociales . . .'[14] We have already seen that Beaumarchais is not quite consistent in his opinions on this point, for he does not always base morality *on* nature, but sometimes sees it pitted *against* nature — hence the unhappiness of man.

[11] NR, p. 34.
[12] NR, p. 65.
[13] NR, p. 116.
[14] NR, p. 70.

Before leaving Beaumarchais's beliefs about the general nature of the
human condition, we must note two more disparate elements in the
situation. So far we have seen man as subject to egoistic instinct, and
thwarted by society, yet saved by pity. He is also the possessor of two
other gifts — reason and a sense of dignity. Like Rousseau once more,
Beaumarchais cannot opt for an integrally sentimentalist view of conscience, but relates it to reason. He does so in a somewhat tautological
way: 'La conscience est un jugement éclairé de la raison sur ce qu'on doit
ou ne doit pas faire.'[15] As for the concept of human dignity, which is
neither quite rationalistic nor altogether sentimental, we have the whole
tone of Beaumarchais's work as evidence of his adherence to this idea. He
may not often speak of it in so many words, though in fact he does go so
far as to claim that in this lies the whole significance of *Tarare*: 'La dignité
de l'homme est donc le point moral que j'ai voulu traiter, le thème que
je me suis donné.[16] But the *drames bourgeois*, the comedies and the *Mémoires*
are proof enough of Beaumarchais's sensitivity to any kind of humilia-
tion inflicted on his fellow men. Indeed he expresses this as part of a
moral doctrine in the *Notes et Réflexions* when he writes: 'De tous les
moyens de nous corriger, le pire est de nous confondre.'[17]

What I have so far said is sufficient, I think, to show the sort of theoretical background against which Beaumarchais thought. It is neither original
nor completely coherent as a philosophy of ethics, but this need not deter
us. Obviously Beaumarchais did not work from theory to practice, but
rather speculated occasionally about the theory of what he practised. In
this way he guarded against self-deception, and guaranteed the freshness
and authenticity of his judgment. That his theory, in so far as it existed,
was pessimistic, seems clear, but the interest of this lies in the very contrast
between theory and practice, in the fact that there is so little metaphysical
anxiety in Beaumarchais. As Monsieur Van Tieghem has put it: 'Le *Tout
finit par des chansons* est la réponse sceptique qu'imposent la forme bouf-
fonne de la comédie et l'optimisme de l'auteur à l'inquiétude métaphysique du siècle.'[18]

We may now leave this field of theory, and consider Beaumarchais's
attitude towards the specific moral beliefs of his contemporaries. This falls
into two parts, the personal standards of the individual, and the relationships between the latter and society.

One would have expected the author of *Eugénie* and *Les Deux Amis* to

---

[15] NR, p. 117.
[16] *Aux Abonnés de l'Opéra*, p. 374.
[17] NR, p. 91.
[18] Philippe Van Tieghem, *Beaumarchais par lui-même*, Editions du Seuil, 1960, p. 121.

have been an apostle of sentimental effusion, but, true believer in sensibility though we shall later find him to be, it is of interest here to note a certain stoicism, a certain cult of reticence, which shows itself from time to time in the *Notes et Réflexions*. For example, he is not impressed by the morality of self-accusation, regarding it as a possible form of escape, though it is difficult to see what could replace it. He does not, it is true, condemn it outright, but simply wishes to throw suspicion upon it: 'Il y a beaucoup de gens assez rusés pour se faire honneur sur leurs fautes d'une spécieuse ingénuité, sachant bien que celui qui s'accuse le premier émousse la pointe des accusations d'autrui . . .'[19] This may well be the judge in Beaumarchais expressing himself, the man who has learnt much from confrontations with those brought before him during his sessions at the Louvre, and who has learnt not to confuse generosity with justice. A similar attitude towards communicativeness is forcefully expressed by Mélac père in *Les Deux Amis*, but this time not in relationship to guilt, but to innocence. Once more the will is put at the centre of moral action, and whatever weakens it is condemned, even if it be the very sociability which lies at the heart of moral relationships: 'Mon ami, l'expérience de toute ma vie m'a montré que le courage de renfermer ses peines augmente la force de les repousser; je me sens déjà plus faible avec vous que dans la solitude.'[20] Together with this unexpected insistence on the reticence and solitude which were so rare in Beaumarchais's own life, goes a certain fatalism with regard to the individual's status in this world, a conservatism which runs counter to the reformist tendencies in the plays. In *Tarare* we read:

> Vouloir être ce qu'on n'est pas,
> C'est renoncer à tout ce qu'on peut être.[21]

while a note intended for *Les Deux Amis* insists on the necessity for class distance between men: 'Moins il y a de distance entre l'état des hommes, plus ils pointillent pour le faire remarquer, comme on voit aux frontières de chaque nation les rixes plus communes que dans l'intérieur des pays.'[22] The attitude behind such observations is clear: it is the antithesis of the 'social pressure' theory of morality, and again echoes Rousseau's dictum that the conscience makes itself heard best in solitude and 'dans le silence des passions'. Beaumarchais can hardly be suspected, with Rousseau, of wishful thinking on this issue, for he was completely at home in company. Yet here we see him making a plea for tranquillity and solitude as the best

[19] NR, p. 135.
[20] *Les Deux Amis*, IV, 7, p. 130.
[21] *Tarare*, V, 7, p. 447.
[22] NR, p. 106; cf. *Les Deux Amis*, I, 11, p. 92.

foundations for moral judgment and strength, as against the tumultuous realities of his personal existence. Not, however, that the opportunity for deliberation which quietude gives is necessarily good in itself. Almaviva is not alone, of course, in the above sense, but he is isolated by his social position, and he has the power which makes genuine personal choice possible. If he abuses his power, it is not, Beaumarchais reminds us, through thoughtlessness. On the contrary, his conscience, by disturbing him and forcing him to reflect, far from acting more as a deterrent, serves as an irritant. So we have once more evidence of the self-contradictory nature of morality itself — in action this time: 'Qui donc m'enchaîne à cette fantaisie? j'ai voulu vingt fois y renoncer ... Étrange effet de l'irrésolution! se je la voulais sans débat, je la désirerais mille fois moins.'[23] Judgment passed on oneself is therefore, as before in the quotation about confession, no guarantee of anything. How much more so in the case of judgment passed on other people, whether in personal relationships or at law! Judgment is, it would appear, a destructive force. For example, it undermines friendship when it demands too high a standard: 'La vie est un jugement continuel; et quelles sont les unions qui peuvent résister à une sévérite de tous les moments?'[24] And the judgment of the law is no less destructive of morals, in so far as one acts, not so much in disregard of it, but in defiance of it. Like Almaviva's conscience, the law acts as an irritant: 'Dans une débauche licencieuse, on se révolte avec fureur contre les préceptes, et la loi, faite pour nous rendre plus justes, ne sert souvent qu'à nous rendre plus coupables.'[25]

There is much in the *Notes et Réflexions* which recalls Montesquieu. I will mention only, in this context, the idea that, in so far as rewards and punishments are concerned with the maintenance of public morals, they must be regarded as having no absolute propriety in themselves, but as deriving whatever appropriateness they have from their close relation to the actual state of the society to which they refer: 'Dans les temps vertueux, il faut punir les vices pour empêcher la vertu de dégénérer. Dans les siècles corrompus, il faut laisser une punition inutile et récompenser les vertus pour arrêter la pente universelle qui porte aux vices.'[26]

Another somewhat unexpected aspect of Beaumarchais is revealed in the severity with which he denounces luxury. Discussion of this question was of course frequent in the eighteenth century, and Rousseau had given a strong lead in favour of simplicity. But Beaumarchais, the capitalist and

---

[23] *Le Mariage de Figaro*, III, 4, p. 307.
[24] NR, p. 127.
[25] NR, p. 103.
[26] NR, p. 153.

the lover of the good life in all its aspects, and a disciple of Voltaire into the bargain, nevertheless comes back again and again to the demoralizing effects of luxury. He has, of course, an eye on the ostentatious luxury of the aristocracy, but he writes with the conviction of a man explaining a universal truth: 'Les vices qu'entraînent les richesses croissent encore plus que les richesses mêmes, comme un fleuve débordé roule plus de limon qu'il ne grossit ses eaux.'[27] And with wealth, the inequality which goes with it is to be deplored. In fact the moral effect works both ways: gross inequality, such as we find under a political despotism, produces luxury: 'L'esclavage fomente toujours le luxe. Plus le despotisme rend les hommes petits, plus ils veulent paraître grands. La ridicule vanité des habîts magnifiques y est toujours substituée à la noble fierté de la vertu.'[28] And with luxury, slavery, from which there is no issue: 'Avec l'âme des esclaves, on sort difficilement de la servitude. Le feu sacré de la liberté ne peut être entretenu que par des mains purs. En vain un homme s'élèverait pour inspirer à sa patrie, épuisée de luxe et d'esclavage, des sentiments patriotiques. On peut farder une vieille femme, on ne la rajeunit pas.'[29] It will be readily apparent that Beaumarchais is here expressing an ideal which comes in direct descent from Montesquieu, through Rousseau, and blossoms out into the political Romanticism of popular late eighteenth century thought. But it is interesting to emphasize it here, since it contrasts so strongly with the widespread image we have of Beaumarchais, built so largely upon the gaiety and sensuality of the comedies.

Beaumarchais is perceptive enough to see that wealth can lie in personal gifts as well as in material possessions, and that, in so far as the former still belong to the world of 'avoir' rather than 'être', they are to be regarded with some suspicion, and certainly not to be placed above moral values. Here again, one recalls the oft-repeated view of Rousseau on the same issue, dating from the first *Discours* at least. Beaumarchais writes in similar vein: 'Quand les talents ont envahi les honneurs dus à la vertu, chacun veut être un homme agréable et nul ne se soucie d'être un homme de bien. De là naît cette inconséquence qu'on ne récompense dans les hommes que les qualités qui ne dépendent pas d'eux, car nos talents naissent avec nous et nos vertus seules nous appartiennent.'[30] That is, as Kant was to put it, there is nothing good but the good will.

We have seen so far, then, that Beaumarchais was critical of some of the normal types of moral judgment to be found in his (and our) society, that

[27] NR, p. 54.
[28] NR, p. 57.
[29] NR, p. 54.
[30] NR, p. 68.

on both a personal and a social level he was detached enough to question the assumptions hidden in our everyday reactions. Above all the attitude of the doctrinaire is completely alien to him. What now has he to say in the way of positive affirmations about man?

Though we shall not, of course, expect to find any assertions of a metaphysical nature, we soon come across beliefs which imply metaphysical assumptions, and the most striking of these is the conviction that man is a free agent. Yes, in spite of what was said at the beginning of this article about man's bondage to his body, Beaumarchais can still believe in a principle of freedom within himself, and there can be no doubt at all that it is at the very centre of his life: again he shows himself to be essentially a pragmatist. As early as his *Essai sur le Genre Dramatique Sérieux* he writes: 'Toute croyance de fatalité dégrade l'homme en lui ôtant la liberté, hors laquelle il n'y a nulle moralité dans ses actions.'[31] It is, however, not a blind assertion that man can work miracles by breaking the chain of cause and effect within himself, or by enjoying an absolute liberty of action. I find only one jotting which squarely faces up to the difficulties of belief in freedom, and this suggests a much more recondite form of liberty — one which lies in the *style* with which we inhabit our own slavery: 'Les événements sont à la fortune, mais la manière dont nous les prenons est à nous. Or le moyen le plus certain de conserver son bonheur et sa liberté au milieu du fatal enchaînement des choses et de leur servitude inévitable, est de secouer ce qu'elles ont d'arbitraire et surtout d'accorder sur soi le moins d'influence possible à la manière dont les événements qui nous arrivent frappent au peuvent frapper les autres; tout cela nous est étranger.'[32] All this, of course, is confused, as philosophy, since it leaves the self which is free beyond reach of cause and effect, yet able to influence it in some obscure way. But it is unfair to approach the 'philosophy' of a man of letters in this way, for his philosophy is better described as a personal ideology; it is a moral position rather than an intellectual one. Within such a context Beaumarchais knows clearly where he stands, and expresses it with vigour and imagination. For instance, 'free will' implies will, and Beaumarchais, abandoning for the moment any idea of the morality of nature, admits that man's ethical status is dependent on a constant effort of the most unnatural sort: 'La nature nous ramène sans cesse à l'égoisme qui est l'antipode de toutes les vertus sociales. Et semblable à l'oiseau pesant que sa gravité ramène en volant vers la terre si un nouveau coup d'aile, qu'un effort sans cesse renouvelle, ne le soutient en l'air à la hauteur de sa direction, il faut à l'homme vertueux, pour soutenir ce caractère, une

[31] *Essai sur le Genre dramatique sérieux*, p. 9.
[32] NR, p. 146.

attention perpétuelle, pour éteindre, repousser au loin ses affections qui tendent toujours à se resserrer, à se concentrer en lui-même.'[33] Man is seen as a centre of creative energy, of generosity — a characteristic which vividly recalls the verve of the two great plays, the intentions of the lesser ones, and the constant witness of Beaumarchais's own life. We are far from any morality of rules and regulations, far from any pharisaism. Beaumarchais, in despising external constraint, does not replace it with the slavery of sentimentality: the *enthousiasme* of which he speaks is to be thought of in conjunction with the effort just referred to; it is not a mere animal reaction, but the flaring up of an energy at the centre of the mind: 'L'homme qui s'enthousiasme des vertus de son état va presque toujours trop loin, mais son exemple frappe et entraîne beaucoup de monde, comme on voit dans les troupes un chef de file faire l'exercice d'une manière gigantesque et forcée devant un corps entier dont il dirige tous les mouvements sur les siens. C'est encore ainsi que survient qu'une seule goutte de liqueur forte met en fermentation tout un vase de liqueur tranquille.'[34] Here, as before, the accent is on activity rather than passivity, though we shall see that the latter has its uses. Beaumarchais is not referring to mere physical action, but to a movement of the mind which he regards as its very life: 'L'occupation est l'aliment de l'âme. La curiosité n'en est que la faim.'[35] Whether we are speaking of the field of moral action or of intellectual or artistic pursuits, life knows no such thing as absolute rest.

So far we have seen that Beaumarchais is far from envisaging man as a thorough-going sensationalist psychology would conceive him. He is a long way from the statue of a Condillac, and much more intransigent than Helvétius's man. Whatever the logical difficulties may be, Beaumarchais has no doubt whatever that within him, somewhere, there is a seat of freedom, of creation. He expresses it in the pompous language of the *drames bourgeois*, but also in his most flippant mood, as when, for example, in the *Vaudeville* to the *Mariage de Figaro*, the thought suddenly bursts forth:

L'esprit seul peut tout changer.'[36]

What does he mean by *esprit* here? Surely not mere wit, nor a superficial cleverness, but rather *mind* in its widest sense — the power to see things from an objective point of view, and thus to free oneself from *le préjugé* and *le fanatisme* — remember he is referring to the power of Voltaire's

[33] NR, p. 150.
[34] NR, p. 175.
[35] NR, p. 53.
[36] *Le Mariage*, p. 363.

writings. It is this capacity which Mélac Père claims when he says: 'Non,
Monsieur, j'ai prononcé, comme un tiers l'aurait fait, en préférant non ce
qui me convient, mais ce qui convient aux circonstances; non ce que je
puis, mais ce que je dois.'[37] But Beaumarchais sometimes refers to this
faculty as *le cœur*, and opposes it to *l'esprit*, then taken in the sense of a
tactless and pedestrian rationalism. There is no doubt that in the following
passage he is speaking of a centre of judgment, not of a blind affectivity:
'N'écoutons que notre cœur. C'est lui qui ne manque jamais. L'esprit veut
quelquefois le contrefaire, mais il manque, il se trompe, il bronche à tout
moment. Ses allures ne sont point égales et les gens éclairés par le cœur ne
sauraient jamais être trompés à son expression.'[38] And sometimes, of
course, he refers to it as *le sentiment*, as when he writes: 'La vertu, comme
le bonheur, est le fruit du sentiment et non de la raison.'[39] Allowances
must be made for the inevitable philosophical 'cliché', which however, I
would not take at its face value in this case. Certainly, if Beaumarchais
seems to be, with his contemporaries, an apostle of *la sensibilité*, it is with
no *fadeur* or mawkishness, but because he considers sentiment to be the
companion of the will. Moreover, if we are to activate the latter, we must
first of all remove the inhibition which *fear* of emotion imposes on it:
'L'homme qui *craint* de pleurer, celui qui *refuse* de s'attendrir, a un vice dans
le cœur...'[40] Beware of the man who is gentle with every one, he may
well be merely callous: 'L'homme indifférent est tranquille. Sa tranquillité
le fait passer pour doux; comme il n'est touché de rien, il fait grâce à
tout.'[41] Beware also of the wise calm of 'experience' — it may well be
no more than a canker in the soul: 'Les maux du corps deviennent plus
poignants à mesure qu'ils vieillissent. Les vices de l'âme, en s'y incorporant,
le tourmente de moins en moins jusqu'à l'insensibilité qui est la gangrène
de l'âme.'[42]

Freedom, judgment and sentiment, therefore — three facets of the same
thing, which constitutes our essential humanity, and which takes us beyond
any purely utilitarian conception of morality. Beaumarchais's distinction
between *l'honneur* and *la probité* makes his position quite clear, and reveals
him as a true idealist: 'L'homme de probité remplit strictement ses engage-
ments. L'homme d'honneur va plus loin: il les chérit et ne restreint pas ses
devoirs dans les bornes que la loi prescrit, il les étend. La probité est fille de
la loi, l'honneur est fils des mœurs. L'engagement d'une femme est d'être

[37] *Les Deux Amis*, IV, 7, p. 129.
[38] NR, p. 72.
[39] NR, p. 187.
[40] *Essi sur le Genre dramatique sérieux*, p. 12. My italics.
[41] NR, p. 119.
[42] NR, p. 101.

fidèle, la femme d'honneur est plus, elle est chaste.'[43] But having described the possibilities which he sees open to us, we must, to be fair, consider also the limits which Beaumarchais sees encompassing all human activity.

Firstly, it can hardly be claimed that Beaumarchais was an apostle of the perfectibility of man, if we understand by this doctrine the possibility of definitive moral progress from one generation to the next. Though he is obviously in favour of social change, he has no doubt that the individual must always start from a moral zero. Freedom of the will implies permanent instability, and it is improbable that all men should ever all choose rightly: 'Les vices, les abus, voilà ce qui ne change point...'[44] The doctrine is familiar, traditional and pessimistic. While the general trend of contemporary materialism was to draw optimistic conclusions from the belief in the malleability of human nature, Beaumarchais viewed such projects with distrust: 'L'éducation ne mord point sur le caractère. Elle le modifie dans la forme. Il reste le même pour le fond.'[45] Yet he did not despair. If a facile and automatic progress was not to be envisaged, there was always the long-term possibility which freedom always implied — that of learning from experience and choosing to apply the lesson. The last word is with the will, and therefore he is not being inconsistent when he writes: 'Il n'est pas ridicule de penser que le monde devant durer si longtemps, les hommes y sont encore jeunes, faibles et bornés.... Sans doute qu'à force de se culbuter, rouler, maltraiter en tous sens, ils se lasseront et en viendront à sentir que leurs jeux ne sont point du tout plaisants....'[46]

Meanwhile what is the wise man to do? There can be no question of a facile hedonistic ethic: 'La vertu ne rend pas heureux, mais elle apprend à se passer de l'être.'[47] Neither can there be the expectation of success all the time, and the effort of which Beaumarchais speaks is not to be confused with hopeless and undignified struggling — it may be the opposite. It is not without significance that he should have chosen as the epigraph to his *Deux Amis*:

Qu'opposerez-vous aux faux jugements, à l'injure, aux clameurs?
— Rien.[48]

It may seem difficult — even ridiculous — to envisage Beaumarchais preaching renunciation, and we must not imagine that he ever considered defeatism as a way of life! Far from it. But in the *last analysis*, he has to accept a position which is remarkably non-utilitarian, remarkably stoical

[43] NR, p. 105.
[44] *Le Mariage, Préface*, p. 235.
[45] NR, p. 188.
[46] NR, p. 79.
[47] NR, p. 186.
[48] From iv, 7, of the same play.

and self-sufficient. Examples are numerous: 'Heureux l'homme qui reçoit d'un même œil les faveurs qu'il mérite et les disgrâces qu'il ne méritait pas.'[49] Or again 'Si l'homme sage s'élève au-dessus du préjugé par la pensée, le chef-d'œuvre de la sagesse est de s'y soumettre dans ses actions.'[50] Unoriginal, of course, but interesting enough for Beaumarchais to write them down, and revealing indications for us of his affinities. In the same tone is the observation concerning the distribution of good and evil in the world: 'Sur cela comme sur tout le reste le bien et le mal sont également répartis. Peut-il y avoir un ingrat sans qu'il y ait en même temps un bien-faiteur?'[51] All this is in contrast to the impression of Beaumarchais which one gets from his tumultuous life, of his unremitting fight for himself, his family and his friends against the forces of oppression. But there is no reason why the two attitudes should not exist side by side in the same man, expressing themselves on the one hand in the actions of everyday life, and on the other in the encompassing vision of his own fundamental status. To call this ambivalence a philosophy would be to confer on it a dignity which it does not require, and which Beaumarchais himself would no doubt have repudiated. Though it is incontestable that he was a disciple of the *philosophes*, he was too independent to be a partisan, and too close in spirit to the people to have pretensions to intellectualism. One wonders whom he is teasing when he writes: 'La philosophie peut aller son train sans risque: le peuple ne l'entend pas ou la laisse dire et lui rend le dédain qu'elle a pour lui.'[52] As a moralist his ultimate faith seems to lie in his own uncommonly sound common-sense, which is serious, practical and generous, devoid of fatuous professionalism, free from the mania of sys-tematisation, or the vain pursuit of novelty, realistic without cynicism, humanistic without arrogance. Behind the multifarious activities of Beau-marchais's career there is a man of admirable integrity and judgment. Our final thoughts on reading his reflexions might well be that for him life itself seemed remarkably similar to life at court: 'A la cour, on s'oublie soi-même, entraîné dans le tourbillon des autres, quoique le fond de tout se rapporte à soi. Mais on s'y fait une habitude d'y être si caché, si envelop-pé qu'on a toutes les peines du monde à se reconnaître pour le but des mouvements qu'on se donne.'[53] Only occasionally does the recognition come, and that is the moment to take out our notebook.

[49] NR, p. 30.
[50] NR, p. 188.
[51] NR, p. 179. Cf. Le Mariage, Préface, p. 136: 'Ne pouvant y avoir un ingrat sans qu'il existe un bienfaiteur, ce reproche même établit une balance égale entre les bons et mauvais cœurs; on le sent, et cela console.'
[52] NR, p. 22.
[53] NR, p. 73.

8

E. T. DUBOIS

Léon Bloy, Paul Claudel and the Revaluation of the Significance of Colombus

... j'ai pensé à Christophe Colomb, à ce personnage qui me han-
tait depuis un certain temps, depuis la lecture du livre de Léon Bloy
... comment ça s'appelle-t-il? *Le Découvreur de la Terre* ... je ne me
rappelle plus exactement. C'était le héros d'une idée que j'ai toujours
eue, cette idée du rassemblement de la terre, de la réunion des différentes parties éparses de l'humanité, et Christophe Colomb me semblait, à ce sujet, un véritable champion et, on peut dire, un saint, tel
que l'avait rêvé le livre de Léon Bloy. (P. Claudel, *Mémoires improvisés*,
Gallimard, 1954, pp. 325-326).

*L*e *Livre de Christophe Colomb*, Claudel's last play, was written, as he
states in *Mémoires improvisés*, p. 327, by way of 'un achèvement du
Soulier de satin', when 'il me restait encore ... l'émotion de la pièce'.
It completes Claudel's writing for the theatre begun with *Tête d'or* in 1889.
Multiple threads link the play with Claudel's activities and preoccupations;
the figure of the conqueror and leader is present in many of his plays beginning with Simon Agnel in *Tête d'or* whose conquest was doomed to
failure as it relied on human strength alone. Gradually the idea of a vocation is woven into the theme of conquest; this is already apparent in
L'Annonce faite à Marie, although other themes dominate the play. In
Partage de midi the idea of adventure, leadership and vocation is spread over
all three main characters only one of whom eventually recognizes the real
purpose of his destiny. Rodrigue in *Le Soulier de satin* was also 'un conqué-
rant' although not 'un découvreur'; however, both he and Columbus
were 'des rassembleurs de la terre' (*Mémoires improvisés*, p. 327). Yet
another theme which runs through Claudel's plays appears also in *Le Livre
de Christophe Colomb*: the role of the woman as a kind of mediatrix, an
instrument of grace in the fulfilment of man's vocation. The emphasis in
Claudel's last play has considerably shifted from earlier treatment: the sin-
ful relationship in *Partage de midi* which only eventually and almost in spite

131

of the partners leads to eternal salvation, the restless search and final separa-
tion of the lovers in Le Soulier de satin (although with the promise of
eternity before them), is purified in Le Livre de Christophe Colomb. Isabella
intuitively understands Columbus's vocation and helps him to fulfil it, but
their relationship is none other than that of queen and subject although
spiritually they are closely linked in the symbolic figure of the dove.

It is perhaps also noteworthy that Claudel wrote Tête d'or (second version) and Le Livre de Christophe Colomb while he held posts in the States.
On a merely human plane, the theme of search for new lands, departure
for foreign shores, the resulting instability of the lives of Claudel's heroes
reflects no doubt something of his own diplomatic career.[1]

The play owed its creation to the request of Max Reinhardt;[2] it was
from the beginning intended to be set to music. Claudel preferred to work
with his friend Darius Milhaud[2] rather than with Richard Strauss, as
suggested by Reinhardt. The fate of the play was in fact that it was performed as an opera at the Berlin Staatsoper in 1930 and had as such a successful run before it was staged as a play (with music and screen projections) in 1953 by J. L. Barrault at the Marigny theatre.

However, we are not concerned here with the history of Claudel's
writing for the stage but with the history of an idea. The idea of spanning
the globe, of gathering together the whole of the universe had always been
dear to Claudel (cf. Mémoires improvisés, p. 327[3]); he thus projected into
Columbus, this 'rassembleur de la terre' something of his own ideals. He
was not only to be the geographical discoverer of a hitherto unknown part
of the earth but was to carry out a divine mission in bringing innumerable
souls to the light of Christ. This is closely bound up with the symbolic
interpretation of the name: Christopher, as he wrote it himself XPO-
ferens and Columbus as the 'colombe', symbol of the Holy Spirit. The
Explicateur (Le Livre de Christophe Colomb, p. 43)[4] heralds the hero as

[1] As. J. L. Barrault explains in Cahiers, 1, Claudel had this 'goût du départ'; in fact it is a
recurring theme in his plays: Anne Vercors in L'annonce faite à Marie, Louis Laine in l'Échange
and most of all Rodrigue in Le Soulier de satin.

[2] Correspondance Paul Claudel — Darius Milhaud, in: Cahiers Paul Claudel, 3, Gallimard,
1961, pp. 78 et seq.; letters of 16th April 1927 and 2nd August from Washington and Brangues
respectively.

[3] '... "rassembleurs" de la terre, ce qui m'a toujours été extrêmement sympathique puisque,
étant tout jeune encore, quand, des hauteurs de mon village, je voyais pour ainsi dire toute la
terre se déployer devant moi, j'avais l'idée de cette vocation qui s'impose à certains hommes
de rassembler tout ce qui s'offre à leur vue et d'en faire l'objet d'une espèce de conquête.'

[4] An Italian translation by A. Grande was produced in Genoa in 1951: Libro di C. Colombo;
cf. H. Bédarida, 'Christophe Colomb, héros de quelques drames français,' in Annales de
l'Université de Paris, 1951, no. 4. The article briefly outlines some melodramatic versions of the
Columbus story, written by French playwrights of the first half of the nineteenth century, in
the wake of J. J. Rousseau's libretto La Découverte du nouveau monde, 1740.

'Colombe et Porte-Christ'. It is true that Columbus himself never lost sight of this missionary aspect of his discovery although at times it appears to be lost in the dark tangle of the uglier motives of lust for power and hidden wealth which prompted those who helped him.

Columbus belonged to that intermediary period that falls between the end of the Middle Ages and the beginning of modern times, to Claudel's mind a rich and exciting epoch. To him the Renaissance was 'une des périodes les plus glorieuses du catholicisme', during which the Church completes 'ses conquêtes dans l'espace et dans le temps'. *Le Soulier de satin* spans the sixteenth century where *Le Livre de Christophe Colomb* introduces it, although it was composed on the ebb of the wide sweep of inspiration that produced the first of the two plays.

It was in the nineteenth century that the figure of Columbus was 're-discovered' and at least in France his missionary work reappraised.[5] The impulse was given by count Roselly de Lorgues, who included an essay on Columbus in a work published in 1845: *La Croix dans les deux mondes*. This was followed by several other books the most important of which is *Christophe Colomb, histoire de sa vie*, 1856. For this the author had the support and encouragement of Pius IX, as is shown by a letter, dated 10th December 1851, prefaced to the first edition of the biography. About the mid-century the question of the possible beatification of Columbus was raised, for which Roselly and subsequently Bloy worked fervently, not without support from some members of the hierarchy. The fourth centenary of the discovery was envisaged as a suitable date; Roselly, encouraged by the success of the biography, drew up a *Mémoire pour solliciter la béatification de Christophe Colomb* in 1870. A commission of the first Vatican Council considered the cause of Columbus and rejected it on moral grounds.[6] This prompted Roselly to some sharp and not well grounded attacks in *Satan contre Christophe Colomb*, 1876, and *Histoire posthume de Christophe Colomb*, 1885.

Léon Bloy's *Le Révélateur du globe*, 1884, quoted by Claudel, was in fact largely inspired by Roselly's work; Bloy espouses Roselly's convictions, prejudices and later grievances when he recasts the biography of Columbus, adding some of his own interpretations. He too pleads for the beatification of his hero; in 1890 he exposes the enemies of Columbus in

[5] Two important studies of Columbus appeared in the nineteenth century outside France: Washington Irving's *The Life and Voyages of Christopher Columbus*, 1827, the documentation of which is partly based, like Roselly's, on Navarrete: *Colección de los viajes y descubrimientos que hicieron pos mas los Españoles*; Alexander von Humboldt: *Kosmos, Entwurf einer physischen Weltbeschreibung*, Stuttgart, Cotta, 1845–62. Humboldt is only concerned with the scientific aspect of the discovery and deals with Columbus mainly in volumes 2 and 4.

[6] *Catholicisme*, 11, 1315, article on Columbus.

Christophe Colomb devant les taureaux (his venom is directed against the unworthy bull breeding descendants of the 'Saint') and addresses, the same year, in Latin, an 'encyclical letter' to the hierarchy of France, pleading the cause of the beatification of Columbus.[7]

The actual commemoration of the centenary of the discovery was publicly acknowledged by the then reigning pope, Leo XIII, in a letter *Quarto abeunte saeculo*, dated 16th July 1892. It gives Columbus due appraisal without further reference to the possibility of raising him to the altar.

When Claudel took up the subject in the late twenties of our century he had already sampled or was about to sample Bloy's other exegetic and apologetic writings. Among these the most important, as far as Claudel is concerned, are *Le Salut par les Juifs* and *Le Symbolisme de la Salette*. The symbolic exegesis, however doubtful its orthodoxy may be,[8] practised by Bloy, largely under the influence of his one-time confessor, abbé Tardif de Moidrey, corresponded to Claudel's own tendencies and inclinations. He was subsequently to edit abbé Tardif de Moidrey's meditation on *Le Livre de Ruth* (1938) with a substantial introduction. Much of the ideological, or rather spiritual background of *Le Livre de Christophe Colomb* stems from this curious blend of literary symbolism and Biblical exegesis.

Before Roselly undertook the rehabilitation of Columbus Lamartine included a study of his life in *Le Civilisateur* (1852–4: *Les Grands Hommes*). Lamartine claimed Columbus as 'un homme de génie' even though he conceded him the God-willed purpose of the undertaking. Roselly knew Lamartine's work, as he knew Irving's, but his approach differs considerably from Lamartine's. For Lamartine Columbus is 'l'instrument de l'histoire' (p. 253); his whole study points to the emergence of 'un homme de génie'. His achievement, and here his point of view and that of Roselly and his successors diverge, was the creation of a 'unité géographique terrestre' (p. 255). Lamartine, in his own rather unorthodox belief, recognized Columbus as an 'envoyé de Dieu' (p. 273), as the prior of Robida had seen him, and also acknowledges the double aspect of the discovery: the spreading of Spanish power and the introduction of the Cross to the new continent. His attitude to the religious belief of the natives, whom he idealizes after the model of the 'bon sauvage', is diametrically opposed to Claudel's. Where Lamartine sees 'une religion évangélique par la simplicité et la pureté de sa morale, émanation mystérieuse . . .' (p. 357), as described by

---

[7] 'Lettre encyclique à tous les évêques de France, les priant de plaider la cause de la béatification de Christophe Colomb auprès de la cour de Rome,' dated 4th October 1890. In it Bloy complains against: '. . . artes pessimas et infernales contra Heroem christianum numero Beatorum adscribendum. . . .'

[8] Cf. C. Charlier: Paul Claudel et la Bible in *Bible et vie chrétienne*, Sept./Nov. 1955, pp. 32–46.

the traditional 'vieillard' of Voltairian ancestry, Claudel ridicules the old Mexican gods remorselessly in the scene *Les Dieux barattent la mer*. Lamartine extols this pre-conquest 'Eldorado' and deplores the subsequent enslavement of the native population whilst Roselly, Bloy and Claudel focus their interpretation on the eternal salvation brought across the *mare tenebrosum*. In the evaluation of the figure of the queen, however, Lamartine and the later writers meet. He stresses the part of enthusiasm and intuition that led to Isabella's decision and distinguishes between her motives and the king's: '... elle croyait servir la cause de Dieu lui-même, ignoré de cette partie du genre humain qu'il allait conquérir à la foi.' ... 'Ferdinand y voyait un royaume terrestre.' To put it in Claudelian terms, *anima* perceives a deeper significance where *animus* only follows the outward phenomenon.

In his summary of this 'véritable grand homme' Lamartine draws a portrait of Columbus which is at once romantic and humanist in its inspiration: 'génie, travail, patience, obscurité du sort, vaincue par la force de la nature, obstination douce mais infatigable pour le but ... confiance dans l'étoile, non d'un homme, mais de l'humanité ... amour immense, ardent et actif de l'humanité ...' He sees Columbus's task as carried out with 'la sagesse d'un législateur et la douceur d'un philosophe' (p. 391).[9] Even though he accepts that Columbus shared in a work of God, he sees his achievement in the 'unité morale du genre humain' (p. 391), in fact a work of civilisation.

Roselly gave the real impetus to the revaluation of Columbus's discovery. A now largely forgotten historian, he belonged to the spiritual family of de Maistre and has, to some extent, through Bloy, stood as godfather to the Catholic revival of the turn of the century. Roselly centres his treatment of the subject around the providential character of the discovery: 'conquête du catholicisme', 'l'œuvre de la Foi' ('Sainteté de Christophe Colomb' in *La Croix dans les Deux Mondes*, Paris, Rivert, 1845, pp. 437, 462). The historical event is overshadowed by the manifestation of providence and Columbus seen as 'Révélateur, apôtre de la croix, messager du catholicisme' (*Christophe Colomb, histoire de sa vie et de ses voyages*, Paris, Didier, 1856, p. 412). Roselly also revives the idea of the fulfilment of a prophecy[10] and sees in Columbus something of a precursor as John

---

[9] Lamartine's work inspired the Spanish writer Luis Mariano de Larra y Wetoret who dedicated his own *La Agonía*, 1861, to Lamartine 'quien engrandeció y poetizó la figura de Colón...'

[10] A. Ballesteros Beretta: 'Cristóbal Colón,' in *Historia de América*, t. 4, Barcelona, 1945, pp. 684 sqq., quotes Columbus's own interest in the prophecies pointing to his own discovery; he himself referred to Jeremiah, Baruch, Ezekiel, Daniel, Hosea in *Descripción del libro de las Profecías que juntó el Amirante Don Cristóbal Colón, con copia de las cartas que éste dirigió al Padre Don Gaspar Gricio y a los Reyes*, begun in 1501 and completed after the fourth journey.

the Baptist was, a 'messager du salut' (op. cit., p. 445). In support he quotes Isaiah, lx, 12[11] and Seneca, *Medea*, II, v. 371.[12] Where Roselly has perhaps given the most decisive directive is in respect of the symbolism of the name. Salvador de Madariaga, in *Vida del muy magnífico señor Don Cristóbal Colón*, (Editorial Sudamericana, Buenos Aires, 1940, p. 37) quoting from Las Casas supports the interpretation of the first name: 'Llamóse, pues, por nombre, Cristobal, conviene á saber, Christum ferens que quiere decir traedor ó llevador de Cristo ... el primero que abrió las puertas deste mar Océano, por donde entró y él metió á estas tierras tan remotas y reinos, hasta entónces tan incógnitos, á nuestro Salvador Jesucristo.' The reading of the first name has been and can be easily adapted to Columbus's discovery. Opinions as to his surname are divided. Roselly makes the meaning of 'colombe' an integral part of his presentation and so do after him both Bloy and Claudel. In fact Roselly takes his interpretation to the furthest possible length when he states: 'Saint Pierre était fils de la Colombe, et Christophe de Colomb' (op. cit., p. 468).[13] Madariaga, on the other hand, continues in the already quoted passage: 'Tuvo por sobrenombre Colón, que quire decir poblador de nuevo ...' and points to the appropriateness of the name. In a later chapter, significantly entitled 'Cristóbal La Cruz, Colón la Bandera', he underlines this twofold aspect of Columbus's achievement and further devotes a chapter to 'Colombo contra Colón'. This to him is, however, merely a question of the writing of the name in Italian and Spanish,[14] for Roselly, Bloy and Claudel it is the key to the real understanding of their hero which stands or falls by it.

So convinced is Roselly of Columbus's mission that he endeavours to eliminate the possibility of a 'scientific' discovery, seeing it rather as a direct result of meditation and divine inspiration; Columbus has 'la foi complète, implicite et ardente du Moyen-Age avec son caractère militant et chevaleresque' (op. cit., 467), stands 'à l'ouverture de l'ère de la Renaissance, la devance sous le rapport de l'intuition et de la Science' (ibid.).

One other point in Roselly's evaluation of Columbus has borne fruit in the later writings on the subject: his view of the part played by Isabella.

[11] 'Every nation and kingdom that refuses thee homage shall vanish away, whole provinces empty and forlorn.' (Roselly sees the fate of America, before Columbus, as Isaiah saw that of his people.)

[12] '... venient annis Saecula suis, quibus Oceanus Vincula rerum laxet, et ingens Pateat tellus ... ultima Thule.'

[13] Bar Jona 'filius Columbae'; Thomas Aquinas, *Super Matthaeum* XVI, 17, defines: 'scilicet spiritus sancti quia haec confessio non poterit fieri nisi a Spiritu Sancto'.

[14] A. Ballesteros Beretta, op. cit., p. 161, also takes the same view: 'Así, era Colombo en italiano, Colomb o Coulon en francés, Colón en espanol y Columbus en latín.' It is true that Roselly refers to the meaning of *colón* (*Histoire* ..., p. 452) but to him this is only an unimportant one.

Indeed her intercession on behalf of Columbus seemed to Roselly renewed by the empress's interest in his 'cause'. Roselly ends his biography thus: 'Sa Majesté Eugénie se trouve l'unique Espagnole et la seule Française qui ait effectivement désiré la réparation due au Révélateur du Globe. ... L'amitié de la catholique Isabelle, restée si fidèle à Colomb, semble ainsi ressuscitée sur le trône. ...' For what it is worth it underlines the trend of thought which will be so largely developed in later writings.[15]

Roselly had a more influential supporter in cardinal Donnet, archbishop of Bordeaux and Metropolitan of the French West Indies, who helped him to plead in Rome. Pius IX was thought to be specially prepared to hear a postulation, which Barbey d'Aurevilly was to call 'le procès-verbal d'une canonisation future', since he had personal knowledge of (South) America, thanks to a minor diplomatic post he had held in Chile. If the Commission sitting in Santa Maria sopra Minerva had to reject the 'cause' of Columbus the Church did not fail to acknowledge his work as: 'aditum Evangelio per novas terras novaque maria patefacere (Leo XIII *Quarto abeunte saeculo*). The whole spiritual impact had already been stressed by Alexander VI who, addressing himself to their Catholic Majesties (*Inter cetera*, May 1493), referred to the purpose of the discovery as: 'Vocare Indorum genus ad instituta christiana'. Leo XIII's letter did, however, put an end to all hopes of beatification; the Devil's advocate had triumphed and Roselly, and Bloy after him, did not mince their words in attacking him in the person of a certain Genoese cleric who became the unfortunate hero of *Satan contre C. Colomb*. Just as Léon Bloy's book led Claudel to take up the subject of Columbus, so was the reading of Roselly's book for Bloy 'un des événements les plus considérables de ma vie intellectuelle' (*Christophe Colomb devant les taureaux*, p. 116). *Le Révélateur du globe*, 1884, was not Bloy's only historical study, though it was his first published one; he had already written *La Chevalière de la mort* (Marie-Antoinette) and was to interest himself later in Napoleon (*L'Ame de Napoléon*), in Joan of Arc, and in Byzantine history (*L'Épopée byzantine*). He formulated his very personal view on history through Marchenoir, the almost autobiographical hero of *Le Désespéré*. For Bloy history is essentially detached from time, it is a manifestation of and participation in eternity. God writes his revelation through history in an 'infini désordre'. Here it seems that Claudel's introductory quotation of *Le Soulier de satin* (*Deus escreve direito por linhas tortas*)

---

[15] This rather childish parallel ties up with Roselly's statement: 'la vérité a besoin de la France' (borrowed from Joseph de Maistre), which introduces the book and serves as epilogue. It is well known of course that the Catholic revival of the late nineteenth and the early twentieth century is bound up with this curious chauvinism. It was very much after Bloy's own heart.

comes very close to Bloy's conception of history. It is a kind of second revelation which manifests itself in the temporal events. This eschatological view of history is closely linked to Bloy's symbolic exegesis to which he was introduced by abbé Tardif. The story of Christ's life on earth and the story of the mystical body throughout the ages belong to the same instant in eternity. The dogma of the Communion of Saints is a necessary counterpart to this highly personal view of history. In this metaphysics of history Bloy sees the work of God but also the power of Satan. All the first part of *le Révélateur du globe* is taken up by the idea of Satan's power 'l'empire illimité de Satan', over 'la multitude des affreux enfants de la liberté humaine'. There remains, however, 'la liberté crucifiée avec Jésus-Christ' over which Satan has no power. Human history, after the manner of Christ's life is 'une histoire crucifiée', and so is man's individual history.[16] On this Bloy builds 'la symbolique des larmes' (largely connected with the Apparition of La Salette); in *Christophe Colomb devant les taureaux*, p. 192, this *mystique* of tears is, though clad in an old Germanic legend, applied to Columbus's experience of failure during his life and unjust treatment after his death.[17] Linked with his philosophy of history is a highly personal theology which is based on the belief of the coming of the reign of the Third Person of the Trinity. Thus Columbus is seen as 'la solitaire colombe de l'océan' symbolizing 'la troisième personne divine' (*Christophe Colomb devant les taureaux*, p. 116).

Three strands of thought run through Bloy's 'revised' biography of Columbus. His was a 'mission providentielle et unique'; like Roselly before him, Bloy sees in his hero 'un des hommes les plus inouïs qu'on ait jamais vus, un prédestiné dont la grandeur colossale déconcerte l'imagination, un patriarche et un prophète à la façon de Moïse et du Précurseur' (*Christophe Colomb devant les taureaux*, p. 35). His mission truly fulfilled divine revelation in a part of the world left in the hands of Satan. Claudel transposes this conception into his farcical interlude on the Mexican gods in *Le Livre de Christophe Colomb*. Columbus is seen as 'l'Apôtre du Nouveau Monde' (*Christophe Colomb devant les taureaux*, p. 45), the patriarch of foreign missionaries, whose dates show some mysterious and symbolic connection with those of St Francis Xavier (he was born seventeen days before Columbus's death; cf. *Le Révélateur du globe*, ch. V).

The symbolism of the names is for Bloy, more even than it was for Roselly, an integral part of the Columbus story. He takes up from his predecessor the reference in *The Song of Songs* to 'columba mea' and evokes a

---

[16] Cf. Béguin: *Bloy, Mystique de la douleur*, Paris, Labergerie, 1948.

[17] It is true that Columbus himself had said in one of his letters (quoted here from *Le Livre de Christophe Colomb*, p. 181): 'Que le Ciel me fasse miséricorde et que la terre pleure sur moi.'

picture of his hero as 'cette blanche et gémissante colombe portant le Christ'! Thus the symbolism of the name is linked to the idea that Christ's suffering is relived in every human being. Columbus's special position is that he also represents the Third Person of the Trinity. Like Roselly, and perhaps to an even higher degree, Bloy whitewashes his hero so as to fit him into the pattern of his interpretation, that is, to see him as the unjustly suffering 'amplificateur de la création'. Claudel's approach will be much more realistic even though he takes over the bulk of the mystical symbolism.

Columbus's life also bears some likeness to that of Our Lord in that he is the innocent victim of popular persecution: 'je crus apercevoir dans un lointain excessif, dans le crépuscule suranné des très vieux ans, la Face douloureuse et calme, la haute figure mélancolique et si douce du Christophore!' (*Christophe Colomb devant les taureaux*, p. 17). In another Biblical image Bloy sees 'le Révélateur du Globe' as '. . . l'indigent Lazare qui gît à sa porte, plein des ulcères que lui ont faits l'ingratitude et la calomnie, et si lamentable, que les chiens eux-mêmes . . . en auraient pitié' (ibid., p. 111).

The failure of Columbus's life, at least the lack of appropriate recognition of his achievements is due to the power of Satan, in his modern shape of freemasonry, as well as to the so-called scientific approach to his discovery. In his very characteristic prose Bloy counterattacks Columbus's enemies, or should one say persecutors, and through them the 'scientific' spirit of his age, so distasteful to him: 'Les bouviers d'ignominie durent affluer en ces pâturages. . . . Les savantasses pharisiens de la bibliographie, les scribes du pédantisme universitaire, les princes des prêtres de la cuistrerie voltairienne et les sycophantes académiciens du diable accoururent à ce Mécène [count of Veragua, descendant of Columbus] de leur turpitude et s'abattirent autour de lui comme les cantharides de la mort autour d'un cadavre' (*Christophe Colomb devant les taureaux*, p. 4).

Although Bloy did not consider history in the light of time but of eternity, he saw the significance of Columbus's epoch. He still inherited 'la ferveur militante du Moyen-Age' (*Le Révélateur du globe*, 2e partie) but it ended with him. He was also 'Messager d'une terre nouvelle et de nouveaux cieux' (*Le Révélateur du globe*, 1ère partie), with him the Renaissance begins and the Reformation is close at hand. Here Claudel meets his predecessor; although the picture drawn of the Renaissance is much more evident in *Le Soulier de satin* than in *Le Livre de Christophe Colomb*.

Le Livre de Christophe Colomb, although clearly under the influence of Bloy and indirectly of Roselly, strikes a very different note. Apart from the dramatic form, in fact it includes a range of arts, music, cinema, dancing and the spoken word, Claudel's presentation is realistic in spite of the symbolic undercurrent. It is a play of hope, of fulfilment (if one considers it *sub specie aeternitatis*, the only possible way of reading any of his works) in the face of enormous material difficulties. At a certain level Claudel's Columbus reminds one of Lamartine's *homme de génie*. Claudel, unlike Roselly and Bloy, is no apologist, he never idealizes his hero; he sees him as carrying out a special mission, 'l'ambassadeur de Dieu', but 'aux prises avec les créanciers, les courtisans, les pédants, les jaloux et les railleurs' ('Le drame et la musique,' p. 33). The dramatic account of Columbus's life is presented in a kind of *dédoublement* whereby the hero is at once actor and judge of his own destiny: *Christophe Colomb II* looks at *Christophe Colomb I* until in the penultimate scene the dying, almost destitute old man joins his other self at the threshold of eternity.

The life of Columbus, as it unfolds from the fifth scene onwards, is throughout submitted to the scrutiny of the chorus, the *Défenseur* and the *Opposant*. These two figures, the one defending the cause of Columbus, the other attacking him in the name of Ferdinand and Isabella, are no doubt borrowed from the procedure of canonisation, although no reference is made. The *Opposant* has everything of the Devil's advocate when he addresses Columbus (p. 52) as 'charlatan, ignorant, halluciné, marchand d'esclaves, menteur, révolté, incapable, calomniateur!' The chorus, as Claudel explains in the prefatory essay, 'Le drame et la musique', lends the play something of its character of 'drame universel'; 'Ce n'est plus le chœur du drame antique.... Ou plutôt c'est ce même chœur, tel que l'Église après le triomphe du Christianisme l'invita à pénétrer dans l'édifice sacré et à se faire intermédiare entre le prêtre et le peuple, l'un *officiant* et l'autre *officiel*. Entre la foule muette et le drame qui se développe à la scène, et, si je peux dire, à l'autel, il y avait besoin d'un truchement officiellement constitué' (pp. 34–5). The chorus, whilst occasionally assuming a liturgical character as in the recital of the *De profundis* in the fifth scene of the second part, represents something of the *vox populi* as well as the *vox Dei*. It also underlines the human circumstances of the drama: Columbus is seen as struggling with his own particular vocation, as any other man might be with his. He has ceased to be the — unsuccessful — candidate for beatification; his life is a struggle with society as much as with himself. As P.A.M. Carré points out in his article 'La Vocation de l'autre monde', in *Cahiers de la Compagnie Madeleine Renaud — J. L. Barrault*, 1, 1954, 'Christophe Colomb est chacun d'entre nous', all of us who have, in Claudel's words 'la vocation de l'Autre Monde'. Columbus is destined to struggle with the mediocrity of life, as it surrounds us, without ever receiving the reward he deserves.

Anyone familiar with the work of Claudel will immediately be reminded of so many other characters of his plays in whom the idea of a vocation is similarly exemplified. Claudel always stresses the two aspects of every human life, the earthly and the eternal; sometimes, as in *Partage de midi*, the hero only discovers at the end of the play the meaning of *his* vocation that had so far been obscure to him. Rodrigue in *Le Soulier de satin*, perhaps closest to Columbus as a Claudelian character, is almost entirely absorbed by the enormous human task before him. The play is dramatically framed by the indication of Rodrigue's eternal destiny, for which the dying Jesuit Father offers up his last prayer. But perhaps nowhere else in Claudel's dramatic work can we see the close intertwining of the two planes of man's life throughout the play. Columbus is aware of his divine mission as well as the material circumstances of his task from the beginning. This other dimension of Claudel's theatre, the transcendental, is dramatically heightened by the *dédoublement* of the main character of which we have spoken earlier. As the last scene of the play is set 'au paradis de l'idée' where Columbus will find his fulfilment: '. . . il [atteint] enfin ce que les deux ailes de son désir cherchaient, vous, ô Portes Eternelles!', we have an almost visual picture of the two dimensions.[18] The medieval division of the stage into the mansions representing this life and the hereafter is replaced by modern scenic devices, such as the screen which is used for the very same purpose.

Although Claudel's interpretation is free from the somewhat extravagant special pleading of Bloy and Roselly and rather closer to Leo XIII's letter, yet the symbolism of the names acts as a *leitmotiv* throughout the play. It is introduced early in the play in the second scene, 'Prière', by the *Explicateur* who acts as a commentator of the book: 'je dis la vie de cet homme prédestiné dont le nom signifie Colombe et Porte-Christ. . . .' It receives its full significance in the last scene where Claudel uses a double symbolism: 'colombe' is the dove of the flood, Genesis, viii, 9–11, and the 'columba' of the Song of Songs. In fact here Claudel brings together several aspects of the play: the Christian symbolism of the dove[19] and man's redemption through a woman (Isabella). Human love and divine love become identical, as the chorus sings at the end of the play: 'Veni, Columba ad Columbam!' Elsewhere in the play Claudel widens the meaning of 'colombe' to include the idea of enthusiasm, inspiration, which he had endeavoured to analyse in the *Cinq grandes odes*. Columbus II addresses

[18] 'Et ce qui était réel dans l'Eternité est infiniment plus réel que ce qui est réel sur la carte,' (p. 47), is Columbus's comment to posterity.

[19] The dove is frequently used in Christian symbolism for Christ, alternatively with the fish and the lamb, for the Holy Spirit, as a symbol for peace and wisdom (cf. *Catholicisme: Hier Aujourd'hui Demain*, article 'Colombe'); the *Encyclopaedia Biblica*, article 'Dove', lists all the references, the most significant of which, after Genesis xv, 9, is Matthew iii, 16.

himself to Columbus I, as the dove flies across the stage: 'ah! je suis vieux, mais je sens dans mes veines la même flamme, le même enthousiasme!' It is the driving force not only of the poet but of every human action, as Claudel says elsewhere: 'Rien de grand ne s'est fait, avoue Voltaire — Voltaire lui-même! — sans un peu d'enthousiasme.'

The fusion of the theme of the dove-Columbus, and of Columbus's redemption through Isabella, takes place early in the play, when the dove explains to Isabella, after the defeat of the Moors, her new role as the instrument of salvation for the people across the sea. She is reminded of a certain ring which she had attached to the foot of a dove; this ring comes into the possession of Columbus who, instead of returning it to his sovereign at the end of his life, sends her his old mule, now richly adorned, on which she is to ride across the carpet prepared by him, the carpet that is America. The ring is no doubt a symbol for the close relationship between the queen and her subject whose purpose and vocation she alone fully understands. But are we really to interpret their relationship as 'une relation amoureuse', as M. J. Madaule indicates in his article 'Le poète dramatique' (La Table ronde, April, 1955, p. 84)? It seems rather that Claudel has, in this last play, stripped his characters of a relationship that brings such unbearable suffering to some, as in Le Soulier de satin or in L'Otage, or is an occasion of sin to others, as in Partage de midi. It is true that Isabella sends a last message to the dying Columbus: . . . 'dis-lui que je l'aime et qu'il me rende mon anneau'. But surely this is hardly anything other than the affection she bears for one she calls 'mon frère Christophe Colomb', as she is about to enter eternity. There seems something serene about Le Livre de Christophe Colomb, free as it is precisely of that human relationship whereby, in almost all of Claudel's plays, ill suited partners are driven together and true lovers separated in this life. It seems in another way, too, to stand at the end of a long series of works which more or less explicitly reflect Claudel's own search for his vocation. This search for the meaning of his life, as a poet, as a Christian, as a diplomat (his place in society) haunted his early work; later he projected some of it into a distant historical period (as in the cycle beginning with L'Otage) or indeed into Le Soulier de satin. But Columbus had always doggedly clung to his vocation, he was not unsure of himself, he only had to suffer through the lack of understanding of others. Claudel says in Conversations dans le Loir-et-Cher (contemporary with the composition of Le Livre de Christophe Colomb): 'Si la Terre est un seul temple consacré à la gloire de Dieu, la première chose est de le réunir . . . d'y apporter la croix' and he visualizes 'toute la terre comme un temple unique'. This corresponds closely to the scene entitled 'La Vocation de Christophe Colomb', where Columbus II says: 'Oui! . . . l'Humanité qu'il faut réunir, l'œuvre de Dieu qu'il faut achever. ....' This is the one clear purpose of the hero throughout the play and it is in this sense that he exemplifies each one of us. Columbus is not the seeker of an ideal or an idea, but he fulfils the purpose of his life. His achievement would seem, on the part of Claudel, a final and decisive answer to a problem that had always remained with him. Into Columbus he was able to project the solution. It is true that Columbus reaches his goal only through suffering, frustration, even apparent failure and gains nothing but the ingratitude of all men. If Claudel uses the figure of Columbus to exemplify man's destiny, he also shows him precisely as a follower of Christ who will receive his [eternal] life through this redemptive suffering. Columbus represents the Christian way of life.

But the play is by no means confined to the figure of Columbus and those around him. The world into which he is to penetrate in order to win it for Christ is seen in its original, unredeemed state. The scene entitled 'Les Dieux barattent la mer' serves as a key to one of the philosophical aspects of the play. The ultimate purpose of the play is the redemption of a continent in which Columbus is merely an instrument. The treatment of the pagan world is farcical, it is a piece of buffoonery; unlike the sixteenth century *conquistadores* who saw in the false gods of the Aztecs manifestations of the Devil,[20] Claudel destroys the world of Aztec civilisation by ridicule. He sees them as 'dieux de sang et de ténèbres' who will be shaken out of a hitherto comfortable existence ('Ah! on était si confortable depuis la création du monde dans cette belle Amérique!'). Their names are distorted to make them even more clown-like. M. J. Soustelle (in his capacity as ethnologist) takes Claudel to task, rectifies the misstatements and corrects the names (*Cahiers de la Compagnie Madeleine Renaud* — J. L. *Barrault*, I, pp. 97 sqq.) under the title 'Respects aux Dieux morts', or rather respect for an old civilisation. There is no doubt that M. Soustelle pleads on behalf of scientific truth, but he does not see Claudel's point which is to represent the truth of God.[21] Claudel evokes the kind of *Goetterdaemmerung* which is about to take place, in the words of the *Appariteur*: 'Arrivez ici! . . . les dieux de la racine et de la feuille! les dieux

[20] Cortés said of them: 'no son dioses sino cosas malas que se llaman diablos'.

[21] Columbus answers the *Opposant* (scene 6) who accuses him: 'Il ne savait pas ce qu'il avait découvert.' 'Je savais beaucoup plus que vous ne savez!' It is of course a different kind of knowledge. It ought perhaps be added that, as we were not concerned with the geographical and scientific aspect of the discovery, the literature on the subject, considerable in recent years, was not taken into account. The most interesting studies are no doubt: S. E. Morrison, *Christopher Columbus, Admiral of the Ocean Sea*, O.U.P., 1945, and the scholarly edition of the English translation of the *Journal of Christopher Columbus*, by C. Jane, revised by L. A. Vigneras, London, 1960. The authors who came under discussion here used the figure of Columbus to express their *Weltanschauung*.

de la cendre et de la bouillie . . . les camarades à becs de perroquets et de tapirs . . . la danse monstrueuse de l'Antarctique!' The contrast between the symbolism of the dove as the manifestation of the spirit of God, and the absurd and cruel deities who appear under the name of *Vitzliputzli* and *Huichtlipochtli* is quite deliberate. For Claudel the manifestation of divine truth and the redemption of a whole continent supersede all merely human feelings.

If the Columbus of Lamartine was 'un homme de génie', the Columbus of Roselly and Bloy an unacknowledged saint, the Columbus of Claudel is a man (and Claudel refers to him as 'un homme seul avec toutes les voix de la mer, du ciel et de la nature autour de lui'[22]) who gives himself completely to the task entrusted to him by God. It may have been a unique vocation by its very scope and impact, but Claudel wanted to convey that every Christian vocation is a unique one. Columbus seems the Claudelian character who has triumphed over all his other dramatic figures.[23]

[22] *Correspondance Paul Claudel — Darius Milhaud,* letter of 17th December 1927, *Cahiers Paul Claudel,* 3, Gallimard, 1961.

[23] A recent article by Weston Flint, 'Colón en el teatro español,' in *Estudios Americanos,* vol. XXII, no. 3, Nov.-Dec. 1961, outlines the history of the treatment of the Columbus theme in the Spanish theatre. In a concluding paragraph (pp. 185–6) the author refers to Claudel's play which, in his opinion, includes all the elements of the Columbus story. The article seems to be taken from the author's thesis, *The Figure of C. Columbus in French, Italian and Spanish drama,* University of North Carolina, 1957, which has come to my notice too late to be discussed in this article.

9

RICHARD N. COE

Stendhal and the Art of Memory

HENRI BEYLE was one of the most inveterate autobiographers in the history of literature. From the early volumes of the *Journal*, begun when he was scarcely more than a first-year student at the École Polytechnique, to the *Souvenirs d'Égotisme*, the *Vie de Henry Brulard* and the innumerable marginal scribblings and jottings which marked the closing period of his life, he wrote unceasingly about himself. In consequence, we know at least as much about the consul and the exile, the lover and the dandy as we know about the writer — so much so, in fact, that for some of the greatest *stendhaliens*, the man in the long run has come to overshadow the novelist. Indeed it is all too easy, in reading the two notable volumes of Henri Martineau's *Cœur de Stendhal*, for instance, or even Professor Del Litto's monumental *Vie intellectuelle de Stendhal*, to overlook altogether the fact that this same Henri Beyle who lived and travelled and jotted was also the author who conceived *Le Rouge et le Noir* and *La Chartreuse de Parme*, and that, were it not for these, all the rest of what he wrote, and all that he was, might very likely have been forgotten. The earliest generation of *stendhaliens* discussed the works with little reference to the man; their successors, inspired by the exemplary scholarship of Paul Arbelet, studied the man and sometimes forgot about the works. It seems now to have fallen to the lot of the latest generation to follow in the footsteps of Jean Prévost and to attempt a synthesis. These recent critics — Georges Blin and Jean-Pierre Richard among others — have not merely aimed at a rather more balanced perspective; they have realised that the almost inexhaustible store of knowledge which we possess concerning the particular man whose name was Henri Beyle offers an unrivalled opportunity for trying to solve that most intriguing and elusive of all problems: the relationship between the writer and his work.

How much of Stendhal's actual experience, in fact, was embodied directly or indirectly in his novels? In the terminology of the textbooks, Stendhal is classified as a 'realist', as a 'subjective writer', and as one of the pioneering theorists of French romanticism. Yet no writer more consistently defeats the customary definitions. Was it a 'realist' who wrote *La Chartreuse*? And what are we to make of the self-confessed 'romantic' of

Racine et Shakspeare or of the *Vie de Rossini* who preferred the eighteenth century to the nineteenth, who deliberately modelled his style on Montesquieu, Helvétius and the Président de Brosses, who detested Madame de Staël and who considered Lamartine, as a poet, distinctly inferior to Béranger? Or of the 'subjective' novelist who adhered all his life to the belief, inherited from Cabanis and Destutt de Tracy, that truth could only be apprehended through the severe discipline of objective scientific analysis? Clearly there is no simple answer. The metamorphosis of 'reality' into 'literature', of experience into art, in Stendhal's case, is an extremely complex process, and the presence of incidents based *directly* upon personal reminiscence — Julien Sorel's misspelling of the word 'cela', the description of the abbé Blanès in his tower,[1] or the picture of the nail-making industry at Verrières[2] — should not blind us to the fact that even the 'petit fait vrai' rarely has more than a corroborative value; it is an additional detail of evidence added to a general picture whose essential elements are conjured up out of the imagination. The point to remember about the famous opening sequence to *La Chartreuse* is that Stendhal was *not* present at the battle of Waterloo. On the other hand, of course, there is nothing conventionally 'fictitious' about the description, since he had heard and read innumerable accounts of the Waterloo campaign, and had himself taken part in the battle of Bautzen and in the crossing of the Berezina.

Thus the balance between memory and imagination is very delicate indeed, the more so as the most direct 'reminiscences' often relate to events which took place twenty years or more before they found their final place in the novels. The 'cela' incident (*Le Rouge et le Noir*, 1830) dates in reality from Henri Beyle's first contact with Pierre Daru, in January 1800; the idea of disguising Fabrice del Dongo as 'un marchand de baromètres' (*La Chartreuse*, 1839) goes back to Stendhal's reading of Silvio Pellico's *Ser Barometro*,[3] probably in 1817–18 or thereabouts. Again and again, between the man and the novelist, we find this singular time-lag. Henri Beyle, soldier, administrator and dilettante, had to all intents and purposes completed the bulk of his personal experience of life by the time he was

---

[1] Cf. Bruno Pincherle, 'Le R. P. Maurice, ou la Lunette de l'abbé Blanès'. To be published in the *Proceedings* of the *Journée stendhalienne de Paris du 23 mars 1962*.

[2] Based on what Stendhal had observed in the autumn of 1811, passing through Morez on his way to Milan. Vide: *Journal* (ed. Martineau, in the *Œuvres Intimes de Stendhal*, Bibliothèque de la Pléiade, 1955), p. 1111.

[3] *Chartreuse de Parme*, ed. Martineau, Paris (Garnier) 1957, p. 31 et seq.; cf. *Courrier Anglais*, ed. Martineau, Paris (Divan) 1935–36, vol. I, pp. 314–5. Silvio Pellico was arrested for political reasons by the Austrian authorities in October 1820, and sent to the fortress of Spielberg, where he remained until 1830; at the time of his arrest he left *Ser Barometro*, 'un roman très amusant dans le genre du *Gil Blas*,' unfinished. Stendhal can only have had knowledge of it during the period of his acquaintance with Pellico, i.e., during the years 1817–9.

forty; Stendhal the writer was nearing fifty before he turned to the novel. This curious 'gap' is both puzzling and significant, and I would suggest that it is by no means accidental. The transmutation of Beyle into Stendhal raises problems which concern the very essence of the creative imagination and it may be that it is precisely the existence of this 'gap' which offers us the most promising of clues, if we are to hope to understand the meta-morphosis of memory into art.

One thing at least is clear, and that is that Stendhal's imagination was never, in the literal sense of the word, 'creative'. That is to say, he was not capable (save perhaps towards the very end of his life) both of *inventing* his material and of working it — emotionally or technically — into literature. Essentially, he needed to find his basic material waiting for him, ready-fashioned; whereupon his imagination would proceed to organise it and, to use his own term, to 'embroider' it to his own delight and satisfaction. More often than not, he would find his factual material already written down, in books and periodicals — in the assize reports of the trial of Antoine Berthet, for instance, or in Giuseppe Carpani's *Lettere su la Vita e le Opere del celebre Maestro Giuseppe Haydn*, or in the *Origine delle Gran-dezze della Famiglia Farnese*, or in Vasari's *Vita dei Pittori* — and in the early stages at least, he borrowed so freely that he was accused, and justifiably so, of straightforward plagiarism. The emotional material of his novels, on the other hand, he found largely in his own experience, and here the process, while still essentially one of transposition and embroidery, is very much more complex. For, ultimately, the mainspring of much of Stend-hal's greatest writing is an attempt to relive a vanished emotional experi-ence and to annihilate absolutely the passage of time.

The nearer one comes to the heart of Stendhal's creative processes, the closer appear his affinities with Proust. His problems are simpler than those which inspired *À la Recherche du Temps Perdu*, but essentially they are the same problems. Nor, as we shall see, does it seem to be a mere coincidence that both writers were fascinated by the evocative powers of music, and that both found their deepest satisfactions in art. Both are profoundly con-cerned with the problem of time; both are dissatisfied with the results achieved by the mental process usually known as memory; both are obsessed with the need to re-create in time a total experience which — apparently — has vanished irretrievably and for ever. But whereas, if we attempt to discover the nature of those fundamental experiences which Proust was trying to recapture, we find a disparate multitude of pheno-mena, insignificant and unimpressive in themselves, but endowed with meaning by the basic fact of having been experienced by the particular 'moi' — in time or out of time — that was Proust, in the case of Stendhal we find a rather more coherent type of raw material. The categories of experience which Stendhal is trying to 'relive' can, in fact, be reduced to three in number: the experience of love; the experience of nature, or, more specifically, of landscape; and the experience of a certain type of freedom. The first of these is that which is chiefly involved with the problem of time; the second, with space;[4] the third, the most complex of the three, implying as it does the evolution of the self in the context of a whole society and a whole code of manners, inspires the ultimate fashioning of an idealised Italy, from medieval Florence with its 'energy' to modern Milan with its 'bonhomie', and lies beyond the scope of this present study.

For Stendhal, there is no 'problem of time' in so many words; there is, however, constantly present a 'problem of memory', which, in the long run, comes to the same thing. For as early as 1802 (when he was 19), but more especially in the autumn of 1805, we find Stendhal in his diaries and his letters completely haunted by his failure to relive his more vivid experiences through the normal processes of memory. To begin with, there is the fact that Stendhal possessed, or at any rate claimed to possess, an unusually bad memory, at least as far as everyday reality was concerned. 'Je n'ai pas de mémoire de faits' is a constant refrain throughout his life, for all that we may suspect a certain amount of deliberation behind this assertion, since, for Stendhal, the simple 'accumulation of facts' — as opposed to the careful selection of 'les petits faits vrais' — was a dreary and stultifying process, and he took good care *not* to remember more than was necessary. Still, even assuming that he possessed a moderately competent 'memory for facts', he could not remember *all* the facts, and it was the totality of the facts which constituted the experience. Very rapidly, the memory of the facts would decay, and the emotional experience would decay along with it. On the other hand, the nature of factual perception and the nature of emotional experience were as different from each other for Stendhal as, for Descartes, matter was different from mind; and he soon discovered that the very process — essentially intellectual — of trying to memorise the facts actually *destroyed* the experience itself. Either way, therefore, the experience was lost.

This early discovery is so significant in the light of Stendhal's later development, that it is worth looking at in greater detail. One of Stendhal's 'moments de bonheur suprême' at this time was a walk in the fields at Montfuront, in the neighbourhood of Marseille, with Mélanie Guilbert.[5]

---

[4]Vide: the author's 'Quelques Réflexions sur Stendhal Paysagiste', to be published in the *Proceedings* of the *Journée stendhalienne de Paris*.

[5] *Journal*, 17 brumaire XIV (8th November 1805). Ed. Pléiade, pp. 754 et seq.

Immediately, in his diaries, we find him faced with the manifold problems of retaining this experience, of defending it against decay in time. Filling out to some extent his own analysis of the experience, we can discover four primary elements which constitute its 'total reality': there is the fact of his love for Mélanie, without which all the rest would be meaningless; there is the 'pure' emotional experience in Stendhal's mind; there is a certain displacement of his 'moi' in space in relation to other objects; and finally there are the material facts — the fields, the ditch, the 'pommier (petit) sous lequel nous avons déjeuné', the words spoken, the contours and colours observed. Now, essentially, these four are inseparable; they cannot exist apart, only as a totality do they constitute an experience in time and space as Stendhal felt and knew it; any one taken separately is *not* the total experience, is nothing.

So that, since all are given significance in the first place by the fact of love for a particular person, it would seem that, once that love had withered, the experience was dead for all time. That this *could* happen is shown some three years later, in a letter to Pauline Beyle, when Stendhal discovers a whole experience to have been annihilated by the evaporation of the love he had felt for its central figure — in this instance, Adèle Rebuffel:

> Je m'aperçois d'une chose assez triste: en perdant une passion, on y perd peu à peu le souvenir des plaisirs qu'elle a donnés. Je t'ai conté qu'étant à Frascati, à un joli feu d'artifice, au moment de l'explosion, Adèle s'appuya un instant sur mon épaule; je ne puis t'exprimer combien je fus heureux. Pendant deux ans, quand j'étais accablé de chagrin, cette image me redonnait du courage et me faisait oublier tous les malheurs. Je l'avais oubliée depuis longtemps; j'ai voulu y repenser aujourd'hui. Je vois malgré moi Adèle telle qu'elle est; mais, tel que je suis, il n'y a plus le moindre bonheur dans le souvenir.[6]

This might seem the simple, if disappointing, answer to the whole problem; but in fact it is not so, for Stendhal was one of those happy people who are seldom completely out of love with any woman they have once really cared for — as is evidenced by the cluster of initials which he scraped nostalgically in the dust with his stick one day beside Lake Albano. More especially is this true after the Angelina Bereyter episode, for if, up to that time, the women he had loved had been fairly worthless (not excluding the Countess Daru), later on he was far less easily satisfied (Angelina having contrived to disillusion him for ever with sex for its

---

[6] *Correspondance*, vol. III, ed. Martineau (Le Divan, 1933), pp. 27–8, letter to Pauline Beyle of 26th March 1808.

own sake), and the women he loved tended to be not only more intelligent, but strong and even violent personalities in their own right. Angelina herself he had probably ceased to love by June 1812:

> Il y avait depuis *six weeks* un vide *in my heart. A passion who lived in it since two years* est morte tout à coup vers le 13 du mois passé *by the sight of the mediocrity of the object*;[7]

but Métilde Dembowski-Viscontini he never ceased to love, nor the Countess Curial, nor 'Madame Azur', nor Giulia Rinieri, nor perhaps even Mélanie Guilbert.

Consequently, the primary element in the experience — the fact of love — *can* be revived; Stendhal *can*, given the right circumstances, actually live through once again, twenty or thirty years later, his experience of love for a particular woman. On the other hand, it is equally evident that this particular aspect of reliving a past emotional experience is passive; it cannot come into being of its own accord, still less can it call into being anything else. It must be revived by some outside agency; it cannot be reconstituted at will.

No more so, obviously, can the second element involved — the 'sentiment pur' of a particular 'mouvement d'âme'. Here Stendhal is categoric. This is the core of the experience itself; it is overwhelming, it verges on the mystic — it is an *angoisse* and a joy of the spirit . . . but essentially it is an abstraction, almost a Beckettian *Unnamable*, there are no words for it, no images to reveal it, no precise and identifiable sensations — and consequently *no memories*. 'On n'a pas de souvenirs des sensations pures,' he notes in the *Journal* on 8th September 1811;[8] and ten days later again: 'J'éprouve bien que ce qui est sentiment pur ne laisse pas de souvenirs'.[9]

This means that, setting aside for the moment the movement of the 'moi' in space, the reliving of a vital emotional experience now depends exclusively on Stendhal's ability to memorise the brute material facts which constituted its setting — a process at which, as we have seen, he was notoriously incompetent, and which, moreover, he despised. The only remedy for a memory thus afflicted was to write down immediately after the event those facts which he desired to remember — and here it became straight away apparent that the cure was more fatal than the disease. 'Si je n'écris pas, j'oublie tout',[10] he notes in the *Journal*, and elsewhere, 'Il faut que j'écrive, de peur (. . .) d'oublier (. . .)'.[11] But to submit a total experience

---

[7] *Correspondance*, vol. IV (1934), pp. 52–3, letter to Pauline Beyle of 14th July 1812.
[8] *Journal*, 8th September 1811. Ed. Pléiade, p. 1116.
[9] Ibid., 20th September 1811, p. 1144.
[10] Ibid.
[11] Ibid., 8th September 1811, p. 1115.

to the slow intellectual process of analysis, selection, organisation and partial memorising, as though it were a school-book lesson in history — and someone else's history at that — was actively and irrevocably to damage and destroy the whole experience, so that the attempt even to preserve it, let alone to re-create it, achieved nothing but its immediate annihilation. And rather than submit to this, Stendhal was prepared to stop writing altogether and for ever. 'Je cesse de décrire, parce que j'ai observé que je *gâtais* mes souvenirs',[12] he notes in 1805; and six years later he is still worrying away at the same problem: 'Si je décris mon sentiment, je me fais de la peine'.[13] That this was still true later is demonstrated by evidence still more incontrovertible, for, of the greatest emotional experience of his life, the 'grande phrase musicale' of his love for Métilde Dembowski-Viscontini, which lasted from 1818 to 1821, that indefatigable scribbler Henri Beyle has left us scarcely a single line.

In fact, as early as 1805, Stendhal had already discovered that there were two kinds of memory: that which is direct, analytical and rational and consists of recording and memorising facts, and 'la mémoire sensible' — the Proustian 'involuntary memory' — which is the far more delicate and complex process of reliving an experience *in toto*. The former he mistrusts progressively more and more all his life, so that in the end it comes to symbolise the diametrical opposite of all that he values; it is the enemy of 'l'imagination' and of 'le génie', the stultifier of 'la sensibilité', the destroyer of creativity and inspiration. Before long, moreover, this type of memory, 'la mémoire des faits', is linked with erudition, which similarly he holds in unspeakable contempt — witness his tirades against Berton, that 'learned musician', in the *Vie de Rossini*, or the cascades of epithets he unloads upon the erudite Monsignore Majo, of the Vatican Library, whose sole offence it was to have invented the art of deciphering palimpsests.[14] To his contempt for memorising also we may attribute the chronic inaccuracy which is so characteristic of his critical work, as he reveals with disarming candour in a late marginal jotting on the fly-leaf of a copy of the *Histoire de la Peinture en Italie*:

> Le travail de l'érudition lui faisant perdre absolument le peu d'oreille qu'il a reçu de la nature, Dominique a écrit de mémoire, sauf à vérifier les faits[15]

— the latter qualification, by the way, being more in the nature of wishful

---

[12] Ibid., 9 thermidor XIII (28th July 1805), p. 741.
[13] Ibid., 20th September 1811, p. 1144.
[14] *Rome, Naples et Florence* (ed. Champion, 1919), vol. I, p. 279.
[15] *Histoire de la Peinture en Italie* (ed. Champion, 1924), vol. I, pp. 295–6.

thinking than anything else. Similarly to his fear of memorising we must attribute the striking absence of any description of remembered scenes in his novels, even when, as in *La Chartreuse*, the story is set precisely among those landscapes which he loved better than any in the world:

> Dès que je cherche le moins du monde à me souvenir, mon talent diminue. Il diminue en proportion de l'embarras des sources; s'il en faut combiner deux ou trois, je suis perdu.[16]

On the other hand, the fact remains that, not only did Stendhal's 'souvenirs' continue to furnish the most valuable and spiritually exalting part of his experience, but further, that without them, he could not create. They were the emotional raw material, which subsequently he could 'embroider' with his own art, or which, alternatively, could be used to fashion the 'embroidery' upon another element of experience — upon a piece of music, for example:

> Mes sentiments *brodent* sur un chant ce qui, d'après la passion dominante, peut faire le plus de plaisir à mon âme (. . .) Tout ce qui est médiocre n'intéresse plus mon coeur, le pouvoir de broder cesse et l'ennui apparaît. Si je perdais toute l'imagination, je perdrais peut-être en même temps mon goût pour la musique.[17]

This passage from the *Journal* of 1811 is remarkable as furnishing one of the earliest illustrations of the working of Stendhal's creative imagination. In this particular instance, it is the music which is 'embroidered' by the 'sentiments' in relation to the 'passion dominante'; but, as we shall see, the 'passion dominante' is just as likely to be an emotion re-created out of the past as it is to be a 'live' emotion experienced in the present. Thus we arrive at the harsh paradox which seems to have preoccupied Stendhal for the better part of ten years (1801–11): he was unable to create except by using material derived from his own past emotional experience, while at the same time, any active process of memorising promptly killed both the emotion and the creative ability. By 1811, it was quite clear to Stendhal that what he needed to develop was a special technique for re-creating and reliving past experience without recourse to any conscious effort of memorising.

It would be almost pathetic, were it not so fascinating, to watch Stendhal's struggles with the problems of preserving and reliving experience, particularly during the Mélanie Guilbert episode of 1805. In the instance

[16] *Journal*, 1 July 1814. Ed. Pléiade, p. 1292.
[17] Ibid., 31 August 1811, p. 1102.

referred to earlier, we find him reduced — significantly — to using the one remaining element of the experience — the relation of the 'moi' to its context in space — in order to preserve what he can of the totality, and his *Journal* at this stage is strewn (as is later the *Vie de Henry Brulard*) with rough and exasperated sketch-maps which show the *locality* of the 'moment de bonheur suprême', all else having failed absolutely.

The next crisis in this 'art of reminiscence' came in 1811, and the reason may easily be guessed. The greatest emotional experience hitherto in Stendhal's life had been his first journey into Lombardy in 1800–1, combining as it did all three major emotional elements — love, landscape and Italy. Much of this experience he had been striving to relive, with a greater or lesser degree of success, through memory ever since. In 1811, however, he returned to Italy, rediscovered Milan and its society, and at last became the lover of that same Angela Pietragrua whom he had last seen ten years earlier. The problem was now as follows: when an experience has been — more or less — relived in memory, what is the relationship between this experience *relived*, and the same, or at least a very similar experience *renewed*? The results were discouraging in the extreme. Each, in fact, helped to kill the other. On the one hand, if at any point the renewed experience failed to correspond in every particular with the memory of it (and Angela failed very seriously to correspond with Stendhal's idealised version of her), then the memory of the past could leave nothing but regret. All he could feel now was what he had formerly felt on attempting to re-read La Fontaine: 'Cela me touchait autrefois (. . .)'.[18] But there was worse, for he now noticed for the first time that any deliberate cult of a 'memory' would actually destroy any attempt to renew the experience in reality. From 1811 onwards, this becomes a recurrent theme in Stendhal's writing, growing almost into an obsession in the years 1822–3, and forming an important background to his critical writing. In the opening pages of the *Vie de Rossini*, for instance, we find:

> La musique n'a d'effet que par l'imagination. Or il est une chose qui paralyse sûrement l'imagination, c'est la *mémoire*. A l'instant qu'en entendant un bel air, je me rappelle les *illusions* et le *petit roman* qu'il avait fait naître en moi à la dernière fois que j'en fus ravi, tout est perdu, mon imagination est glacée, et la musique n'est plus une fée toute-puissante sur mon coeur.[19]

This theme recurs in one form or another in almost every chapter, so that,

[18] Ibid, 23rd September 1806, p. 857.
[19] *Vie de Rossini* (ed. Champion, 1922), vol. I, p. 16.

some 250 pages later, for instance, we find almost the identical words:

> Et vous savez que rien ne coupe les ailes à l'imagination comme
> l'appel à la mémoire (. . .)[20]

It is probably this same experience with memory which is responsible
for one of the odder features of Stendhal's critical work, namely, his cult
of *novelty*, almost at any cost, and despite such contradictory evidence as
his own life-long passion for Mozart and Shakespeare. For him, Paris was
the capital of the universe, for there and there alone could a man be certain
of acquiring 'quatre idées nouvelles par jour'; yet paradoxically, he also
sees this cult of novelty as one of the features of his idealised Italy:

> J'ai tiré du maître à musique [de Livia B . . . , à Ancône] la con-
> firmation entière d'une idée à moi. *Bisogna novità pella musica*. Voilà
> en Italie une règle sans exception, et qui s'accorde très bien avec la
> sensibilité de ce peuple né pour les arts.
>
> Si l'on donnait un opéra de Cimarosa (. . .), à la première mesure de
> chaque air tout le monde le reconnaîtrait, et l'opéra ne pourrait
> durer (. . .)[21]

There is no need, obviously, to stress the importance of this idea, particularly in relation to the romantic theories of 'genius' and 'originality'.
But 'la nouveauté', while it avoids the encumbrances of a memorised and
stultifying past, is obviously unsatisfactory in itself as a creative principle
— paradoxically, for the very reason that it carries over *nothing* from the
past, and therefore is unrelated to those 'sensations sublimes' which caused
Stendhal to create. The past relived, let it be said once again, is the basis of
Stendhal's creative imagination; and as early as 1802, when he was working
on his abortive epic, *La Pharsale*, he noted, with a phenomenal prevision
of his own later development: 'Les choses nouvelles ne sont point tou-
chantes, car elles n'ont point de souvenirs'.[22] So once again we are back
with the same problem: if there are two completely distinct ways of
recalling the past, namely memorising ('la mémoire des faits') and *reliving*
('la mémoire sensible'), how are we to call the latter into being, preferably
at will, without interference from the former?

The discovery of the solution began during Stendhal's period of office
as a Napoleonic administrator in Germany in 1806, but the main 'programme of research' (if one may so call it) into the techniques of reliving
the past was carried out between 1811 and 1821. The 'mémoire sensible',

---

[20] Ibid., vol. I, p. 254.
[21] *Journal*, 19th October 1811. Ed. Pléiade, p. 1197.
[22] *Mélanges de Littérature* (ed. Martineau, Le Divan), vol. I, p. 332.

Stendhal came gradually to realise, could not be called into being directly, nor by any immediate effort of will; but it could be conjured up through the agency of a catalyst, and this catalyst was invariably *art*. All types of art were potential catalysts in this respect, but for Stendhal some were more powerful than others, and each had its own prescribed function. For the 'sensation pure' of love, the catalyst was primarily music; for emotions derived from landscape and the sense of space, the catalyst was painting (*not*, however, let it be noticed, landscape painting: no more here than in music is there any question of direct, 'affective' association); for the experience of freedom, there is something to be gained from poetry (Byron, Dante, Shakespeare, or the dialect poets of Milan), much from history (Sismondi, the Italian chroniclers, the *Mémorial de Sainte-Hélène*, the *Mémoires* of Retz, Besenval, etc.), perhaps something also from the ballet, at least from the choreography of Salvatore Viganò. But we must conclude further: for not only was this *one* of the functions of art, it was *the* function of art, it *was* artistic experience. In other words, art, for Stendhal, was not in itself a primary object of, or occasion for, emotion; it was invariably a means to an end, and this end was the evocation of the 'mémoire sensible', or the reliving in the present of the 'sensations pures' of past experience.

(Let it be stated here, in parenthesis, that this does not mean — as critics have all too often asserted — that Stendhal's art-criticism, considered as such, is worthless. Far from it. In general, only the greatest art could fulfil the function which Stendhal demanded of it, and the elements of art capable of evoking past emotion were so complex, so totally unrelated to direct association,[23] and so immediately dependent upon a super-refined aesthetic sensibility, that Stendhal's reactions to art, and above all to painting, are usually valid as pure aesthetic criticism, even though pure aesthetic experience is not their object.)

Some warning such as this is necessary if we are not to read too much aesthetic incompetence into the sort of statement which Stendhal was constantly making concerning the nature of art, such as this one which comes from a letter to the Baron de Mareste in 1818:

> Mon thermomètre est ceci: quand une musique me jette dans les hautes pensées sur le sujet qui m'occupe, quel qu'il soit, cette musique est excellente pour moi (. . .) Toute musique qui me laisse penser à *la musique* est médiocre pour moi.[24]

[23] There are, of course, occasional unhappy exceptions — cf. Stendhal's raptures over Baron Steuben's painting, *La Mort de Napoléon*, in *Courrier anglais* (ed. Martineau, Le Divan), vol. III, pp. 464–5.

[24] *Correspondance*, vol. V, p. 114, letter to Mareste of 21st March 1818.

From this quotation, it would appear that *any* subject can become the material for 'high thoughts' under the influence of music; but elsewhere it is made abundantly clear that almost all Stendhal's major experiences of great music are concerned with reliving past emotions in the present. For the exceptional occasions where he notes that music had the effect of making him concentrate upon problems of style, or even upon 'le moyen d'armer les Grecs',[25] there are dozens where he observes, as in *Rome, Naples et Florence*, that

> la musique plaît, quand elle place le soir votre âme dans une position où l'amour l'avait déjà placée dans la journée,[26]

or more specifically, as in *De l'Amour*:

> Imaginez une figure de géométrie assez compliquée, tracée avec du crayon blanc sur une grande ardoise: eh bien! je vais expliquer cette figure de géométrie; mais une condition nécessaire, c'est qu'il faut qu'elle *existe déjà* sur l'ardoise: je ne puis la tracer moi-même.[27]

The 'figure traced on the slate' is Stendhal's past emotional experience; the art can 'explain' it, develop it, reconstruct it, but it cannot create it in the first place. This, I would suggest, is the real theme of the *Vie de Rossini*: a re-creation, through music, of the experience of Métilde Dembowski. At this point, moreover, we can glimpse a solution to the paradox concerning 'la nouveauté': 'Les choses nouvelles (. . .) n'ont point de souvenirs'. The art-experience itself does not have to belong to the past in order to be capable of re-evoking that past. If the memory of the past could only be recalled by (say) music which had previously been associated with it, the experience would be valueless:

> Si un air que nous avons entendu il y a dix ans nous fait encore plaisir, c'est d'une autre manière, c'est en nous rappelant les idées agréables dont alors notre imagination était heureuse; mais ce n'est plus en produisant une ivresse nouvelle.[28]

Nor would there be much value if the recalled memory remained that and nothing else — a memory. There may be pleasure of a secondary order in the phenomenon of memory; but it can never represent that 'exaltation' that Stendhal is seeking. The 'ivresse' must specifically be 'nouvelle' — that is, the old emotion has not merely to be recalled through an old,

---

[25] *De l'Amour* (ed. Champion, 1926), vol. I, p. 69.
[26] *Rome, Naples et Florence*, vol. I, p. 81.
[27] *De l'Amour*, vol. II, p. 269.
[28] *Vie de Rossini*, vol. I, p. 18.

associated melody re-heard; it must literally be re-created as a *new* experience, through a *new* aria, a new opera, a new painting. This experience is to be lived through all over again as though it had never been — and yet at the same time it retains the charm and the nostalgia and the familiarity of the old: it becomes 'une chose touchante'. Thus, ideally, the art-medium itself must be new, precisely in order to avoid direct associations from the past — further, it must itself be continually *renewed*, if it is not to breed memory-associations out of its own imaginative evocations. A 'new' aesthetic experience, because it is barren of affective associations, is free to use the power of art to create its own 'memories' out of the *listener's* past experience:

> On ne jouit réellement de la musique que par les rêveries qu'elle inspire. Cet effet magique augmente pendant les huit ou dix premières représentations; ensuite on ne va plus demander que des plaisirs de réminiscence à tel opéra qui autrefois donnait des transports d'admiration (. . .)[29]

What the foregoing suggests is that Stendhal's art-criticism and music-criticism represent an essential stage in the development, not only of his style (which has long been recognised), but also of his creative imagination. Regardless of whether or not this criticism is valid in its own right as an aesthetic statement, its essential function is that it bears witness to Stendhal's discovery of a means for reliving his emotional past, just as, in a similar way, the reliving and refashioning of the emotional experience of Italy can be traced through *Rome, Naples et Florence*, through the *Promenades dans Rome* and through a vast amount of historical reading — a long process of re-assimilation and re-creation which was necessary before it could be creatively exploited in the *Chroniques Italiennes* and the *Chartreuse*. If we accept this hypothesis, then Stendhal's life as a whole assumes a very clear and coherent pattern. From 1800 until 1821 (when he left Milan to return to Paris), he is mainly concerned with *living*, and the bulk of his 'expérience vécue' is accumulated during this time. For a middle period (overlapping in one direction at least: 1814–28) he is involved above all in developing a technique for evoking and exploiting his 'mémoire sensible', and to this epoch belong the majority of his critical and travel writings; and finally, from 1827 until his death, there comes a period of creative activity, when he has discovered how to recover from the past his own emotional experience in sufficiently living and actual a form for his imagination to be able to make use of it.

---

[29] *Notes d'un Dilettante*, in *Vie de Rossini*, vol. II, p. 325.

How, then, is the transition effected from the second stage to the third? I think it will be fairly obvious, from what I have already written about Stendhal's process of 'imaginative embroidery' about a given theme — the way in which his imagination, working in a context of art, creates emotional variations on a pre-existent 'sensation pure' — that this is parallel to, or rather represents a further stage in the process which he termed 'la cristallisation'. In fact, if we study the famous chapters on 'la cristallisation' in *De l'Amour*, it will be seen how closely Stendhal's analysis of the process of 'falling in love' corresponds to his own, much more scattered, analysis of the creative process.

In *De l'Amour*, the prerequisite 'raw material' is present in the form of the chosen woman with her initial physical and mental attraction for him. Upon this primitive material, his imagination proceeds to 'embroider', gradually endowing her with idealised qualities which cling to her and bit by bit conceal the original form altogether — just as in the old mines at Salzburg, where 'la cristallisation du sel recouvre les branches noirâtres d'un rameau avec des diamants si brillants et en si grand nombre, que l'on ne peut plus voir qu'à un petit nombre de places ses branches telles qu'elles sont'.[30] Until, in the end, the lover loves a woman whom he has transformed now entirely with qualities of his own imagining. Is she, or is she not, still the same person? Yes, because beneath the imaginative embroidery, she is there, unchanged, as in the past. No, because the lover's imagination has in fact created *new* attributes for her, and henceforward she, as an image to be loved, as an 'erotic object', to use more modern terminology, is inseparable from those attributes. What is slightly different in *De l'Amour* is the role played by the element of time. The 'real woman' beneath the embroidery *is* present here and now, is still (theoretically at least) as accessible as she was in the past; whereas when music re-creates and endows with additional qualities a 'sensation pure', the original cause and circumstances which brought about that sensation, and thus, in a sense, the original sensation itself, are lost forever; and indeed, the sense of loss is itself one of the additional qualities with which the re-created sensation is now endowed. Strangely enough, in *De l'Amour*, which was Stendhal's most immediate lament for his lost love for 'Méthilde', there is very little sense of loss; whereas in the *Vie de Rossini*, which is that same lament transformed through music, the sense of loss is everywhere. And it is precisely this awareness of a reality that has vanished which takes the process of 'la cristallisation' a stage further.

In fact, throughout the *Vie de Rossini* and, to a lesser extent, throughout the 1826 version of *Rome, Naples et Florence*, the sense of loss is acute and

[30] *De l'Amour*, vol. II, pp. 291–2.

all-pervading. If the 'mémoire sensible', working through music, is able to re-create *in toto* and despite the passage of time an original emotional experience, an awareness of the unreality of that experience is an inseparable part of it in its new form. In this, Stendhal's awareness of the nature of time is, for once, truly and characteristically 'romantic': the pathos arising from the contrast between 'what was', 'what is' and 'what might have been', the muted tragedy of time and change, is one of the hall-marks of the romantic mind, from Young and Ossian, by way of *Le Lac* and *Lorenzaccio*, to its final exaggerated and degenerate form in, typically, J. M. Barrie's *Dear Brutus*. For the romantic mind, this particular awareness of time was in itself a 'sublime' experience; it was 'la douce mélancolie' which, in cruder imaginations, found its expression in Gothic ruins and in antique ivy-mantled towers, but which, for Stendhal, had been incarnated once and for all in the greatest music of all time: that of Mozart. It was the existence of this sense of loss in Mozart's duets and arias which, in the end, raised him to a pinnacle of greatness in Stendhal's estimation, higher than Rossini, higher than Bach or Haydn, higher even than Cimarosa; and in the new reality of the imagination created through music — above all through Mozart's music — 'la mélancolie' forms an additional and now essential attribute:

> C'est quand l'âme a des regrets, c'est durant les premières tristesses des jours d'automne de la vie, c'est quand on voit la méfiance s'élever comme un fantôme funeste derrière chaque haie de la campagne, qu'il est bon d'avoir recours à la musique (. . .) Cet art donne des regrets tendres en la *vue du bonheur*; et faire voir le bonheur, quoique en songe, c'est presque donner de l'espérance (. . .)[31]

But great art is also by definition (or was, at least, in Stendhal's time) beauty; art, therefore, which re-creates in time a past experience, and which further endows that experience with a new and poignant sense of loss, simultaneously transforms this 'douleur' into a thing of beauty in its own right. Where there had been merely a sense of waste, futility and impending death, now (through the transformation of art) there is a 'tristesse regrettante' which, for Stendhal, is the most moving incarnation of 'la mélancolie' (shorn now of every element of 'sécheresse' and 'haine impuissante') and the supreme and ultimate pleasure of 'le souvenir'. In this sense, therefore, an experience relived through art carries with it also the 'crystals' of a higher idealisation: its own sense of loss and its own consolation —

> Pourquoi a-t-on du plaisir à entendre chanter dans le malheur?

---

[31] *Vie de Rossini*, vol. II, pp. 118–9.

C'est que, d'une manière obscure, et qui n'effarouche pas l'*amour propre*, cet art nous fait croire à la pitié chez les hommes: il change la douleur sèche du malheureux en douleur *regrettante*; il fait couler les larmes.[32]

In other words, the re-created experience is *not* completely identical with the original: it carries new and additional elements which increase both its intensity and its poignancy, without in any degree detracting from the old. Art — to summarize the process — first re-evokes a vanished or vanishing emotion; it conjures up the 'mémoire sensible' which re-creates a lost experience, yet stresses the anguish inherent in that loss; and finally, through its own beauty, it transforms 'la douleur sèche' of anguish into a 'tristesse regrettante' which is an additional emotion in itself. Thus, in the process of reviving what existed in the past, it not merely 'creates anew' in the present, but creates an experience of still greater intensity and power than that which existed before. The 'memory' (if that word now still applies) is actually deeper, richer, more fully to be experienced, than the original experience which gave it birth. And one step more: for as, through the medium of art, a *new* experience has been created out of the past, so that experience can now no longer quite be contained within the art which produced it. Being deeper, different, more intense than it was, it will in turn react upon the art, and make a song, a painting — who knows, even a novel — through which at last it can express itself:

> Un jeune Italien, plein d'une passion, après y avoir réfléchi quelque temps en silence, pendant qu'elle est plus poignante, se met à chanter à mi-voix un air de Rossini, et il choisit, sans y songer, parmi les airs de sa connaissance, celui qui a quelque rapport à la situation de son âme; bientôt, au lieu de le chanter à mi-voix, il le chante tout haut, et lui donne, sans s'en douter, l'expression particulière de la nuance de passion qu'il endure. Cet écho de son âme le console; son chant est, si l'on veut, un miroir dans lequel il s'observe; son âme était irrité contre le destin, il n'y avait que la colère; elle va finir par avoir pitié d'elle-même.
>
> A mesure que ce jeune Italien se distrait par son chant, il remarque cette couleur nouvelle qu'il donne à l'air qu'il a choisi; il s'y complaît, il s'attendrit. De cet état d'âme à écrire un air nouveau, il n'y a qu'un pas (. . .)[33]

Perhaps in a manner not wholly dissimilar from that of 'ce jeune Italien'

---

[32] *Rome, Naples et Florence*, vol. II, p. 76.
[33] *Vie de Rossini*, vol. I, pp. 9–10.

were the emotional experiences of Henri Beyle transformed into the novels of Stendhal.

Not, however, without one final crisis. We saw earlier the disastrous results which ensued when an experience memorised unsatisfactorily through the 'mémoire de faits' came into conflict with a similar experience renewed in reality. Both suffered, but what would happen when an experience properly reconstituted through art and the 'mémoire sensible' was set beside a similar experience renewed in reality? That this must have happened in Stendhal's experience during the period 1823-8 seems fairly probable, since his whole life was overshadowed at this time by the memory of 'Méthilde' (who died in 1825), while at the same time he was experiencing a very real love, first for the comtesse Curial, later for Alberthe de Rubempré, whom he called 'Madame Azur'. Unhappily, the *Journal* has ceased by this stage, while his correspondence on the whole reveals very little. So we must go back to an earlier period, when his technique of reviving past experience through art was still in a fairly primitive stage. Nonetheless, even in 1811, the pattern is clear. Art is the only force powerful enough to re-create the 'mémoire sensible'; but as soon as an emotion identical with, or even similar to, the re-created emotion is encountered (a new love, a new landscape), the relived experience pales into insignificance, and at the same time, *all the power of art is lost also*:

> Mes souvenirs étaient charmants, vifs; ils se changèrent en réalité (...) Dès lors, mille petites circonstances qui m'intéressaient à Milan pâlirent. Les cloches, les arts, la musique, tout cela charmant un coeur inoccupé devint fade et nul quand une passion le remplit. (...) Il sera utile pour Mocénigo [i.e., Stendhal's 'moi'] que je me rappelle comme quoi le charme de Milan disparut tout d'un coup, quand les souvenirs devinrent assez forts pour se changer en réalité, et l'explication que j'en donne, par les nombreuses sources de *plaisir de souvenir* qui se trouvèrent taries, aussitôt que je ne vis dans les choses que ce qui pourrait servir ou nuire à ma passion naissante (...)[34]

If Stendhal was more than a little regretful, even in 1811, to sacrifice all his 'plaisir de souvenir' and all his love of art, for the experience of a present passion which was, to say the least of it, unsatisfactory, how much more intensely may he be presumed to have felt the same loss in 1824 or 1825, when almost all he valued in his life was now wrapped up in memory and art? Moreover, as we have seen, the supreme experience in Stendhal's world was no longer love as such, but the 'final crystallisation':

---

[34] *Journal*, 11th September 1811. Pléiade, pp. 1128-9

love plus melancholy plus beauty, relived through art. The actual experience of love, therefore, could only be attained through the sacrifice of an emotion more intense and more poignant still — yet without the renewed experience of actual love, there could, in the future, be no further past experience to re-create, and consequently no experience of art and no prospect of ultimate creativity. 'Sans amour, je ne vaux rien.'

The outcome of this crisis seems to have been, in fact, that Stendhal did (consciously or subconsciously) consent to sacrifice his love of art. Suddenly, from about 1827 onwards, his interest in music — save in the music he remembered from the past — just fades away. His interest in painting subsists, in a muted form, somewhat longer, but this may have been due more to his close friendship with Abraham Constantin in Rome than to any form of internal compulsion. Of ballet and the other arts (with the notable exception of history) there is scarcely a mention after 1830; but at the same time he continues to love, to remember — and to create. In other words, by becoming his *own* creative artist, he managed to fuse in one the actual experience, the re-created experience and the catalyst — and the final dilemma was solved. But the essential principle of memory still abides. For Stendhal the novelist just as clearly as for Beyle the dilettante, factual reminiscence — except in matters of detail — still killed stone dead the creative imagination, and so the 'mémoire de faits' must needs be set aside. What then remains? What Stendhal relives now, through the medium of his own art, is the 'mémoire sensible' of an experience *already relived* through the medium of another art in an earlier period — so that the climactic instants of experience in the lives of Julien Sorel and Mathilde de la Mole, of Fabrice del Dongo and Clélia Conti, while they are unquestionably in origin the 'sensations pures' of Stendhal himself, are presented in terms of that experience already once relived in terms of music — that relived experience now being re-created at yet a third remove from its original accompanying facts. And if the final catalyst in the process of abolishing time is now the art of Stendhal himself, still traces of the earlier art remain. It is to the miraculous strains of *Quelle pupille tenere* that Fabrice and Clélia find their ultimate quietus, while Mathilde similarly relives, not only the exaltation of her creator's original emotional experiences, but also his exaltation in the music through which those experiences had already before been reconstituted out of the past — the music of Cimarosa:

> Du moment qu'elle eut entendu cette cantilène sublime, tout ce qui existait au monde disparut pour Mathilde (. . .) Son extase arriva à un état d'exaltation et de passion comparable aux mouvements les plus

violents que, depuis quelques jours, Julien avait éprouvés pour elle. La cantilène (. . .) occupait tous les instants où elle ne songeait pas directement à Julien. Grâce à son amour pour la musique, elle fut ce soir-là comme Madame de Rênal était toujours en pensant à Julien . . .[35]

These scattered observations and hypotheses do no more, obviously, than touch the fringes of a very complicated problem. Perhaps in the end all that might be firmly concluded is this: that Stendhal the creator, no less than Proust, emerges from a lifelong struggle to re-create and to relive in the entirety of its reality the experience of the past; and that the novelist we know is rarely content simply to reminisce about his own experience, but prefers — or rather is compelled — to relive during his final epoch as a creative writer experiences already once relived during his middle period as a critic and a dilettante. In other words, for Stendhal, the supreme experience of the 'complete man' is experience already once abstracted and relived through the 'mémoire sensible'; while the supreme experience of the creative artist is to relive yet again the experience of the 'complete man'.[36]

---

[35] *Rouge et Noir* (ed. Champion), vol. II, p. 222.

[36] Since this article was written, the author has had knowledge of Professor Georges Poulet's important essay, 'Stendhal et le Temps' (*Revue Internationale de Philosophie*, 16e Année, Nos. 61–2, Fasc. 3–4, 1962, pp. 395–412). Although Professor Poulet is more immediately concerned with the phenomenon of instantaneity in Stendhal than with the problem of re-living the past, the two aspects of Stendhal's thought are closely interrelated, as will be seen from this extract from Professor Poulet's conclusion: 'Condamné à vivre — et à revivre —, isolément, les moments de son existence, Stendhal n'est ni capable, ni même désireux, de transformer ces moments en un temps continu de l'être. Non, son idéal profond, l'espoir sans cesse déçu et sans cesse renaissant de sa pensée, ce serait de conférer à chacun de ces merveilleux moments une sorte d'éternité indépendànte et particulière. Le rêve, ce serait de garder chacun de ces moments, frais, disponibles, prêts à être revécus dans l'esprit à volonté. Utiliser indéfiniment en n'importe quel instant nouveau, les quelques instants qui valent la peine d'être répétés, voilà ce que Stendhal souhaite, et que, par une infinité de processus variés, il tâche d'accomplir' (p. 411).

10

G. HAINSWORTH

Schopenhauer, Flaubert, Maupassant: Conceptual Thought and Artistic 'Truth'

SCHOPENHAUER's numerous sources and analogues in world literature make it difficult, except in respect of certain anti-Hegelian and
Darwinian features and his views on love and women, to distinguish
exactly his 'influence', a fact which clearly emerges from Baillot's thesis.[1]
Fortunately we are less concerned here with such influences as Baillot
considers than with an attempt to elucidate, partly in the light of Schopenhauer, the implicit ideas of certain texts of Flaubert and Maupassant, and to
examine in general the problem of the artist's 'thought' as opposed to that
of philosophers.

If Flaubert is recognized nowadays, it is largely for qualities he would
have disclaimed, and his pretension to the title of 'triple thinker' would
normally be received with a smile, for it is an eloquent commonplace of
French criticism that he, and his followers for that matter, are lamentably
deficient in 'ideas', as if, in this respect, a void stretched between Stendhal
and Proust — or should we rather say Paul Bourget? — and as if imaginative literature were to be prized only in so far as it approaches conceptual
thinking, its opposite. We may here adduce Schopenhauer himself when,
with reference to genius, artistic or otherwise, he contrasts the meagreness
and poverty of conceptual thinking with that original thought which
works in images and that profound knowledge which is rooted in the
perceptive apprehension of things.[2]

Baillot shows no regard for such distinctions and applies to Flaubert the
same treatment as to Taine and Renan, for example. Moreover, while he
is probably right in making no great claims for Schopenhauer's 'influence'

[1] A. Baillot, *Influence de la philosophie de Schopenhauer en France* (1860–1900), Paris, 1927.
What little we owe to this study will be indicated as the occasion arises.
[2] *Sämtliche Werke*, Stuttgart/Frankfurt am Main, Cotta-Insel, 1960–3, 4 vols.; vol. II,
p. 488. Our references to Schopenhauer will be to this edition, apart from those sections of the
Parerga not included in it, for which we shall refer, as *Parerga*, to Deussen's fifth volume of the
complete works (München, 1913).

on Flaubert, his examination of the evidence, as also his parallel between the two men, may appear insufficiently rigorous.

He affirms: 'La doctrine de Schopenhauer lui a été révélée au plus tôt par Challemel-Lacour ou, plus vraisemblablement, par les premières traductions.'[3] By the latter, he must mean, although he does not say so, Salomon Reinach's version, published in 1876, of *Uber die Freiheit des Willens* and A. Burdeau's translation (1879) of *Über die Grundlage der Moral*, since his remark is based on a letter of Flaubert's dated June 1879 and since no other texts of Schopenhauer, at least outside periodical literature, were available in French before Cantacuzène's *Parerga et Paralipomena, Aphorismes* (1880) and J. Bourdeau's *Pensées, maximes et fragments* of the same year, *Die Welt als Wille und Vorstellung* not of course appearing in French before 1886. Now, as A. Burdeau's translation would seem to have appeared late in 1879,[4] Flaubert may not after all be alluding to it in the abovementioned letter to Mme Roger des Genettes:

> Connaissez-vous Schopenhauer? J'en lis deux livres. Idéaliste et pessimiste, ou plutôt bouddhiste. Ça me va.[5]

We know from Descharmes[6] that Flaubert borrowed from the library of Rouen, in February 1879, the *Revue française* for December 1856, which contained a translation or partial translation by Alexandre Weill of the chapter on *Animalischer Magnetismus und Magie* from *Über den Willen in der Natur*. It is possible that this is one of the 'works' mentioned by Flaubert in his letter. However, while this text and the essay on free will justify Flaubert's phrase *idéaliste et pessimiste*, the epithet *bouddhiste* is hardly to be explained by them and would make much more sense either as an expression of what Flaubert already knew of Schopenhauer or as a reference to *Die Grundlage der Moral*, which is of course strongly Buddhist in inspiration. In the latter event, one would have to suppose, as one may readily do, that one of the 'works' Flaubert had before him in June 1879 was Weill's partial translation of *Die Grundlage der Moral* which had also appeared in the *Revue française*, in the year 1857.[7]

Baillot merely *quotes* Flaubert's remark as a proof that he read Schopenhauer in 1879.[8] He also notes Flaubert's earlier allusion: 'Mon opinion sur

---

[3] P. 216. Challemel-Lacour: 'Un bouddhiste contemporain en Allemagne, Arthur Schopenhauer,' *Revue des Deux Mondes, mars-avril,* 1870, pp. 296-332.

[4] Cp. *Bibliographie de la France,* 13th September, 1879.

[5] *Correspondance, nouvelle édition augmentée,* Conard, vol. VIII, p. 272.

[6] *Autour de Bouvard et Pécuchet,* Paris, 1921, p. 297.

[7] These translations of Weill are merely mentioned by Baillot (p. 88), without any discussion of their importance for the question of Flaubert. Cp. also *Jahrbuch der Schopenhauer-Gesellschaft,* 1932, pp. 271-4.

[8] P. 221.

Schopenhauer est absolument la vôtre. Et dire qu'il suffit de mal écrire pour avoir la réputation d'un homme sérieux!'[9] To be exact, Baillot omits the *et* before *dire*, as Thibaudet does,[10] and resembles Thibaudet and, later, Digeon,[11] in taking the remark for a condemnation of Schopenhauer, which is by no means proven. The *et* has its importance, and the following context, in which Flaubert congratulates Mme Roger des Genettes on her liking for Lucretius has hardly an anti-Schopenhauerian ring. In any event the question remains: what is the reference of the letter, to Th. Ribot's rather unsympathetic study of Schopenhauer (1874) or what? And *did* Flaubert remain ignorant of Schopenhauer until 1876?

Without wishing to insist on this factual side of the matter, we may regret that Baillot gives no detailed chronological account, from 1850 onwards, of Schopenhauer's penetration into France. Challemel-Lacour's article, covering as it does, if somewhat stiltedly, the main points of Schopenhauer's idealism, ethics, aesthetics and attitude towards love and women, no doubt counts for the seventies. But, prior to 1870, Baillot is content to mention, along with Weill, one or two articles (out of many!) in the *Revue des Deux Mondes*, including Saint-René Taillandier's,[12] a book by Bartholmèss published in 1855,[13] Foucher de Careil's *Hegel et*

---

[9] *Correspondance*, vol. VII, p. 153 (June 1874); Baillot, p. 220.

[10] *Gustave Flaubert*, Paris, 1935 ed., p. 173.

[11] *Le dernier visage de Flaubert*, Paris, 1946, p. 46, n. 1.

[12] 'L'Allemagne littéraire' (1st August 1856).

[13] *Histoire critique des doctrines religieuses de la philosophie moderne*, Paris, 1855, 2 vols. This text is remarkable as quoting, fifteen years before Challemel-Lacour, Schopenhauer's views on women (cp. Baillot, p. 161, n. 2, where his source is Schopenhauer's conversations with Bähr). This might have some relevance when one considers Flaubert's remarks to Feydeau in 1859 (*Correspondance*, vol. IV, pp. 303-4): 'Je n'admets pas que les femmes se connaissent en sentiment. Elles ne le perçoivent jamais que d'une manière *personnelle* et relative. Il ne faut se fier en femmes (en fait de littérature) que pour les choses de délicatesse et de nervosité. Mais tout ce qui est vraiment haut et élevé leur échappe' (cp. also Flaubert's remarks on the Immaculate Conception, *le culte de la mère*, ibid.). Cp. Schopenhauer, *Über die Weiber* and also vol. II, p. 553 (the ridiculous Germano-Christian veneration of women). One might be tempted, elsewhere in Flaubert, to compare certain details textually with Schopenhauer: thus in *Bouvard et Pécuchet* (Charpentier, pp. 265-6), the development on magic ('Il y a une essence, un agent secret et universel. Si nous pouvions le tenir, on n'aurait pas besoin de la force, de la durée. Ce qui demande des siècles se développerait en une minute; tout miracle serait praticable et l'univers à notre disposition. (. . .) Comment devenir magicien? (. . .) Un régime préparatoire est indispensable') (cp. also *Saint Antoine*, Charpentier, p. 15) resembles Schopenhauer in *Animalischer Magnetismus*(vol. III, pp. 453-4), quoting Horst: 'Die magische Kraft setzt den, der sie besitzt, in den Stand, die Schöpfung (. . .) zu beherrschen und zu erneuern; so daß, wenn viele in einer magischen Kraft zusammenwirkten, die Natur paradiesisch umgeschaffen werden könnte (. . .) Wie wir zu dieser magischen Kraft gelangen? In der neuen Geburt durch den Glauben (. . .)' However, the parallel is by no means conclusive. In general we have refrained from this sort of inquiry (for which in any case our apparatus is inadequate). Such matters may well seem of secondary importance: thus Flaubert's general agreement with Schopenhauer in his attitude towards Hegel, for example (*Bouvard et*

Schopenhauer (1862), and 'an article read by Taine in the *Revue germanique* for 1862'. He partly makes up for this in 1932 by reprinting, along with extracts from Bartholmèss, Saint-René Taillandier and Alexandre Weill, an anonymous article, still earlier, from *L'Athénæum français* (1854).[14] At no stage does he mention, for example, De Sanctis's article on Schopenhauer and Leopardi in the *Revue contemporaine* for December 1858. Now reference to Flaubert's correspondence or even to the index under *Athénæum français*, *Revue contemporaine*, *Revue des Deux Mondes*, *Revue germanique*, will confirm that Flaubert was in a position, as a subscriber or otherwise, to know most of the articles mentioned above, while, as for Bartholmèss and Foucher de Careil, there is every reason for supposing that his interest in religions and in Hegel would bring these volumes into his hands.[15] In any event, it is manifest that one who cultivated Taine, Turgeniev and Renan in the sixties could not have remained ignorant of Schopenhauer until 1870, 1874 or 1876.

While in no way claiming to derive Flaubert's opinions from Schopenhauer, let us note his general concurrence with the German philosopher in what concerns the evil of the world and human imbecility.

For Flaubert, suffering is the rule, not the exception, in life: 'Nous sommes nés pour souffrir, puisque la vie se passe à cela.'[16] The 'truth' about man is to be found in hospitals, existence being a long struggle with the forces of decay: 'A peine nés, la pourriture commence sur vous, de sorte que toute la vie n'est qu'un long combat qu'elle nous livre, et toujours de plus en plus triomphant de sa part jusqu'à la conclusion, la mort. Là, elle règne exclusive'.[17] The *grand trou noir* is implicitly alluded to throughout Flaubert, and the view of death and generation as correlatives is as characteristic of him as of Schopenhauer, so that the cemetery of Jaffa with its corpses and its fruit trees strikes him by its perfect symbolism.[18] Long before the time when Louise Colet imagined she was with child by him, Flaubert conceives a horror of procreation: 'A quoi bon faire sortir du

---

Pécuchet, Charpentier, pp. 289–91), is what possesses intrinsic significance — whether or not the resemblance be accidental.

[14] *Jahrbuch der Schopenhauer-Gesellschaft*, 1932, pp. 252–79.

[15] Yet they do not figure in the inventory of his library published by R. Rouault de la Vigne (*Revue des sociétés savantes de Haute-Normandie*, 1957, pp. 73–84).

[16] *Correspondance*, vol. VI, p. 380; see also vol. III, pp. 16 and 275. This is a point of doctrine with Schopenhauer: 'Wenn nicht der nächste und unmittelbare Zweck unsers Lebens das Leiden ist; so ist unser Daseyn das Zweckwidrigste auf der Welt.' (*Parerga*, p. 317: *Nachträge zur Lehre vom Leiden der Welt*). So as not to multiply our references, we will confine ourselves to stating that most of Flaubert's ideas as quoted in the paragraph above have analogues in that essay.

[17] Vol. III, p. 269 (hospitals); vol. III, p. 145.

[18] Vol. III, p. 137.

néant ce qui y dort?'[19] Love itself, satisfied or unsatisfied, leads to suffering in Flaubert's opinion,[20] and he refers the *faiseurs d'élégies* to prostitution as to a true mirror of the nothingness of human relations.[21] If one adds to this scheme of things the ferocity of men towards each other,[22] it will follow that the idea of earthly happiness is not only an illusion, but positively harmful, an invention of the Devil, as compared with a resolute pessimism.[23]

From the point of view of intelligence, man distinguishes himself by 'la rage de ne pas vouloir voir la vérité, l'amour du factice et de la blague'.[24] Instead of accepting what is, he seeks at every step to 'conclude' in the sense that he is intent on reaching precise notions, in terms of cause and end, for example, concerning human affairs, expecting of them a logical and clear-cut character which they do not possess.[25] At the same time, he takes shadows for realities, as in his attitude towards honour, fame, distinctions.[26] Flaubert's well-known axiom: 'Les honneurs déshonorent, le titre dégrade, la fonction abrutit'[27] involves not only the stupidity and incompetence of those who accord distinctions, the multiplicity of the latter and their lack of intrinsic value, but also the idea that to have gained the approval of *the many* testifies directly to one's worthlessness.

Our rational being thrives on logomachy:

> Nous rions, nous autres, du réalisme et du nominalisme (. . .) Une république moderne et une monarchie constitutionnelle sont identiques. N'importe! on se chamaille là-dessus, on crie, on se bat.[28]

Politics, incidentally, are the despair of Flaubert who, while a revolutionary at heart, considers universal suffrage to be as extravagant as divine right or papal infallibility, given the fact that 'le peuple est un éternel mineur'.[29] As a mandarinate remains an idle dream, Flaubert's criteria are expediency and the maintenance of the *status quo* in the teeth of all utopists.[30]

Belief in progress, comparable to the belief in the possibility of individual happiness, supplies, of course, in Flaubert's eyes, the final ironic touch to

---

[19] Vol. I, p. 355 (1846).
[20] Vol. II, p. 44; vol. III, p. 202; vol. IV, p. 353.
[21] Vol. III, p. 216.
[22] Vol. V, p. 112; vol. VI, p. 135; vol. VII, p. 400.
[23] Vol. II, p. 55; vol. III, pp. 204 and 403.
[24] Vol. VI, p. 148.
[25] Vol. II, p. 239; vol. IV, p. 357, etc.
[26] Vol. II, pp. 321, 64 and 427. Cp. *Aphorismen zur Lebensweisheit*, vol. IV, pp. 420–82.
[27] Vol. VIII, p. 184, also p. 407; and *Supplément*, vol. IV, p. 137.
[28] Vol. VI, pp. 281–2.
[29] Vol. VI, pp. 33, 138, 228, etc. Cp. Schopenhauer, *Zur Rechtslehre und Politik* (*Parerga*, p. 271).
[30] Vol. III, p. 17. Cp. *Parerga*, p. 280.

the picture of human folly.[31] Man's fluctuating ideas, his agitated and repetitive existence no more argue for such optimism than does the larger rotation of history.[32]

While the pessimistic views of Flaubert and Schopenhauer thus run largely parallel, and perhaps constitute what is basic in them (even in Schopenhauer, in spite of interpretations for the best in the last seventy years) the two men present in certain particular fields — morals, aesthetics, metaphysics — along with material resemblances, striking differences of approach and emphasis.

For practical purposes, 'love one another' and *Tat tvam asi* play no part in Flaubert's declared opinions. It is with joy that, in connection with the idea of progress, he notes the *service* rendered by the theory of evolution in disposing once and for all of any idea of a millennium.[33] His reactions elsewhere[34] to disasters — natural cataclysms or war — involve no doubt in part the pleasure, which Schopenhauer might have shared,[35] of discovering confirmation of his own views and salutory correctives of those of the multitude, and could thus be related to his love of truth, but it would be difficult to deny the presence of positive hatred, not of *bêtise*, not of the bourgeois, but of mankind:

> J'aime à voir l'humanité et tout ce qu'elle respecte, ravalé, bafoué, honni, sifflé. C'est par là que j'ai quelque tendresse pour les ascétiques.[36]

In the same breath, moreover, he dissociates himself from mankind: 'Va te faire (. . .) , troupeau; je ne suis pas de la bergerie' and from ideas of charity (fundamental, however, in Schopenhauer): 'ces belles blagues de dévouement, sacrifice, abnégation, fraternité et autres, abstractions stériles et dont la généralité humaine ne peut tirer parti'.[37] Flaubert deplores Christian ideas, humanitarianism, a general sentimentality, as clouding all issues and leading to an inadequate sense of proportion in matters of elementary justice, justice being for Flaubert a sufficient criterion in questions of behaviour.[38]

Nor does asceticism assume in Flaubert the ethical character it has in

---

[31] Vol. II, p. 466; vol. III, p. 17; vol. V, p. 112; vol. VI, p. 155. Cp. *Parerga*, p. 283.

[32] Vol. III, p. 60 ('Votre coin de culture disparaîtra sous l'herbe, votre peuple sous d'autres invasions, votre religion sous d'autres philosophies'); vol. VI, p. 163 ('Les Latins sont finis! maintenant c'est au tour des Saxons, qui seront dévorés par les Slaves. Ainsi de suite') and p. 201 ('Paganisme, christianisme, muflisme'). Cp. *Parerga* (*Nachträge* . . .), p. 318.

[33] Vol. VIII, p. 108.

[34] Vol. III, p. 276; vol. V, p. 229; vol. VI, pp. 139 and 259.

[35] Cp. *Nachträge zur Lehre vom Leiden der Welt* (*Parerga*, p. 319).

[36] Vol. IV, p. 33; cp. also vol. III, pp. 396-7.

[37] Vol. III, p. 275; cp. also p. 210.

[38] Vol. VI, pp. 296-7; vol. V, pp. 348-9.

Schopenhauer. Revulsion from the flesh is not coloured by any feeling of sin in the writer who considers that *la haine du bordel* irrevocably stamps a man as beyond the pale, who condemns vice for its stupidity alone and sees in lust, the depths of which he has plumbed, just another quest for the absolute.[39] Though Flaubert may aspire to a nirvana, he certainly does not subscribe with Schopenhauer to any doctrine of original sin, atonement for the fact of existence itself, *el delito mayor del hombre, haber nacido.* Abstinence, for him, is admirable as a mark of will-power, not in itself.[40] The religious instinct, religious fanaticism and *le fanatisme de l'art,*[41] which correspond to the conviction that there exists 'something superior to life', are to be prized on these lines and as an age-old characteristic of humanity less repugnant than the prosaic materialism which he accuses French positivists of teaching:

> Nous ne valons peut-être quelque chose que par nos souffrances, car elles sont toutes des aspirations.[42]

Yet it is implicit in Flaubert that aspirations, by definition, remain unsatisfied.

With Flaubert, renunciation — relative seclusion and immobility and self-macerations having for object his phrases and paragraphs — requires no other rationale than disgust with life, belief in the consequent superiority of contemplation, and the notion *ars longa.* Schopenhauer's view of art, whether in respect of its creation or its enjoyment, as a peculiarly moral activity — for it suspends the movement of the Will — is hardly characteristic of Flaubert, who, rather than making of aesthetics a dependency of ethics, as the German does, subordinates ethics to art and sees in abstemiousness the condition of artistic creation.[43] Obviously, even here, the idea of detachment is involved, and at times, in reply to accusations of egoism, Flaubert depicts as altruistic his efforts to identify himself with humanity for the sake of art, refers to the selflessness of the artist ('cette disposition à planer sur soi-même') as being perhaps the source of all virtue,[44] and sees literary creation as leading eventually to 'une espèce de sainteté, qui est peut-être plus haute que l'autre, parce qu'elle est plus désintéressée'.[45] He

[39] Vol. III, p. 77; vol. IV, p. 234 ('Je déracinais l'homme à deux mains'); vol. III, p. 216; vol. IV, p. 170; vol. III, p. 270; vol. IV, p. 313; and cp. vol. V, p. 274 ('La femme est l'ogive de l'infini').

[40] Vol. V, p. 250. Here, perhaps, rather than Schopenhauer, we should recall Spinoza's distinctions between the passive and the active side of behaviour.

[41] Vol. III, p. 149; cp. also p. 201; vol. IV, pp. 170 and 232.

[42] Vol. IV, p. 232; vol. VIII, p. 107 (positivists); vol. III, p. 149. Cp. *Parerga*, pp. 283 and 319.

[43] Vol. IX, p. 3.

[44] Vol. II, p. 407.

[45] Vol. IV, p. 171.

emphasizes equally, however, the pleasure accruing to the artist.[46] Else-where he modestly considers art as a refuge from the bitterness of life,[47] or compares it, in importance, to a game of skittles, dominoes or Binet's hobby.[48] It would seem that Flaubert 'believes in' art hardly more than in anything else.[49] He certainly does not distinguish his own vocation from any other aspiration or quest of the absolute in respect of its finality and, rather than 'turning against the Will', he would appear to be redirecting it, while continuing to realize the vanity of all effort.

Flaubert's remoteness from any foundation in ethics and his conviction that all forms of activity are ultimately a matter of indifference coincide with his metaphysics proper, if it be permitted to use the term in connection with him, for he never really goes beyond systematic doubt, *Que say-je?* and *Ne pas conclure* being his favourite slogans. He classifies himself as an idealist:

> Est-ce que vous avez jamais cru à l'existence des choses? Est-ce que tout n'est pas une illusion? Il n'y a de vrai que les 'rapports', c'est-à-dire la façon dont nous percevons les objets.[50]

Moreover, unlike Schopenhauer in his theory of the Will, at all times Flaubert stresses the impossibility of our arriving at the thing-in-itself. This is particularly evident in his attack on the pet dichotomies of the philo-sophers: soul and body, form and substance, matter and mind,[51] distinc-tions which, echoing perhaps Spinoza, he rejects as unproven. He is so far sceptical as to question atheism and materialism, while ridiculing 'ceux qui ont le bon Dieu dans leur poche'.[52] 'Quel orgueil que celui d'un dogme quelconque!'[53] he exclaims, and elsewhere: 'Saisirons-nous jamais l'absolu? Il faut, si l'on veut vivre, renoncer à avoir une idée nette de quoi que ce soit.'[54]

Through idealism, phenomenalism, pyrrhonism, Flaubert thus makes his escape from metaphysics, not surprisingly when one thinks of *le Garçon*, the *Dictionnaire des idées reçues* and the *Sottisier*.

What then are 'truth' and 'reality' in Flaubert's vocabulary? Clearly nothing other, in abstract terms, than that all is illusion, a matter of 'relations', no absolute being attainable, and humanity being destined to

---

[46] Ibid.; cp. also vol. II, p. 395 and vol. III, p. 210.
[47] Vol. III, p. 107; vol. V, pp. 146 and 378.
[48] Vol. II, pp. 329 and 355; vol. VII, p. 2.
[49] Vol. II, pp. 13 and 51.
[50] Vol. VIII, p. 135.
[51] Vol. IV, pp. 313 and 357; vol. III, p. 271; vol. V, p. 367.
[52] Vol. VIII, pp. 173 and 327.
[53] Vol. VIII, p. 231.
[54] Vol. IV, p. 181.

perpetual evolution and transformation in this vale of tears.[55] Flaubert's art, the fact that he mirrors the world and makes a picture of the picture, far from appearing inconsistent with such notions, is an unmistakable act of adherence to them.

The artistic truth of his work is to be sought in an indirect communication, embodied in an image of the world, of this radically nihilistic point of view, but with the important proviso that, in so far as he refrains from 'concluding', the artist, by this return — or descent — from thought to experience, has furnished the only available data for any conclusion and eliminated to some extent, for all these matters are relative, the possibility of error, half-truth, pure verbalism. Axiomatically, Flaubert's novels refer beyond his 'opinions' to his original experience and his personal vision, and if these last appear abnormal, one can only adduce Flaubert's *conscious* and conscientious striving after what is *general* or, in the last resort, quote jesting Pilate.

The 'sincerity' of Flaubert can hardly be brought into question. Just as any act of artistic creation implies by its very existence a judgment on the importance of 'real life', so Flaubert's aspiration to the contemplative state, his experience of hallucination, whether as victim or as one who sought artificially to induce it,[56] and in general his cult of the purely cerebral — as real as anything else, obviously, in his scheme — involved already, quite apart from any express opinions of his, a questioning of the importance to be ascribed to the external world. At the same time his perception of this external world, his actual sight, is marked, not only by a peculiarity of perspective, partly explained by the detachment of one who is spectator, not actor, but also, according to certain texts, by a stereoscopic quality which superimposes on particular impressions other images drawn from the past or the future, thus underlining the ephemeral and meaningless character of phenomena and at the same time embracing apparently in some way something more than the purely phenomenal. We may quote from the correspondence his impression, on going to the theatre, of rows of skeletons filling the auditorium,[57] or his remark: 'Je n'ai jamais vu un enfant sans penser qu'il deviendrait vieillard, ni un berceau sans songer à une tombe. La contemplation d'une femme nue me fait rêver à son squelette.'[58] His reactions at the baptism of his niece in 1846 present a more complicated character: 'Je me faisais l'effet d'assister à quelque cérémonie d'une religion lointaine exhumée de la poussière (. . .) Ce qu'il y avait de

[55] Vol. II, p. 51; vol. IV, p. 184.

[56] Vol. II, p. 395; vol. III, pp. 210 and 270; vol. V, p. 350; etc.

[57] *Supplément*, vol. II, p. 95.

[58] Vol. I, p. 221. Quoted by Faguet (*Flaubert*, 3e éd., Paris, 1913, p. 27) as romanticism and *goût de la tristesse*!

plus intelligent, à coup sûr, c'étaient les pierres qui avaient autrefois compris tout cela et qui, peut-être, en avaient retenu quelque chose.'[59] Such texts sufficiently explain Flaubert's meaning when he declares the test of an artistic vocation to be that 'les accidents du monde, dès qu'ils sont perçus, vous apparaissent transposés comme pour l'emploi d'une illusion à décrire.'[60] At the same time, the vision involved is in many ways analogous to that ascribed by Schopenhauer to one who has escaped from the Will.[61]

This tendency to look before and after (which Flaubert, within certain limits, attributes — for it is a human characteristic — to his protagonists themselves, along with hallucination, dream, day-dream and dissociation of personality), this multiple and complex vision stamps Flaubert's whole work and, taken in conjunction with his aesthetic recipes (*faire général, acceptation ironique, ne pas conclure, refonte plastique, faire rêver*), provides a better guide to his writings and to their meaning than any abstract ideas of ours or his. This is so far true, that literally Flaubert's 'thinking' in the novels takes on a catholicity not characteristic of the correspondence, and embraces, for example, notions of pity, charity and the identity of all creatures, disclaimed by Flaubert the letter-writer, in which fact, of course, far from wishing to see the *part de Dieu*, the *mens divinior* which Du Bos declares absent from Flaubert,[62] we find merely corroboration of the latter's belief in the superior truth of art.

Unless no importance at all is to be attached to an author's intentions, it must be postulated in the case of Flaubert that any interpretation which reduces such and such a work of his to a simple formula is an erroneous distortion of it, and this applies even to those works which at first sight may appear the least plastic, like *La Tentation de Saint Antoine* and *Bouvard et Pécuchet*.

To define the first of these works as 'emanatist panpsychism'[63] or as 'Spencer's doctrine of the Unknowable',[64] is an *a priori* substitution of discursive reasoning for aesthetic appreciation, and rank Philistinism.

---

[59] Vol. I, pp. 202–3. Cp. also Thibaudet, p. 78.

[60] Vol. VI, p. 487.

[61] 'Die Gaukelbilder dieser Welt, die (. . .) jetzt so gleichgültig vor ihm stehn wie die Schachfiguren nach geendigtem Spiel oder wie am Morgen die abgeworfenen Maskenkleider, deren Gestalten uns in der Faschingsnacht neckten und beunruhigten. Das Leben und seine Gestalten schweben nur noch vor ihm wie eine flüchtige Erscheinung, wie dem Halberwachten ein leichter Morgentraum, durch den schon die Wirklichkeit durchschimmert und der nicht mehr täuschen kann' (vol. I, p. 531).

[62] *Approximations*, Paris, 1922, pp. 167–8; the whole article is singularly lacking in any kind of sympathy, grafting itself on Proust's essay on Flaubert's style, interpreted for the worst.

[63] Baillot, p. 221.

[64] Digeon.

Debates on the 'precise meaning' of Saint Antoine's last monologue, which represents, for Faguet,[65] a deplorable abdication of the reason, for Thibaudet,[66] 'le panthéisme d'en bas, après celui d'en haut' and also something analogous to Flaubert's aspirations to impersonal contemplation, for Baillot, on the contrary,[67] interpreting for the best, intelligence victorious over matter, underline a radically insufficient method and the determination to simplify at all costs.

It is obvious that this speech is susceptible of yet other interpretations than those mentioned above. Fischer put his finger long ago on what is solid and palpable when he suggested, with unnecessary diffidence — if we remember the opening scene of Faust — that we have to do here with the cry of one weary of reflection and immobility, an aspiration to action, movement, animal existence, man being after all an animal.[68] Another line of approach is suggested by the Goncourt Journal,[69] according to which Flaubert referred to this last page as 'la défaite finale du saint, due à la cellule, à la cellule scientifique'. This, we think, is understandable only if we suppose that Saint Antoine, who has just made out minute protozoa ('de petites masses globuleuses, grosses comme des têtes d'épingles et garnies de cils tout autour'[70]) beginning to vibrate ('une vibration les agite'), is elated at the thought of having discovered the origin of life, is then led, under the influence of his emotion, into a dithyramb on all forms of *non-rational* existence, including the most curious ('souffler de la fumée, porter une trompe'), while, tacitly until 'pénétrer chaque atome, descendre jusqu'au fond de la matière', he returns to a consciousness of his point of departure, realizing that the cell, and even the sight of the inanimate becoming animate, provides no last word, whereupon, with the wish *être la matière*, he expresses simultaneously his thirst for absolute knowledge and a peevish renunciation of all knowledge.[71] A mad conclusion indeed for those who like their philosophy clear, but appropriate in a work subtitled by its author *le comble de l'insanité*.

This impression of vain agitation, contrary attitudes, circular move-

[65] P. 62.
[66] P. 173.
[67] P. 218.
[68] E. W. Fischer, Études sur Flaubert inédit, Leipzig, 1908, p. 117.
[69] Vol. IV (Charpentier), p. 352.
[70] Cp. the ciliated monera discussed and illustrated in Haeckel, Histoire de la création des êtres organisés d'après les lois naturelles, Paris, 1874, p. 166: 'petites boules muqueuses invisibles à l'œil nu ou, si elles sont visibles, de la grosseur d'une tête d'épingle (. . .) rayons très fins (. . .)' For Haeckel (p. 308) they offer strong proof of spontaneous generation. This particular volume obviously cannot be Flaubert's source in Saint Antoine.
[71] This grotesque and ironic trend distinguishes the passage from the materially analogous development in Par les champs et par les grèves quoted at length by Fischer (p. 114).

ment, general instability, is not contradicted but confirmed by the following context: in a sky which takes on the appearance of an altar, the sun rises, displaying in its disc the face of Jesus Christ. The sun here, in our opinion, is linked with the ciliated monera of the previous page, whether as hallucination on the part of Saint Antoine or as figuring life and eternal life. At the same time the juxtaposition of sun and protozoon creates a relativist system relevant to the question of man's stature and limitations, while the start of a new day — 'encore un jour!'[72] — and Saint Antoine's return to his prayers take up again and project into infinity the endless cycles, transformations without finality, which have been the matter of the text.

The fact that Saint Antoine is or thinks he is in a state of grace at the end has, of course, no more significance in itself than any other of his passing moods,[73] in this ironic and comic picture of the imbecility of man, a prey to the flesh, frustrated in his aspirations, led on and on by his chimera ('qui s'éloigne en décrivant des cercles'[74]). It is that image which constitutes, for one part, the 'general truth' of the work. Clearly, it is basic, too, in all Flaubert's novels. Egoism, vanity, stupidity, lust, carnage, suffering, perpetual agitation and striving, such elements make up his real world, as in the case of Candide or Schopenhauer's account of the objectifications of the Will. If we seek to go further and discover a more particular 'thought' here, we should not address ourselves to any formula employed by the interlocutors, not even the dilemma put forward by the Devil:

La Forme est peut-être une erreur de tes sens, la Substance une imagination de ta pensée.

A moins que le monde étant un flux perpétuel des choses, l'apparence au contraire ne soit tout ce qu'il y a de plus vrai, l'illusion la seule réalité.[75]

Rather, starting from the text as a whole and attempting to account for all its parts, should we consider that most of the episodes — opening descriptions, dreams proper, heresies, procession of the gods, evocation (including what is fabulous) of the animal, vegetable and mineral realms — converge towards the same point: the instability and variety of all forms. In the dissolving perspective thus created, all 'reality', apart — ironically — from a hankering after the possession of reality, disappears, so that hallucination and true vision, man's behaviour and the phenomena

---

[72] Cp. Saint Antoine's first words (Charpentier, p. 2).
[73] For Faguet, 'l'œuvre s'achève en poème chrétien' (p. 63).
[74] P. 282.
[75] P. 261.

of the external world, cease to be differentiated. We have here, not the abstract statement: 'All is illusion', strictly meaningless and conveying nothing, but a *plastic* evocation of the averred foundations for any such remark, the text thus expressing what is otherwise incommunicable and embodying, by a reversal of normal modes of thought, a truth concerned simultaneously with object and knowing subject and derived, as it were, from outside this world.

From Flaubert's point of view, and indeed logically, the *multiplicity* of phenomena has here in itself the force of an argument, a fact which explains also one aspect of *Bouvard et Pécuchet*, presumably the only work of fiction to embrace at one and the same time metaphysics, morals, aesthetics, literature; theology and comparative religion; politics and political economy; education, grammar; astronomy, chemistry, geology, palaeontology, botany; agriculture, horticulture; anatomy, pathology; memnotechnics, mesmerism, phrenology, magic; ornamental gardening, drawing, gymnastics; prehistory and history; the future of the world, the end of the world, an account of heaven, etc. The work attempts to embody, in as plastic a form as possible, not only, as Demorest says,[76] 'le vaste ensemble des problèmes qui ont préoccupé l'homme de tout temps et le Français du XIXe siècle', but the detailed content of human knowledge and the varied forms of human activity, restored to their context, the phenomena of the external world.

Glad of the opportunity to conduct the discussion solely on the level of ideas, critics like Faguet, Thibaudet, Descharmes and Digeon set at a discount everything in *Bouvard et Pécuchet* which is not science, philosophy or religion, suppose it to have no importance in Flaubert's eyes other than that of *making it appear* he is writing a novel, and see in the different chapters only the particular topic under discussion. Yet such passages as the exploration of man's internal organs,[77] the evocation of the different shapes of the human skull,[78] the concise object-lesson in pathology,[79] and another series to which belong the ornamental garden, the museum, a description of *objets de piété* and the antics of the two heroes as gymnasts,[80] have every appearance of being part of the author's plan, like the recurrent stylized descriptions of nature in its movement and diversity as also in its continuity. Although they cannot be considered as didactic or as fitting at all precisely into the author's 'argument', they still make sense, if only as

[76] *A travers les plans, manuscrits et dossiers de 'Bouvard et Pécuchet'*, Paris, 1931, p. 153.
[77] Pp. 78–80 (Charpentier).
[78] Pp. 357–8.
[79] P. 258. Cp. also, in this vein, the dead dog (p. 297), the scalded cat (p. 373), the crucified owl (p. 381).
[80] Pp. 62, 125–7, 312, 246–7.

demonstrating the infinite variety of phenomena and questioning by implication our notion of reality. To quote the text, we will refer, not to Bouvard's doubts about distinctions between the 'mineral realm' and the organic ('Tout passe, tout croule, tout se transforme. La création est faite d'une manière ondoyante et fugace'[81]) but to their reading of Thiers on the Revolution, one summer day of 1845, in their garden:

> La haute tribune de la Convention dominait un nuage de poussière, où des visages furieux hurlaient des cris de mort. Quand on passait au milieu du jour, près du bassin des Tuileries, on entendait le heurt de la guillotine, pareil à des coups de mouton.
>
> Et la brise remuait les pampres de la tonnelle, les orges mûres se balançaient par intervalles, un merle sifflait. En portant des regards autour d'eux, ils savouraient cette tranquillité (. . .)
>
> A force de bavarder là-dessus, ils se passionnèrent. Bouvard, esprit libéral et cœur sensible, fut constitutionnel, girondin, thermidorien. Pécuchet, bilieux et de tendances autoritaires, se déclara sans-culotte et même Robespierriste.[82]

Such a passage, with its fusion, or non-differentiation, of past and present, its juxtaposition of real (?) differences and academic ones, its picture of the two men transformed for the moment the one into the other merely because of the fact that they are engaged in discussion, its evocation of nature, *irrational* (!) and calm, albeit in motion too, serves to epitomize all Flaubert's nihilism, without offering the least semblance of discursive reasoning.

The so-called chapter on politics (VI) is largely an account of 1848–51 in Chavignolles, calculated to *show* how, with the movement from monarchy to republic and back again, error becomes truth in 1848 and error again in 1851,[83] and of course, clearly, in our opinion, the main plan of the book, the trajectory followed by Bouvard and Pécuchet, is concentric with this chapter: the two copyists, aspiring to other activities, meet with frustration in each successive field and finally withdraw, returning to their copying.

According to the plans of the unfinished part, examined by Demorest,[84] there is a hint, even in this last stage, of the sort of movement which characterizes the main body of the work. The two men begin by copying

[81] P. 121.
[82] P. 150.
[83] That this main aspect, as in the case of Flaubert's earlier treatment of the same topic (*L'Éducation sentimentale*), should go unnoticed, speaks eloquently against the *a priori* approach to literature.
[84] Pp. 92–3.

anything at all, then conceive the idea of a classified form, which leads to their *recopying* their copy in another ledger, and to certain knotty problems at times, especially when they are faced with the difficulty of classifying a letter of Vaucorbeil's declaring them to be two harmless imbeciles:

> Qu'allons-nous en faire? Pas de réflexions! Copions! Il faut que la page s'emplisse, que 'le monument' se complète — égalité de tout, du bien et du mal, du Beau et du Laid, de l'insignifiant et du caractéristique. Il n'y a de vrai que les phénomènes.

This ending, in which the two men abandon the role of actor in favour of that of spectator, far from constituting a mere detail of characterization,[85] enriches *Bouvard et Pécuchet* with yet other 'meanings' than those embraced by such formulae as 'lack of method' (Dumesnil), 'the sore travail and the grief entailed by thought' (Descharmes), 'the relative character of knowledge' (Digeon). It expresses indirectly the superiority of art to life[86] (thus announcing discreetly the conclusion of *A la Recherche du Temps perdu*) and, generally, a doctrine of renunciation.[87]

However, as in the case of *La Tentation*, we must seek at a deeper level, in a depiction of general human nature, a less intangible and a richer truth.

The tendency of critics to see in *Bouvard et Pécuchet* pure ideas, and not men thinking and acting, is accompanied — quite comprehensibly, for otherwise the critic's own position would appear insecure — by a strong disinclination to believe that the two protagonists are other than exceptions, whether as too obtuse, too primary, too old, too impatient or too

---

[85] Even Demorest (p. 46) does not quarrel with Descharmes's curious argument (p. 152) that this proves that Bouvard and Pécuchet had no gifts or liking for pure knowledge. Invaluable for its documentation on Flaubert's sources, Descharmes's book otherwise exemplifies the dangers of ratiocination applied to literature.

[86] A. Thorlby (*Gustave Flaubert*, London, 1956, pp. 53-4) sees the ending as alluding to art, but not in terms of art as opposed to life: 'This is the ultimate stroke of satire against his own novel and the labour of realism — if indeed satire is still the right word' [*sic*]. What truth there is in this remark (for which cp. also Thibaudet, p. 198) cannot redeem the incredible narrowness of the interpretation. The writer reaches his conclusion purely deductively in the following steps, if we read him aright: (*a*) Flaubert is a realist (in art); (*b*) he is (mistakenly) a nihilist (in thought); (*c*) therefore art is not real; (*d*) therefore this dilemma constitutes the only 'real' subject of his works. Although the argument appears consonant with certain modern trends, it should be possible to declare one's dislike of an author without constructing systems of this type.

[87] L. Trilling's interpretation of the ending ('Flaubert's Last Testament', *Partisan Review*, Nov.-Dec. 1953, pp. 605-30) as 'saintly abnegation of Bouvard and Pécuchet', is generous, acceptable in what it affirms, unacceptable in what it excludes. The ending is complex (involving negation of life, a doctrine of withdrawal and an irony on this doctrine in the form of an image of perpetual recommencement) and hardly serves to temper the pessimism of the work, as Trilling suggests. This critic, who has considerable feeling for the generality of *Bouvard et Pécuchet*, arrives, somewhat deviously, at the definition: 'an attack on culture itself', which still does not exhaust the book.

desultory. Yet Flaubert's aesthetics require that Bouvard and Pécuchet should represent humanity generally. Obviously Bouvard is the sanguine type, Pécuchet the bilious, and both are gifted, or afflicted, with a thirst for knowledge not characteristic of the majority, whose opinions are a mere by-product of self-interest. But such distinctions have little importance once one is prepared to consider the secondary roles as more than mere *utilités*, and to have regard for the whole tenor of the work, which necessitates the juxtaposition of metaphysician, scientist, empiricist, of peasant, bourgeois and priest.

To consider here only Bouvard and Pécuchet and only in their capacity of 'intellectuals', is it really so difficult not to see them as extraordinary when, as anatomists or ascetics, they dress for the part,[88] when, as metaphysicians, they are lost in financial problems, or, as scientists, in statistics, classifications, nomenclatures? The thinker who has not experienced the pleasure to be derived from argument for argument's sake and from persecuting his fellow-men with his opinions and his acquired knowledge,[89] the historian who has never failed clearly to make out what is going on in his own house,[90] or the teacher who has never presumed to impart what he has not fully mastered himself,[91] these, if such exist, may declare Bouvard and Pécuchet abnormal.

Demorest is one of the few to recognize this general character of *Bouvard et Pécuchet*. 'Satire du *genus homo*', including Flaubert himself, he declares.[92] He might have used even stronger terms, the upshot of both aspects of the book, in our estimation, tending to *utter derision* of *homo sapiens*. As with Schopenhauer, the reason appears here, when applied to practical ends, a somewhat imperfect tool (by comparison with instinct), in *all* its working subordinated to a more or less remote self-interest, and as a guide to 'truth', powerless by definition. Its epiphenomenal character is brought out, not only by the 1793 episode quoted above, but in other particular passages, for example Pécuchet's long debate with Jeufroy on the early martyrs and the *victims* of Catholic persecution respectively, with regard to their relative numbers and the degree of suffering they endured. This academic argument, introduced by the spectacle of Pécuchet catching Jeufroy alone on the highway and dragging him into conversation against

[88] Ch. iii and ch. ix. Cp. Demorest, p. 59.

[89] Ch. ix and *passim*.

[90] Ch. iv.

[91] Ch. x. Far from attributing to the author's 'arbitrary plan' (Digeon, p. 142) the fact that Bouvard and Pécuchet embark, after all their own frustrations, on pedagogy, one should ask oneself if this is not precisely what men do. On this question of the plan, Demorest points out well (p. 50) how Flaubert's aesthetic scruples require that the different topics should *not* be arranged rationally and methodically.

[92] P. 61.

his will, is interwoven with references to a gathering storm, which eventually breaks, constraining the two men to shelter under the *curé*'s umbrella and eventually to come to a halt, 'face à face, ventre contre ventre, en tenant à quatre mains le parapluie qui oscillait'[93] — without ceasing to argue, drenched as they are. We have to do here with the theme *tantum religio potuit suadere malorum* accompanied by the parody of this theme in the present exchange of 'ideas', while the material proximity of the two men, their solidarity in the rain, which involves from one point of view a parody of martyrdom, stresses above all the essential nature and fundamental identity of the two, thus drawing attention still further to the basic irrelevance of their so-called differences of belief. Some pages further on,[94] the bitter *quarrel* between the 'Christians' and Pécuchet, when the latter declares that he would as soon embrace Buddhism, is on similar lines (such wrangling being inconsistent with either doctrine, no more importance can be attached to these people's 'ideas' than to a battle-cry) but without the affirmation *Tat tvam asi*.[95]

In these circumstances, what Schopenhauer refers to as the Will, takes on in Flaubert much of the importance it had in his predecessor. Chapter VII, in which Faguet and Thibaudet[96] choose to see mainly Pécuchet's misadventure with Mélie, such is their determination to reduce the text to clichés and shine at the expense of their author, offers in its beginning, with the episode of Mme Castillon abandoned by her lover Gorju, the grimmest and the most moving picture of the tender passion, one which suffices to lift the whole chapter far above the level of *Candide*. In chapter X, the episode of Mme Bordin and the peacocks presents a sort of minia-ture of Schopenhauer's world as Will and Representation. One idyllic spring day, Bouvard and Mme Bordin, surrounded by sheets hung out to dry, exchange brief remarks which principally serve to cloak their basic inclination towards each other, and finally hold each other's hand. There-upon the wind lifts up the washing and reveals to them themselves, as it were, in the form of a peacock wooing its female. Gouy's old horse, startled by the peacocks, drags the clothes-line away and is cruelly ill-treated by its master, although Bouvard protests in the name of kindness to animals. The children Victor and Victorine have been present at this scene, which ends in general recriminations.[97] The changes of view-point here (Bouvard watching Mme Bordin, both watching the birds, Victor watching both

---

[93] P. 330.
[94] Pp. 344–6.
[95] We have here that *comique des idées* to which Demorest refers, without illustrating it (p. 74). In this case the inspiration recalls Molière's Mme Pernelle.
[96] 'Des gravelures (. . .) au-dessous de tout' (Faguet, pp. 131–2); Thibaudet, p. 191.
[97] Pp. 366–70.

the human and the animal couple) and the generalizing series: adults, birds, horse, children, seem to direct the attention, beyond the veil of appearances, towards some deeper reality, the blind play of instinct, with its alternation of creative and destructive impulses. At the same time, just as the Mme Castillon episode constitutes a significant prelude to the chapter on love, this object-lesson on the world as it is prepares ironically Pécuchet's lecture on morality in the context following.

However, even if we suppose that the sheets here allude comically to the veil of Māyā, it is not indispensable to consider the episode as an adaptation of Schopenhauer.

The changing point of view and the varying angle, within a general framework of *prospection* alternating with retrospection, stamp all Flaubert's work and suffice, with that heightening, which we noted in *Saint Antoine*, of the effect of instability already given in phenomena, to undermine our confidence in appearances. The opening chapter of *L'Éducation sentimentale* and especially the first chapter of Part III, the 'tour in the forest', where the characters themselves are visited by a vague uneasiness, constitute, amongst other things, a pure exposition of phenomenalism.

As regards its material elements, the episode of Mme Bordin and the peacocks might appear as not much more than the quintessence of the *Comices agricoles* chapter in *Madame Bovary* (rational superstructures, basic lust and self-interest, brutality of man to man, and man to animal). At no point, for that matter, had Flaubert viewed love apart from its complementary image, the fact of death and destruction. *Madame Bovary* is strongly marked by this double vision, and *Salammbô*, with *Hérodias* later, will appear, from one point of view, as demonstrations on such lines. The same might be said of *Saint Julien*, which is so far general that it could be interpreted almost indifferently in terms of De Sade, Schopenhauer, Buddhistic thought or Christianity.

With the veil of Māyā, the identity of all creatures, its corollary charity, and the doctrine of renunciation, we have to do, of course, with Vedantic and Buddhist themes to which Schopenhauer has no proprietary claim. Although the apparently increasing importance given to animals in *Un Cœur simple*, *Saint Julien* and *Bouvard et Pécuchet*, may seem significant, one should not forget the lions (for example) in *Salammbô*, Fox the dog in the first *Éducation sentimentale*, Djalioh in *Quidquid volueris*. The identity of man and man, as in the 'martyrdom' scene, reaches back, through *Un Cœur simple* (Mme Aubain and Félicité 'satisfaisant leur douleur dans un baiser qui les égalisait') and *L'Éducation sentimentale* (Frédéric by the corpse of Dambreuse[98]), to *Madame Bovary* itself, where Homais and Bournisien,

---

[98] We examined this episode in *Comparative Literature*, 1951, pp. 130–3 and 150.

during their vigil, succumb to sleep: 'après tant de désaccord se rencontrant enfin dans la même faiblesse humaine; et ils ne bougeaient pas plus que le cadavre à côté d'eux qui avait l'air de dormir.' While the theme of altruism appears only late in Flaubert (*Un Cœur simple*, *Saint Julien*), the doctrine of renunciation is implicit from the beginning. If *La Tentation* and *Madame Bovary* (with the role of Justin) put forward in their conclusion an image of perpetual recommencement, this is ultimately little more than irony in relation to the positive tenor of the work, which manifestly declares the vanity of all action. The end of *L'Éducation sentimentale*, which involves a return to the beginning like that of *Bouvard et Pécuchet*, should be compared to the latter in respect of its 'lesson' also. When Frédéric turns his back on Mme Arnoux in their last interview, he is repeating his behaviour at la Turque's in 1837, but this time from awareness — reached by thirty years' experience — of a fact precociously grasped by his creator: that man errs, not on a point of method, but in consenting to participate at all in a game which, according to Schopenhauer's favourite phrase, is not worth the candle. The injunction *Abstiens-toi* is far more relevant to Flaubert's 'meaning' here than the strictly limited ideas Thibaudet reads into the text,[99] and we may add that the injunction and its basis attain maximum expression only with this brutal but not ill-considered comparison of life with a *maison close*.

We must not forget that Flaubert is handling images, not ideas. Any attempt to bring him in line, from a moral point of view, for example, does violence to his intentions which remain firmly representational and to his vision which inevitably makes of each work, even reduced to its simplest definition (an evocation of perpetual flux in which is included, as its miniature,[100] an impression of human nature and behaviour seized in their general aspect) a monument to *l'éternel néant de tout*.

Flaubert bequeaths to Maupassant, as well as the theory of an impersonal

[99] P. 156. Cl.-Edm. Magny (*Les Sandales d'Empédocle*, 1945, p. 143) is presumably referring to Thibaudet's interpretation when she roundly declares of Flaubert's last chapter: 'Ce n'est pas une découverte bien sensationnelle.' In a preface of 1949 (cp. S. Cigada, 'Un decennio di critica flaubertiana', *Ist. Lombardo di Sc. e Lettere, Rendiconti*, 1957, p. 670) Robert Kemp still sees in the last page 'une espèce de gaminerie outrancière, faussement cynique'. The nature of Mme Durry's approach (*Flaubert et ses projets inédits*, 1950) precludes almost of necessity any consideration of this last page, which also applies to J.-P. Richard (*Littérature et Sensation*, Paris, 1954). E. Wilson had understated its meaning in *The Triple Thinkers* (1938) as 'a damnation of their whole society'.

[100] We may note here Flaubert's remarkable mania for the reduction of opposites, far remote from any *Hegelei*, and tending towards pure negation of reality. We are thinking of the sort of *chassé-croisé* involved when, in *L'Éducation sentimentale*, Mme Arnoux and Rosanette eventually exchange roles, or in *Bouvard et Pécuchet*, the two protagonists (like Don Quixote and Sancho) react on each other and are at times transposed, as also of the basic inspiration of *La Spirale, Une Nuit de Don Juan* and *Harel-Bey*.

and general art, the theme of illusion–disillusion and human imbecility, with a form which, whether or not presenting that circular pattern to which the subject lends itself, is at all times deliberate.[101] In contrast to the Goncourts, Zola, Daudet, who are interested in the particular, the exceptional, the pathological, almost envisaging the 'document' as an end in itself, and adopt a form which might be defined as that of the broken line and the suspension mark, Flaubert and Maupassant are concerned, over and above any question of mere style, evocation of details, or effects of pathos, with the beauty proper to the work of art, derived from its catholicity and its whole inner arrangement and proportions. It is evident that *Boule de Suif* and *Une Vie*, for example, continue Flaubert in these respects.

However, just as already in *Boule de Suif* the form is quaternary rather than ternary and just as Maupassant will later escape altogether (*Bel-Ami*) from the limitations of Flaubert's mould, so *Une Vie* corresponds to a vision not utterly identical with Flaubert's. With its four generations, its copious symbolism and the role played by nature and animal life, the novel presents characteristics one might perhaps associate more specifically with Zola: 'les hommes, les bêtes et les choses, en pleine coulée de la vie universelle (. . .) un monde où l'homme ne serait qu'un accident.' In addition to *bovarysme*, *Une Vie* involves, pessimistically orientated, Darwinism, Schopenhauerian notions of the identity of all creatures, the blind and ceaseless striving characteristic of the Will, and mechanistic conceptions. The nearest model we can think of for this in Flaubert is the episode of Mme Bordin and the peacocks, which, while announcing much that is characteristic of Maupassant's vision,[102] seemed, precisely, to invite comparison with Schopenhauer.

Schopenhauer's 'influence' on Maupassant, that is explicit or obvious allusions to Schopenhauer in Maupassant's journalistic essays and elsewhere, has been sufficiently examined by Neubert, Vogl and more recently Vial.[103] There is no need here to expand on the references Maupassant makes to the German whenever it is a question of human egoism, sexual relations, the will of the species, women, etc. This is so far true that a difference of opinion may well appear more enlightening than their general agreement. For example, Maupassant considers wives naturally unfaithful, and takes it as a matter of course, whereas Schopenhauer con-

---

[101] Cp. our article on Maupassant (*French Studies* V, 1951, pp. 1–17).

[102] Cp. our above-mentioned article, p. 7.

[103] F. Neubert, *Zeitschrift für Französische Sprache und Literatur, Supplementheft* VIII (1914), pp. 1–78, and IX (1919) pp. 1–130; A. Vogl, ibid., 1938, pp. 83–108; A. Vial, *Guy de Maupassant et l'art du roman*, Paris, 1954. However, if it is a question of *dating* Maupassant's contact with Schopenhauer, *Les Dimanches d'un bourgeois de Paris* and *Héraclius Gloss* would deserve far more attention than they have received.

siders fidelity the rule,[104] and deplores adultery on the part of the wife. In general terms, we have to do on one hand with a moralist, a preacher of asceticism, and on the other with one to whom such attitudes are quite foreign. If Schopenhauer explains the infidelity of the husband, the faithfulness of wives and pederasty by reference to the interests of the species,[105] while advocating total abstinence, Maupassant is capable at one moment of recommending voluntary sterility and alembicated modes of intercourse, for a *greater satisfaction* of the senses and as a way of *besting* Nature, and capable at other times of following the *divin marquis* in depicting cruelty and murder as logically falling in with nature's plan. In such a scheme, if one adds that the points listed by Neubert and Vial as illustrating Maupassant's 'pity' would be better classified as notations on the sufferings of the world, not only do morality and renunciation undergo an eclipse, but we enter a labyrinth of scepticism — *l'abîme effrayant du scepticisme* in Pécuchet's phrase[106] — which makes it the more desirable to appeal from what the artist says to what he shows.

As in the case of Descharmes on Flaubert, the dangers of an *a priori* approach to literature are amply illustrated by Vial's account of Maupassant. This scholar, who notes almost every aspect of Maupassant's 'ideas', in so far as expressly stated, and every view that could be classified as Schopenhauerian, and who at the same time postulates that Maupassant's aesthetics follow on Flaubert's, nevertheless gives of Maupassant's texts an interpretation so narrow that neither Schopenhauer's nor Flaubert's worldview survives with any completeness and Maupassant is imprisoned in the abstract idea and in the particular.

So as not to dwell unduly on Maupassant, we shall confine ourselves to one or two texts. Vial rightly sees *Amour* as alluding to the ineluctable urge of the species whether human or animal[107] (the male dies out of its attachment to the female). Yet this is only part of what the author sets before us. What of the *fait-divers* mentioned at the beginning ('Il l'a tué, puis il s'est tué, donc il l'aimait'), the relator's remarks on his passion for the chase (literally for *la bête saignante*) and on the marsh, now frozen, with which he associates normally ideas of heat, life and spontaneous generation? The tale, like *Saint Julien*, manifestly concerns not only love but blood-lust, both the procreative and the destructive aspect of the Will, at the same time hinting at the ambivalence of the sexual instinct itself. With its opposition of cold and heat, death and life, destruction and love, and

[104] *Metaphysik der Geschlechtsliebe* (vol. II, p. 693); *Parerga* (vol. IV, p. 440).
[105] Vol. II, pp. 678–727.
[106] *Bouvard et Pécuchet*, p. 283.
[107] P. 196.

with the series: birds, dogs, men, infinite space, *Amour* is a complex of images composing a *generalization* on the universe which might be *approximately* defined as 'Schopenhauer's world as Will', but certainly not in any abstract formula such as that employed by Vial: 'un traité de l'amour absolu dans le règne animal'.[108]

In *Bel-Ami*,[109] Norbert de Varenne's thoughts on death and on the curse of intellect, his advice to Bel-Ami, of all people, to liberate himself from the slavery of the Will, are noted as Schopenhauerian by Vial,[110] who refers[111] to the death of Forestier as being in the same key, that is, concerned with destruction and decomposition. He does not allow for the fact[112] that the latter episode has a double nature, depicting not only the ultimate goal of all striving, but also, in their full power, the workings of the Will in Bel-Ami and Madeleine. For this critic, as for Thibaudet,[113] Maupassant's novel as a whole is the story of 'une vie qui se fait', analogous to the story of Rastignac. 'Duroy réussit,' says Vial.[114] Rather than accept this conception of *Bel-Ami* as a success-story, the pessimism of which is to be sought only in the mean and corrupt nature ascribed to the hero, we prefer to insist on the *bergauf bergab* image borrowed from Schopenhauer by Norbert de Varenne and to see in *Bel-Ami* a diptych of which the second part, unwritten and implicit, is nevertheless strongly and eloquently suggested. The death of Forestier should be related to the whole text in the same way as the *pied bot* chapter relates to the rest of *Madame Bovary*. Such an interpretation alone permits us to credit Maupassant with true originality of form and with a theme and a meaning which would have satisfied Flaubert's requirement of generality.

Like *Amour* and *Bel-Ami*, *Pierre et Jean* has suffered from an encroachment upon aesthetics of what amounts to a principle of simplification prepared to seize, if need be, to the exclusion of all the rest, on the secondary aspect of a text, if this aspect offers an apparent conformity with accepted ideas. We may note that the itch to 'classify' Maupassant's fiction (on the basis, for example, of geographical setting, the social status, sex or other particular qualities of the main characters) having led to the discovery that many of his works are concerned with the illegitimate child and the unfaithful wife or mistress, critics often complete the circle, when returning to *Pierre et Jean* (or *Le Champ d'oliviers* for that matter), by finding

---

[108] Pp. 473–4.
[109] Conard, pp. 206–13.
[110] P. 125.
[111] P. 223.
[112] Cp. for this our article in *Comparative Literature*, 1951, pp. 133–7.
[113] *Nouvelle Revue Française*, November 1932, pp. 746–52.
[114] P. 358.

within the work no more than is indicated on the label they themselves have arbitrarily devised. Vial goes to extreme lengths here, firmly maintaining that Maupassant's last three novels can be sufficiently characterized in a short and simple abstract formula. Thus *Pierre et Jean* is 'l'adultère et l'enfant adultérin agents de désorganisation de la famille'.[115] As proof of his idea, he adduces Pierre's reflection: 'Il se trouvait condamné à cette vie de forçat vagabond uniquement parce que sa mère s'était livrée aux caresses d'un homme.' In Vial's interpretation this means 'because his mother had committed adultery'. Yet the most important allusion of the sentence, whether or not Pierre should be taken as realizing it, is to the torments of existence[116] consequent on the fact of having been born at all. One step further on, and Cogny will credit Maupassant with a profound conviction of *le devoir sacré de la paternité* and the belief that all begetting of children outside matrimony is a crime.[117] *Pierre* may consider with Schopenhauer, whose opinion on women, on the vanity of human activities and on the domination of the rational by the instinctive self he also shares, that: 'Quand la femme est devenue mère, son devoir a grandi, puisque la nature lui confie une race. Si elle succombe alors, elle est lâche, indigne et infâme.'[118] But Pierre is not Maupassant, and we would say that, far from appearing intelligent and far from analysing himself lucidly until he reaches the point where, nothing remaining for him to discover, the novel necessarily ends,[119] Pierre explores certain upper levels of the subconscious, as described by Schopenhauer,[120] but is condemned to perpetual error in that he fails to trace back his own behaviour and thoughts to their real root, the brute will of the species.

In this connection, as indeed for the whole tenor of the work, the role of the secondary characters is essential and organic — Pierre is not, *pace* Vial, the whole subject of the novel. What this subject is, in all its generality, we have attempted to describe elsewhere:[121] it is on the lines of *Amour* and the Mme Bordin episode from one point of view, on those of *Boule de Suif* and *Bouvard et Pécuchet* from another. From the latter angle, we have to do with a work in which, more subtly perhaps than was the case in *Bouvard et Pécuchet*, ideas have become plastic notations, a generalized study of the limitations of the human reason and of its role as a mere tool of the Will.

[115] P. 368.
[116] Cp. *Parerga*, p. 327 (*eine Strafanstalt, a penal colony*).
[117] *Pierre et Jean*, Garnier, 1959, pp. xlviii and liii.
[118] Ch. v.
[119] Thus Vial, p. 405.
[120] Cp. e.g. vol. II, pp. 174–5.
[121] *French Studies*, 1951, pp. 15–7.

The following passage, with its echoes of Flaubert's phenomenalism and the suggestion of universal illusion (the variegated elements of the description, the dissolving imagery, Pierre's confused sensations) and with its Schopenhauerian pattern — objects meaningless and indifferent viewed from outside the stream of willing (for Pierre is absorbed in his own thoughts) take on importance again for one reimmersed in the Will — may serve to epitomize the two aspects of the novel:

> Sur la grande dune de sable jaune, depuis la jetée jusqu'aux Roches Noires, les ombrelles de toutes les couleurs, les chapeaux de toutes les formes, les toilettes de toutes les nuances, par groupes devant les cabines, par lignes le long du flot ou dispersées çà et là, ressemblaient vraiment à des bouquets énormes dans une prairie démesurée. Et le bruit confus, proche et lointain des voix égrenées dans l'air léger, les appels, les cris d'enfants qu'on baigne, les rires clairs des femmes faisaient une rumeur continue et douce, mêlée à la brise insensible et qu'on aspirait avec elle (. . .)
>
> Il les frôlait, entendait, sans écouter, quelques phrases; et il voyait, sans regarder, les hommes parler aux femmes et les femmes sourire aux hommes.
>
> Mais tout à coup, comme s'il s'éveillait, il les aperçut distinctement; et une haine surgit en lui contre eux, car ils semblaient heureux et contents.[122]

We have not sought, in the field of art, to explain Maupassant in terms of Flaubert. While presenting formal and thematic resemblances with the master, the disciple shows himself capable of a freedom of design, a use of homely materials, a mastery of the sustained tragic, not strictly characteristic of Flaubert. Nor has our purpose been to establish the influence of Schopenhauer on Flaubert's ideas — Flaubert was in many ways formed by 1838, as witness the last pages of *Mémoires d'un fou* — nor that of Flaubert and Schopenhauer on Maupassant's. The three are not identical in strict metaphysics, Flaubert the sceptic contrasting both with Schopenhauer and with the ultimately materialist Maupassant, and the two French writers show little trace of the quasi-Christian ethics of Schopenhauer, in their express opinions. The general identity of all three would only become apparent, once again, in a descriptive scheme of human behaviour on the lines: pessimism, including a conviction, increasingly profound, of the limitations and ancillary character of the reason, and, consequent on these, resort to intuition, contemplation and the pure mirroring of phenomena — a system which the optimist would no doubt more pithily characterize as sour grapes.

The main link between the three, on the level of ideas, is their conception of art as impersonal, general, and involving a communication of 'truth' quite beyond the power of discursive thinking. Our aim has been to corroborate their theories (a) negatively, by drawing attention to the debates, the misinterpretations and the distortion which arise from an approach to literature implying the opposite of such views, (b) positively, by attempting to show that in very truth Flaubert's and Maupassant's novels have more to say than either author ever said in the first person, and by suggesting the richness and multiplicity of 'meanings' — albeit in this case pessimistically coloured — presented by true works of art.

The fact that these 'meanings' have not been self-evident, and indeed have not been arrived at here without difficulty, constitutes no argument if one realizes that these texts were not meant to be analysed, but to be grasped intuitively.[123] That they are so grasped by the average reader who approaches them without preconceived ideas, we would be prepared to wager! As to our own approach, if it has been — inevitably — analytic and discursive, it has at least attempted to do justice to the original, pre-conceptual data, to mirror, not to abstract, the work in question, and to have regard for the *whole*.

That our findings should appear strange and unacceptable, that the authors we have been dealing with should appear retrospectively as limited and 'dated', can be explained in terms of, and serve to corroborate, their own thought (on the inadequacy of the reason, its *practical* orientation and the illusion of progress).

It is appropriate, in more ways than one, for our discussion, that Proust, to whom few if any will refuse the title of thinker, Proust who, aware of the tendency of literary generations to destroy each other,[124] condemns equally so-called realism and the literature of ideas,[125] and denies the competence of *l'intelligence raisonneuse* in the judgment of matters of art,[126] should have expounded a theory of art and life which strongly echoes Flaubert and Schopenhauer:

> Ce travail de l'artiste, de chercher à apercevoir sous de la matière, sous de l'expérience, sous des mots quelque chose de différent, c'est exactement le travail inverse de celui que, à chaque minute, quand nous vivons détourné de nous-même, l'amour-propre, la passion,

---

[123] Cp. Schopenhauer, *Über das innere Wesen der Kunst* (vol. II, p. 522).
[124] *Le côté de Guermantes* (Pléiade), vol. II, p. 469.
[125] *Le Temps retrouvé*, vol. III, pp. 881–2.
[126] Ibid., p. 893.

l'intelligence, et l'habitude aussi accomplissent en nous, quand elles [*sic*] amassent au-dessus de nos impressions vraies, pour nous les cacher entièrement, les nomenclatures, les buts pratiques que nous appelons faussement la vie (...) C'est ce travail que l'art défera, c'est la marche en sens contraire, le retour aux profondeurs où ce qui a existé réellement gît inconnu de nous, qu'il nous fera suivre.[127]

Now, with its atomization of character, its relativism, its correspondences, its insistence on flux and transformation, Proust's incomparably elaborate picture not only materially resembles the world of Flaubert but, as pure thought, comes to no more than *une leçon d'idéalisme*,[128] followed (as with Schopenhauer) by an intuition of the thing-in-itself, here situated partly in art (compare Flaubert), partly outside time and even space (compare the Will in Schopenhauer).

The positive elements of this thought are expressed with a vagueness sufficient to make them appear consoling, but what deserves attention above all is the fact that, after liberally interweaving generalizations into the main body of the narrative, the relator adds to his picture an abstract account of what it means. It must be largely for this reason that Proust, especially after the last volumes appeared, became officially a thinker, although all he has to say is fully contained in the non-discursive sections of the work. It is for this reason, and because of an inveterate belief in progress in all spheres, that, when this or that feature of Flaubert or Maupassant is noted as 'anticipating Proust', it is with a sort of surprise that such writers could be so 'modern', and even as if they were basking in a glory *borrowed from Proust*.[129]

What Flaubert would have said of Proust's last volume would be a foregone conclusion, were it not for the fact that the scholia of *Le Temps retrouvé* may be at least in part ironic, given Proust's sense of the ridiculous and his remark, at this very point:

> Une œuvre où il y a des théories est comme un objet sur lequel on laisse la marque du prix.[130]

---

[127] P. 896. Proust goes on to insist on the necessity of envisaging things under their general aspect.

[128] P. 910.

[129] J. Pommier, *La Mystique de Marcel Proust*, 1939; G. Poulet, *Études sur le temps humain*, 1949, ch. xv; Margaret Mein, 'Flaubert, a Precursor of Proust', *French Studies*, 1963, pp. 218–37. It is one thing to declare the ideality of Time, quite another to speak of pure, solid or elastic time, or of renewing, recapturing, defying or conquering time. But the ultimate crime is to imprison any *artist* within such abstractions.

[130] Vol. III, p. 882.

G. W. IRELAND

Prolegomena to a Study of Inspiration in Gide

A T the outset of Proust's great spiritual adventure, his hero tells us how he would sometimes lose in sleep all sense of his own identity. He would feel that he *was* the subject-matter of the book he had been reading as he fell asleep: 'une église, un quattuor, la rivalité de François Ier et de Charles-Quint'. When he awoke his sense of this loss filled him with anguish; but 'comme un secours d'en haut pour me tirer du néant d'où je n'aurais pu sortir tout seul', memory would come to his aid and, by permitting him to recognize certain familiar objects in his room, 'recomposaient peu à peu les traits originaux de mon moi'.[1]

The self that is thus restored to him is anterior to the moment of anguish and independent of the experience which gave rise to it. It may have been temporarily in abeyance; but once restored to him it reasserts its absolute autonomy by marking the radical division that separates it, as subject, from the objects that surround it.

In Gide, consciousness reacts very differently to confrontation with something other than itself. It tends to move in precisely the opposite direction — towards the condition, in fact, in which Proust's sleeping hero no longer distinguishes himself from the subject-matter of his book. The critical psychological movement is, in fact, reversed.[2]

The self, in Proust, is fortified by confrontation with an object; in Gide it is challenged. Frequently Gide is far more aware of the appeal — the active solicitation — of that which presents itself to his awareness than he is of any positive act of consciousness on the part of an autonomous self. He says explicitly that our ideas are formed independently of our will and

---

Unless otherwise stated references are to the fifteen volumes of the *Oeuvres Complètes* [OC] published by Gallimard (1933–9) except in the case of the *Journal* and other personal writings, for which references are to the two volumes of the *Pléiade* edition (Gallimard 1948, 1954). Such abbreviations as are used will be self-explanatory.

[1] *A la Recherche du Temps perdu*, Bibliothèque de la Pléiade I, 3–6.

[2] Contrast, for example, with Proust's position, Gide's declaration: 'L'espoir de me réveiller quelqu'un d'autre m'engage à laisser s'endormir qui je suis.' [*J*, I, 982].

that their survival depends on 'une sorte de "struggle for life" ' *among themselves*.³

And this is true, of course, not only of ideas. The passive way in which the Gidean self participates in experience in general is suggested by innumerable passages throughout his work. Contact with an object, he tells us, '(je ne dis pas: objet matériel seulement,)' rarely produces in him a simple and unified reaction: 'Le plus souvent [. . .] *s'offre aussitôt en moi* la série complète.'⁴ On finding himself, for example, in the course of an Alpine journey, unexpectedly face to face with Mont Blanc, he describes how 'j'ai *entendu s'élever en moi* vingt interjections confuses [. . .]';⁵ and the *Journal* is full of such incidents.

It is made abundantly clear that, on these occasions, the self does not attribute to itself the initiative in experiencing whatever emotions or ideas the situation may call forth. This circumstance is in no way regarded as a defeat. It engenders no feeling of anguish or even of frustration. Gide is perfectly satisfied to feel '[. . .] au contraire de l'égoïsme et du souci d'égocentrisme [. . .] une quasi complète indifférence à l'égard de *ma* façon de sentir'.⁶

So complete, in fact, is this indifference and so strong Gide's sense of the role played by the *non-moi* in initiating experience that he is led to make a very striking suggestion:

> Cette violence, cette impétuosité des désirs, il ne nous semble point tant qu'elle soit en nous, mais plutôt en l'objet même de nos désirs [. . .].⁷

What is evoked in this crucial text is something more and other than mere inadequacy on the part of the self. It would be perfectly possible to conceive of a feeble self reacting weakly to experience and capable only of tepid emotions or commonplace ideas, but which would yet be the centre and fountainhead of this mediocrity. In Gide, on the other hand, the debility of the self by no means excludes violent emotions or daring ideas. It is rather that, to the presence of such ideas or emotions, the presence of the self as such seems wholly irrelevant. The self may, in fact, appear to be

---

³ *J*, 2, 114. My italics. Commenting on the programme for one of the Pontigny *décades*, at which the debate between Christianity and Humanism was to be discussed, Gide explains to Desjardins: 'C'est celui même qui se livre en moi, auquel je me livre (dans le sens de "se donner en pâture").' [Letter to Paul Desjardins in the Gide-Du Bos correspondence, p. 107.]

⁴ *Caractères*, OC, 12, 5–6.

⁵ Ibid. My italics.

⁶ Letter to Jean-Marc Bernard, OC, 6, 472. Gide's italics.

⁷ *J*, 1, 960.

literally absent. However poetically it is made, the suggestion is perfectly serious:

> Est-ce bien moi qui suis assis dans cette petite cour de mosquée, moi qui respire, et moi qui t'aime? Ou rêvé-je seulement de t'aimer? Si *bien réellement j'étais*, aurait-elle volé si près de moi cette hirondelle?[8]

Extreme as this position may sound, it is attested again and again. 'Il m'est très difficile,' he writes to a friend, 'de te parler de moi [. . .] *je* n'existe plus';[9] and these words find many echoes throughout his work. When he say of his wife, for example: 'il me semble que, sans elle, je n'aurais jamais *riens* été',[10] '[. . .] je ne vivais que par elle'[11] or: 'elle était ma réalité',[12] he means quite literally what he says; and the famous declaration from the *Journal des Faux-Monnayeurs* is no less literal:

> [. . .] dans la vie, c'est la pensée, l'émotion d'autrui qui m'habite; mon cœur ne bat que par sympathie.[13]

It is therefore, so to speak, outside the self — outside the self as subject — that Gide's experiences tend characteristically to take place. This situation is inevitably pregnant with potential distress. For the experiences which thus escape identification with the self are still *his* experiences. They are not only all the contact he has with life; they are his only means of identifying himself to himself; and they are woefully inadequate. 'Je me sens,' he exclaims, 'désespérément loin de moi-même.'[14] He seems to witness from a distance those experiences which are his only by proxy and to recognize himself with the greatest difficulty in their protagonist. This sense of being separated, as it were, from himself ('De moi à moi quelle distance'[15]) is a permanent source of uneasiness, though it can degenerate into a form of lightheaded complacency or, on the other hand, be sublimated into a form of inspiration. This is not a case of a simple romantic *dédoublement*. What this state above all betrays is a fundamental incapacity on the part of the self to identify itself with its own experiences or, in other words, to come to grips *directly* with life:

> [. . .] Je ne colle pas, je n'ai jamais pu parfaitement coller avec la

---

[8] *J*, I, 401. My italics.

[9] Lettre à A . . . R . . ., OC, 2, 481. Gide's italics.

[10] *J*, 2, 1154. Gide's italics.

[11] *J*, 2, 1155.

[12] *Ainsi soit-il*, *J*, 2, 1164. It is not, of course, exclusively to Madeleine that this experience is related. In his *Journal* Gide quotes from one of his own letters to Marc Allégret: 'Par crainte de trop vivre à travers toi, j'ai voulu me passer de toi pour un temps; je ne vis plus.' [*J*, I, 908.]

[13] *Journal des Faux-Monnayeurs*, OC, 13, 49.

[14] *J*, I, 366.

[15] *J*, I, 365.

réalité. Il n'y a même pas, à proprement parler, dédoublement qui fasse que, en moi, quelqu'un reste spectateur de celui qui agit. Non: c'est celui même qui agit ou souffre, qui ne se prend pas au sérieux. Je crois même que, à l'article de la mort, je me dirai: tiens! il meurt.[16]

From time to time, particularly in his youth, Gide's sense of the nebulous character of the self provokes in him a reaction of protest. In its very feebleness the Gidean *ego* is flattered and seduced by Schopenhauer's description of the self into just those 'prétentions à l'égocentrisme' which he more characteristically disavows. Schopenhauer had said that the subject, knowing all while being itself unknown, was therefore, 'le support du monde' and the adolescent André Walter brandishes like a banner 'cette pensée orgueilleuse'.[17] More than half a century later, however, Gide returns to this very text and deals more characteristically with the pretensions it puts forward:

> Lors de mon initiation à la métaphysique allemande, j'étais resté longtemps tout émerveillé devant la phrase de Schopenhauer: 'Je suis[18] donc le support du monde . . .' Il m'en souvient fort bien, après plus d'un demi-siècle: rien n'existait qu'en fonction de moi. C'était grisant. A présent la question se retournait: Tout existait et continuait d'être sans mon aide. Le monde n'avait aucun besoin de moi. Et durant un assez long temps (cela dura, je pense, un quart d'heure) je *m'absentai*; il me semble que je n'étais plus là; et ma disparition passait inaperçue.[19]

The very tone of this commentary ('C'était grisant'!) amounts to a wry confession of the petulant, almost wilful, character of the youthful enthusiasm; but it is not necessary to wait for the end of Gide's life to see that Gide's adoption of Schopenhauer's claims, as he understood them, owed more to wistfulness than to conviction. Already in *André Walter* there is a febrile quality in the expression of this incitement to a metaphysical heroism which betrays a mind of a very different temper from that of Schopenhauer. It is too little to say that the words with which Gide's hero tries to bolster up his resolution fail to convey any real sense of confidence. They are expressions of despair, intimations of impending surrender. Schopenhauer's position is, perhaps, the one which *would be* called for ('L'âme agissante, *voilà le désirable* [. . .]');[20] but to maintain one-

---

[16] *Ainsi soit-il, J*, 1226–7.
[17] *André Walter*, OC, 1, 100.
[18] The change to the first person indicates clearly in what sense Gide understood Schopenhauer's text.
[19] *Ainsi soit-il, J*, 2, 1177.
[20] *André Walter*, OC, 1, 36. My italics.

self in it would demand an effort which Gide's hero knows in his heart he cannot sustain. It is because defeat stares him in the face that he must avert his eyes:

> Il ne faut pas que la ferveur faiblisse — sinon tout retombe aussitôt; il ne faut même pas y songer [. . .][21]

This wilful blindness is the last ditch. The subjective world — the world of which the will of the subject is the only prop — can be maintained intact only by a refusal to respond to solicitations from without.

> Si j'arrivais à contempler la chimère avec assez de fixité pour que mes yeux éblouis du mirage n'aient plus un seul regard pour les réalités ambiantes, la chimère inventée m'apparaîtrait réelle [. . .].[22]

The conditional mood is a confession. The 'réalités ambiantes' are not to be denied.

For the self, which André Walter called upon somewhat plaintively to resist or at least to ignore them, demonstrates at every turn its helplessness to defend its integrity against their encroachment. It is 'extrêmement (et peu s'en faut que je ne dise déplorablement) accessible à la sympathie [. . .][23] It is at the mercy of every chance encounter. The beauty of natural objects 's'infiltre en moi jusqu'au cœur';[24] the warmth of the sun 'entre en moi, monte en moi comme de la sève'.[25] Images of penetration, of invasion, of porosity such as these never cease to testify to the self's defencelessness:

> [. . .] la nature me pénétrait [. . .] je ne sentais plus à mon corps de limites; il se continuait plus loin; ou parfois, voluptueusement, devenait poreux comme un sucre; je fondais [. . .].[26]

Here the word 'voluptueusement' suggests very clearly how ill-adapted this self is to the heroically defensive role in which André Walter would have cast it. Certain passages from Gide's reading, even, were 'si voluptueusement pénétrantes que je sentais la phrase entrer comme matériellement dans mon cœur'.[27]

In personal relations Gide is even more aware of '[. . .] cet absurde besoin de me livrer, sans armes, sans malice, au premier venu'[28] and the images

---

[21] Op cit., 151.
[22] Op. cit., 114.
[23] J, I, 1219.
[24] J, I, 136.
[25] J, I, 216.
[26] Nourritures terrestres, OC, 2, 102. Hereafter referred to as NT.
[27] J, I, 198.
[28] J, I, 245.

which evoke this surrender are, if possible, more striking still. At the foyer for Belgian refugees to which Gide gave his services during the First World War, 'je me sentais *bu* par autrui.'[29] A still more violent image tells how, during his journey through the Congo, crowds of natives thronged about him:

> Et tout ce peuple vous enveloppe, s'empresse pour la joie de serrer la main qu'on leur tend; tous avec des cris et des rires, une sorte de lyrisme dans les démonstrations d'amour. *C'est presque du canni-balisme.*[30]

The defensive position into which Schopenhauer led André Walter is besieged, so to speak, by whole herds of Trojan horses. Its fall is inevitable and Schopenhauer's youthful disciple is duly buried under the wreckage. Like Alissa, like the companions of Urien, he had nothing to offer but a '*vertu de résistance*'[31] and for Gide this virtue will no longer serve. A fortress is, by its very nature, partially a prison. With the overthrow of the fortress the prison is also destroyed. The self may have lost in Walter a quixotic champion but at least it is now freed from the tyranny of the will. The mood of exaltation that had inspired Walter's desperate resistance gives way to a more realistic appraisal of its limitations and possibilities:

> L'âme humaine (et pourquoi craindre d'employer ce mot pour désigner ce faisceau d'émotions, de tendances, de susceptibilités dont le lien n'est peut-être que physiologique) reste de contours vaporeux, changeants, insaisissables, constamment modifiés et modifiables au gré des circonstances, des climats, des saisons, de toutes les influences, de sorte que la volonté la plus tendue et la plus vigilante a bien du mal à y maintenir un semblant de cohésion.[32]

The tone may still be a little wistful; but there is no real sense of bitterness in this defeat. Indeed, in order to convert defeat into glory, Gide has only to substitute for the bankrupt pretensions of egocentrism a scale of values which not only replaces but transcends them. By virtue of his own nature, the solution lies directly in his path; but he finds in the Bible a precious aid (and what he would no doubt have called an authorisation) in the task of formulating his own vision. No other writer leans more heavily on quotation than Gide does; yet one text recurs throughout his writing

---

[29] *J*, 1, 500. Gide's italics.
[30] *Voyage au Congo, J*, 2, 768. My italics.
[31] 'Notre vertu, Seigneur, est toute faite de résistance [. . .].' [*Le Voyage d'Urien*, OC, 1, 331.] '[. . .] une vertu de résistance à l'usage des jours de pluie [. . .]' [*La Porte étroite*, OC, 5, 166.]
[32] *J*, 2, 133.

with far more frequency than any other. It is as if he saw in it the key to his whole position as a man and as an artist:

> Celui qui aime sa vie, qui protège sa personnalité, la perdra: mais celui-là qui en fera l'abandon *la rendra vraiment vivante* [. . .][33]

The implications of this text for Gide, on many levels of meaning, are so momentous that it may well be considered as the starting-point of his experience of inspiration. It offers him in the first place the possibility of transposing a fundamental psychological movement from a key of abjection to one of ecstatic lyrical abandon; and, more important still, it teaches him that in yielding to his most deeply-rooted impulses he is not impoverishing his response to life, but, on the contrary, making for himself a life more intense and more abundant. Almost every page of the *Nourritures terrestres* furnishes a litany for this new creed.[34]

> Nathanaël, que chaque attente, en toi, ne soit même pas un désir, mais simplement une disposition à l'accueil. Attends tout ce qui vient à toi; mais ne désire que ce qui vient à toi [. . .] L'unique bien c'est la vie.[35]

Since, in principle, no limit is set to this 'disposition à l'accueil', the self becomes, as it were, an 'open city' offering no resistance to invasion. Into it from every side pour wave after wave of sensual experiences, metaphysical suggestions, spiritual promptings, social attitudes, solicitations of every kind, jostling each other for pride of place, each striving for the exclusive adoption which would enable it to drive the others from the citadel and reign alone. As the overcrowding proceeds unchecked the confusion becomes more and more intolerable.

> C'est dans ma tête un fouillis inextricable; chaque pensée nouvelle, en se déplaçant, remue toutes les autres. Rien n'est délimité précisément, et cette absence de contours, qui fait peut-être les rapports plus perceptibles, fait aussi que tout se confond dans ma tête et que chaque concept s'accroche un peu à tous les autres.[36]

As early as 1891, Gide suggests with rare precocity that 'cette complexité inextricable des émotions, et ces systèmes de vibrations' which had oppressed him on the eve of writing *André Walter*, 'c'est peut-être l'état

---

[33] OC, 11, 262. My italics. Gide, as we shall see later, insists on this precise formulation.

[34] This theme is, of course, not restricted to the *NT*, any more than the *NT* is restricted to this theme; but for obvious historical reasons it plays a particularly prominent part in that work.

[35] *NT*, OC, 2, 73-4.

[36] *J*, 1, 30.

qui toujours chez moi précédera la production nouvelle et suivra les longs repos'.[37] But although this state may precede each new work of art clearly it cannot, in itself, conduce to literary creation.[38] In itself it amounts to a state of complete paralysis:

> Ah! si pouvait se simplifier ma pensée [. . .] Je reste là, parfois tout un matin, ne *pouvant* rien faire [. . .].[39]

In this confusion of 'lignes dans tous les sens, et pas de direction'[40] he has certainly found an abundance of life; but '[. . .] mes richesses s'entrenuisent:[41] 'Ce qui m'empêche d'écrire [. . .] c'est la complexité inextricable des émotions plus encore que leur multiplicité [. . .]'[42]

It was in order to achieve a rapturous sense of plenitude that consent had been given to the self's surrender.[43] Now, as the sense of confusion, of overcrowding, of suffocation grows more and more paralysing, it grows more and more evident that 'le sentiment de la complexité peut devenir une stupéfaction passionnée', amounting to a state of anguish: '[. . .] car enfin ma tête en éclate de la pression des émotions accumulées'.[44]

What has gone wrong? The fact that these swarming emotions should *accumulate* implies the existence of a *place* which can contain them; and their co-habitation will produce *pressure* only if this place has definite limits. Consent to the surrender of the self, it is clear, does not entail — or at least does not necessarily achieve — its total suppression. For it is only against a framework provided by the self that this pressure can be built up:

> Il est aisé de considérer l'âme comme cette *particule de terrain* où maintes plantes distinctes croissent et tant d'insectes vivent. Il y a surabondance, il y a lutte, il y aura donc suppression. C'est trop, c'est trop! Si l'on n'arrache celle-ci elle étouffera celle-là. Si vous n'arrachez rien, la nature va disposer de la lutte.'[45]

As we have already suggested, 'l'âme humaine' appears in Gide less as the protagonist or subject of experience than as the scene of a swarming activity for which it is not responsible but which it is powerless to resist.

[37] *J*, I, 19.
[38] *J*, I, 1,029.
[39] *J*, I, 47. Gide's italics.
[40] *J*, I, 842.
[41] *J*, I, 717.
[42] *André Walter*, OC, I, 104–105.
[43] '[. . .] ce qui nous exalte, c'est le sentiment de la plénitude.' [*J*, I, 39.]
[44] *André Walter*, OC, I, 104.
[45] *J*, I, 93–4. My italics.

So independent indeed does the self appear of the ideas and emotions which overrun it that, as the tension and complexity caused by their proliferating mount, Gide envisages again and again nothing less than a total withdrawal of the self from the situation!

> Il arrive un moment où tout devient par trop compliqué. A force de tirer des fils d'un point à l'autre, d'établir des rapports, des inter-dépendances, des relations, le moindre acheminement de l'esprit dans cette toile ébranle tant de considérants qu'il reste en surplus, immobile, et *voudrait sortir du jeu*, recommencer à neuf, ignorer [. . .].[46]

> [. . .] Je sens en moi toujours assemblée, une foule contradictoire; certaines fois, je voudrais agiter la sonnette, me couvrir et quitter la séance. Que m'importe *mon* opinion?[47]

> Ah! je voudrais crier: 'Pouce,' *sortir du jeu*.[48]

> Fuir! habiter pour un temps je ne sais quelle région abstraite, creuse et démeublée, où *s'abstenir de vivre* [. . .][49]

The very form of these emotional outbursts, however, makes it clear that they do not offer a serious proposal for overcoming the sense of oppression against which they protest. If, by withdrawing from the situation, the self can only 's'abstenir de vivre' such a withdrawal is not an escape. On the other hand, if no way is found to relieve the pressure which is building up against the limits of the self, these limits will be literally exploded:

> Je mourrai par éclatement [. . .][50]

At the point of anguish, indeed, one form of total suppression of the self appears, not as a catastrophe, but as the most seductive of temptations. For if it were possible for the self to oppose literally no resistance at all to an external stimulus, if the subject were to lose itself so completely in the object as to be indistinguishable from it, no pressure of the one upon the other could be maintained. The temptation is exquisite and it is exquisitely evoked:

> Dès que l'air est suffisamment tiède et le ciel bleu, je souhaite m'évaporer dans la nature entière, emporté par la brise qui passe [. . .][51]

[46] *J*, I, 1,265. My italics.
[47] *Caractères*, OC, 12, 5–6. Gide's italics.
[48] *J*, I, 1,261. My italics.
[49] *J*, I, 1,243. My italics.
[50] *J*, I, 639.
[51] *Feuillets d'Automne, J*, I, 1,084.

The image of liquefaction followed by evaporation recurs again and again:

> Mon cœur naturellement aimant *et comme liquide* se répandait de toutes parts . . .[52]

> [. . .] j'éclate, je fonds, je m'évapore, me subtilise dans l'azur.[53]

> Il aurait voulu être goutte d'eau, se disperser comme une buée subtile [. . .].[54]

> [. . .] je me sens évanouir dans une tendresse infinie qui se répand sur toute chose. Quel moment ineffable où la monade abandonnée se dissipe comme une brume . . .[55]

But, however rapturous the sense of relief may be, it is soon apparent that it is only the *moment* of abandon that is 'ineffable'. It is the *process* of evaporation that is delightful. Once the dissolution of the self is completed experience is at an end.

Having sought to achieve communion with Emmanuèle by just such a total surrender of the self, André Walter finds himself face to face with inevitable failure:

> Je sens la confusion de nos âmes; je ne sens pas nos âmes se confondre. Pour que la mienne, se mêle à la tienne il faut que je perde la notion de sa vie résistante, la conscience d'elle-même: L'âme devient passive alors. Ainsi le Nirvana n'est un bien qu'avec la saveur du néant goûtée dans le non-vivre même. Il y a négation. La communion ne sera jamais parfaite; ou, parfaite, elle ne se sentira pas.[56]

The sense of relief on which these raptures depend exists only in function of the pressure experienced and relieved. When this pressure is altogether absent the tensions to which it gave rise are replaced by 'un morne engourdissement de l'esprit [. . .]'[57] which is scarcely more tolerable. In this condition Gide describes himself as 'vegetating'[58] and says of himself that:

> [. . .] sitôt que son esprit n'était pas surtendu, il retombait dans un engourdissement torpide et dont il lui semblait alors que même le bruit du canon proche ne le sortirait pas.[59]

[52] *NT*, OC, 2, 118. My italics.
[53] *Mopsus*, OC, 3, 7.
[54] Fragments de la *Nouvelle Éducation sentimentale*, OC, 1, 4.
[55] *Notes d'un Voyage en Bretagne*, OC, 1, 13.
[56] *André Walter*, OC, 1, 73.
[57] *J*, 1, 144.
[58] Ibid.
[59] *J*, 1, 484.

This condition is no more viable than the extremes of tension whose place it has taken:

> [. . .] dès que je ne suis plus tendu vers quelque chose, je m'embête à mort et n'ai plus de plaisir à vivre.[60]

And, of course, he finds himself in no better posture to undertake the creation of a work of art. When this 'torpeur végétative' takes possession of him, he is 'perdu pour le travail'.[61] 'Très loin du ciel; et même, simplement, de la terre,'[62] he hovers in limbo, '[. . .] las de *ne pas être*.'[63]

Neither through aggressive self-assertion nor through total surrender before the multiple solicitations of external life can a path be found that will lead to the creation of a work of art. The only conceivable starting point for such an undertaking must be the plenitude of experience to which we have already referred. But merely to say so is to recall to mind the difficulties with which that state confronts us.

> L'ennui d'écrire, car écrire quoi? Pourquoi plutôt une que l'autre de toutes ces émotions qui réclament leur forme [. . .]?[64]

Even if it were possible to choose between conflicting claimants, Gide is notoriously committed in principle to a refusal to make such a choice. How, in any case, could such a choice be made? The claims of each of these emotions exactly balance the claims of any other.

Of all the compliments ever paid him, Gide was perhaps proudest of Claudel's description of him as 'un esprit sans pente'.[65] But this state of equilibrium has two phases. To the second of these we shall come in due course. For the moment, equilibrium presents itself as a state of inertia, the essential immobility of which is vividly rendered by Gide's description of it as 'une stupéfaction passionnée'.

In order to impart motion to this locked mass, this first phase of equilibrium must somehow be upset: a bias, an inclination must be created, for a total 'absence de pente', Gide himself tells us, makes it impossible for him to write anything at all.[66]

If there is nothing which can plausibly motivate the introduction of such a bias, Gide has only one course open to him. He must simply dispense with motivation. Much has been said and written about the

---

[60] *J*, 2, 42.
[61] *J*, 1, 217.
[62] *J*, 1, 803.
[63] *J*, 1, 253. Gide's italics.
[64] *André Walter*, OC, 1, 104.
[65] *J*, 1, 257.
[66] *J*, 1, 362.

notorious 'acte gratuit' in *Les Caves du Vatican*; but, in the universe of Gide, it is not Lafcadio who performs the archetypal 'acte gratuit': it is the Adam of the *Traité du Narcisse*. Bored with the symmetrical, unchanging perfection of Paradise, Adam rebels:

> Un geste! un petit geste, pour savoir, — une dissonance, que diable! — Eh! va donc! un peu d'imprévu.[67]

In Gide this gesture may occur almost fortuitously, as mood or occasion give to a particular idea, emotion or value-judgment a provisional pre-eminence which is, in reality, merely an effect of perspective. Or, since Gide is always insisting that his various works are written after he has emerged from the crisis they reflect, it may appear purely arbitrary.

The impulse which follows the inclination thus produced is not a trend of *thought*. The process we are seeking to describe is an inclination of the whole personality and bears only a superficial resemblance to that by which an abstract thinker, faced with a rational dilemma, experimentally postulates a hypothesis. Gide's thought itself is not of a nature to survive such an operation.

> Abstraite, ma pensée même s'éteint [. . .][68]

> C'est aussi que je ne peux attacher prix à une pensée tout abstraite et comme déshumanisée. Inconséquences de la raison sont souvent conséquences du cœur.[69]

The warmth of life may compromise the purity of the thought, but without this warmth the thought is sterile and inoperative. Ideas, in a work of art, must be presented in function of the human personality which nurtures them and from whose destiny their effective sense is insepar-able.[70]

> La pensée abstraite est glacée; et de ce qui reste froid, je n'ai jamais rien su faire. Elle se compromet en se tiédissant et s'humanisant, mais prend vie; c'est seulement alors qu'elle peut devenir active.[71]

Among the wealth of rival claimants for election to this role of *porte-parole*, Gide yields the stage to one — selected, as we have suggested, arbitrarily if not at random.

[67] *Traité du Narcisse*, OC, I, 211.
[68] *J*, 2, 113.
[69] *J*, 2, 211.
[70] The compliment that Gide pays Dostoïevsky is a declaration of principle: 'Il n'aborde jamais [une question] d'une manière abstraite, les idées n'existent jamais chez lui qu'en fonction de l'individu [. . .].' [*Dostoïevsky*, OC, 11, 150.]
[71] *J*, 1, 1,222-4.

The best way of describing the nature of the surrender that Gide makes in this way to one aspect of his personality rather than to another, is to say that it is *lyrical*, defining this term in as Gidean a sense as possible. The first element of such a definition is provided by a passage of the *Faux-Monnayeurs*:

> Chacun de nous assume un drame à sa taille [. . .] [Douviers] manque de lyrisme [. . .] il ne s'oublie jamais dans ce qu'il éprouve, de sorte qu'il n'éprouve jamais rien de grand [. . .] je crois que j'appelle lyrisme l'état de l'homme qui consent à se laisser vaincre par Dieu [. . .].[72]

The surrender of the self is still called for; but now that surrender is made not to an object outside the self but to a *subject* no longer co-extensive and identifiable with it. In a text of rare penetration Gide makes this subtle distinction clear:

> Savoir se mettre 'à la place des autres'. X. s'y met bien . . . Mais c'est toujours *lui* qu'il y met.[73]

Such a proceeding, it is clearly implied, falls far short of his own requirements:

> Rien n'est fait si, ce personnage que j'assume, je n'ai pas su vraiment le devenir, jusqu'à me donner le change et me dépersonnaliser en lui jusqu'à encourir le reproche de n'avoir jamais su portraiturer que moi-même, si différents que soient entre eux, Saül, Candaule, Lafcadio, le pasteur de ma *Symphonie* ou La Pérouse ou Armand. C'est revenir à moi qui m'embarrasse, car, en vérité, je ne sais plus bien qui je suis; ou, si l'on préfère: je ne suis jamais, je deviens.[74]

This assumption of a 'personnage' is made in the interests of the work of art. The very awareness that it *is* an 'assumption' spontaneously disappears or is deliberately suppressed; and even if it is not entirely lost from sight[75] it is not allowed to inhibit the free expression of his *personnage's* 'own' emotions, for it was in order to make this expression *subjective* that the assumption was made in the first place.

> Et puis, d'autres vies! d'autres vies; tout ce que nous pourrons

---

[72] *Les Faux-Monnayeurs*, OC, 12, 444–5. This particular text continues: ' — N'est-ce pas là précisément ce que signifie le mot: enthousiasme? — Et peut-être le mot: inspiration. Oui, c'est bien là ce que je veux dire.'

[73] *J*, 1, 1,101. Gide's italics.

[74] *J*, 1, 829–30.

[75] 'Le véritable artiste reste toujours *à demi* inconscient de lui-même, lorsqu'il produit. Il ne sait pas *au juste* qui il est.' [*Dostoïevsky*, OC, 11, 161. My italics.]

vivre d'elles, *nous-mêmes*, et (sachant que c'est une erreur) savourer
d'émotions pour les dire.[76]

At the same time the fact that he does not speak in his own name enables
him to describe his work as 'objective' since 'Le triomphe de l'objectivité,
c'est de permettre au romancier d'emprunter le "je" d'autrui'.[77]

We are thus confronted with something like a subjective objectivity!
But this apparent contradiction in terms offers no real occasion for
embarrassment:

> [. . .] — objective? subjective? Ces mots perdent ici tout leur sens;
> car s'il m'arrive de peindre d'après moi [. . .] c'est d'abord que j'ai
> commencé par devenir celui-là même que je voulais portraiturer.[78]

The act by which Gide contrives to 'objectiver le sujet (avant d'avoir
à assujettir l'objet)'[79] may call for a considerable effort of the imagination;
but this effort is richly rewarded. For the life of the characters thus projected outside the self often attains an intensity which the nebulous
character of the self would otherwise preclude. As in the case of Dostoïevsky, Gide's characters draw him, as it were, in their wake, into regions of
experience which they discover in their own right. By making him aware
of a life ('their' life!) which is far more intense and varied than he, in his
own person, is capable of knowing, these characters satisfy the most profound of all Gide's psychological needs: '[ils] le font entrer pathétiquement
dans la vie'.[80]

In their capacity as instruments of discovery they even bring forward
ideas which, from any starting point other than that which is peculiar to
them, would be literally *inconceivable*. In *The Devils*, for example, Kirilov's
ideas could be conceived only in a mind sick as Kirilov's was sick; but
's'il est nécessaire que Kirilov soit malade pour les avoir, c'est aussi bien
pour que nous, nous puissions les avoir ensuite, sans être malades'.[81]

The feelings, the ideas thus *'obtained'* are not a fortuitous addition
grafted on to a stem of experience which would be capable of bearing a
work of art without them. The Gidean self is far too feeble to speak, as it
were, in its own name for the emotions and ideas that throng his work.
The difficulty he experiences, for example, in writing *Geneviève*, is
explained by his inability to

> [. . .] faire endosser par un 'héros' quantité de ratiocinations *qui*

[76] *J*, I, 37–8. Gide's italics.
[77] *J*, I, 759.
[78] *J*, I, 737.
[79] *Journal des Faux-Monnayeurs*, OC, 13, 15–16.
[80] Lettre à Charles Du Bos, OC, 10, 550.
[81] *Dostoïevsky*, OC, 11, 302.

m'ont élu pour domicile et que je me suis trouvé *comme contraint* d'assumer [. . .] ainsi que précédemment j'avais fait des nietzschéennes avec mon *Immoraliste*, des chrétiennes avec ma *Porte Étroite*'.[82]

Without such a 'héros' to whom he can delegate the responsibility for the ideas which have chosen to inhabit him, Gide remains, in his own striking formula: 'pris au jeu (ou au "je")'[83] — obliged to speak, if he is to speak at all, in his own name. This is enough to reduce him to silence, and not merely to silence — to impotence, to 'aphasia'. It is precisely in these terms that, towards the end of his career, he accounts for the decline of his creative powers:

> L'extraordinaire difficulté que je trouve à m'exprimer aujourd'hui ne vient-elle pas aussi de ce que plus aucun personnage imaginaire ne m'habite et que c'est en mon nom propre que je cherche à parler? Je le crois volontiers et que le meilleur moyen de triompher de cette impuissance (j'allais dire: de cette aphasie) serait d'inventer de nouveau un héros responsable (ayant soin de le douer de certaine faculté d'élocution!).[84]

The key word here is 'responsable'. For if Gide had to accept responsibility in his own name for all the ideas which might suggest themselves to him, he could no longer 'les pousser à bout, à l'absurde'[85] as he could do in a work of fiction. In a work of fiction, indeed, he would find himself more or less obliged to do something of the kind, since merely to select a single unifying point of view from amongst the wealth of possibilities that crowd the self is already to exaggerate.

> Simplifier, c'est exagérer ce qui reste. L'œuvre d'art est une exagération.[86]

> L'œuvre d'art c'est une idée qu'on exagère.[87]

The author's lack of responsibility for the excesses of the *personae* he projects outside himself is an invitation if not an incitement to extremism. Michel's 'immoralism', for example, can be carried to the limits of catastrophe only because Gide does not have to underwrite it. On the contrary, he can regard its *reductio ad absurdum* as a salutary form of purgation.

[82] *J*, I, 1,160. My italics.
[83] Ibid.
[84] *J*, I, 1,043.
[85] *J*, I, 1,160.
[86] *J*, I, 33.
[87] *Réflexions*, OC, 2, 424.

In a letter to Scheffer, Gide sums up both of these aspects of the creative process:

> Que de bourgeons nous portons en nous [. . .] qui n'écloront jamais que dans nos livres! Ce sont des 'œils dormants' comme les nomment les botanistes. Mais si, par volonté, on les supprime tous, *sauf un*, comme il croît aussitôt, comme il grandit! comme aussitôt il s'empare de la sève! Pour créer un héros ma recette est bien simple: Prendre un de ces bourgeons, le mettre en pot — tout seul — on arrive bientôt à un individu admirable. Conseil: choisir de préférence (s'il est vrai qu'on puisse choisir) le bourgeon qui vous gêne le plus. On s'en défait du même coup. C'est peut-être là ce qu'appelait Aristote: la purgation des passions. Purgeons-nous [. . .] purgeons-nous! Il en restera toujours assez.[88]

Under conditions of perfect liberty, however, with nothing at all to check the rate or extent of its growth, that growth would soon exhaust itself 'par son exagération même'.[89] In the same way, if it is allowed to break free from the tension to which it owes its vitality, 'l'œuvre brusquement cède et se décompose'.[90] It is precisely the business of art to rescue the artist from that 'horreur (ou peur) de la liberté'[91] from which Gide's life suffered and his art benefited so greatly. The exigencies of art, and not only the *formal* exigencies, are there to provide a salutary check on the freedom that is otherwise liable to 'plonger l'âme dans une sorte de détresse'.[92] The work of art militates by its very nature against the worst excesses of exaggeration. 'L'art comporte une tempérance et répugne à l'énormité;'[93] and the artist may quite well accompany his characters to the brink of catastrophe without being obliged to follow them over it. Outside his lyrical commitment to their point of view, outside his 'espousal' of their emotions, he retains somewhere 'ce peu de bon sens qui me retient de pousser aussi loin qu'eux leurs folies.'[94]

The driving force behind each of Gide's characters is a centrifugal impulse. In the course of a very remarkable preface to *Les Fleurs du Mal*, Gide takes for granted that, confronting the cohesive power by virtue of which, as Spinoza puts it, 'l'individu tend à persévérer dans son être', there is another power, 'centrifuge et désagrégeante, par quoi l'individu tend à

---

[88] OC, 4, 616–7. Gide's italics.
[89] *Dostoïevsky*, OC, 11, 226.
[90] *Les Limites de l'Art*, OC, 3, 408–9.
[91] *J*, 1, 737.
[92] *J*, 1, 893.
[93] *Voyage au Congo, J*, 2, 1,692.
[94] *Journal des Faux-Monnayeurs*, OC, 13, 52.

se diviser, à se dissocier, à se risquer, à se jouer, à se perdre . . .'[95] That this tendency is omnipresent in Gide himself is self-evident and there can be no doubting the power with which, at times, it manifests itself. The very idea of constancy on the part of the self towards itself — consistency in the psychologist, *durée* in the historical phenomenon, consequence in the moralist — is invariably apprehended as a constraint and not infrequently as an oppression. Against the sense of confinement which it inspires in him, Gide reacts characteristically. He almost never, as he puts it, occupies the centre of his cage. His whole being 'afflue vers les barreaux'.[96] But once again, with unfaltering virtuosity, he has chosen the *mot juste* to describe this process. His life is not lived in the centre of his cage; but, in his own name, he never quits it. It is from the centre that his being moves outwards *towards* the bars. Gide is well aware of the danger of seeking a limitless empire. He points himself to the example of Napoleon who was willing, in order to conquer Russia, to risk France. Gide will not make that mistake. Conscious all the time of the 'nécessité de relier la frontière au centre', he is acutely aware that as soon as any movement away from that centre is in danger of tearing itself loose, 'il est temps de rentrer'.[97]

But the most effective check on the extremist tendencies of any one of Gide's projections is quite simply the well-known dialectic process by which the development of one point of view provokes automatically the development of its opposite, 'l'excès de l'un trouvant dans l'excès de l'autre une permission secrète et tous deux se maintenant en équilibre'.[98]

From all that has just been said it would seem that the balance thus achieved quite clearly represents a victory for common sense, the 'peu de bon sens' that *recognises* excess and *allows* its expression in any direction only on condition that it be balanced by a similar manifestation in the opposite direction. To this form of common sense Gide does not hesitate to give the name 'banality' and banality is a form of repose.

Have we then come full circle? Are we once more in that state of paralysed stupefaction from which only a 'gratuitous action' like that of Adam enabled us momentarily to emerge? Was that action itself vain? On the contrary. What we have gained is almost measureless. For the banality to which we have now attained is a 'banalité supérieure' which we could have reached in no other way and which represents nothing less than the highest achievement of the highest art. Whereas each of the fashionable

---

[95] OC, 7, 503–4.
[96] J, 1, 1,006.
[97] J, 1, 352.
[98] J, 1, 365–6. This process is too well known to require much discussion here. Cf. *inter alia*, G. W. Ireland: *Gide*, Oliver and Boyd, 1963, pp. 23ff.

writers and artists among Gide's contemporaries had a *manner* of his own,

> [. . .] le grand artiste classique travaille à n'avoir pas de manière; il
> s'efforce vers la banalité. S'il parvient à cette banalité sans effort, c'est
> qu'il n'est pas un grand artiste, parbleu! L'œuvre classique ne sera
> forte et belle qu'en raison de son romantisme dompté.[99]

The last sentence is decisive. Scores of texts echo this definition of classi-
cism (of which, it will be remembered, Gide considered himself to be the
finest living representative), insisting always that the value of classical art
is in direct proportion to the strength of the 'romantic' elements on which
it imposes the measure, cohesion and clarity that make them seem 'banal'.

It is the great triumph of Gide's art — the triumph, he would claim, of
all truly classical art — that in it the reign of equilibrium does not involve
the suppression of lyrical fervour. Precisely the reverse is true. Equilibrium
in Gide is created and maintained by tension; and this tension, in its turn,
is produced by the fervour with which conflicting emotions are simultaneously indulged. Each of these tendencies is 'dompté' because they meet
together in a state of deadlock and not in a state of inertia. A state of
equilibrium which depended on anything less — indifference, say, or
compromise — would be at once insipid and unworthy:

> Cet état d'équilibre n'est beau que sur la corde raide; assis par terre
> il n'a plus rien de glorieux.[100]

Only on 'la corde raide' does the work of art reach the degree of intensity at which it acquires that power to fortify and to ennoble which allow
it to be invested with authentic *moral* value. That is why Gide is able to
close the circle of his inspiration by returning precisely at this juncture to
the biblical text which was his starting point.

As he seeks to define this 'banality' which is the artist's crowning
achievement, he weighs his arguments and does not find them wanting:

> Dois-je citer le mot de l'Évangile? — Oui, car je ne pense pas le
> détourner de son sens: Celui qui veut sauver sa vie (sa vie personnelle)
> la perdra; mais celui qui veut la donner la sauvera (ou, pour traduire
> plus exactement le texte grec: *la rendra vraiment vivante*).[101]

He will raise it, in fact, to the level of a work of art.

---

[99] *Billets à Angèle*, OC, II, 36–7.
[100] *J*, I, 364.
[101] *Billets à Angèle*, OC, II, 37. Gide's italics.

12

STEPHEN ULLMANN

Images of Time and Memory in 'Jean Santeuil'

'Tous les à peu près d'images ne comptent pas. L'eau, dans des conditions données, bout à 100 degrés. A 98, à 99, le phénomène ne se
produit pas. Alors mieux vaut pas d'images.' On reading *Jean
Santeuil*, the student of Proust's imagery is often reminded of these words
which he wrote many years later, in his preface to Paul Morand's *Tendres
Stocks*. The pages of *Jean Santeuil* are densely packed with similes and
metaphors; indeed, the richness of the figurative element is, if anything,
greater than in the *Temps perdu*;[1] its quality, however, is very uneven.
There are many images of great poetic beauty, intellectual brilliance and
an unmistakably Proustian ring, but there are also many others which do
not quite come off, which fail to convince and to illuminate, or which do
not play any useful part. Gide once complained in his diary: 'Quoi de plus
fatigant que cette manie de certains littérateurs, qui ne peuvent voir un
objet sans penser aussitôt à un autre';[2] in *Jean Santeuil*, we see the inex-
perienced young writer yielding all too frequently to this temptation.

Even if one bears in mind the immaturity, the lack of polish and revision,
which are so obvious in the style of *Jean Santeuil*, the profusion of idle and
abortive analogies is somewhat surprising in a novel which shows the
author fully alive to the dangers of imagery. In *Jean Santeuil*, Proust did
not yet have a coherent theory of metaphor such as he was to evolve in
the *Temps perdu* where it is closely linked to the process of involuntary
memory; nor did he yet believe, as he was to proclaim much later, that
metaphor alone can confer a 'kind of eternity' on style.[3] There are a
number of references to imagery in the novel, but most of them are either
ironic or openly critical. The most sweeping condemnation of rhetorical
images comes from Beulier, the 'professeur de philosophie' who is

---

[1] This at least is the conclusion reached in Elfi Zeblewski's unpublished thesis, *Prousts
Bildersprache in 'Jean Santeuil'*, Marburg, 1957, summarized in an article by the same author,
'Zur Bildersprache in Marcel Prousts *Jean Santeuil*', *Die Neueren Sprachen*, NF, vii (1958),
pp. 324–37: p. 324.
[2] 20th August 1926 (p. 822 of the Pléiade ed.).
[3] 'A propos du "style" de Flaubert,' *Nouvelle Revue Française*, xiv, 1 (1920), pp. 72–90.

modelled on Proust's own teacher Darlu: 'Il faudra soigneusement bannir toutes ces métaphores, toutes ces images qui, mieux choisies que les vôtres, peuvent plaire au poète, mais que même alors la philosophie ne tolère pas. Mais même pour le professeur de lettres, ne grossissez pas la voix pour dire des banalités'.[4] Beulier himself carefully avoids the vice against which he warns his pupils: 'Jean . . . ne trouva dans toute la leçon aucune de ces images splendides et parfumées auxquelles il aurait pu pendant cette rude course intellectuelle faire halte comme auprès d'un reposoir de fleurs' (I, 241). Jean, on the other hand, has a juvenile infatuation for this kind of imagery. He adorns his French essays with images borrowed from various poets (I, 115); he looks for two things only in poetry: 'la richesse de leur sens' and 'l'éclat de leurs images' (I, 129). When reading Le Capitaine Fracasse, he is intoxicated with 'certaines phrases retentissantes à la fois et imagées' (I, 178), much as the young narrator in the Temps perdu will be fascinated by the striking metaphors of Bergotte.[5] In Leconte de Lisle, 'les images brillantes, le style enflammé . . . excitaient en lui une ardeur matinale' (I, 123), but he is a little disturbed by the style of Colomba 'où à tous moments une facétie venait empêcher la vague poésie des images de le ravir' (I, 196).

Proust is equally critical of another type of idle imagery: the similes and metaphors with which the conversation of certain intellectuals is sprinkled. A Professor of the École des Sciences Politiques hazards the image: 'une orchestration fouillée de main d'ouvrier', which strikes a more conservative colleague as a little unusual: 'L'image est un peu hardie, . . . cela ne s'écrira pas, ni vous ni moi ne nous risquerions même à le dire' (III, 25; cf. III, 23). In the Temps perdu, the same idea will be developed in the linguistic caricature of Professor Brichot. Even more interesting is the case of Bergotte, who is a painter, not a writer, in this novel. When listening to music, Bergotte will note certain passages on which he can comment with an unexpected epithet or a prettily turned comparison, whereupon he will lose interest in the music and think of other things (III, 196).

All these remarks on the more superficial aspects of imagery show that the young writer had given some thought to these matters. On the deeper implications of the problem there is still very little in Jean Santeuil. There are, however, two passages which foreshadow the role of analogy in the process of involuntary memory. In a description of hawthorns, which was later on transmuted into one of the great metaphorical themes of the Temps perdu, the author speculates on the reasons for Jean's interest in pink

[4] Jean Santeuil, 3 vols., Paris, Gallimard, 1952: I, 244.
[5] Du Côté de chez Swann, I, 95. All references to À la recherche du temps perdu are based on the Pléiade ed., repr. 1961-2.

hawthorns: 'Était-ce qu'ayant vu auparavant de l'épine blanche, la vue d'une épine rose dont les fleurs ne sont plus simples mais composées le frappa à la fois de ces deux prestiges de l'analogie et de la différence qui ont tant de pouvoir sur notre esprit?' (I, 204). In the later work, Proust's technique will be far more subtle and effective; as Professor Cocking has put it, we shall be given 'not the wherefores of the experience, but the experience itself'.[6] More closely related to the literary image is another passage which, though banal in itself, is of some interest in the light of Proust's later ideas on the role of metaphor in the recapture of the past: 'les objets qui furent aimés pour eux-mêmes autrefois sont aimés plus tard comme symboles du passé et détournés alors de leur sens primitif, comme dans la langue poétique les mots pris comme images ne sont plus entendus dans leur sens primitif' (III, 279).

Another passage shows that Proust was aware of the ambiguity of the term 'image', and of the danger of confusion between the sense 'mental picture or impression' and other meanings of the word. It is in the former sense that 'image' must be taken in this simile which Proust was to use again, with slight modifications, in *Combray*:

> C'est roulées pour ainsi dire dans cette image qu'il emportait ses pensées, comme un jeune pêcheur rapporte au soleil sans qu'il en souffre, sous un lit frais d'herbe, de l'herbe arrachée au fond de l'étang où il l'a pris, le poisson qu'il vient de pêcher. Ainsi ne connaissant pas encore ses idées, il les gardait cachées sous l'image qu'il voyait devant ses yeux (III, 299).[7]

He goes on to develop the same idea, and at one point finds it necessary to emphasize that 'image' does not mean anything 'symbolic' in this context: 'Une fois devant son papier il écrivait ce qu'il ne connaissait pas encore, ce qui l'invitait sous l'image où c'était caché (et qui n'était en quoi que ce soit un symbole) et non ce qui par raisonnement lui aurait paru intelligent et beau' (III, 301).

I

The imagery of *Jean Santeuil* has a twofold interest for the critic. It can be studied — to borrow two terms from modern linguistics — 'synchronic-

[6] J. M. Cocking, *Proust*, London, 1956, p. 48. See also by the same scholar: '*Jean Santeuil* et *A la recherche du temps perdu*', *Bulletin de la Société des Amis de Marcel Proust*, no. 6 (1956), pp. 181–97: pp. 190 ff.

[7] Cf. *Swann*, I, 179: '... cette chose inconnue ... je la ramenais à la maison, protégée par le revêtement d'images sous lesquelles je la trouverais vivante, comme les poissons que, les jours où on m'avait laissé aller à la pêche, je rapportais dans mon panier, couverts par une couche d'herbe qui préservait leur fraîcheur.'

ally' and 'diachronically': in its own right, without any reference to the major work that followed, and as an important stage in the development of Proust's metaphorical vision. The purpose of the present article is to examine it synchronically, by concentrating on a significant group of intellectual images: those which describe the workings of memory and time. First, however, it might be useful to consider briefly some of the diachronic problems raised by the imagery. In the words of one critic, to move from Proust's early exercises 'to the shapeless mass of *Jean Santeuil* is to enter the workshop where the real labour is going ahead'.[8] In the field of figurative language this approach is particularly fruitful since it can grant us unique insights into the emergence of individual images and of some of the tendencies which govern the movement of Proust's imagery as a whole.

One is struck, first of all, by the fact that some experiences already have the same, or very nearly the same, metaphorical expression as in the *Temps perdu*. The mother's good-night kiss is already described as 'le doux viatique, attendu si fiévreusement que Jean s'efforçait de ne penser à rien en se déshabillant, pour franchir plus vite le moment qui l'en séparait' (I, 65–6). Another great Proustian theme, the 'petite phrase' — identified here as coming from a Saint-Saëns sonata — is also presented in metaphorical terms which all readers of the cycle will immediately recognize: 'Il écoutait cette phrase dont le divin sourire déjà au temps de leur bonheur lui paraissait désenchanté . . . ils la sentaient passer comme une caresse . . . à la phrase désolée qui disait que tout passe, la tristesse paraissait rester aussi légère' (III, 223–4).[9] A similar persistence of metaphorical motifs is found in the passage on hawthorns, which has already been mentioned. These crucial experiences obviously found their figurative equivalents at an early stage, and the images in which they were clothed remained firmly associated with them in the author's mind.

More incidental analogies may also persist, either because of their graphic quality and expressive force or because of their emotive over-tones. Take these descriptions of two women listening to music: first Madame Cresmeyer in *Jean Santeuil*:

> . . . qui depuis le commencement du morceau balançait sa tête avec son corps très vite et sans presque la déplacer, comme un balancier très rapide mais s'écartant si peu de son centre de gravité qu'il semblait plutôt trembler par lui-même (III, 198);

[8] Cocking, *Proust*, p. 12.
[9] On the role of the 'petite phrase' in *Jean Santeuil* and in the *Temps perdu*, see P. Costil, 'La construction musicale de la *Recherche du temps perdu*, II,' *Bulletin de la Société des Amis de Marcel Proust*, no. 9 (1959), pp. 83–110.

then Madame de Cambremer in *Du Côté de chez Swann*:

> ... battant la mesure avec sa tête transformée en balancier de
> métronome dont l'amplitude et la rapidité d'oscillations d'une épaule
> à l'autre étaient devenues telles ... qu'à tout moment elle accrochait
> avec ses solitaires les pattes de son corsage (I, 328).

There are obvious differences, but the basic image is the same. Similarly
we see in *Jean Santeuil* 'les arbres stériles s'adresser au ciel avec des gestes
immenses' (II, 259), and in *Combray* 'le peuplier de la rue des Perchamps
adresser à l'orage des supplications et des salutations désespérées' (*Swann*, I,
152). At Étreuilles, as at Combray, the flies perform a kind of 'chamber
music' on a hot summer's day, and the whole setting is almost exactly the
same: Jean lying on his bed, the shutters drawn against the sun, and the
sleepy stillness of the afternoon punctuated only by the noise of hammering
in the street (I, 162–3; *Swann*, I, 82). Even a rather far-fetched mythological
simile is preserved in the passage from *Jean Santeuil* to the *Temps perdu*. At
the very end of the former, Jean, in the midst of all his social activities,
looks in on his mother 'comme Thétis visitée par son fils Aristée au fond
des eaux' (III, 328), whereas at the beginning of Combray the same analogy
is used to describe the two vastly different worlds in which Swann moves
(*Swann*, I, 18).

It also happens that Proust has not yet found, in *Jean Santeuil*, the metaphorical equivalent which will eventually satisfy him although the
ingredients are all there. Thus the lilacs in the park at Étreuilles remind him
of a fairy in an eastern tale (I, 136), and there is a variation on the same
theme in a later passage: 'ces beaux lilas, de sang persan, ... sveltes
Shéhérazades immobiles entre les branches' (I, 197). The final stage in the
development of this image will not be reached till *Combray*: 'ces jeunes
houris qui gardaient dans ce jardin français les tons vifs et purs des minia-
tures de la Perse' (*Swann*, I, 135). Even more remarkable are the metamorphoses of another flower. At Étreuilles, 'un coquelicot ... dressait sur
le cordon tendu de sa mince tige verte sa fleur éclatante et simple ... le
vent courbait, faisait trembler à l'ombre sa flamme rouge ... donnant au
rare passant qui aperçoit tout d'un coup son pavillon rouge et élancé le
plaisir d'une découverte' (I, 167). In *Combray*, these metaphors are gathered
up and developed until they form a striking and unified image:

> ... la vue d'un seul coquelicot hissant au bout de son cordage et
> faisant cingler au vent sa flamme rouge, au-dessus de sa bouée grais-
> seuse et noire, me faisait battre le cœur, comme au voyageur qui
> aperçoit sur une terre basse une première barque échouée que répare

15

un calfat, et s'écrie, avant de l'avoir encore vue: 'La Mer!' (*Swann*, I, 138–9).

Even more significant than the first appearance or gradual crystallization of particular analogies is the presence in *Jean Santeuil* of some of the fundamental forms and tendencies of Proust's imagery, only a few of which can be mentioned here.[10] He is already fond of borrowing similes and metaphors from chemistry, physics and other sciences. Some of these are brief and incisive:

La pensée est une espèce de télescope qui nous permet de voir des spectacles éloignés et immenses (III, 322);

... le désir de l'un avait découvert le désir de l'autre, et, comme le soufre s'unissant au phosphore, s'en était enflammé (II, 246).

Elsewhere the analogy is more fully developed. In the introductory chapter we are told that the author of *Jean Santeuil* never wrote letters to friends: 'Il les considérait comme des sortes de paratonnerres qui tirent à l'esprit son électricité et ne lui permettent pas de s'accumuler jusqu'à ces véritables orages intérieurs où peut seulement jaillir le véritable éclair du génie, où la parole humaine prend une puissance qui la fait retentir au loin comme le tonnerre' (I, 38–9).

As in the *Temps perdu*, some of the scientific analogies in *Jean Santeuil* have an ironical twist resulting from the contrast between the grandeur of the image and the mediocrity of the subject described. Thus Jean's father is thrilled to hear of a society scandal which had been common knowledge for many years, 'comme nous trouvons du plaisir en recevant la lumière d'une étoile en voyage peut-être depuis des milliers d'années' (III, 55).

Medicine is already an important source of imagery in *Jean Santeuil*, as it was to remain in the *Temps perdu*. Some of the medical analogies are almost technical in their precision:

... ces paroles qu'elle redisait si souvent étaient comme la petite dose de morphine qui ayant peu à peu anesthésié sa conscience, la faisait vivre en paix avec elle-même (III, 59).

The association between illness and love, which was to become the main

---

[10] On the part played by these types of imagery in the *Temps perdu*, see J. Mouton, *Le Style de Marcel Proust*, Paris, 1948, ch. 3, and my book, *The Image in the Modern French Novel*, Cambridge, 1960, ch. 3. On scientific images, see esp. R. Virtanen, 'Proust's Metaphors from the Natural and the Exact Sciences,' *Publications of the Modern Language Association of America*, lxix (1954), pp. 1038–59.

Cf. also V. E. Graham, *The Imagery of Proust*, which will appear shortly in the *Language and Style* series (Oxford, Blackwell).

metaphorical theme of *Un Amour de Swann*, is already in evidence in *Jean Santeuil*:

> ... cet amour n'était plus. On pouvait le toucher aux points jadis sensibles sans que Jean éprouvât rien, comme une peau morte que nous portons encore avec nous mais qui désormais ne ressentira plus ni caresses ni piqûres, qui n'est plus nous, qui est morte (III, 16);

> ... pareilles à ces maladies d'où un jeune homme se relève plus fort mais auxquelles succombe le tempérament épuisé de celui qui a derrière lui une longue vie, ces querelles, qui rafraîchissent et exaltent un amour naissant, conduisaient de plus en plus vite à sa fin leur amour qui avait tant duré (III, 222–3).

Images from the various arts are already very prominent in *Jean Santeuil*. Flowers, for example, are repeatedly likened to works of art:

> Chacune était large et brillante comme une rose et sa couleur safranée transportait comme dans un tableau l'inspiration hardie, l'infaillible hardiesse d'un coloriste délicieux (III, 179);

> ... le petit duvet finement organisé des pistils qui étaient au cœur de la fleur, comme une sorte d'obscur et mystérieux chœur au sein d'une éclatante basilique (I, 137).

In this last example one wonders whether the homonymy of *cœur* and *choeur* was not the starting-point of the image.

There are already one or two parallels between paintings and human beings, as in this description of M. Beulier: 'Cette essence d'âme, toute la personne de M. Beulier en était comme enduite, comme certains personnages du Titien sont comme enveloppés d'une beauté qui est la beauté de la peinture, et aussi de la vie' (I, 333). This imagery, however, is still in a minor key: it is a long way from the precise and highly differentiated pictorial analogies in the *Temps perdu*, from the constant parallels which Swann draws between human beings and works of art, and from the close association between certain people and pictures: Odette and Botticelli's Zephora, the kitchen-maid and Giotto's Charity, and others.[11]

---

[11] Cf. André Maurois's remarks in the preface to the Gallimard edition of *Jean Santeuil*: 'La peinture et la musique jouent ici un rôle moindre et l'on ne trouve point d'images empruntées à Carpaccio, à Mantegna; point de Zephora, fille de Jethro; point d'anges musiciens, point de guerriers appuyés sur leur lance. Ce sera Ruskin qui formera Proust à dérouler ses périodes avec la grâce de vagues lentes ou de chevelures florentines, et à incruster d'améthyste et de corail les plus simples descriptions de fleurs, de reflets sur l'eau ou de bœuf en daube' (I, 26). Cf. also Zeblewski, loc. cit., p. 327. On art images in the *Temps perdu*, see esp. M. E. Chernowitz, *Proust and Painting*, New York, 1945; J. Monnin-Hornung, *Proust et la peinture*, Geneva/Lille, 1951; M. Hindus, *The Proustian Vision*, New York, 1954.

Proust's later habit of comparing culinary masterpieces to the major arts is foreshadowed in an image, developed in great detail, where a dinner is compared to an art-gallery: 'Un dîner est une sorte de musée de la gourmandise où les différentes œuvres, auxquelles notre imagination a souvent rêvé ... se trouvent à notre portée' (II, 317).[12]

Similes and metaphors from mythology are, as Professor Seznec has recently reminded us,[13] one of the most persistent motifs of Proust's imagery. There are various examples in *Jean Santeuil*, some quite short:

Comme Jupiter, son crâne semblait contenir le monde (II, 217);

... portant plus légèrement qu'Atlas le monde entier sur ses épaules (II, 218);

others developed into an epic simile:

Au plus fort de la mêlée et quand la position devenait vraiment dangereuse, un dieu prenait Ajax par les cheveux et le dérobait aux coups de ses ennemis dans un nuage. C'est ce nuage divin qui flotta pendant quelques jours autour de l'esprit de Marie (II, 110).

Another essential motif of Proust's imagery, personification, is also noticeable in *Jean Santeuil*, though not always with very happy results:

... ce devant quoi rôde et aboie notre pensée (III, 135);

L'habitude l'attendait dès la porte et l'ouvrait gaiement pour lui (II, 175).[14]

Synaesthetic analogies between the various senses, which Baudelaire's *Correspondances* had erected into an aesthetic principle and which were to play a crucial part in the description of music and other experiences in the *Temps perdu*, occur repeatedly in *Jean Santeuil*:

... ce que lui chantait le soleil qui l'accompagnait à son tour de toutes les choses illuminées comme d'instruments retentissants, frémissants d'une musique divine (III, 165).

Yet another great metaphorical theme of the later work, the *mystique* of

<hr>

[12] Cf. P. Aschkenasy-Lelu, 'Les sens mineurs chez Proust,' *Bulletin de la Société des Amis de Marcel Proust*, no. 9 (1959), pp. 44–68: pp. 56 ff. Cf. also G. Matoré, 'Les images gustatives dans *Du Côté de chez Swann*,' *Mélanges de linguistique et de littérature romanes à la mémoire d'István Frank*, Universität des Saarlandes, 1957, pp. 685–92.

[13] J. Seznec, *Marcel Proust et les dieux* (Zaharoff Lecture), Oxford, 1962, pp. 9 ff.

[14] Cf. Zeblewski, loc. cit., pp. 331 ff.

proper names, is adumbrated in a dithyrambic passage on the name Fontainebleau:

> Fontainebleau, nom doux et doré comme une grappe de raisin sou-
> levée ... ses lettres portent sur le timbre de la poste, comme une
> obscurité de sous-bois, ce nom glorieux et doux Fontainebleau (II,
> 317-8).

It is clear, then, that many characteristic tendencies of the imagery of the *Temps perdu* are already present in *Jean Santeuil*, either in a fully developed or in an embryonic form. Needless to say, there are also very great differences between the two works, both in the quality of the images them-selves — in their appropriateness, precision and novelty, in the density and complexity of their texture — and in the way in which they are used. In the *Temps perdu*, many of the major metaphorical themes — hawthorns, the 'petite phrase', parallels between love and illness and between people and paintings, certain forms of personification, the magic of proper names, and others — are closely integrated into the structure of the work; some recurrent images act very much like Wagnerian *leit-motivs*. In *Jean Santeuil*, the integration of imagery into the structure of the novel does not arise since the novel has no structure in the proper sense of the term. As Proust himself says in the epigraph, 'ce livre n'a jamais été fait, il a été récolté'. Looked at in this light, the images in *Jean Santeuil*, like other elements of the book, are no more than raw material waiting to be fitted into the grand design of the cycle.

II

According to one critic, 'le principal plaisir qu'on prend à lire *Jean Santeuil* naît de ces promesses, souvent répétées, du chef-d'œuvre futur'.[15] It would, however, be wrong to consider the book solely as a prefiguration of what was to follow; in this way one might miss certain valuable features which were not subsequently embodied in the *Temps perdu*. We shall therefore examine an important group of images in the novel from a strictly 'synchronic' point of view, irrespective of whether or not they passed into the later work. Time and memory play a prominent part in *Jean Santeuil*;[16] they are complex, elusive and highly abstract experiences

[15] R. Pomeau, '*Jean Santeuil* et le temps retrouvé', *Annales Publiées par la Faculté des Lettres de Toulouse*, vi, 1-2 (1957), *Littératures V*, pp. 59-66: p. 64.

[16] See esp. E. R. Jackson, 'The Genesis of the Involuntary Memory in Proust's Early Works,' *Publications of the Modern Language Association of America*, lxxvi (1961), pp. 586-94: pp. 588 ff.

On the further development of this imagery, see now E. Gülich, 'Die Metaphorik der Erinnerung in Prousts À la Recherche', *Zeitschrift für französische Sprache und Literatur*, lxxv (1965), pp. 51-74.

about which one can hardly talk, and whose essence one can hardly grasp, in other than figurative language. It is therefore of considerable interest to see how, by means of what analogies, Proust tried to formulate these difficult problems at this stage of his development. Many of Proust's images are connected with water, the sea and allied phenomena,[17] and it was inevitable that these analogies should suggest themselves to him when he was talking of the passage of time. The basic theme of this imagery, the traditional metaphor of the 'flow of time' — the Heraclitean πάντα ῥεῖ[18] — appears already in the epigraph to the novel: 'Puis-je appeler ce livre un roman? C'est moins peut-être et bien plus, l'essence même de ma vie recueillie sans y rien mêler, dans ces heures de déchirure où elle découle.' Waves in particular provide Proust with three interesting images in which the continuity of time is evoked on three different planes. One of them depicts the apparent stagnation of one period in a man's life:

> ... comme un homme assis dans une barque qui reste immobile, les yeux fixés sur les petits flots qui passent autour, peu à peu victime d'une sorte de vertige croit que les flots conspirent à pousser la barque et qu'elle avance, ainsi le temps en passant lui semblait préparer le jour qu'il attendait (II, 113).

Another wave-image, which concludes the whole novel, describes the biological processes which are constantly at work in our lives and which can be most directly observed in a sleeping man:

> ... sa poitrine se soulevait régulièrement, ballottée comme une chose inerte sur ces flots de la vie qui le portaient et venaient se briser si près de Jean et de sa mère avec un bruit égal ... L'œuvre de vie et de mort, l'œuvre du temps ne s'arrêtait pas (III, 334).

A little earlier, the change of generations had been pictured in similar terms:

> ... vous avez vu l'histoire se faire devant vous, c'est-à-dire à deux générations l'espèce humaine se transformer, comme vous ne pouvez pas rester au bord de la mer quelques minutes à regarder le flot se soulever, se jeter en avant, reculer et recommencer, sans voir, marquée par les flots eux-mêmes qui semblaient n'être que des flots sans rapport qu'avec celui qui le précédait et le suivait, l'indication plus vague

[17] See V. E. Graham, 'Water Imagery and Symbolism in Proust,' *The Romanic Review*, l (1959), pp. 118–28, esp. pp. 124 and 126.

[18] Cf.G. Poulet, *Études sur le temps humain*, Edinburgh, 1949, p. 10. The formula may, however, be apocryphal; cf. B. Russell, *History of Western Philosophy*, 3rd impr., London, 1948, p. 64. See also H. Meyerhoff, *Time in Literature*, Berkeley/Los Angeles, 1960, pp. 14 ff.

en apparence, mais au fond plus certaine, plus vaste, de la marée (III, 323).

A few lines further on, the same image is developed into a personification: '. . . si c'est la loi de ces générations . . . de se laisser tendrement dominer par celle qui vient après elles, comme la vague s'infléchit caressante sous la vague qui bondit joyeusement sur elle et la réduit' (ibid.).

Memory and oblivion are also compared to certain experiences at sea:

> . . . les époques de notre cœur sont comme des îles qui s'engloutiraient dans l'océan au moment où le voyageur les quitte et dont . . . il ne pourra plus retrouver la trace (III, 228);

> . . . le nom prêt à être accueilli par la mémoire ouverte, eût été comme ces épaves glissantes qu'aucun clou ne peut accrocher, renvoyées par le reflux du doute sur la mer de l'inconnu, en proie à des remous sans nombre (III, 35).

Some of these water images have a slightly precious air. A mind which has remained youthful in an ageing body is likened to fresh water underground (I, 334), and the night is visualized as pouring oblivion into our open mouths from its 'outres d'oubli' (I, 148).

Among other forces of nature, the wind plays a vital part in the romantic reveries of Jean Santeuil. In an important passage on involuntary memory, the wind acts as a kind of 'magic carpet'[19] which takes him back into the past, reawakening long-forgotten pictures of seaside holidays:

> . . . le vent dont le premier bruit . . . avait gonflé ses ailes, comme s'il était de la race des mouettes et se sentît appelé vers les tempêtes . . . l'enfant bien-aimé qu'il avait assis sur ses ailes immenses, caoutchoutées et froides comme des nageoires et bercé de son bruit . . . qu'il avait ainsi conduit partout où il y avait une idée, quelque chose à trouver, un sentiment qui valait la peine qu'il le déterrât dans le sable (II, 226).

In more simple language we are told: 'Le vent en lui soufflant à sa [sic] figure n'entrait pas seulement dans sa poitrine. L'âme de Jean respirait en même temps le souvenir' (II, 218).

Other natural phenomena also suggest analogies for the obscure processes of involuntary memory. When we rediscover a past experience in a present one, we do so by virtue of an 'essence' which the two have in common. These 'eternal' essences, thanks to which we transcend the limit-

---

[19] See Jackson, loc. cit., p. 589.

ations of time (cf. II, 233), occupy a key position in Proust's idealistic philosophy, and he sums up their nature in a simple but expressive simile: '... essence qui nous trouble en ce qu'elle est nous-même, ce nous-même que nous ne sentons pas au moment, mais que nous retrouvons comme un miel délicieux resté après les choses quand elles sont loin de nous' (II, 339). Flowers which take us back into the past seem to have 'une expression morale': they are like an image of an earlier period of our life, which we recognize in them (I, 138). In the same way, a piece of music will carry the memories associated with it, just as a wood keeps the secrets it has overheard (I, 166).

Animal images are also brought into play to portray these experiences. The moments fly past, one after another, 'l'aile basse, emportant au néant le message dont chacun était chargé pour Jean et qu'il n'avait pas eu l'énergie de prendre au vol et d'essayer de comprendre' (I, 308). Other animal images are somewhat bizarre:

> ... les souvenirs lui dressaient une échelle par où, s'il avait la force de la saisir, il pouvait de réflexion en réflexion ou de créature en créature, s'évader dans ce champ de l'espérance et des siècles, où l'esprit peut courir comme un poulain lâché (I, 72);

> ... comme une poule que sa nature, sans lui faire connaître si elle réchauffe des œufs de poussin ou des œufs de serpent, force pourtant à leur donner sa vie, il couvait cet avenir inconnu, et sa douteuse espérance, avec toute la chaleur infatigable de son âme attentive (III, 245).

The scientific bias of Proust's mind comes to the fore in several images connected with memory and time. One of these is drawn from geology, a science which was to become a prolific source of analogies in the *Temps perdu*:

> Il fallait ... que dans le fond de son passé et de son oubli, qui sait peut-être dans de récentes alluvions de sa mémoire, saignât encore quelque plaie qu'elle lui avait faite (III, 88).

The alleged timelessness of certain human types is compared to a chemical formula:

> On dit noble de 1830, on dit journaliste de 1880, mais comme le chimiste qui sait que le soufre et le phosphore se combineront éternellement dans les mêmes proportions (III, 324).

In a passage on the miraculous speed of memory, electric currents and telephones are incongruously associated with medieval pictures of angels:

> L'électricité ne met pas moins de temps à conduire à notre oreille penchée sur un cornet téléphonique une voix pourtant bien éloignée, que la mémoire, cet autre élément puissant de la nature qui, comme la lumière ou l'électricité, dans un mouvement si vertigineux qu'il nous semble un repos immense, une sorte d'omniprésence, est à la fois partout autour de la terre, aux quatre coins du monde où palpitent sans cesse ses ailes gigantesques, comme un de ces anges que le Moyen Âge imaginait (I, 80).

Proust is fully aware of the fact, which has been emphasized by some modern philosophers and linguists,[20] that we tend to picture time in terms of space. His spatial metaphors can have an abstract, almost geometrical precision:

> Il ne cherchait pas à se demander ce qu'elle avait été avant lui, ce qu'elle serait après, le temps ressemblant pour lui à l'espace et toute la partie qui ne tombait pas immédiatement sous son rayon visuel étant cachée derrière cet horizon vague que l'œil, en arrière ni en avant, ne cherche pas à pénétrer (III, 126);

> Sentiment qui peut-être ne sera pas conservé, mais se rit de l'être comme si la conservation si longue qu'elle soit était dans cette sphère du temps, si au-dessus [sic] de la zone indéterminée dans laquelle il plane (II, 232).

Elsewhere, the image becomes impressionistic and heavily charged with emotion:

> J'use du bout des doigts tous ces moments qu'aujourd'hui m'apporte encore sans pitié, l'un après l'autre. Que la nuit vienne au plus vite enceindre à jamais de ses murailles gigantesques, mettre une forme éternelle et fuyante à aujourd'hui, passer lentement sur lui son noir déluge (I, 93).

As was only to be expected, Proust's absorbing interest in art colours also his ideas about memory and time. He draws a number of images from the visual arts, including two interesting analogies suggested by photography:

> . . . les lieux changent moins vite que les hommes pour qui le rideau de saules, le chemin montant ou le remous de l'eau sous le pont entre

[20] Cf. esp. B. L. Whorf, *Language, Thought, and Reality*, Cambridge, Mass., 1956. On spatial metaphors see G. Matoré, *L'Espace humain*, Paris, 1962. Cf. also G. Poulet, *L'Espace proustien*, Paris, 1963, esp. pp. 135 ff. and 182 ff.

les nénuphars sont comme les photographies qui restent dans une maison, que ne reconnaissent pas ceux qui ne les ont pas connues (II, 337);

... la photographie de tout cela avait pris sa place dans les archives de sa mémoire, des archives si vastes que dans la plus grande partie il n'irait jamais regarder, à moins d'un hasard qui les fît rouvrir (III, 201).

In one of the main passages on the rediscovery of the past, the contrast between involuntary and ordinary memory — 'la triste mémoire', as Proust once calls it (II, 233) — is brought out by a series of analogies from painting and drawing. Ordinary memory keeps merely 'les croquis rangés du présent', but in some privileged moments of our life the past comes back to us in a flash and we relive our experiences in the fullness and richness of reality: 'au lieu de la tristesse de quelqu'un qui n'a que des collections, ... je sens la trame de ma vie d'autrefois, ... non point plates comme une image mais pleines comme une réalité et vagues comme un sentiment' (II, 231-2).

In a different context, the similarity between people belonging to the same generation is compared to that between portraits from the same period in an art-gallery (III, 323). Elsewhere, sculpture furnishes a somewhat unexpected analogy: 'les mauvais jours ... persistant seulement dans son souvenir comme ces morts dont nous ne pouvons plus contempler que l'impuissante statue' (II, 112).

In two images, memory is likened to a jewel case and, in rather questionable taste, to a relic:

... trésor qui ne peut se conserver que dans un seul écrin, la mémoire, et ne peut se faire présenter aux autres que par une sorte d'illusion, la poésie (II, 337);

Un nom qui contient de la voix de ma mère, du temps même en train alors de s'écouler, ... je le vénère, il contient pour moi plus de divin, d'irréfaisable à n'importe quel artiste ou philosophe, que la relique qui contiendrait du sang du Christ (I, 184).

Proust even finds a comparison from his own craft to describe the effects of time on our memories: 'Les années de notre vie que nous avons vécues avec le plus de passion, une fois révolues, sont pour nous comme un roman que nous avons lu jusqu'à la fin: une fois lu, nous n'avons plus de plaisir à le relire' (II, 214).

Although music is one of the principal agencies of involuntary memory, it does not provide many analogies for the description of these processes.

In a curious passage, which is difficult to reconcile with what we shall be told later on about the 'petite phrase', Proust argues that 'natural music', which has no timeless and universally valid message to convey, will preserve more vividly than human music the atmosphere of the place and time where we heard it. And he goes on:

> ... ces humbles musiques naturelles ont un rapport profond, une harmonie cachée avec la saison où elles ont été entendues. Nées d'elle, cris d'adieu de l'hirondelle de ses premiers froids, ou bourdonnement des mouches de sa chaleur, c'est bien naturellement que ces musiciennes nous parlent d'elle puisque c'est elle-même qui nous parle dans leurs chansons (I, 166).

Another musical image embroiders on the connexion between age and memory:

> On dit qu'en vieillissant nos sensations s'affaiblissent. Peut-être, mais elles s'accompagnent de l'écho des sensations plus anciennes comme ces grandes chanteuses un peu vieilles dont un chœur invisible renforce la voix affaiblie (II, 10).

In a very different key, time and memory are sometimes compared to humble everyday objects. An old cloak which his mother used to wear does not simply remind Jean of his own youth but looks like an image of it: 'Troublé, il regarda le manteau qui, dans ses couleurs encore fraîches, son velouté encore doux, ressemblait à ces années qui ne servaient plus à rien, sans rapport avec la vie, mais pas fanées, intactes dans son souvenir' (I, 309–10). Even an ordinary handkerchief can become an effigy of time:

> Chaque heure lui devenant troublante et sacrée, comme ayant reçu l'essence de sa personne et les secrets de son intimité, il la respirait en tremblant ainsi qu'un mouchoir où elle aurait en le tenant dans sa main laissé un peu de son odeur (III, 242–3).

The contrast between an old body and a young mind is also presented in deliberately prosaic similes: the body will be worn out as an old dressing-gown which is not part of one's personality; it will, however, be kept healthy by the mind just as the freshness of meat is preserved by a grain of salt (I, 334).

The alphabet suggests an unusual image in a discussion of the way in which a writer utilizes the raw material of his experience: 'notre vie, quelle qu'elle soit, est toujours l'alphabet dans lequel nous apprenons à lire et où les phrases peuvent bien être n'importe lesquelles, puisqu'elles sont toujours composées des mêmes lettres' (II, 11–2).

Other images drawn from everyday experiences are more poetical. A new day is likened to a mysterious New Year's present:

> Demain n'est-il pas là, qui déjà, tandis qu'il dort, repose encore tout enveloppé, comme le grand cadeau mystérieux où une carte se dissimule sous la ficelle, sous la lampe, le matin du jour de l'an (I, 92).

Towards the end of *Jean Santeuil*, a parallel is drawn between sleep and a journey — a motif which will be more fully exploited in the *Temps perdu*:

> ... comme en voyage on se réveille dans un tout autre pays que celui où on s'était endormi, ainsi notre pensée est dans un tout autre site quand nous nous réveillons que quand nous nous sommes endormis ... Il a tant voyagé depuis, pendant cette nuit, que tout a bien changé en lui (III, 295).

A little earlier, dreams about the remote past had been evoked in more romantic terms:

> Comme une nuit obscure mais momentanément éclairée, ils (ses rêves) étaient pleins de signes et de présages. La chaîne des circonstances, la suite des temps ne pesant pas sur eux comme sur la vie de la veille, ils convenaient sans doute à cette dernière entrevue, à ce dernier rendez-vous avec un passé déjà trop lointain pour être ressaisi dans la vie. Ce fut donc sous le porche plein d'ombre d'un rêve que Françoise revint une dernière fois à lui (III, 229).

Personification plays a conspicuous part in the description of time and memory in *Jean Santeuil*. At one point, time itself is endowed with a soul:

> ... comme si les années passées vivaient encore ..., comme si l'âme de ce temps flottait encore dans des jardins pareils (II, 46).

The quiet hours of the past are personified and presented as purposeful human beings: '... ouvrage inappréciable qu'auraient ouvré des doigts aimés, ces douces étoffes vertes où sont engainés ces tuyaux au fond du bassin, ... qu'ont tissées ces mêmes heures silencieuses' (I, 184).

To meet a flower which can talk to us of the past is like seeing an old friend: 'nous avons senti ... dans ces bonnes fleurs blanches quelque chose qui nous parlait, comme quand nous rencontrons dans un défilé une personne aimée qui nous sourit, nous fait bonjour' (I, 137–8).

Places we have seen are similarly personified and given a physiognomy of their own: 'Les lieux sont des personnes, mais des personnes qui ne changent pas et que nous retrouvons souvent après bien longtemps ... des personnes à qui l'humanité qui est en nous a donné une physionomie' (II, 336–7; cf. II, 225).

Elsewhere the personification is more discreet, hardly more than a vague attempt to present an abstract phenomenon in a concrete form. In this passage on the role of imagination in involuntary memory, the verb *flotter*, not very metaphorical in itself but strengthened by repetition, provides the key-note of the whole experience:

> Serait-ce que la beauté, le bonheur pour le poète, c'est dans cette substance invisible qu'on peut appeler l'imagination, ... qui *flotte* seulement autour de la réalité passée qui se trouve prise dans une réalité présente? De sorte qu'entre elle et l'œil qui la voit, qui la voit aujourd'hui et autrefois, *flotte* cette imagination divine (II, 230).

And the same motif recurs once more at the end of the chapter:

> Nous ne savons pas quel jour où nous chercherons la beauté dans une montagne ou dans un ciel, nous la trouverons dans le bruit d'une roue de caoutchouc ou dans l'odeur d'une étoffe, dans ces choses qui ont *flotté* sur notre vie où le hasard les ramène *flotter* encore (II, 234).

From the examples which have been quoted it is clear that the imagery of time and memory in *Jean Santeuil*, though uneven and at times vague and uncertain, contains many valuable elements some of which will recur in the *Temps perdu*, in a more or less modified form. But it is equally clear that the really great images and symbols on these two central themes have not yet taken shape: the powerful metaphorical orchestration of the *madeleine* episode; the almost Einsteinian vision of a four-dimensional space-time continuum; the geological structure of our memories; the tragic predicament of man who is the mine where his own past lies buried, as well as the miner who alone can extract it; the nightmarish picture of the ever-growing stilts of time on which we are perched until we finally topple over, and many more. There is, of course, also another fundamental difference: by the very nature of things, we do not find in this imagery those significant patterns of recurrent analogies and those variations on a metaphorical theme which will be so characteristic of the later work.

Two general impressions emerge from our study of a few selected aspects of the imagery of *Jean Santeuil*. On reading this novel one is alternately amazed to see how much had already been achieved and how much still remained to be done. The problem of involuntary memory, and the imagery clustering round it, are examples in point. Proust was well aware that he had had his predecessors in this field; in *Le Temps retrouvé* he mentions Chateaubriand, Nerval and Baudelaire[21], and modern scholarship has added several other names to the list.[22] Proust himself was already exercised by these problems in *Les Plaisirs et les jours*,[23] and in *Jean Santeuil* there are, as we have seen, many detailed and penetrating analyses of these experiences, and the author has also evolved a rich and varied metaphorical language in which to talk about them. But the decisive step still had to be taken: Proust's ideas, and the images in which they were couched, had not only to be further developed but had to be transmuted into a work of art. In this as in other respects, he still had to accomplish all the labours which his narrator foresaw in *Le Temps retrouvé*: 'cet écrivain . . . devrait préparer son livre minutieusement, avec de perpétuels regroupements de forces, comme une offensive, le supporter comme une fatigue, l'accepter comme une règle, le construire comme une église, le suivre comme un régime, le vaincre comme un obstacle, le conquérir comme une amitié, le suralimenter comme un enfant, le créer comme un monde' (III, 1032).

The imagery of *Jean Santeuil* also serves to remind us of a truth which, though obvious enough, is apt to be overlooked. Images, like other elements of style, do not exist in isolation. In a novel without structure, individual figures of great artistic beauty or expressive force may arise, but the imagery as a whole is bound to be shapeless and without any structural value. In the passage immediately following the lines which have just been quoted from *Le Temps retrouvé*, the narrator tentatively compares his future book to a cathedral, and although he dismisses the analogy as too ambitious, there can be no doubt that Proust liked to picture his cycle in that way. The images of *Jean Santeuil*, talented but inchoate and amorphous like other elements of that novel, had to be transferred from the workshop into the cathedral, they had to be fitted and integrated into the architecture of a highly complex composition, before they could shine forth in their full lustre and significance.[24]

[21] III, 919-20.
[22] See esp. J. O'Brien, 'La mémoire involontaire avant Marcel Proust,' *Revue de Littérature Comparée*, xix (1939), pp. 19-36; E. Czoniczer, *Quelques antécédents de 'À la recherche du temps perdu,'* Geneva — New York — Paris, 1957; M. Mein, *Proust's Challenge to Time*, Manchester, 1962.
[23] See Jackson, loc. cit., pp. 586 ff.
[24] I am greatly obliged to Professor J. M. Cocking for bibliographical information and for lending me two fascicules of the *Bulletin de la Société des Amis de Marcel Proust*, and to Professor H. Flasche, of Marburg/Lahn, for enabling me to consult Miss Zeblewski's thesis referred to in n. 1.

Economics, Politics, Philosophy

13

M.-L. THYSS

Le Débat sur la Concurrence dans le Fret des Marchandises ou Un Aspect de la penseé économique, sociale et humanitaire du XVIIIème siècle

BIEN que la plupart des controverses soulevées par les théories de l'Ecole physiocratique aient été déjà longuement étudiées, peut-être serait-il intéressant cependant de se pencher à nouveau sur un épisode de la campagne pour la liberté du commerce, connu sous le nom de 'Débat sur la Concurrence dans le Fret des Marchandises'.[1] Ce débat, qui va dégénérer en une véritable querelle, car le ton s'élève et l'intégrité intellectuelle ne sera pas toujours respectée, va s'étendre sur plusieurs années: il commencera avec la victoire des Physiocrates, consacrée par l'Edit de 1764, puis couvrira une période d'hésitations et de reculs dans l'application de la politique de liberté, et finira, un peu court, il est vrai, quand en 1768, l'opinion sursaturée des théories physiocratiques et rendue prudente par la puissance de leurs adversaires, soit préférera s'abstenir, soit se désintéressera complètement de la chose.

'La question de la concurrence des Etrangers dans le transport de nos grains n'est point une question isolée: elle tient à tous les principes de l'administration économique.'[2] Bien plus, elle tient aussi à tous les fondements de la science économique, car nous verrons évoquer tour à tour les problèmes de la liberté et du monopole, de la production et de la consommation, des droits naturels et de l'intérêt particulier, et même du bonheur des peuples et de la fraternité des nations. Voici les faits:

La Déclaration du 25 Mai 1763 avait établi la libre circulation des

---

[1] Le débat s'étend sur 27 pièces dont nous avons établi la bibliographie complète à la fin de cet article, et numérotées 1 à 27. Les notes se rapporteront donc à cette numérotation. Comme presque toutes les pièces ont été publiées dans les deux périodiques *La Gazette du Commerce* et le *Journal de l'Agriculture, du Commerce et des Finances*, nous nous contenterons de mentionner ces périodiques par les initiales de *G.C.* et *J.A.C.F.* respectivement.

[2] **27**, pp. 99 et 100.

grains à l'intérieur du royaume; l'Edit de 1764 consacrait à son tour la liberté d'exportation et d'importation de ces mêmes grains; il comprenait cependant quelques restrictions: en particulier, toute exportation serait interdite si le prix du quintal dépassait douze livres dix sols; le transport de ces grains était réservé aux vaisseaux et équipages français, et le nombre des ports d'où partiraient ces bâtiments était fixé à 27. C'est le second point qui fait l'objet du débat: les physiocrates réclamant la libre concurrence, donc l'admission des étrangers à la voiture des grains, tandis que leurs adversaires voulaient, par le principe de l'exclusion, réserver les profits de la voiture aux Français et se servir du privilège pour développer et affermir la marine française. En fait, tous les grains que la France pouvait exporter après la récolte de 1764, furent exportés, et ce, par des bâtiments français qui suffirent à assurer le transport. Mais le prix du fret français s'avéra passablement plus élevé que ne l'aurait été celui du fret hollandais ou anglais.

Le principe de la liberté d'exportation ne sera jamais contesté ici, et les partisans de l'exclusion ne seront point des mercantilistes mais des esprits éclairés[3] et certes avisés des méfaits des monopoles et de la guerre des tarifs. Ils seront prudents et réalistes beaucoup plus qu'antiphysiocrates. Dans la discussion, l'accent sera mis tout d'abord sur le désir de faire jaillir la lumière, et l'opinion publique sera juge et partie:

> Le public sera juge de la dispute et sera mis à portée de prendre un parti. La question est assez importante pour mériter son attention. Peut-être s'élèvera-t-il de nouveaux athlettes de part et d'autre; les deux premiers quittes de leur engagement se retireront pour être spectateurs du combat, pour applaudir et se féliciter de la lumière qui doit en résulter.[4]

Ce public sera composé de gens de robe, d'armateurs, de commerçants, d'un intendant du Roi, et de gens de lettres, représentant assez exactement la classe cultivée du XVIIIème siècle. Ils pourront tous ainsi exprimer leurs idées, mais la querelle n'aurait guère reçu une telle publicité si elle n'avait permis aux physiocrates d'étaler leurs théories, car, au début du moins, ils dirigeaient les journaux qui vont la publier. C'est ainsi qu'ils pourront essayer de convaincre encore une fois une opinion toujours

---

[3] 'Je m'estimerai heureux si mon travail donne occasion aux Citoyens éclairés d'agiter de part et d'autre cette importante question, de la développer sous ses différents rapports et d'ajouter leurs vues à celles que je présenterai. C'est de la discussion que la vérité tire son évidence et son éclat, c'est de la contradiction que sort la lumière comme l'étincelle du caillou que le fer a frappé avec violence.' Letrosne, 5 G.C. 23 Février 1765, p. 125.

[4] 7 J.A.C.F. Juillet 1765, pp. 46–47.

récalcitrante[5] que la terre est la seule source de richesse, que son plus haut revenu possible est obtenu par le plus haut prix possible pour la vente de ses produits, et que ce dernier ne peut être atteint que grâce à la concurrence libre et entière. Le débat sera aussi prétexte à belles paroles et phrases bien rythmées, à assaut d'éloquence et d'esprit, à la manière du XVIIIème siècle.

Les véhicules de la querelle sont principalement les deux périodiques la *Gazette du Commerce*[6] et le *Journal de l'Agriculture, du Commerce et des Finances*[7] que nous appellerons respectivement la Gazette et le Journal dans la suite de cet article. La lettre aux auteurs, insérée dans un numéro, avec ou sans notes de la rédaction, incitera à la réponse sous la même forme; certains morceaux cependant dépasseront de beaucoup le cadre d'une lettre, même longue, et seront beaucoup trop polis pour être autre chose que de véritables pamphlets qui sont soit destinés à être lus en communication à de savantes académies, soit dignes de figurer plus tard dans un recueil séparé.[8] Le ton vivant de cette 'correspondance' fait accepter plus facilement certains passages plutôt longs et verbeux et donne parfois un piquant et une ironie fort agréables pour les lecteurs. Il serait bon d'ajouter ici que les rédacteurs des deux périodiques prennent souvent la plume eux-mêmes, soit ouvertement au moyen de notes, d'avertissements, de résumés ou même de 'mains directives' placées dans les marges, signalant les points contestables selon eux, soit sous couvert de l'anonymat.[9] Mais les rédacteurs ne seront pas toujours les mêmes pendant les quatre années du débat, aussi certains points contestables pour les premiers peuvent-ils bien devenir paroles d'évangile pour les suivants.

Les premiers rédacteurs forment un groupe qui comprend des personnalités telles que le Docteur Quesnay, le Marquis de Mirabeau, l'abbé Roubaud et Pierre Samuel Dupont de Nemours, tous physiocrates convaincus et de ce fait, partisans de la concurrence pleine et entière. Dupont de Nemours, qui deviendra en 1765 le rédacteur en chef du Journal, est vraisemblablement responsable des commentaires et des notes; de plus, il

---

[5] 'Je ne doute pas que la majeure partie du public ne soit d'un avis contraire au mien, non seulement sur la question principale, mais même sur plusieurs autres telles que l'unité de la source du revenu, les effets de la grande valeur des denrées, la nature des travaux de l'industrie . . .' 12, pp. 35–36.

[6] Fondée en avril 1763, elle deviendra en juin 1765 la *Gazette du Commerce, de l'Agriculture et des Finances*, et à partir de 1769 la *Gazette d'Agriculture, Commerce, Arts et Finances*.

[7] Fondé en juillet 1765, il a les mêmes rédacteurs que la Gazette; c'est une publication parallèle, pour permettre de présenter avec l'étendue nécessaire ce que la Gazette ne fait qu'indiquer. Le Journal publie des mémoires plus que des éléments pratiques, et est destiné à 'répandre le goût et à contribuer aux progrès de la science économique.'

[8] Voir **15, 17** et **27**.

[9] Voir **18**.

descendra lui-même dans l'arène sous l'anonymat de M. C.[10], afin de donner plus de poids à sa pensée. Ami de Turgot, futur député à l'Assemblée Nationale, sa plume ne cessera jamais d'attaquer les 'fauteurs intéressés de prohibitions et de réglements qui s'efforçaient de raisonner leurs concitoyens avec la formule patriotique de la protection due au travail national'.[11] Mais après novembre 1766, alors que la liberté d'exportation a de nouveau été réduite et que triomphent les adversaires des physiocrates, la rédaction passera aux mains de Véron de Forbonnais et de l'abbé Yvon qui vont essayer de minimiser l'importance de la question et se permettront d'ailleurs de ne plus donner que des extraits des lettres, voulant ainsi enterrer une querelle qui n'est plus d'actualité. Véron de Forbonnais peut, de plus, apporter tout le poids de son autorité: auteur des *Elémens du Commerce*, ouvrage classique d'un mercantilisme modéré, il attire encore le respect par sa longue expérience et son activité dans le domaine du commerce.[12]

Il nous paraît nécessaire d'établir chronologiquement les différentes étapes du débat et de présenter les antagonistes. Mais pour l'étude critique des idées exprimées sur la question de la concurrence, il nous a semblé préférable d'adopter un plan plus synthétique: cette étude en effet, serait fort gênée par des redites et des répétitions aussi lassantes qu'irritantes si nous devions suivre pas à pas chacun des mémoires, d'autant que certains morceaux n'ont pas été publiés dès leur envoi au Journal et que des réponses à des auteurs différents se croisent et s'entrecroisent sans cesse; aussi la rédaction avait-t-elle été forcée de numéroter les mémoires 'pour' et 'contre' afin d'y voir clair.

S'il nous faut trouver un point de départ précis à ce débat, nous pourrions commencer avec la note fort abondante que M. Letrosne, avocat du Roi au bailliage d'Orléans, associé de l'Académie Royale des Belles Lettres de Caen, membre de la Société Royale d'Agriculture, insère dans son *Discours sur l'Etat actuel de la Magistrature*[13] à propos de la prospérité qu'il souhaite à la France, prospérité qui devait avoir pour base

---

[10] Il n'y a aucun doute sur l'identité de Monsieur C. car certains morceaux publiés d'abord sous cette signature seront reproduits plus tard, le nom de l'auteur figurant en clair. Il en est de même pour Monsieur G., Monsieur M. et Monsieur K. qui sont respectivement Le Mercier de la Rivière, Letrosne et Guérineau de Saint Péravy, tous physiocrates convaincus.

[11] Daire (E.), *Les Physiocrates*, (série des principaux économistes), Paris, 1846, p. 314.

[12] Inspecteur général des monnaies, il prit une part active à l'administration des finances sous Silhouette, le Contrôleur Général des finances en 1759; plus tard, conseiller au Parlement de Metz, il continuera une correspondance fournie avec les intendants des finances: l'Abbé Terray, entre autres, responsable de l'Arrêt de 1770 qui allait supprimer la liberté d'exportation.

[13] Prononcé le 15 Novembre 1763 et publié en 1764. La note va de la page 69 à la page 75 incluse.

l'agriculture. Il croit nécessaire de reprendre en vingt-deux propositions les principes qui résument le 'tableau économique' du Docteur Quesnay. Cette note est si importante que les auteurs de la Gazette trouvèrent bon de la reproduire avec un court commentaire sous le titre de *Réflexions sur la Culture des Terres*.[14] La Gazette fait paraître ensuite le *Réquisitoire*[15] de Monsieur de La Chalotais, Procureur Général au Parlement de Bretagne, prononcé devant le dit parlement le 20 août 1764 à fin de faire enregistrer L'Edit de liberté de circulation des grains. La Chalotais accepte les idées de Letrosne tout en maintenant que la France devrait un jour suffire seule au transport de ses grains. Les *Réflexions* vont provoquer les premières réactions sous forme d'une lettre de M. Girard (dont l'identité ne sera dévoilée que plus tard); avocat du Roi au Parlement de Bretagne, établi à Quimper, il va attaquer Letrosne, et en particulier la dix-huitième proposition, au nom des faits qu'il connaît par son expérience bretonne.[16] Letrosne répond et défend sa proposition, mais au nom de la théorie générale.[17] Girard réplique, plus longuement cette fois.[18] Letrosne reprend la plume, mais dans le Journal nouvellement créé, et expose à nouveau ses vues.[19] C'est alors qu'apparaît un nouvel antagoniste: M. A. Il envoie lui aussi ses *Réflexions d'un Citoyen*:[20] c'est un 'homme très profond dont on doit louer la modération et le style'.[21] Monsieur A. restera anonyme, mais de la connaissance qu'il a des délibérations du Bureau du Commerce, nous pourrions facilement déduire qu'il s'agit d'un personnage officiel, peut-être d'un intendant d'une province maritime? Le même Journal publie encore une autre lettre de M. Girard.[22] Maintenant se manifestent, en octobre et novembre 1765, deux autres partisans de l'exclusion. Tout d'abord, M. B.; celui-ci nous donne suffisamment de détails sur sa carrière pour qu'il soit possible de reconnaître en lui Daniel Trudaine;[23] conseiller au Parlement de Paris, intendant d'Auvergne, puis Intendant des finances et Directeur des Ponts et Chaussées, enfin Directeur du Commerce et des Manufactures, il est certes le plus qualifié comme le plus

[14] 2 G.C.
[15] 3 G.C.
[16] 4 G.C.
[17] 5 G.C.
[18] 6 G.C.
[19] 7 J.A.C.F.
[20] 8 J.A.C.F.
[21] 8 J.A.C.F., p. 139.
[22] 9 J.A.C.F.
[23] 10 J.A.C.F. Toutes les bibliographies s'accordent à attribuer la lettre 'B' à Daniel Trudaine. M. B. nous dit en effet qu'il a lutté 30 ans (depuis 1734) pour obtenir la liberté, qu'il a eu la satisfaction de soumettre ses idées aux premières personnes de l'Etat et qu'il a été le premier à en discuter. Tout ceci correspond exactement à la carrière et aux services de Daniel Trudaine.

intelligent peut-être de nos auteurs, et son style est posé, concis et clair. Le second est un autre anonyme, M. X., dont nous aurons également un deuxième mémoire en août 1766.[24] Nous découvrirons qu'il est plus 'affermi dans la politique du commerce par des connaissances pratiques qu'exercé dans la discussion'.[25] Il est colérique et conscient de son importance, a des intérêts en Espagne et au Portugal et semble si bien connaître la marine et les marchés des ports qu'il pourrait bien être un armateur. Sa pensée est vive, rapide et souvent ironique.

'Notre querelle qui ne présentoit d'abord qu'une question particulière s'est étendue sur toutes les parties de science économique',[26] car le même Journal publie encore un mémoire de Letrosne et un autre de M. G., c'est-à-dire de Le Mercier de la Rivière, ancien intendant de la Martinique et ami du Docteur Quesnay et du Marquis de Mirabeau. Mais hélas, malgré les compliments des rédacteurs, car voici enfin des renforts pour Letrosne, le mémoire est long, ennuyeux et beaucoup trop général.[27]

Peut-être devrions-nous ajouter ici le mémoire de M. K.[28] qui parut en septembre 1766, bien que reçu par le Journal dès décembre 1765. Ce mémoire est le plus brillant, le mieux composé et le plus intéressant de tous les articles des partisans de la liberté; M. K. n'est autre que Guérineau de Saint Péravy, littérateur, ami de Dupont de Nemours et collaborateur du Marquis de Mirabeau. Si son mémoire ne parut que plus tard, c'est que les rédacteurs trouvaient bon alors d'enterrer la querelle: Letrosne, lui-même, qui est bien le meneur de jeu, voulut ridiculiser une bonne fois ses adversaires et en finir, en transmettant au Journal, qui le publia en décembre 1765, le *Projet de Requête des Rouliers-Voituriers d'Orléans*: c'est une plaisanterie, comme il le reconnut lui-même plus tard, mais il y assimile les marins à ces ridicules rouliers d'Orléans qui veulent être les seuls à voiturer le vinaigre et le vin de la région.[29]

Mais ce n'est qu'une trève de trois mois; la querelle repart de plus belle dans sa troisième phase. M. Rouxelin, secrétaire de l'Académie Royale des Sciences, Arts et Belles Lettres de Caen, avait lu en communication à la séance de la dite académie le 6 mars 1766, un mémoire qui prétendait résumer et conclure la querelle. Les membres de l'académie jugeant cette pièce remarquable, la communiquèrent au Journal qui ne put s'empêcher de la publier, car fort habilement, elle finissait par donner raison aux

[24] **11 et 19**.
[25] Lettre à M.M. *J.A.C.F.* juillet 1766, p. 124.
[26] **12** p. 34.
[27] **13** *J.A.C.F.* voir note 10 pour l'identification de M.G.
[28] **20** *J.A.C.F.* voir note 10 pour l'identification de M.K.
[29] **14** *J.A.C.F.* M.M. qui communique le *Projet* n'est autre que Letrosne.

physiocrates.[30] Les lettres reprennent, se croisent, se répondent: d'un côté Letrosne, puis M. C., c'est-à-dire Dupont de Nemours, et M. K.; de l'autre M. Girard, M. X., et un nouveau venu, M. S.[31] Ce dernier réclame pour lui la qualité de négociant, ce qui lui donne autorité pour parler de transactions commerciales vérifiées: ironique, piquant, parfois violent, mais fort sensé, il frappera Letrosne au point faible de la théorie que n'assure pas la pratique.[32] Pour répondre à ses coups, les rédacteurs font alors paraître en novembre 1766, une *Lettre d'un Commerçant de Marseille*: à négociant, négociant et demi![33] M. S., furieux déjà de la manière dont la rédaction a osé résumer son mémoire, dénoncera alors l'artifice: que voilà fort à propos un commerçant 'résident auprès du Journal', car sa lettre ne peut être partie de Marseille, vu les délais du courrier, et qu'il est bien peu informé des faits pour être commerçant! Jusque là nous avions pu croire, avec M. S., à la bonne foi des auteurs; mais après cela que penser de leur intégrité intellectuelle? La querelle s'est exaspérée: sans doute les physiocrates sentaient-ils la fin prochaine de leur politique, car c'est avec le Journal suivant, celui de décembre 1766, que la rédaction change: Véron de Forbonnais se dépêchera de terminer la querelle. S'il publie encore deux lettres de M. S., dont la dénonciation du 'Commerçant de Marseille',[34] il ne donnera plus que des extraits d'une lettre de M. Girard. Quant à Letrosne, il lui faudra se résoudre à faire paraître son dernier mémoire en réponse à M. S. dans un recueil à part, et ceci seulement en 1768.[35] Ainsi finit la querelle, non point faute de combattants, mais faute d'arguments nouveaux et surtout d'intérêt de la part de l'opinion publique.

Ayant ainsi présenté les antagonistes de la querelle, nous pouvons enfin aborder l'objet de leur long débat. En fait le principe qui sert de base à toute la discussion n'est autre qu'une des *Maximes générales du Gouvernement* du Docteur Quesnay:

Qu'on maintienne l'entière liberté du commerce: car la police du

[30] 15 *J.A.C.F.* Le rédacteur ajoute à la lettre de l'académie cette remarque, p. 65: 'Il ne peut être qu'infiniment avantageux pour notre ouvrage périodique d'avoir de pareilles obligations aux Académies; et il doit être bien doux pour tout bon Citoyen de voir que l'étude de la Science Economique pénètre jusques dans le sanctuaire des Muses, et que les hommes les plus instruits et les plumes les plus éloquentes s'occupent de l'examen des questions qui intéressent la Patrie.'

[31] D'un côté: 17, 18 et 20; de l'autre: 16, 19 et 21. *J.A.C.F.*

[32] M.S. nous révèle qu'il habite à 100 lieues de Paris, vraisemblablement à Nantes, un des plus grands ports français de l'époque.

[33] 23 *J.A.C.F.* Cette lettre ne pouvait pas matériellement partir de Marseille et arriver à temps pour la publication en réponse à M.S.

[34] 24 et 26 *J.A.C.F.*

[35] 27 dans *Recueil de plusieurs morceaux économiques sur la Concurrence des Etrangers dans le transport de nos grains*. Paris 1768.

commerce intérieur et extérieur la plus sûre, la plus exacte, la plus profitable à la Nation et à l'Etat, consiste dans la pleine liberté de la concurrence.[36]

Letrosne la reprend pour lui-même dans sa 18ème proposition sous cette forme:

Il faut décharger le Commerce de toute espèce de droits au dedans et au dehors du Royaume, car tout impôt donne aux Etrangers avantage sur nous; il faut donc lui laisser la plus grande liberté au dedans et au dehors, pour l'entrée et pour la sortie, pour les Regnicoles et les Etrangers car qu'importe qui nous débarrasse de notre superflu et qui voiture nos denrées. Le grand intérêt d'une Nation agricole, est de vendre et de procurer à ses productions des débouchés à moindre frais qu'il est possible, parce que les frais sont pris sur la chose, diminuent le bénéfice, et sont un grand obstacle à la sortie. Elle doit donc établir la concurrence entre ses Voituriers et les Voitures [sic] étrangers et ne pas restreindre son exportation pour vouloir profiter seule du mince bénéfice de la voiture, surtout lorsqu'elle n'a point assez de Vaisseaux pour y suffire, et que les Etrangers ont le fret moins cher.[37]

Voici donc le problème posé. Au nom de l'intérêt de l'Etat, qui est de produire et d'écouler ses denrées par la vente, comme au nom du bon sens, qui conseille aux agriculteurs de vendre au meilleur prix, la circulation des grains à l'extérieur du royaume ne doit souffrir aucune restriction. Et maintenant que le 'système fatal des Prohibitions paroît abandonné sans retour,'[38] système fatal qui défendoit aux Sujets d'un même Souverain de se prêter un mutuel secours et qui interdisoit entre la France et les autres Nations cette communication dans les échanges du superflu et du nécessaire, qui est si conforme à l'ordre de la Providence,'[39] pourquoi laisser subsister une protection particulière et accepter les restrictions de l'Edit?

Ce n'est que prudence et sagesse, répondent MM. Girard, A. et B. Nous avons affaire à une période de transition et il ne faut point aller trop vite. Le 'Gouvernement a déferré à des craintes populaires qui bien que peu fondées sont naturelles à l'indigence. Il a pensé peut-être que des préjugés enracinés par une longue habitude devraient plutôt être détruits par l'expérience que par l'autorité.'[40] Il a pris le 'parti mitoyen et c'est générale-

---

[36] Maxime XXV de l'édition de 1758, citée par E. Daire, op. cit.
[37] 2 G.C., p. 571.
[38] L'Edit est dit 'perpétuel et irrévocable'.
[39] 3 G.C., p. 612.
[40] 3 G.C., p. 618.

ment le parti du sage'.[41] D'ailleurs, ne pourrait-on pas rapprocher ou concilier les parties en leur présentant l'intérêt de l'Etat 'dont elles ne sont que des membres, intérêt qui les frappe peut-être moins qu'un intérêt personnel mal entendu, mais qui leur est d'autant plus important que cet intérêt personnel ne doit et ne peut subsister qu'autant qu'il se peut concilier avec l'intérêt général et y contribuer lui-même'.[42] M. A. et Letrosne seraient-ils d'accord? Non, car si la liberté d'exportation va lever les barrières contraires aux fondements de la société et si le blé ne sera plus l'objet d'un trafic de contrebande ou de profiteurs, cela ne veut pas dire que l'on doive à tout prix exporter en toute saison, ni que l'on doive abandonner le 'mince' bénéfice de la voiture s'il est possible de le garder pour soi. De plus, l'exclusion des voituriers étrangers, favorisera la marine française. Enfin les théories ne s'accordent pas toujours avec les faits.

Ainsi, avec M. de La Chalotais, 'examinons la question sans prévention et sans intérêt' et 'ne craignons point d'entrer dans les détails: l'expérience est la base de tout ce qui est physique; le calcul en est la mesure. On ne parvient à des maximes générales que par la connaissance de faits particuliers.'[43] C'est précisément ces faits particuliers que va nous présenter M. Girard, et nous aborderons tout d'abord le problème le plus factuel, celui de la marine.

Partant de l'axiome 'point de marine, point de commerce, et point de commerce, point de marine' que M. B. tient pour véridique, nous arrivons tout de suite à considérer le premier point: la marine est nécessaire et désirable. Mais s'ensuit-il que l'on doive protéger une marine en particulier? Pourquoi protéger la marine française?

Parce que la marine française trouvera ainsi une raison de se développer et de s'affermir, ensuite, parce que tout gain pour les marins français est un gain pour la France. Ce sont là deux arguments que Letrosne lui-même considère comme sérieux, tout en se proposant de les réfuter.

Tous les auteurs contre la pleine concurrence sont d'accord pour constater que la marine française ne tient plus la place qu'elle avait tenu au XVIIème siècle, et qu'il serait bon qu'elle la reprenne. En effet, vers 1760, les bâtiments de commerce français étaient peu nombreux et de petit tonnage, car on préférait les petits bâtiments aux grands, les risques étant ainsi mieux répartis.[44] Or les grains sont une marchandise lourde et encombrante, et les hollandais avec leurs flutes lourdes et vastes pouvaient les transporter plus aisément; ils gagnaient en encombrement ce qu'ils

[41] 8 *J.A.C.F.*, p. 141.
[42] 8 *J.A.C.F.*, p. 148 et 149.
[43] 3 *G.C.*, p. 613.
[44] 10, p. 28.

perdaient en célérité. Il fallait donc construire des bâtiments du même genre, mais pour que les armateurs fussent tentés de le faire il fallait aussi leur assurer l'utilisation de ces nouveaux vaisseaux. C'est justement ce qu'a fait l'Edit: M. Girard nous assure qu'il n'est 'pas de port en Bretagne où l'on n'y construise depuis la paix' et 'si les récoltes augmentent, les constructions augmentent en proportion'.[45] Fort bien, répond Letrosne, construisez et réduisez le prix de votre fret; mais en attendant, votre fret est plus cher et vous n'avez pas assez de bateaux. Cette dernière affirmation est fausse, s'écrient MM. Girard, X. et S.; tout le superflu de la récolte de 1764 et même de celle de 1765 a bien été exporté par des bâtiments français qui ont pu suffire aux transport; une marine bien encouragée suffira également à transporter un plus grand superflu. Quant au fret, les entraves infligées à la marine française sont cause de sa cherté. Enlevez les entraves, disent-ils au gouvernement, afin de pouvoir rivaliser sur un pied d'égalité avec les Hollandais. Nous apprenons alors que non seulement les bâtiments français doivent circuler avec un équipage beaucoup plus nombreux que celui des Hollandais, mais que les matelots français sont moins sobres, donc consomment plus, et sont moins endurants; la grande Ordonnance de 1681, destinée à former une pépinière de matelots dans une marine presque inexistante est devenue inutile et onéreuse.[46] Il ne faut point partir de l'argument qu'il n'y a pas assez de vaisseaux pour qu'il n'y en ait jamais assez: une terre à défricher ne peut-elle jamais l'être, simplement parce que le paysan manque d'outils? D'autre part Letrosne n'a-t-il pas imprudemment avoué dans un autre écrit que la marine 'manque de bras et qu'il faut repeupler nos ports'?[47] La marine marchande est la pépinière de matelots qu'utilisera à son tour la marine de guerre; les pêcheurs ne suffisent pas car beaucoup d'entre eux ne pratiquent qu'une navigation côtière, évitant la haute mer et le mauvais temps. Un matelot ne peut se faire avec de l'argent mais seulement grâce à une longue expérience. N'est-ce point là ce qui poussa l'Angleterre à promulguer son Acte de Navigation en 1660?

> Le Seigneur ayant voulu par une bonté particulière pour l'Angleterre que sa richesse, sa sûreté et ses forces consistassent dans sa Marine, le Roi, les Seigneurs et les Communes assemblés en Parlement ont ordonné que pour l'augmentation de la Marine et de la

---

[45] 9, p. 188.
[46] 21 M.S. donne en effet en grand détail toutes les différences existant entre un équipage français, anglais et hollandais pour un bâtiment de même sorte: un vaisseau français navigue avec 64 matelots par exemple, contre 44 anglais et seulement 15 ou 18 hollandais sur des vaisseaux de même tonnage et de même catégorie.
[47] G.C., p. 160, 5 mars 1765.

Navigation, l'on observera dans tout le Royaume les réglemens suivants.[48]

Moyennant quoi, l'Angleterre s'est assuré la suprématie sur les eaux en refusant de laisser des bâtiments autres que les siens enlever ses denrées et a vu sa marine s'accroître considérablement.[49] Et n'est-ce point justement 'l'exclusion que nos voisins ont eux-mêmes donnée à nos propres vaisseaux'[50] qui force la France à l'exclusion des étrangers dans le transport de ses grains? Car il ne faut pas compter jamais trouver de réciprocité chez les Anglais quant à la concurrence dans le transport. L'exclusion est donc le seul moyen, les entraves étant ce qu'elles sont, d'empêcher les nouveaux vaisseaux français de pourrir dans les ports.[51]

Enfin cette exclusion ne fait pas qu'encourager la marine elle-même, mais bien toutes les autres classes de métiers qui travaillent de près ou de loin à la construction des vaisseaux: charpentiers, voiliers, cordiers, forgerons et même mineurs par exemple, ou encore les paysans qui produisent le lin ou le chanvre, tous contribuent autant à la richesse du pays que le cultivateur de blé, chacun apportant un effort essentiel.

Voilà donc la cause de l'exclusion plaidée en faveur de la marine. Mais les physiocrates répondent à tous ces points:

Les entraves existent, il est vrai, mais au lieu de s'entêter à attendre qu'elles soient enlevées, il faut faire œuvre de citoyen intelligent et s'efforcer de gagner les autorités aux théories physiocratiques. Les ordonnances forcent la marine marchande à demander un fret trop coûteux, 'mais je regarde ces obstacles comme nuls, parce que je sçais aussi que dès que nos Armateurs ne verront plus d'espoir aux profits contre nature de l'exclusion et du monopole, ils seront très empressés à solliciter la révocation de ces droits que rien ne justifie, et parce que je sçais encore que l'administration est trop éclairée pour ne pas se rendre à cet égard à leurs justes demandes dès qu'ils prouveront leur patriotisme en ne sollicitant plus de privilèges exclusifs'.[52]

Mais tous ne partagent pas l'optimisme excessif de M. de Saint Péravy. Les armateurs auraient-ils jamais pu d'ailleurs obtenir le rappel de la grande Ordonnance de 1681? Ils auraient dû former une ligue autrement puissante que celle dont on les accuse d'être les membres. Tous les armateurs sont dispersés par toute la France et ne communiquent guère entre

---

[48] Cité par M. Girard, **16**, p. 147. Préambule de l'Acte de Navigation.
[49] **16** Sous Charles Ier, l'Angleterre avait moins de 3 vaisseaux de 300 tonneaux. Sous Charles II, l'Angleterre avait plus de 400 vaisseaux de 300 tonneaux.
[50] **9**, p. 189.
[51] **9**, p. 197.
[52] **20** note 7, p. 105.

eux; ils ont d'autres idées en tête; l'un met des bornes à la cupidité de son voisin, nul armateur n'aimant voir son vaisseau pourrir au port, et c'est une concurrence assez forte que celle de deux mille armateurs jaloux et rivaux.[53] Il ne faut pas confondre ici une exclusion qui à l'intérieur d'un état (telle une manufacture) surcharge tous les citoyens au bénéfice d'un seul, avec l'exclusion à l'extérieur du royaume qui assure aux membres de l'état le bénéfice que ferait l'étranger.[54]

Mais, nous dit-on, tout privilège, tout monopole, toute exclusion est contraire à la vie en société, et tout ce qui prétend à isoler les nations est contraire aux lois sacrées de la Nature.[55]

> Les hommes ne sentiront-ils jamais qu'ils ne peuvent se passer les uns des autres, qu'ils sont dans une dépendance mutuelle ordonnée par la Providence pour resserrer les liens de la Société, et assurer la subsistance de tous, que le commerce ne consiste pas seulement dans une communication de biens, mais dans une communication de services; que pour l'entretenir, il ne faut pas vouloir tout faire, tout entreprendre, tout gagner, mais laisser aux autres leur part du profit; que c'est rompre tout commerce que de prétendre tout vendre et ne rien acheter, tout embrasser et ne point laisser d'occupation aux autres, voiturer chez eux et les exclure de chez nous, vouloir se passer d'eux et leur être nécessaire; que pour une Nation agricole cette œconomie est aussi ruineuse que le seroit celle d'un Laboureur qui supprimeroit une partie de ses Domestiques pour gagner leurs gages.[56]

Mais les lois sacrées de la Nature, et parmi elles, l'instinct de la propriété, ne mènent-elles pas normalement à un état d'hostilité entre les hommes? Letrosne veut établir une communication de services:

> Ce désir est sans doute celui d'un philosophe dont le monde entier est la patrie; mais si la Providence même s'oppose à cette union en faisant souvent naître des guerres, (...) pourquoi s'occuper d'un objet chimérique pendant que nous devons commencer par nous aimer nous mêmes?[57]

Trop souvent les nations ne s'accordent que lorsqu'épuisées par la

---

[53] **21**, p. 107 et suivantes.
[54] **21**, p. 130 à p. 137.
[55] **13** Le Mercier de la Rivière reprend plusieurs fois le même thème.
[56] Letrosne, **3** G.C., p. 143.
[57] Girard, **4** G.C., p. 215.

guerre, et même, dans leurs accords, s'efforcent d'avoir la supériorité l'une sur l'autre:

Je voudrois comme vous Monsieur, que résolues de ne plus se faire la guerre, elles levassent tous les obstacles qui gênent leur commerce réciproque, mais encore une fois, cela n'est pas dans l'ordre de la Providence: il y aura toujours des guerres comme il y aura toujours des procès et si vous m'en demandez la raison, c'est parce que l'intérêt domine autant une Nation entière qu'un simple particulier.[58]

Nous voilà dans une impasse: l'un invoque la Nature et la Providence, et l'autre la même Providence mais en leur prêtant des desseins différents! Mais c'est justement parce que Letrosne, Dupont de Nemours et consorts désirent une paix universelle et croient en la possibilité de son avènement, que la nécéssité d'une marine de guerre leur paraît presque un nonsens; point n'est besoin pour eux de renouveler continuellement la pépinière de matelots. C'est là que nous est exposée une théorie fort hardie pour l'époque: il était inconcevable en effet pour la France de tirer les matelots nécessaires à la marine de guerre d'une autre source que de la marine marchande ou des inscrits maritimes. Recourir à la presse était considéré comme une pénible nécéssité à éviter dans la mesure du possible. Letrosne va dès le début du débat proposer soit de dissocier les deux marines, soit de se passer purement et simplement de marine de guerre incorporée à l'Etat, et de la remplacer, si tant est qu'elle dût être remplacée, par une marine mercenaire. Sa première idée provoque des objections nombreuses: et les frais? que ferait cette marine en temps de paix? S'il avait réfléchi il aurait découvert l'économie admirable de cette opération par laquelle le Roi entretient aux dépens d'autrui ses gens de mer; leur formation ne lui coûte rien, et c'est 'une économie bien supérieure à ce qui se pratique pour les troupes de terre'.[59] La seconde proposition fait pousser les hauts cris à l'opinion publique: pourrait-on compter sur la loyauté d'étrangers? les frais seront encore plus grands! Laisser échapper l'une sans protéger l'autre équivaut à se laisser emprisonner sur son propre territoire dont la moitié des frontières sont côtières. Tout ceci est si impensable que Letrosne battra en retraite et fera simplement remarquer que les deux marines ne sont pas nécessairement solidaires.

D'ailleurs, dit-il, le véritable problème n'est point là: ce qu'il faut empêcher à tout prix c'est de protéger une classe stérile aux dépens de la

<hr>

[58] 4 G.C., p. 215.
[59] Letrosne n'est pas entièrement suivi en cette matière par ses alliés. Pour eux, et en particulier pour Le Mercier de la Rivière 'qui n'entend rien à la politique', de son propre aveu, la marine militaire est un mal nécessaire pour protéger la marine marchande.

classe productive, et de diminuer ainsi les profits de cette dernière. Car
d'où vient l'argent pour créer une marine, armer les bateaux, payer les
gens de mer, développer les ports et les arsenaux? C'est le revenu
territorial de la France qui pourvoit à ces dépenses; or ce revenu vient du
produit net,[60] qui lui, provient de la vente de première main des denrées.
La France est une nation agricole qui doit avoir des vues plus
hautes que de petites nations maritimes qui n'ont guère de ressources
agricoles.[61] Son revenu est le résultat de l'écoulement d'une production
qui est surtout agricole, c'est donc à l'agriculture qu'il faut apporter ses
soins.

Les adversaires répondent que les agriculteurs ne constituent qu'une
petite proportion de la population française, que les voituriers sont
citoyens eux aussi et font partie au même titre de la nation française, qu'il
est donc de l'intérêt de l'état de leur accorder autant d'attention qu'aux
autres branches de métiers. De plus, en enlevant la voiture aux Français,
les voituriers perdront une source de travail, donc de revenu national.
M. X. nous soumet un simple calcul: un tonneau de froment se vend
200 livres à Lisbonne; sans application de l'exclusion, le cultivateur
recevrait 180 livres et le reste (20 livres) serait perdu pour la France; en
appliquant l'exclusion, le cultivateur n'aurait que 160 livres mais tout le
prix de la voiture, soit 40 livres retournerait à la circulation générale de la
France. Enfin, n'est pas 'stérile' une classe de la population qui par son
commerce et son industrie permet de convertir ses denrées et ouvrages en
objets utiles et en numéraire si nécessaire à la circulation. Les profits de ses
agents deviennent ceux de la Nation par la dépense qu'ils en font lorsqu'ils
consomment à l'intérieur du royaume les denrées de la classe agricole
elle-même; par leur consommation ils participent ainsi au bénéfice de
cette dernière.

Non, réplique fermement Dupont de Nemours: La circulation ne *rend*
pas ce que la voiture a pris à l'agriculture, elle le lui *revend*. Le manque à
gagner de 20 livres de l'agriculteur dans l'exemple de M. X., correspond
à un écu que vous auriez pris à un aubergiste, chez qui vous allez ensuite
consommer du pain et du vin pour la valeur d'un écu: voilà un écu
revendu mais non point rendu. Ces 20 livres sont une perte nette pour le
revenu territorial.[62]

Halte là, s'écrie Girard, vous confondez le revenu *national* avec le

---

[60] Le *produit net* est le revenu provenant de la vente des denrées, *après* remboursement des
avances faites à la culture et paiement du bénéfice dû au cultivateur. 2, 6ème proposition.
[61] 3 Entendez ici les Hollandais.
[62] 11 note 2, p. 16. Cette note est de la rédaction, mais Dupont a repris cet argument
ailleurs.

revenu *territorial*. Le salaire des mercenaires, ces classes réputées *stériles*,[63] ne revient pas tout entier par la consommation à l'agriculture; il sert de base aux impôts, tels la capitation et les taxes personnelles, augmentant ainsi le revenu national.[64] Et qu'importe que le revenu territorial soit grand si les cultivateurs ne peuvent suffire à mettre le royaume en état de se défendre en cas de guerre; et que deviendraient ces cultivateurs et les productions de leurs terres si des ennemis pouvaient venir impunément enlever leurs récoltes?[65]

Puisque M. Girard s'entête à ne point voir l'essentiel, il faut donc revenir au premier point de la théorie, dit Letrosne:

Le point fondamental qui nous divise est de savoir s'il y a une ou plusieurs sources de revenus. Nous soutenons qu'il n'y a source de revenu que là où il y a création et production et que partout ailleurs il n'y a que circulation et dépense; mais nos adversaires croient voir un accroissement de richesses dans la distribution et l'emploi des richesses; ils multiplient la source en autant de branches qu'il y a divers genres d'occupation dans la Société comme un homme qui voyant une infinité de canaux qu'on a tiré d'une rivière voisine (. . .) prendrait tous ces ruisseaux pour autant de rivières séparées, sans remonter à la source dont ils dérivent.[66]

L'industrie est donc comparable à cette infinité de canaux:

L'industrie est un attrait pour exciter à multiplier le revenu par les agréments des jouissances qu'elle varie; elle est en même temps une ressource pour faire subsister sur ce même revenu tout l'excès de la population qui ne peut être employé à le faire naître; elle étend les facultés de l'homme, et la sphère de ses connaissances, et elle exerce et occupe son génie: tels sont les motifs de la considération dont elle doit jouir. Mais on anéantirait tout et on la détruirait elle-même si l'on croyait devoir lui donner le pas sur l'Agriculture, et pouvoir la favoriser aux dépens de celle-ci.[67]

---

[63] Pour les Physiocrates les citoyens se divisent en trois catégories: (a) ceux à qui la terre appartient: propriétaires, Souverain, Grands, Décimateurs; (b) les cultivateurs qui font naître ce qui n'existait point; (c) les artistes, commerçants, artisans, voituriers etc . . . qui constituent la classe stérile, car ils ne font rien naître, mais se contentent de transformer ou de faire circuler les produits de la nature. Les deux autres classes sont productives, soit directement, soit par leurs avances à l'agriculture. Dupont propose de substituer les mots de classe *payée* et *payante* à *stérile* et *productive*.

[64] **4**, p. 191.

[65] **4**, p. 198.

[66] **17**, p. 50 ou **27**, p. 39.

[67] **20**, p. 97.

Si nous admettons que la seule source de revenu est la terre, il s'ensuit
que, des trois éléments qui composent le prix de vente du blé, c'est-à-dire
le prix reçu par le vendeur à l'origine, le remboursement des frais et la
rétribution du commerçant, seul le premier intéresse vraiment la culture,
donc la nation, et contribue à sa richesse véritable. Les deux autres sont
des dépenses stériles, en ce sens qu'elles ne contribuent pas à l'accroissement
ou au renouvellement des richesses territoriales. Il faut donc tendre à
diminuer le plus possible ces dépenses stériles pour augmenter à leur place
la valeur de la vente de première main et obtenir le plus haut prix possible.

'C'est cette première vente qu'il faut principalement et peut-être
uniquement considérer; c'est elle qui décide des reprises des cultivateurs,
du revenu de tous les propriétaires, des salaires et de la subsistance de tout
le reste de la nation'[68] qui ne peut vivre que sur la dépense des classes
productives. De sorte que la nation ne doit jamais craindre de voir ses
denrées à un prix trop haut (la disette à part), parce qu'elle ne doit pas
craindre d'avoir un trop grand revenu.[69] On portera tous ses soins à
établir le taux de la valeur vénale: si la quantité de denrées excède de
beaucoup la consommation nationale, ce superflu n'est plus richesses, il
nuit à la valeur du nécessaire: la valeur vénale baisse à l'intérieur du
royaume. On ira donc chercher ailleurs, par le commerce d'exportation à
qui il appartient de procurer le débit et la valeur. Mais à l'extérieur on ne
vend le blé qu'autant qu'il est vendu au prix général fixé par la concurrence, concurrence qui fait la loi quand il y a plusieurs vendeurs sur le
marché commun extérieur; et de ce prix on doit déduire les dépenses
stériles pour avoir le revenu. Comme ce prix est indépendant du cultivateur, pour avoir un grand revenu il faut d'abord profiter au mieux des
avantages que donne la concurrence dans le transport, et ensuite augmenter
l'exportation.

En effet, une nation qui admet tous les vaisseaux pour exporter a plus de
facilités pour profiter du moment; elle incite les étrangers à avoir des
magasins dans ses ports; la dépense qu'ils y font est un bénéfice net pour la
nation; la voiture des blés peut alors entrer dans la combinaison des
voyages et des retours, alors que maintenant, par exemple, les bateaux
français doivent rentrer à vide d'Angleterre; enfin une nation qui exporte
à moindre frais peut encore exporter quand une autre doit s'arrêter.[70]

Bien loin de permettre l'augmentation de l'exportation, l'exclusion des
étrangers la restreint: parce que les frais sont parfois insupportables; parce
que dès qu'il y a pénurie de vaisseaux, le prix de la voiture étant réglé sur

[68] 20, pp. 64–65.
[69] 2ème proposition.
[70] 27.

le volume et non sur la valeur, on préfère charger une autre marchandise.[71] Alors pourquoi se contenter de la concurrence qui existe entre les armateurs quand on peut en établir une beaucoup plus grande? Et l'effet de la concurrence se fera d'autant plus sentir que l'exportation augmentera. Plus les denrées auront de valeur vénale et plus l'exportation augmentera, plus il y aura de revenu, plus il y aura de dépense, plus la dépense procurera d'ouvrage et de salaire à tous ceux qui vivent de leur travail, et plus la population augmentera, car elle est toujours en raison des moyens de subsistance.[72]

Puisque le prix du blé est la mesure de la valeur de toutes les marchandises et ouvrages aussi bien que des salaires de l'ouvrier, il est donc de l'avantage de l'ouvrier de voir le prix du blé assez haut pour qu'il en soit de même de son salaire et à condition que ce prix soit constant afin d'éviter les craintes et les incertitudes. Or cette constance ne s'établit que par l'équilibre que donne la concurrence internationale.[73] C'est pourquoi l'intérêt des salariés ne peut en aucun cas être contraire à celui des cultivateurs et des propriétaires, car ils vivent de la dépense du revenu de ceux-ci. Ces derniers rendent à l'agriculture ce même revenu par leurs avances, prélèvement fait de leurs besoins. Ainsi les richesses foncières donnent les richesses d'exploitation qui produisent les richesses renaissantes qui font l'abondance de la population.[74] Finalement, une grande population signifie une grande puissance.[75]

Voilà la thèse des physiocrates pleinement développée. Leurs adversaires répliquent à nouveau par des faits.

Augmenter le prix du blé risquerait d'amener les populations à la misère, car le prix du pain est déjà le tiers de ce que l'ouvrier gagne chaque jour.[76] D'autre part si le prix du blé augmente, les salaires augmenteront peut-être, mais le coût de la vie montera aussi. Et il n'est pas dit que le revenu profite à la nation comme il se doit: les propriétaires sont avides et veulent accumuler leurs richesses; quant au colon, il pourrait bien devenir ivrogne et paresseux au lieu de défricher.[77] Enfin pourquoi vouloir à tout prix augmenter l'exportation? Une trop grande exportation ferait tomber les prix du blé à l'étranger alors qu'il serait trop cher pour la population chez nous; ce serait rompre l'équilibre qui seul peut assurer la sécurité: les achats et les envois cesseraient tout à coup et les

[71] 5.
[72] 2, 19 ème et 22 ème propositions.
[73] 2, 20 ème proposition.
[74] 20, p. 91. Saint Péravy oublie que bien des propriétaires ne sont pas gagnés à ses idées.
[75] Théorie populationniste acceptée à l'époque.
[76] 6.
[77] 16, p. 162.

étrangers viendraient nous vendre à nous-mêmes.[78] Ce qu'il faut c'est nous assurer une vente régulière; mais c'est le bon marché qui assure la vente, et procure seul le prompt et grand débit duquel dépend absolument le revenu territorial.[79] Vendre peu, vendre souvent et avec profit, et sacrifier sur le prix ce que l'on peut gagner en régularité, voilà le parti du sage.[80] Non qu'il faille négliger l'intérêt du cultivateur, mais il est subordonné à un intérêt infiniment supérieur, celui du consommateur. Il semble que les physiocrates aient singulièrement négligé ce dernier. Si même la France pouvait étendre son exportation, ce qui est douteux au delà de ce qui a déjà été enlevé, il y a des bornes à tout, bornes que fixe la loi de l'offre et de la demande.

C'est ce que nous rappelle M. B. avec toute son expérience:

Je crois aussi comme M. Le Trosne, que la liberté du Commerce des grains établira une parité de prix dans tous les marchés de l'Europe; mais il ne faut pas penser qu'il résulte de cette parité que la même quantité de grains aura une égale valeur dans tous les marchés; cette parité ne s'établira qu'en proportion

1) Du plus ou moins de superflu de chaque marché
2) Du plus ou moins de besoin connu ou prévu
3) Des frais que les Nations respectives auront à faire, les unes pour chercher la consommation de leur superflu, les autres pour pourvoir à des besoins qui sont de première nécessité.[81]

Si Letrosne et ses alliés se sont attachés à remplir la première condition, à peine ont-ils effleuré les problèmes que posent les deux autres. 'Il est inutile de lui faire comprendre que l'exportation doit être mesurée moins sur l'abondance de la récolte de celui qui exporte que sur les besoins du consommateur'.[82] Disette à l'étranger ne veut point dire abondance chez nous, mais il y a souvent abondance partout à la fois. De plus il existe une chose appelée satiété:[83] Letrosne ne voit point de bornes à l'exportation des grains que pourrait consommer la population de l'Europe, mais que fera la France de ses blés quand personne n'en voudra plus? Le danger est d'aller aux extrêmes, car c'est la régularité dans les échanges qui reste la

---

[78] 6 et 9.

[79] 9, p. 196.

[80] 9, p. 186.

[81] 10, pp. 22 et 23. M.B. donne en exemple l'Italie: si la Sicile ne lui suffit pas, elle achète en Angleterre et en France; mais le transport de Provence est beaucoup moins onéreux. Pour entrer en concurrence avec les Provençaux, le cultivateur anglais devra baisser son prix de tout ce qu'il en coûtera de frais de transport en plus.

[82] 19, pp. 163–4.

[83] 19 M.X. nous donne la preuve des blés français, partis en Espagne et finalement réexportés en France.

seule sauvegarde du commerce d'une nation. D'autre part, le fret français, si cher soit-il, est souvent compensé par la célérité de la livraison, la sécurité de la navigation française et l'assurance meilleure marché de ce fait. Enfin, quelles sont les possibilités de la nation acheteuse? Peut-elle payer en numéraire ou ne faudra-t-il pas avoir recours à un échange de denrées direct ou indirect, impliquant plusieurs transports différents par des nationalités diverses? Toute transaction commerciale considère deux intérêts souvent opposés, production et consommation. Letrosne croit pourvoir aux deux, mais la population est-elle le critère de la consommation et de la richesse?

Chose étrange, c'est du camp physiocrate que nous vient la réponse à cette question purement rhétorique:

> Le nombre des habitants d'un Etat n'est point du tout un indice sûr de sa force, de ses richesses et de sa fertilité. . . . La seule manière infaillible d'estimer la puissance relative des Empires, consiste à examiner si les cultivateurs y sont riches, si toutes les terres y produisent des denrées de haut prix, si tous les habitants, sans égard à leur nombre y jouissent d'une grande aisance fondée sur un grand revenu (. . .)[84]

C'est pourquoi il ne suffit pas d'avoir une grande population. La France est-elle plus riche d'avoir cent mille mendiants? A quoi servent ces cent mille consommateurs qui ne défrichent pas? La pluie d'or ne fertilise rien non plus.[85]

Ayant vu ainsi un de leurs arguments se retourner contre eux, les partisans de l'exclusion lâcheront alors leur dernier trait qu'on ne pourra repousser, car l'expérience a démontré sa véracité: c'est l'exemple anglais. L'Angleterre, par son 'chef d'œuvre de police du commerce'[86] a favorisé l'exportation de ses grains, les a fait transporter sur des bâtiments anglais et a ainsi acquis une importante et fructueuse branche de commerce. Peut-on le nier?

Oui: ce n'est point à cause de sa politique d'exclusion, mais en dépit de celle-ci qu'elle a acquis une fortune. Consciente des possibilités de son agriculture, elle a su développer ses terres en multipliant les avances à la culture et en protégeant l'intérêt de ses fermiers. Mais par son Acte de

---

[84] **20**, p. 98.

[85] A quoi on aurait dû rétorquer que la production sans écoulement prévu ne sert à rien et qu'il confond ici le capital or avec le capital travail. Mais personne, parmi les protagonistes, ne s'en est avisé.

[86] **19**, p. 165.

Navigation elle a rompu le principe de la Fraternité des Nations. Cependant

> L'acte d'hostilité que commet une Nation envers une autre en l'excluant de chez elle par des prohibitions ou des impôts, en violant la loi de la réciprocité du commerce et de la liberté des échanges n'autorise point les *réprésailles*, parce qu'elles ne sont légitimes que dans le cas d'une nécessité indispensable.[87]

Bien plus, si l'on suivait la voie que nous trace la Nature,

> (. . .) tous les Empires n'auroient point de faiblesse masquée, de grandeur factice et de puissance précaire: leur richesse et leur puissance seroient fondées sur leurs productions naturelles, sur une industrie qu'on ne pourroit envier, ni leur enlever; et chacun ne pouvant réussir qu'autant qu'il concoureroit à la prospérité générale, la cupidité ne parviendroit plus à séduire l'ambition pour l'engager à la seconder en embrasant l'Univers.[88]

Après s'être élevé au niveau de la paix universelle par la concurrence il ne reste plus rien à dire si ce n'est se jeter des accusations à la tête. Tout ceci n'est 'que métaphysique qui n'engendre que des systèmes' dira Girard. Vaut-il mieux le raisonnement de M. S. qui 'a élevé dans la lice un tourbillon de poussière, a aveuglé les spectateurs pour se prévaloir de l'obscurité et les a étourdis par des coups bruyants frappés dans l'air'? Mais Girard l'emporte:

> Ne pourrais-je, monsieur, vous comparer à Jean Jacques Rousseau dont on admire encore la force et les grâces du style, mais dont on n'approuvera jamais les principes.[89]

Enfin il restera toujours la ressource de dire tout bonnement: 'Je ne vous entends point.'[90] Où sont donc nos esprits éclairés?

En définitive que conclure de ce long débat? N'est-il pas étrange de constater à quel point tous les auteurs, ayant en main presque tous les éléments d'un système vraiment constructif, soient passés à côté des vérités économiques indiscutables? Sans doute est-il trop facile de condamner les physiocrates pour leurs erreurs; avec la confiance optimiste qui caractérise leurs mémoires, ils nous paraissent si pompeusement imbus

---

[87] **17**, p. 43.
[88] **20**, pp. 56 et 57.
[89] **12** 'Métaphysique bien physique,' dit Dupont en note; **27**, p. 104; et **9**, p. 182, respectivement. Girard s'adresse à Letrosne. Ce commentaire, condamnant Rousseau, date de 1765, et la grande majorité des élites provinciales, ces fameux anonymes, correspondants du *Journal*, pensaient de même.
[90] **12**.

de la doctrine d'une Providence bienveillante et régularisatrice du monde, si retranchés dans la métaphysique d'un système où les mythes du Progrès et de la Bonne Volonté universelle sont tenus pour vrais, que nous serions tentés de ne voir en eux qu'un groupe d'illuminés inoffensifs. Ils sont les enfants du siècle de Rousseau, déjà pourtant rejeté lui-même, et il serait presque vain de tenter de les défendre en un siècle où les problèmes de la production et de la consommation sont choses quotidiennes. Mais aurait-on pu à l'époque concevoir une France autre que la France agricole, avec ses vastes espaces à défricher et toutes ses ressources encore à exploiter? N'était-il pas un fait que c'était là la source probable d'un accroissement de la population et par suite d'une multiplication des consommateurs? Qu'il est dommage cependant qu'ils aient commis cette erreur fondamentale de confondre le capital or avec le capital travail par leur conception des richesses revendues et non rendues. Si seulement M. X. ou M. S. avaient fait un pas plus avant ils auraient démontré clairement, avec Daniel Trudaine pour guide, que le travail n'est point fonction uniquement des avances en argent qu'on lui fait, mais de l'habileté de sa main d'œuvre, des outils qu'il emploie, de la variété de ses ressources et de l'épargne de ses ouvriers, points qu'Adam Smith, qui puisa une grande partie de sa pensée à la source des économistes français, s'empressera d'exposer quelques années plus tard. Hypnotisés comme ils l'étaient par le commerce des grains, les physiocrates n'ont pu concevoir que le commerce des objets manufacturés, tellement plus aisé par sa mobilité et sa variété, viendrait à rapporter un revenu infiniment plus rapide et maniable malgré l'influence d'éléments variables comme la mode et le goût. Conscients du luxe et de ses méfaits 'dans l'ordre physique aussi bien que dans l'ordre moral', [91]ils n'ont pas essayé de circonvenir et d'exploiter un mal qu'ils ne pouvaient détruire. Il est ironique que leurs adversaires, qui détenaient les faits qui auraient dû les aider à placer le problème de la consommation dans une juste perspective, se soient retranchés derrière l'intérêt particulier, même quand ils avaient su détecter que la richesse d'un pays vient du travail, et non point uniquement de la terre. Ils n'ont pu que prolonger le système de la protection et des tarifs dont ils savaient pourtant les désavantages.

Mais malgré tous ces échecs, ces esprits éclairés, avaient déjà, bien avant nos économistes modernes, pressenti la possibilité et même la nécessité d'un Marché Commun de l'Europe.[92] Mais la Communauté Economique

[91] **27** Letrosne.

[92] Monsieur de la Chalotais déplorait que la France, depuis un siècle, ne participât plus 'au prix du marché Commun de l'Europe', ce qui lui semblait de la première nécessité; ce qui prouve que cette notion du marché commun pour l'Europe n'était point nouvelle pour certains esprits.

Européenne qui a su établir la parité des prix si chère à Letrosne, au sein des pays qui en sont membres, a rejeté le principe du plus haut prix possible, pour suivre pas à pas les conseils de Daniel Trudaine. Ainsi, quoiqu'encore éparpillés à travers un long et parfois ridicule débat, les éléments que nous trouverons dans cette querelle vont servir à construire d'autres systèmes qui seront les bases solides des sociétés modernes. Les premiers, nos auteurs ont formulé une théorie des grands marchés: à l'unité de temps et de lieu des foires du Moyen Age, ils ont ajouté l'unité de prix, l'unité d'intérêts, et l'unité des transports. Bien que l'accent ait été porté plus sur la production que sur la consommation, presque toutes les conditions nécessaires à la vente d'un certain produit à un certain moment avaient été envisagées: prix de vente, dispersion des acheteurs, moyens de transport et de diffusion, obstacles géographiques, psychologiques, voire administratifs. Les Etats d'Amérique, dans leur Constitution de 1787 révèleront bientôt leur souci d'unité commerciale entre leurs Etats. Le Zollverein réalisera plus tard de 1834 à 1867 le rêve de Letrosne: la création d'une sorte de contagion du libéralisme dans les Etats Allemands. Enfin avec les Empires coloniaux, la théorie des grands marchés s'élargira jusqu'à englober des conceptions plus complexes, car l'inégalité des forces va modifier profondément les facteurs de liaison. Mais pour nos physiocrates les problèmes étaient simples, puisqu'il suffisait de croire en la Fraternité des Nations, utopie qui a encore cours aujourd'hui, car pour certains, elle est la seule alternative possible à la destruction du monde par 'les intérêts particuliers des Nations ennemies'.

BIBLIOGRAPHIE DU DÉBAT SUR LA CONCURRENCE DANS LE FRET DES MARCHANDISES

1 *Discours sur l'Etat actuel de la Magistrature et sur les causes de sa décadence* (prononcé à l'ouverture des Audiences du Bailliage d'Orléans, le 15 novembre 1763) par M. Letrosne, avocat du Roi, Paris 1764, in-8°, 129 p.

2 *Réflexions sur la culture des terres*, par M. Letrosne. *Gazette du Commerce* du 4 septembre 1764, pp. 569–71.

3 *Réquisitoire de M. de La Chalotais*, prononcé le 20 août 1764 par M. Caradeuc de la Chalotais, G.C. des 22 et 25 septembre 1764, pp. 617–19.

4 *Lettre à l'Auteur de la Gazette*. [par M. Girard, avocat au Parlement de Bretagne], G.C. du 5 janvier 1765, p. 13.

5 *Lettre de M. Letrosne, Avocat du Roi au Bailliage d'Orléans, à l'Auteur de la Gazette*, sur l'exclusion des Vaisseaux étrangers pour la voiture de nos grains, en réponse à la lettre insérée dans la Gazette du 5 janvier 1765. G.C. des 23 et 26 février 1765 et 2 mars 1765, pp. 125–7, 133–7 et 141–4.

6 *Réponse à la lettre de M. Letrosne*, insérée dans la Gazette du 23 février 1765 [par M. Girard]. G.C. des 23, 26 et 30 mars, et 2 avril 1765, pp. 189–92, 197–200 et 205–8.

7 *Lettre de M. Letrosne sur les Avantages de la Concurrence des Vaisseaux Etrangers pour la*

Voiture de nos grains. Journal de l'Agriculture, du Commerce et des Finances. Juillet 1765, août 1765, pp. 45–143, pp. 39–113 et 114–122.

8 *Réflexions d'un Citoyen sur l'admission des Etrangers à la Concurrence dans le Fret pour l'exportation*, par M. A. *J.A.C.F.* septembre 1765, 2ème partie, pp. 138–79.

9 *Lettre de M. Girard. J.A.C.F.* septembre 1765, 2ème partie, pp. 180–204.

10 *Mémoire sur le Commerce des Grains* par M. B. *J.A.C.F.* octobre 1765, pp. 3–30.

11 *4ème Mémoire contre la Concurrence dans le Fret*, de Lisbonne par M. X. *J.A.C.F.* novembre 1765, pp. 6–31.

12 *Réponse de M. Letrosne à M. Girard. J.A.C.F.* novembre 1765, pp. 32–99.

13 *Observations sur le Mémoire intitulé 'Réflexions d'un Citoyen, relativement à l'admission des Etrangers à la Concurrence dans le Fret pour l'exportation de nos grains', ou Lettre aux Auteurs du Journal*, par M. G. [Le Mercier de la Riviere]. *J.A.C.F.* novembre 1765, pp. 100–46.

14 *Lettre à MM. les Auteurs de la Gazette et du Journal*, par M. M. [Letrosne] accompagnée de *Projet de Requête des Rouliers-Voituriers par terre de la ville, fauxbourgs et banlieues d'Orléans*, à présenter à l'Assemblée municipale des habitants de ladite ville, *J.A.C.F.* décembre 1765, pp. 57–85.

15 *Analyse des moyens pour et contre l'exclusion dans l'exportation de nos grains*, lue en séance publique de l'Académie Royale des Sciences, Arts et Belles Lettres de Caen, le 6 mars 1766, par M. Rouxelin (Secrétaire de l'Académie), *J.A.C.F.* avril 1766, pp. 66–105.

16 *5ème Mémoire contre la Concurrence dans le Fret, ou Réponse de M. Girard à la dernière Lettre de M. Letrosne, J.A.C.F.* juin 1766, pp. 146–91.

17 *De l'Utilité des Discussions économiques* par M. Letrosne, et *Résumé des principes de M. Girard, J.A.C.F.* juillet 1766, pp. 8–90.

18 *Lettre aux Auteurs sur le Cabotage dans la Concurrence du Fret* par M. C. [Dupont de Nemours]. *J.A.C.F.* juillet 1766, pp. 177–206.

19 *6ème Mémoire contre la Concurrence du Fret* par M. X. *J.A.C.F.* août 1766, pp. 150–84.

20 *4ème Mémoire pour la Concurrence dans le Fret* par M. K. [Guérineau de Saint Péravy], Réponse à M. A. *J.A.C.F.* septembre 1766, pp. 46–136.

21 *7ème Mémoire contre la Concurrence dans le Fret* par M. S. *J.A.C.F.* octobre 1766, pp. 107–64.

21a *Résumé du Mémoire de M. S.* par les Auteurs du Journal. *J.A.C.F.* octobre 1766, pp. 164–7.

22 *Lettre à M.B. ou Réponse de M. Letrosne au Mémoire contre la Concurrence. J.A.C.F.* novembre 1766, pp. 28–51.

23 *Lettre d'un Commerçant de Marseille à MM. Les Journalistes de l'Agriculture et du Commerce. J.A.C.F.* novembre 1766, pp. 173–93.

24 *Réponse de M.S. au Résumé de son Mémoire. J.A.C.F.* décembre 1766, pp. 113–31.

25 *Extrait d'une Lettre de M. Girard contre la concurrence des Etrangers dans l'exportation de nos grains. J.A.C.F.* janvier 1767, pp. 104–12.

26 *Supplément à la Lettre de M.S. du Journal de Décembre 1766. J.A.C.F.* janvier 1767, pp. 121–9.

27 *De la Concurrence des Etrangers dans la Navigation ou Réfutation du Mémoire de M.S. du Journal d'Octobre 1766.* 3ème Morceau du *Recueil de plusieurs morceaux économiques sur la Concurrence des Etrangers dans le transport de nos grains*, par M. Letrosne, Paris, 1768, in-12, 236 p. (les nos. **17** et **22** de cette bibliographie, réédités alors, forment les premier et deuxième morceaux respectivement de ce Recueil).

14

T. V. BENN

Les «Political discourses» de David Hume et un conte de Diderot

Cette enquête fut, à l'origine, de nature purement bibliographique. Elle a comme point de départ une section des matériaux recueillis à Leeds[1] pour l'étude de l'influence anglaise en France. Cette section se rapporte aux écrivains qui, au dix-huitième siècle, en Angleterre et en France, étaient en train de fonder l'économie politique; parmi eux, David Hume s'est révélé de suite comme une figure de proue, bien qu'il fût précédé par Cantillon l'incompris, et suivi par le géant Adam Smith. Mais la bibliographie mène partout: l'étude des traductions des *Political discourses* de Hume (1752) soulève, en effet, certaines questions:

1° Peut-on se fier aux affirmations de Diderot?

2° Mlle de La Chaux (prénom inconnu), jeune fille émancipée, charmante, et savante, et qui a sa place dans la *Biographie universelle*, a-t-elle jamais existé?

3° Les savants du 19e siècle (et même du 20e) ont-ils créé parfois des livres imaginaires?

Relevé des traductions françaises des «Political discourses» (1752)

1 (a) *Discours politiques de Monsieur Hume* (Amsterdam; Paris, Lambert, 1754, 2 vol.) Traduction de l'abbé Jean-Bernard Le Blanc.

(b) —— (Dresde, Groell, 1755, 2 vol.)

2 (a) *Discours politiques de Mr. David Hume* (Amsterdam, Schreuder, P. Mortier le jeune, 1754). Traduction de Eléazar Mauvillon.

[1] La recherche de ces matériaux, commencée en 1927–33 avec l'encouragement de Paul Barbier fils (chef du département de français à Leeds de 1903 à 1938), a pu être reprise à partir de 1950 grâce à des subventions consenties par M. Clapton. Ces matériaux comportent, au commencement de 1965, pour la période jusqu'en 1839, environ 100.000 fiches. Une collection de livres pour l'étude de l'influence anglaise en France jusqu'en 1805, commencée à Leeds en 1919 par Paul Barbier et Richard Offor (bibliothécaire de 1919 à 1947) et continuée par B. S. Page, bibliothécaire depuis 1947, contient plus de 4.500 volumes.
Je voudrais ici remercier ma femme qui a passé avec moi de longues heures dans une dixaine de bibliothèques à examiner des livres, vénérables et parfois oubliés, d'économie politique.

(b) —— (Ibid., 1761).
(c) —— (Amsterdam, Schreuder, 1767).
3 (a) *Essais sur le commerce,* ... *par David Hume, traduction nouvelle* ...
    (Amsterdam, 1766). Exemplaire perdu, signalé par A.-A. Barbier,
    avec une dédicace par la traductrice; sans «Réflexions».
(b) —— (Amsterdam, 1766). Sans dédicace, avec «Réflexions».
(c) —— (Avignon, 1766). Edition perdue?
(d) —— (Paris, Saillant; Lyon, Delaroche, 1767).
(e) —— Tome VII des *Œuvres philosophiques de M. D. Hume* (Londres,
    1788).
4 (a) *Le génie de M. Hume* (Londres; Paris, Vincent, 1770. Extraits;
    compilateur: Auguste-Pierre Damiens de Gomicourt.
(b) —— (Londres, 1771).
5   Diverses traductions partielles seront indiquées.

La traductrice des «Political discourses»

Les exemplaires des *Essais sur le commerce, le luxe, l'argent* ... *traduction
nouvelle* ..., trouvés jusqu'ici, sont sans nom de traducteur et portent la
date de 1766 ou de 1767. C'est la troisième traduction des *Political discourses* (1752) de Hume; elle est généralement attribuée à Mlle de La Chaux.
Les bibliographes en proposant cette attribution, s'en remettent à Diderot,
qui, dans un conte intitulé «Ceci n'est pas un conte», avait dit, en fait,
tout autre chose. Diderot avait bien spécifié:

Mlle de La Chaux (...) posséda l'anglois au point de rendre en
françois les premiers essais de métaphysique de Hume. (*Œuvres* ...
p.p. J. A. Naigeon, An VI–1798, XII, 390–1; *Œuvres* ... *revues* ...
par J. Assézat, V (1857), 321).

Et plus loin:

(...) sa première tentative littéraire fut la traduction des *Essais sur
l'entendement humain,* de Hume. Je la revis; et, en vérité, elle m'avoit
laissé bien peu de choses à rectifier. Cette traduction fut imprimée en
Hollande, et bien accueillie du public. Ma Lettre sur les Sourds et
Muets parut presque en même temps. ... La traduction de Hume ne
lui avoit pas rendu grand argent. Les Hollandois impriment tant qu'on
veut, pourvu qu'ils ne payent rien. (Naigeon, XII, 402–3; Assézat, V,
328, 329).

Naigeon, ami de Diderot, est seul responsable de cette précision: *Essais
sur l'entendement humain.* Les éditeurs les plus récents, H. Dieckmann et J.
Proust,[2] nous révèlent le texte des trois copies manuscrites retrouvées

2 Diderot *Contes,* ed. H. Dieckmann, 141; *Quatre contes,* éd. J. Proust, 95.

jusqu'ici; elles portent, au lieu du titre de l'ouvrage de Hume, la mention très vague: ' (...) sa première tentative littéraire fut la traduction des premiers ouvrages de Hume.' (Hume avait publié jusqu'en 1751, six volumes).

M. Dieckmann n'a pas craint d'ailleurs (p. 121), d'alléguer que Naigeon avait corrigé le texte de Diderot. On n'a retrouvé ni le texte de Diderot ni la copie de Naigeon.

A l'appui de Naigeon, on peut faire remarquer que les *Philosophical essays concerning human understanding* sont de 1748, qu'ils sont de nature plus 'métaphysique' que les *Political discourses*, et que d'après J. Proust (*Revue des sciences humaines*, 1959, 179-80) Diderot possédait le texte anglais dès 1748.

La Lettre sur les sourds et muets parut en 1751, sans lieu de publication.

Les catalogues ne font aucune mention d'un ouvrage quelconque traduit de Hume à la date de 1751. Qu'une édition se perde, voilà pourtant un incident qui n'est pas rare.

L'affaire en resterait là, si les bibliographes ne s'en étaient pas mêlés.

Une «conjecture» tout à fait légitime fut avancée, en 1822, par A.-A. Barbier, auteur du *Dictionnaire des ouvrages anonymes*. D'après lui, Diderot se serait trompé. C'était peut-être un autre ouvrage de Hume, les *Essais sur le commerce, le luxe* . . ., que Mlle de La Chaux aurait publié; non pas en 1751, mais en 1766. Les observations de Barbier qui aboutissent à cette «conjecture» sont instructives; et tout à l'honneur de Barbier:

1°, en 1806, dans la première éd. du *Dictionnaire* (I. 254, no. 2081), Barbier avait attribué à «de Mauvillon» la traduction des *Essais sur le commerce*, . . . *traduction nouvelle*, édition de 1767. Plus loin (I.510) il se reprend: «ce nouveau traducteur est inconnu; au moins, je n'ai pu découvrir son nom; il est vrai que Mauvillon a traduit le même ouvrage de Hume, mais sa traduction a paru sous le titre de *Discours politiques*» (1754). En effet, ces deux traductions sont différentes, et celle de 1754 a toutes les chances d'être effectivement de Mauvillon.

2°, en 1814, Barbier présente des «Remarques» sur la *Correspondance littéraire de MM. Grimm et Diderot*, dans un *Supplément* à cette correspondance (Paris, Potey, Buisson, Delauney, 1814, 374-6). Il y rapporte l'histoire de Mlle de La Chaux, en suivant assez fidèlement le conte de Diderot. Il ajoute:

> Comme Diderot écrivait ces détails en 1773, vingt ans après la mort de mademoiselle de La Chaux, je crains que sa mémoire ne l'ait induit en erreur relativement à la traduction des *Essais sur l'entendement humain*, de Hume; car il est avéré que cette traduction, qui

est de M. Mérian [*sic*], de l'académie de Berlin, et dont Formey fut l'éditeur, ne parut qu'en 1758 à *Amsterdam*, ou à *Berlin*, suivant M. Denina, qui raconte dans la *Prusse littéraire* (Berlin, 1790, trois volumes *in*-8°.), comment M. de Mérian fut engagé par le président de l'académie de Berlin à traduire les *Essais philosophiques* de Hume.

Rien que de juste dans les soupçons de Barbier; toutefois, rien ne prouve, non plus, que Diderot ait écrit son conte en 1773.[3]

M. Dieckmann (*Contes*, 122) propose le mois de Septembre 1772 comme date de la rédaction finale du conte par Diderot.

Quant à l'autorité de C. G. M. Denina (dans *La Prusse littéraire*, Berlin, 1790–91, 3 vol., III. 13–25) cet auteur avait dit, en fait, autre chose:

> M. Merian [*sic*] n'étoit à Berlin que depuis peu lorsque les Essais philosophiques de David Hume parurent. Frappé des singularités et des paradoxes du philosophe écossois, que l'on a vus ressuscités depuis en partie par Kant, il en parla au président de l'académie [Maupertuis]. (...) Cette traduction, faite d'abord pour le président seul [et avant le 28 févr. 1755 — date d'une lettre de Maupertuis à Le Blanc, publiée par A. Monod-Cassidy], fut imprimée dans la suite, avant qu'il en parût aucune autre en Allemagne, soit en allemand, soit en françois. ... Elle a été imprimée à Berlin en deux volumes. ... Tout cela fut ensuite réimprimé plusieurs fois en Hollande.

Les *Essais philosophiques* dont parle Diderot n'ont pas paru avant 1758 «en Allemagne». Ce n'est pas à dire qu'ils n'aient pas paru ailleurs, comme l'avait affirmé Diderot.

A noter (i) que la recherche d'un premier traducteur amène parfois des surprises (l'abbé Blavet a toujours cru, à tort, qu'il était le premier à traduire *The wealth of nations*, de Smith; un exemplaire de la première traduction complète ne s'est retrouvé qu'en 1906; (ii) que l'édition de Berlin, «avérée» par Denina semble être perdue elle aussi; celle de 1758, *Amsterdam, Schneider*, 2 vol., est elle-même assez rare; (iii) qu'à côté des «ghosts» (livres qui n'ont jamais existé) il y a de véritables revenants — et des ressuscités. Pour un revenant parmi les traductions de Hume, voir L. L. Bongie, *French Studies* XII, 238, et 245, n. 24.

3°, en 1820, Barbier est un peu moins catégorique (*Examen critique et complément des dictionnaires historiques les plus répandus*, 1820, 190): il résume la vie de Mlle de La Chaux racontée dans «Ceci n'est pas un conte», et il ajoute: «Diderot attribue à Mademoiselle de la Chaux la traduction des *Essais sur l'entendement humain* de Hume. (...) Elle n'a pas été imprimée

---

[3] L'un des MS se trouve en compagnie d'autres contes dont un de 1747 ou 1749 (Dieckmann, *Inventaire du Fonds Vandeul*, 1951, 97).

[en dépit des mots de Diderot]; car la seule que nous possédions, parut à Amsterdam en 1758. Elle est de M. de Mérian [*sic*]».

4°, en 1822, Barbier avait fait une découverte (*Dictionnaire des ouvrages anonymes*, 1822-27, I (1822), no. 5913; détails reproduits dans l'édition courante, 1872-79, II (1874), 281): c'est un exemplaire des *Essais sur le commerce*, ... *par David Hume, traduction nouvelle*, Amsterdam, 1766, in-12:

> dédiée à madame d'Arconville, par le traducteur, ou plutôt par la traductrice, son amie intime, probablement mademoiselle de La Chaux. (...) Les exemplaires de cette traduction répandus dans le commerce n'ont pas d'épître dédicatoire, et ils contiennent des réflexions du traducteur, avec l'adresse de Paris et Lyon, 1767. Ces «Réflexions» n'étaient pas dans l'exemplaire de Mme d'Arconville.
>
> Ma conjecture sur le nom de l'amie de cette dame explique un passage de Diderot (...) qui attribue à Mlle de La Chaux la traduction des «Essais sur l'entendement humain» de Hume.
>
> Diderot, qui cite ordinairement d'une manière fort inexacte, aura confondu les «Essais sur l'entendement» avec les «Essais sur le commerce».

Il serait difficile de rejeter le témoignage de Barbier: acceptons qu'il avait bel et bien vu un exemplaire de 1766, in-12, dédié par une dame à Mme d'Arconville (traductrice bien connue), et sans «Réflexions». On verra plus loin qu'il existe une édition des *Essais sur le commerce* de 1766, avec les «Réflexions», que Barbier ne connaissait pas. L'exemplaire vu par Barbier serait-il un tirage à part? Ce n'est pas du tout certain: (i) trois sur quatre des «Réflexions» (qui manquent dans l'exemplaire de Barbier) commencent, dans l'édition de 1766, au milieu de la page; (ii) l'édition de 1766 est un in-8°.

Encore une difficulté que Barbier n'a pas relevée: si le «conte» de Diderot avait réellement été écrit en 1773, la mort de Mlle de La Chaux aurait eu lieu, comme on verra plus loin, vers 1753-55 — plus de dix ans avant la date de la dédicace.

L'exemplaire décrit par Barbier n'est pas mentionné par lui dans les autres catalogues qu'il a dressés (*Cat. . . . Boutourlin, et Cat. des livres de la Bibliothèque du Conseil d'État*, 1803, et celui de la vente de sa bibliothèque 1828).

L'attribution à Mlle de La Chaux dans le «conte» de Diderot, serait établie, si les *Souvenirs* de Mme Thiroux d'Arconville en faisaient mention. «Treize volumes manuscrits» de ces «Souvenirs» existaient en 1826, d'après Hippolyte de La Porte, dans la *Biographie universelle* (Michaud), t. 45, 1826.

Il s'agirait de retrouver ce manuscrit. D'autre part, il ne manque pourtant pas de traductrices en France au XVIIIe siècle.[4]

Reste donc au moins la possibilité qu'une certaine Mademoiselle de La Chaux, connue par un conte de Diderot, ait publié une traduction des *Philosophical essays* de Hume — la première — en 1751, maintenant introuvable; quant à l'exemplaire, peut-être unique, des *Essais sur le commerce, le luxe* . . . , traduction décrite par Barbier, faite par une dame, il est perdu, lui aussi.

Quelle foi peut-on ajouter aux paroles de Diderot? Peut-on trouver, dans son conte, le défaut de l'armure?

«Ceci n'est pas un conte»

Dans le conte de Diderot on trouve d'abord une réclamation inattendue, et ensuite un certain nombre de constatations vérifiables.

Diderot déclare, suivant le texte de Naigeon et celui des manuscrits reproduits dans les éditions de 1963 et de 1964:

> (. . .) le récit qu'on va lire, et qui n'est pas un conte, ou qui est un mauvais conte si vous vous en doutez . . . (Naigeon, XII, 377; *Contes*, p.p. H. Dieckmann, 1963, 124; *Quatre contes*, p.p. J. Proust, 1964, 73).

Cette déclaration se rapporte à l'histoire du voyageur Tanié victime de Mme Reymer, personnages qui n'ont pas encore été identifiés. En tête de la deuxième partie du *Conte*, où se trouve l'histoire de Mlle de La Chaux victime de Gardeil, Diderot insiste de nouveau:

> (. . .) ce que je vais ajouter n'est pas plus un conte que ce qui précède. (Naigeon, XII, 385; Dieckmann, 131; Proust, 82).

Personne jusqu'ici n'a voulu inscrire à la Grande Encyclopédie le voyageur Tanié. Mlle de La Chaux serait-elle également imaginaire? Naigeon ajoute ici (XII, 385-7) une longue note pour appuyer, à propos d'elle, la réclamation de Diderot: son récit est «littéralement vrai», dit-il, y compris la conversation même entre Mlle de La Chaux et Gardeil. Il indique en plus un conseil (invérifiable) que cette jeune fille aurait donné à Condorcet après avoir lu son *Essai sur l'origine des connaissances humaines* (1746)! «Ceci n'est pas un conte» est toutefois classé avec l'œuvre romanesque de Diderot — au tome XL des manuscrits, et dans ses œuvres publiées.

---

[4] Quelques-unes des difficultés suscitées par la conjecture de Barbier sont fort bien exprimées dans la thèse de P. H. Meyer (Columbia), *Hume in Eighteenth-century France*, pas encore publiée. Par contre, L. L. Bongie, dans un article récent (*French Studies*, XV, 216n, juillet 1961), en parlant de la publication alléguée par Diderot des *Essais sur l'entendement humain* en Hollande en 1750 ou 1751, ajoute: «I have found no evidence to support this statement and a certain amount of evidence which seems to question its probability. Perhaps the whole story is a *conte* after all!»

Dans ce conte on apprend qu'«il y a des hommes bien bons, et des femmes bien méchantes» et «des femmes très bonnes et des hommes très-méchants». Diderot choisit pour illustrer la méchanceté de ces derniers la noire ingratitude de Gardeil envers sa maîtresse Mlle de La Chaux. Elle l'aide dans son travail de compilateur, mais sa petite fortune à elle une fois dissipée, il l'abandonne. Le médecin Le Camus, et Diderot, l'encouragent à travailler; elle fait une traduction de Hume, publiée, d'après Diderot, vers 1751; elle écrit un conte, *Les trois favorites*, où il était question de Madame de Pompadour, et qui n'a pas été publié. Elle est morte peu de temps après («il y a près de vingt ans», d'après la *Correspondance littéraire*, avril 1773) — mettons en 1753 ou 1754.

Tout de long de ce conte, Diderot sème des repères. On verra s'ils sont consistents, et s'ils sont vérifiables. (Les références se rapportent à l'édition Assézat et Tourneux des *Œuvres* de Diderot).

1°. *Les personnages* (sauf Mlle de La Chaux) sont connus: M. d'Hérouville publia l'ouvrage projeté («une histoire générale de la guerre»: V. 318-9, 321) en 1757; J.-E. Montucla, né en 1725, publia de même l'*Histoire des mathématiques* (V. 319) en 1758; A. Le Camus (V. 321-31), médecin, connu pour ses bienfaisances, est né en 1722; et il y a Gardeil.

Le «héros de l'aventure» (V. 319), Jean-Baptiste Gardeil, est connu des biographes (p.ex., Chameret dans la *Biographie Universelle* Michaud, XVI, 1816) par sa traduction d'Hippocrate (1801) et par le conte de Diderot. Une notice plus détaillée, obligeamment communiquée par le Conservateur des Archives de la Haute-Garonne, cadre assez bien avec le récit de Diderot. Gardeil, 1726-1808, fait de solides études à Toulouse, «va chez les Oratoriens, à Paris, quitte la robe et se lie avec Diderot et d'Alembert. Pour occuper ses loisirs, il apprend plusieurs langues, étudie les mathématiques, la botanique et la médecine. Il s'absente alors, fait un assez long voyage à l'étranger et revient à Paris où, pendant quelque temps, il collabore à la *Gazette de France*. Mais sa fortune n'étant pas considérable, il se décide à prendre une situation: il s'installe à Toulouse comme docteur, après avoir été reçu bachelier le 16 juillet 1755, et docteur le 28 octobre de la même année.» On le voit, après 1764, «vivre à l'aise», à Toulouse. Ces détails sont tirés de Jules Barbot, *Chroniques de la Faculté de Médecine de Toulouse*, 2 vol., 1905.

D'après «Ceci n'est pas un conte», Diderot et Gardeil auraient appris ensemble le grec, vers 1749 ou 1750 (Gardeil serait donc âgé de 23 ans à peu près, Diderot de 36). «Gardeil n'avait rien, Mlle de La Chaux jouissait de quelque bien; et ce bien fut entièrement sacrifié aux besoins et aux fantaisies de Gardeil» (V. 321). La liaison de Gardeil avec Mlle de La Chaux avait duré «plusieurs années»; elle apprend le grec et l'hébreu pour pouvoir copier et traduire des passages qui allaient servir à la confection de l'ouvrage du comte d'Hérouville (qui employait Montucla et Gardeil comme «nègres»). Mais «Gardeil fut ingrat» (V. 322): il ne veut plus la voir. En réponse aux reproches de Diderot, il dit: «Que voulez-vous que je fasse? je suis aussi gueux qu'elle.» Ici Diderot révèle le mot de l'énigme: elle est atteinte d'érysipèle (V. 326). Cette rupture précède la «première tentative littéraire» de Mlle de La Chaux, et la publication de son travail — d'après Diderot, «presqu'en même temps» que la *Lettre sur les sourds et muets* (V. 328), ce qui eut lieu en février 1751.

Quant à Mlle de La Chaux: «je la nomme de son propre nom, parce que la pauvre malheureuse n'est plus» (Naigeon, 1798, XII, 387; Assézat, V. 319; et *Correspondance littéraire*, 2e édition, II (1812), 440, 1er avril 1773).

2°. *L'itinéraire des personnages* du conte est vérifiable. Déjà en 1773, dans la *Correspondance littéraire*, on apprend que «le conte qu'on va lire est de M. Diderot» (2e édition, II. 437), et l'interlocuteur imaginé par Diderot pour égayer son histoire, lui dit: «Vous demeuriez alors à l'Estrapade.» Diderot reprend: «Lui [Gardeil], rue Sainte-Hyacinthe, et son amie, mademoiselle de La Chaux, place Saint-Michel.»

Or, Diderot habitait 3 rue de la Vieille Estrapade entre 1749 ou avant, et jusqu'en 1754:[5] «A la Vieille Estrapade» ou «rue Vieille-Estrapade», si on en croit les dépositions de police de juillet 1749.[6] La Place Saint-Michel était là où de nos jours se trouve la place Edmond Rostand (boulevard Saint-Michel, anciennement à peu près rue de La Harpe); et la rue Sainte-Hyacinthe était approximativement sur l'emplacement de la rue Malebranche.[7] Les amants vivaient donc à deux pas l'un de l'autre. On apprend (V. 324, édition Assézat) que Gardeil habitait «cette grande maison neuve, la seule qu'il y ait à droite dans la rue Hyacinthe, en entrant par la place Saint-Michel», et que son appartement était au fond de la cour.

Le lendemain du jour où Gardeil avait chassé sa maîtresse, elle se rend chez Diderot. «J'envoyai chercher une chaise à porteurs, car elle n'était guère en état de marcher» (V. 324). Prévenance fort vraisemblable: la rue de l'Estrapade est à 300 mètres de chez Gardeil.[8]

---

[5] D'après A. M. Wilson, *Diderot* ..., New York, 1957, 95, 218, 220, etc., ce serait «rue de l'Estrapade»; son installation rue Taranne eut lieu en 1754 ou 1755.

[6] *Revue d'histoire littéraire de la France*, VI (1899), 204, 208.

[7] Ces rues restent inchangées au XIXe siècle — on les retrouve, p. ex., dans le *New Paris Guide*, 1844, de Galignani.

[8] Assézat (*Intermédiaire*, VIII, 474-5, 10 août 1875) croit que Diderot avait quitté «la place de l'Estrapade» et qu'il habitait la rue Taranne «vers 1752 (*sic*), époque à laquelle se passe l'épisode de Gardeil et de Mlle de La Chaux».

3°. *La concordance des dates* fait croire que le conte de Diderot, dans le texte publié par Naigeon, avait été rédigé, ou revu, vers 1773, date où la *Correspondance littéraire* en avait publié un fragment. Nous savons que Gardeil était déjà à Toulouse en 1755, ou avant. D'autre part, si on suit la carrière de Mlle de La Chaux, alléguée par Diderot, on remarque qu'après avoir été chassée par Gardeil, elle aurait traduit et publié les *Essais* (1751); puis elle est malade (l'érysipèle est une maladie qui peut traîner en longueur); elle en guérit; elle passe ensuite 4 à 5 mois à écrire «un petit roman historique», et 2 à 3 mois à attendre une réponse de Madame de Pompadour; ensuite des mois d'hésitations, puis elle déménage:

(...) je la perdis tout à fait de vue. Ce que j'ai su du reste de sa vie, c'est qu'il n'a été qu'un tissu de chagrins, d'infirmités et de misère. (...) Le docteur [Le Camus] ne l'abandonna point. Elle mourut sur la paille, dans un grenier [«le docteur n'était pas riche alors» (V. 330)], tandis que le petit tigre de la rue Hyacinthe, le seul amant qu'elle ait eu, exerçait la médecine à Montpellier ou à Toulouse, et jouissait, dans la plus grande aisance, de la réputation méritée d'habile homme, et de la réputation usurpée d'honnête homme. (V. 331).

La mort de Mlle de La Chaux pourrait se placer, d'après ces détails, entre 1753 et 1755, ou même, si on accepte le mot «tandis que» littéralement, un peu plus tard, car l'aisance pour Gardeil, n'a pas dû être instantanée.

Diderot s'exclame (V. 320): «Il y a près de vingt ans que tu n'es plus»; c'est-à-dire vers le milieu de 1753[9] ou peu après, si on suppose que Diderot avait rédigé le texte peu avant le mois d'avril 1773.

Cette chronologie ne laisse pas supposer que Mlle de La Chaux — ou qui que ce soit — ait traduit en 1751 ou même en 1753 un ouvrage publié en 1752 (*Political discourses*), ni dédicacé une «traduction nouvelle» de cet ouvrage en 1766.

Et Naigeon qui avait connu Diderot depuis 1764, croit fermement à l'existence de Mlle de La Chaux et à la véracité de son histoire.

La «Lettre à mademoiselle ★★★★★»

La Lettre sur les sourds et muets de Diderot, fut publiée chez Bauche en février 1751. D'autres éditions de 1751 comportent des «Additions, pour servir d'éclaircissemens à quelques endroits de la Lettre ...»; parmi les «Additions», une «Lettre à Mademoiselle ★★★★★». D'après A. M. Wilson,

---

[9] Ce serait «vers 1758», d'après Weiss: *Biographie universelle* (Michaud), *Supplément*, t. 60 (1836).

qui cite le journal manuscrit de d'Hémery, les «Additions» ont reçu une permission tacite le 20 mai 1751.[10]

Or le texte du conte publié par Naigeon en 1798 fait allusion à cette «Lettre» de 1751:

> Ma Lettre sur les Sourds et Muets parut presque en même temps [que la traduction de Hume par Mlle de La Chaux]. Quelques objections très-fines qu'elle me proposa donnèrent lieu à une addition qui lui fut dédiée. Cette addition n'est pas ce que j'ai fait de plus mal. (V. 328, édition Assézat).

La Lettre elle-même commence par les mots: «Non, mademoiselle, je ne vous ai point oubliée.» Vers la fin: «J'apprends que vous mettez en notre langue le *Banquet* de Xénophon, et que vous avez dessein de le comparer à celui de Platon. Je vous exhorte à finir cet ouvrage. Ayez, mademoiselle, le courage d'être savante.»

Ces sentiments (de 1751) cadrent bien avec les données que Diderot a consignées dans «Ceci n'est pas un conte». Diderot, en somme, paraît avoir bonne mémoire, et ses références sont passablement exactes.

Il y a donc là une série de «petits faits vrais» qui font croire à l'existence d'une jeune fille instruite, qui aurait publié une traduction non pas des *Political discourses*, mais des *Philosophical essays concerning human understanding*, pas plus tard que 1751. Ce serait là la première traduction de cet ouvrage en français. On n'en a pas retrouvé un seul exemplaire; mais c'est là un incident bien connu.[11]

L'évolution de la conjecture de A.-A. Barbier

On a remarqué que Barbier s'en tient, après tout, à une «conjecture».

[10] La *Correspondance littéraire* («Nouvelles littéraires» par Raynal; édition Tourneux, II, 67) fait mention de ces «Additions», en date du 31 mai. L'édition de la *Lettre sur les sourds et muets* (1751, in-12), qui se trouve au British Museum (1174. 8. 45), serait composée des anciennes feuilles de février 1751 (pp. x, 241), avec un greffage, qui commence au verso de la p. 241: une table (11 pp. non numérotées), le faux-titre pour les Additions, le verso en blanc, ensuite la p. 241 de nouveau, toujours signée X, et le texte des Additions (pp. 242-400). Cet exemplaire est donc de x, 241, [11 + 2], 241-400 pp., au lieu de x, 400 pp., pagination donnée dans le catalogue du B.M. La «Lettre à mademoiselle ****» se trouve aux pp. 249-310 des exemplaires du B.M. et de la B.N. (Rés. X. 1915-16).

[11] On pourrait croire que «de La Chaux» n'est pas, après tout, le vrai nom de la traductrice. Ce nom ne paraît pas, sauf erreur, dans les mémoires du temps ni dans les ouvrages sur les salons. Restent des sources manuscrites inexplorées. Pourtant Diderot, en 1773, n'avait pas craint de faire circuler à Paris des copies de son conte où se trouve en toutes lettres le nom de Gardeil, ami d'autrefois, son adresse à Paris, et son signalement: modèle de «l'ingratitude de l'homme. (. . .) Un petit homme, bourru, taciturne et caustique, le visage sec, le teint basané; en tout une figure mince et chétive; laid, si un homme peut l'être avec la physionomie de l'esprit.» Il est vrai que ce passage ne fut imprimé qu'en 1812 (*Correspondance littéraire . . . par le baron de Grimm et par Diderot*, II, 440-1 de la 2e édition). Gardeil est mort en 1808.

Charles Weiss, en 1836, fait entrer Mlle de La Chaux dans le Panthéon de la *Biographie universelle* (Michaud), au *Supplément*, t.60, et il y reprend fidèlement, sans inventer le moins du monde, les éléments biographiques fournis par Diderot. Pour les *Essais sur l'entendement humain* il remarque simplement qu'«on ne connaît pas d'autre traduction ... que celle de Mérian». C'est l'honnêteté même.

D'autres, pourtant, critiques ou historiens, passent outre. Il y aurait, d'après eux, une édition (même deux) des *Essais sur le commerce*, traduits par Mlle de La Chaux, et publiés en 1752 ou en 1753, ou les deux. A partir de 1830, c'est le chapitre des erreurs (ou pire).

1°. En 1830, J.-M. Quérard avait déjà rendu à la «conjecture» de Barbier la dignité d'un fait.[12]

2°. En 1847 Eugène Daire et G. de Molinari, dans une «notice sur D. Hume» (*Mélanges d'économie politique*, I. 7–8) nous disent catégoriquement que Mlle de La Chaux est l'auteur de la première traduction des *Political discourses*. «Faite, en 1752 ou 1753, cette traduction, dont on ne retrouve plus les exemplaires primitifs, et portant une Dédicace à Mme d'Arconville [à quelle date?] (...) est, selon toute apparence, la même que celle réimprimée avec la date de 1767, Paris et Lyon, in-12.»

Daire et Molinari inventent donc une date de composition, changent la «conjecture» de Barbier en certitude, et nous dotent d'une édition dédicacée que Barbier n'avait pas proposée. Il fallait bien, sans doute, que la traduction ne soit pas publiée en 1751, avant la parution de l'original (1752). L'édition de 1767 est un in-8; c'est Quérard qui l'indique comme un in-12. Le premier ouvrage connu de la main de Mme d'Arconville est de 1757.

3°. En 1852, Charles Coquelin et G.-U. Guillaumin pillent la «notice» de Daire et Molinari, pour l'article «Hume» de leur *Dictionnaire de l'économie politique*, t.1.

4°. En 1875, dans l'édition des *Œuvres complètes* de Diderot, éditée par J. Assézat et M. Tourneux (I. 396) les éditeurs constatent qu'en 1751 Mlle de La Chaux «venait de traduire les *Essais sur l'entendement humain*, de Hume, traduction que Diderot avait revue.» Au t. V, p. 310, les éditeurs ont trouvé la «conjecture» de Barbier. Là-dessus pourtant ils proposent une nouvelle explication de l'aberration de Diderot: il ne s'est pas du tout trompé en parlant des *Essais sur l'entendement humain*; non, il a «seulement, comme toujours, donné à l'ouvrage ... un titre trop général»! Quoi qu'il en soit, les éditeurs sont catégoriques: «Il s'agit ici des *Political discourses*, formant la deuxième partie des *Essays*. La première traduction de cette

---

[12] J. M. Quérard, *La France littéraire*, IV (1830).

partie (*Essais sur le commerce, le luxe, l'argent*, Amsterdam, 1752, 1753, in-12; Paris et Lyon, in-12) est bien de Mlle de La Chaux.»

Inutile de dire que les *Political discourses* ne forment pas la deuxième partie des «Essays» [*on human understanding*].[13] Les *Political discourses* rentrent, en 1753, dans les *Essays and treatises on several subjects* (4t., 1753) au t. IV; le t. II, lui, (1753) contient les *Philosophical essays concerning human understanding*! (Renseignment dû à l'amabilité de M. A. T. W. Liddell, St. Andrews, qui possède une éd. de 1753 en 4 vol. des *Essays*.

Les deux dates de composition, inventées en 1847, deviennent les dates de publication de deux éditions. Assézat avait pu lire dans *La France littéraire* de J.-M. Quérard (1830), les indications suivantes: «*Essais sur le commerce, le luxe* . . . (dédiés à Mme d'Arconville par la traductrice, Mlle de La Chaux). *Amsterdam*, 1766, in-12. — Nouv. édit. (avec des réflexions du traducteur). *Paris et Lyon*, 1767, in-12.» Il n'y avait qu'à changer les dates et le tour est joué.

5°. En 1902, A. Schatz, *L'œuvre économique de David Hume* (P., Rousseau; p. ix) relève pour 1752–53 une traduction des *Essays, moral, political* (1752), par Mlle de La Chaux, «élégante mais parfois insuffisamment exacte», livre «non mis dans le commerce» — choix d'erreurs assez judicieux.

6°. En 1951, H. Bénac, dans son édition des *Œuvres romanesques* de Diderot, (p. 905) nous assure que «l'aventure de Mlle de La Chaux est réelle . . . elle avait traduit en 1752–53 les *Political discourses*.»

7°. En 1955, au t.I de la *Correspondance* de Diderot, éditée par Georges Roth, la lettre «A Mademoiselle ★★★» est tirée de l'édition de la *Lettre sur les sourds et muets*, 1751; destinataire: Mlle de La Chaux. L'éditeur de la *Correspondance* accepte Mlle de La Chaux comme traductrice des *Essais sur le commerce*, sur la foi du catalogue de la B.N., pour l'édition de 1767, mais il ajoute: «La première édition porte l'indication: Amsterdam, 1752.» Où a-t-il vu cette «première édition»?

8°. En 1959, Jacques Proust, dans la *Revue des sciences humaines*, 1959, 179–80, laisse supposer que les *Essais sur le commerce, le luxe, l'argent*, «Amsterdam, 1752 ou 1753», sont tirés des *Philosophical essays concerning human understanding*. Ce serait cette même confusion qui a pu lui faire dire, dans son *Diderot et «L'Encylcopédie»* (Colin, 1962, 465) que Diderot s'est inspiré peut-être de l'essai sur le luxe, l'un des *Political discourses* de Hume publiés en 1752, lorsqu'il écrivait l'article *Art* de l'*Encyclopédie*, publié en 1751.

9°. En 1963, H. Dieckmann dans sa précieuse édition des *Contes* de Diderot, présente (p. 198) le texte de trois manuscrits (par des copistes

---

[13] Cette supposition est tirée, peut-être, d'une lecture hâtive de l'article «Hume» de la *Biographie universelle* (Michaud), XXI (1818), 49–56.

inconnus) qui font dire à Diderot que Mlle de La Chaux avait traduit les "premiers ouvrages de Hume", et il rejette le texte publié par Naigeon, où il est spécifié qu'elle avait traduit les *Essais sur l'entendement humain*.

M. Dieckmann propose carrément que 'Mlle de La Chaux translated Part Two of the first volume of Hume's *Essays, moral, political and literary*.[14] ... The translation appeared in 1952 in Amsterdam.' Il accepte, par là, pour le fond, l'argumentation d'Assézat, sans donner ses raisons, et il reprend la date de 1752 (au lieu de '1752 ou 1753') alléguée par MM. Roth et Bénac.

★   ★   ★

Un fait remarquable: personne n'a cité, jusqu'ici, en toutes lettres, le titre de l'ouvrage de métaphysique revu, vers 1751, par Diderot.

La traduction des *Political discourses*, de 1752, ou de 1753, apparemment mythique, n'a probablement pas fini d'évoluer. A force d'y croire, on ne croira plus à l'édition des *Essais sur l'entendement humain*, de 1751, si un jour elle ressuscite.

Traductions françaises des «Political discourses» (1752)

Abréviations: Ft: faux-titre. T: page de titre. [R]: imprimé en lettres rouges. □: indique que la ligne n'est pas centrée.

+: exemplaire collationné. L'absence de + implique l'existence d'un ex. d'après un catalogue imprimé.

Leeds A–F: collection «anglo-française» de la bibliothèque universitaire («Brotherton Library») de Leeds.

Goldsmiths': Goldsmiths' Library, Senate House, University of London.

BM; BN: British Museum; Bibliothèque nationale, Paris.

Barbier: A.-A. Barbier, *Dictionnaire des ouvrages anonymes* (Paris, Daffis, 1872–79, 4 vol.).

Quérard: J.-M. Quérard, *La France littéraire* (Paris, Didot, 1827–39, 10 vol.).

Higgs '35: H. Higgs, *Bibliography of economics, 1751–1775, prepared for the British Academy* (Cambridge, 1935).

Jessop: T. E. Jessop, *A Bibliography of David Hume* ... (London, Brown, 1938).

Kress: *Harvard Graduate School of Business Administration: the Kress Library covering material published through 1776* (London, Bailey, 1940). ... *1777–1817* (Ibid., 1957). ... *Supplement to 1776* (1956).

Morellet: *Catalogue des livres de la bibliothèque de Feu M. l'abbé Morellet* (Paris, Verdière, 1819).

---

[14] En effet, on trouve deux éditions des *Essays, moral, political and literary* où les *Political discourses* forment la deuxième partie du premier volume. (Ce sont les éditions de 1760 et de 1770 des *Essays and treatises*, en 4 vol. Il existe sept autres editions de cette édition collective). Corriger l'erreur de rédaction d'Assézat ne saurait pourtant revaloriser son argumentation.

1(a) *Discours politiques*, 1754. Traduction de l'abbé Jean-Bernard Le Blanc. DISCOURS / *POLITIQUES* / DE MONSIEUR HUME / TRADUITS DE L'ANGLOIS. / [Filet 6.7] / □ *Magna pars, ſtudiorum amœnitates quœrimus:* / *quœ verò tractata ab aliis dicuntur immenſœ ſubti-* / *litatis, obſcuris rerum tenebris premuntur.* □ / □ Plin. in Præf. ad Veſpaſ. / [Filet 6.7] TOME PREMIER. [SECOND.] / [Ornement, 1·45 × 1·0] / A AM-STERDAM, / *Et ſe vend à Paris,* / Chez MICHEL LAMBERT, Libraire, rue / & à côté de la Comédie Françoiſe / au Parnaſſe. / [Filet gras et maigre 6.0] / M.DCC.LIV //

I. lviij, 431. a⁸ b⁴–e⁴ f¹ A⁸ B⁴–Mm⁸ Nn⁴.

Ft; T; Préface du traducteur, à Monsieur le docteur Lami, professeur à Florence ... 30 Juillet 1754. [v]–lviij; Discours politiques [1]–330; Réflexions politiques sur l'Etat présent de l'Angleterre principalement à l'égard de ses taxes et de ses dettes, & sur leurs causes & leurs conséquences, traduites de l'anglois de Mylord Bolingbroke. [331]–429; Table [431].

II. [4], 418. [ ]² A⁸ B⁴–Kk⁸ Ll⁴ Mm⁴ Nn¹. La page 84 est numérotée 44.

Ft; T; Texte [1]–382; Notice de quelques-uns des Principaux Ouvrages Anglois sur le Commerce. 383–396; Ouvrages sur le commerce, les finances, &c. cités dans les Notes sur les Discours de M. Hume, & qui ont paru en France depuis deux ans. 397–417; Table [418].

+Leeds A–F 3; +Goldsmiths' 1754; BN. *E. 2976–7; Paris, Fac. de Droit, E 11.5086; +Arsenal 8°S.6206, et 3 autres ex.; École polytechnique; Bordeaux (1830) 19490; Grenoble 11213; Rennes 2189; Barbier (attribué par erreur[15] à Mauvillon); Higgs '35, no. 692; Jessop, p. 24–5.

Le «docteur Lami» à qui l'ouvrage est dédié, est Giovanni Lami, savant de Florence (1697–1770), rédacteur des *Novelle litterarie, pubblicate in Firenze*, 1740–69, 30t. (BM. P.P. 4162).

Les *Discours politiques* ont reçu une «permission tacite» (L. L. Bongie, in: *French Studies*, XII. 234–5).

L'abbé Le Blanc a contribué: (1) une longue dédicace; (2) de nombreuses notes sur le texte; ces notes de Le Blanc reparaissent en 1755 (éd. de Dresde), et un petit nombre en ont été reprises par Daire et Molinari (*Mélanges d'économie politique*, I, 1847), qui laissent supposer qu'elles sont de Hume lui-même; et (3) bibliographie commentée, qui a dû constituer une révélation pour les lecteurs de 1754: dix-huit ouvrages anglais sur le commerce, sans compter plusieurs ouvrages récents publiés en France, traductions ou autres.

Cet excellent ouvrage reçut son baptême de feu le 15 août 1754, dans la *Correspondance littéraire* (éd. Tourneux, II. 393): note acerbe et injuste de Melchior

---

[15] L'erreur d'attribution dans cette 3ᵉ éd. de Barbier (I, p. 1024) est due aux éditeurs Olivier Barbier, et R. et P. Billard. L'erreur ne se trouve pas dans les éd. de 1806 et de 1822.

Grimm; le traducteur anonyme y est nommé en toutes lettres. Vient ensuite un compte rendu en règle dans l'*Année littéraire* de septembre (V. 73–97). Nulle mention de la traduction de M[auvillon], publiée à Amsterdam — la note par Raynal (*Corr.*, II. 178) pourrait se rapporter à l'une ou à l'autre des deux traductions. Le Blanc lui-même ignore l'existence de la traduction de Mauvillon jusqu'en décembre 1754 (Monod-Cassidy, p. 408–411).

P. H. Meyer (p. 182–7) signale cinq comptes rendus de l'original anglais dès 1752–54: les questions commerciales sont à la mode.

1(b) *Discours politiques*, 1755. Traduction de l'abbé Le Blanc.

DISCOURS / POLITIQUES / DE MONSIEUR HUME / TRADUITS DE L'ANGLOIS / *Nouvelle Edition.* / Par MONSIEUR L'ABBÉ LE BLANC / Hiſtoriographe des Bâtimens du Roi de France. / [Filet 7.5] / *Magna pars, ſtudiorum amœnitates quærimus: quæ* / *vero tractata ab aliis dicuntur immenſæ ſubtilitates, ob-* / *ſcuris rerum tenebris premuntur.* □ / □ Plin. in Præf. ad Veſpaſ. / [Filet 7.6] / *TOME PREMIER.* [*SECOND.*] / [Fleuron] / *avec Privilège du Roi.* / A DRESDE, Chez Michel Groell, / Libraire & Marchand d'Estampes. / [Filet orné 5.7] / M.DCC.LV. //

I. [4], [8]; [5]–48; [1]–287. [a]^2 $_{*}^4$ a$^{3-8}$–c^8 A^8–S^8.

(A^2 signée Aji; L^4 sans sign.) Les 8 pages ($_{*}^4$) pour la dédicace auraient été ajoutées après.

Ft; T; Dedication (*sic*; titre courant), 8p. non-chiffrées; Préface [5]–48; Texte [1]–220; Réflexions politiques . . . [221]–286; Table 287.

Dédié «à Monsieur le marquis de Marigny, conseiller du Roy en ses Conseils, Directeur & Ordonnateur Général de ses Bâtimens, Jardins, Arts, Académies & Manufactures Royales», et daté «De Dresde le 1. Avril 1755»; signé «L'Abbé Le Blanc.»
La Préface est datée «De Dresde le 1. Mars 1755». A la p. 286: «Imprimé à Pfœrten, chez Jean Tobie Siefard».

II. [4], 276. [ ]^2 A^8–R^4 S^6. (R^4 est sans sign.).

Ft; T; Texte [1]–249; Notice de quelques-uns des Principaux Ouvrages Anglois . . . 250–259; Ouvrages sur le Commerce . . . 260–275; Table 276.

+BM. 8006. c. 23; +Goldsmiths' 1754 (les Ft manquent); BN. *E. 2978–9 et 8° Nc. 2054; Barbier, I. 1024–5, à corriger; Higgs '35, no. 941 (également sans Ft); Jessop, p. 24–5. Un ex. vendu par Magis (Cat. 35, 1957) porte l'ex-libris de Calonne.

Cette éd. montre, en conformité avec la nouvelle dédicace, quelques changements à la Préface; en plus, de nouvelles remarques sur [Plumart] «de Dangeul» et sur «Fort-Bonnais»: ces deux auteurs, nés au Mans en 1722 «et que l'amitié n'unit pas moins que la parenté» (I.22), «ont le mieux appris des Anglois à traiter des matières du Commerce» (I.35). Le Blanc nomme en toutes lettres Véron de Forbonnais, qui était resté jusque-là dans l'anonymat (I.35; II.262, 263, 272): «il ne doit pas trouver mauvais que je cherche à satisfaire la curiosité du Public» (II.263). Le Blanc signale que la seconde éd. des *Elémens du commerce*, de Véron, qui comporte quelques additions, «s'est débitée avec le même succès que la première» (II.272) — toutes les deux de 1754; et Le Blanc se réjouit particulièrement de ce que Véron avait atténué, dans sa 2ᵉ éd., quelques critiques d'ouvrages anglais.

Le Blanc projetait de faire paraître une troisième édition des *Discours* (lettre adressée à Hume, in: J. H. Burton, *Life and correspondence*, I. 460-1; texte complet, in: H. Monod-Cassidy, 417: lettre de Paris [été 1757]). «L'Edition ne paroîtra pas que je n'aye reçu de vos nouvelles». En effet, cette 3ᵉ éd. est inconnue des bibliographes.

Le Blanc parle (I.10n.) d'une lettre «que Mr. Hume m'a fait l'honneur de m'écrire au sujet de son Discours sur la Population»; il avait communiqué la lettre à Montesquieu, dont il vient d'apprendre la mort (le 10 février 1755). La lettre pourrait se trouver parmi les papiers de Montesquieu; elle n'est pas mentionnée par Greig.

2(a) *Discours politiques*, 1754. Traduction d'Eléazar Mauvillon.

DISCOURS / [R] POLITIQUES / DE / [R] *Mᴿ. DAVID HUME,* / TRA-DUITS DE L'ANGLOIS / *PAR Mᴿ. DE M*****. / [Gravure: Neptune et symboles appropriés: *LFDB. del. F.M. la Cave Sculp.*] / [R] *A AMSTER-DAM,* / [filet 5.5] / Chez J. SCHREUDER, / & PIERRE MORTIER le Jeune. / [R] MDCCLIV. //

[4], 355. [ ]² A⁸–X⁸ Y⁶ Z⁴.

T; Avis du traducteur [ ]²ᵃ; Table [ ]²ᵇ; Discours politiques [1]–355.

+Leeds A–F 3; +BM. 8005.b.15; +Goldsmiths' 1754; +Dijon 16705; Lausanne S71; +Troyes Et. B. 1835; Higgs '35, no. 694; Jessop, p. 24. (Grimm-Diderot, *Corr. litt.*, II. 178, 19 août 1754: cette notice, par Raynal, peut se rapporter également à la traduction de l'abbé Le Blanc).

A première vue, on pourrait croire que les impressions datées de 1761

L'éditeur hollandais Schreuder publia entre 1756 et 1758 une série de cinq volumes sous le titre de *Discours politiques*, tomes II à VI, par différents auteurs. Le «Tome second» (1756, réimprimé en 1769) recèle trois sections tirées du fonds Le Blanc:

(i) II. 251–4: «Avis du traducteur» [des *Réflexions politiques* de Bolingbroke]; ces pages sont tirées du commentaire de Le Blanc sur le *Testament politique de Mylord Bolingbroke*, au tome II des *Discours politiques* (1754 et 1755).

(ii) II. 255–314: la traduction de ces *Réflexions*, faite par Le Blanc (*Discours politiques*, 1754, I. 331–429; 1755, I. 221–286). Cette traduction est dûment attribuée à Mauvillon par Quérard, I (1827), s.n. Bolingbroke, et V (1833), s.n. Mauvillon, avec la date de 1753!

(iii) II. 315–324: la bibliographie commentée, par Le Blanc (*Discours politiques*, 1754, II. 397–417; 1755, II. 260–275), avec quelques changements: omission des notes sur Boling-broke, utilisées ailleurs; l'indication «Amsterdam, Changuion», qui remplace, pour deux ouvrages (King et Plumart), le nom de l'éditeur de Paris donné par Le Blanc; un ouvrage de Coyer (1756) est ajouté pour la vraisemblance. Le Blanc avait indiqué que les ouvrages en question avaient «paru en France depuis deux ans». Schreuder, lui, ajoute «depuis deux à trois ans» — et ce texte reste inchangé jusqu'en 1769.

Nulle mention de l'abbé Le Blanc; il est pourtant connu comme traducteur des *Discours* dès 1755, même avant.

On recontre souvent dans les catalogues l'indication d'une édition des *Discours politiques de Mr. D. Hume* en 5 volumes, 1754–57. En fait, le nom de Hume, comme de raison, ne paraît que sur le titre du premier volume de la série: ce titre, d'ailleurs, ne porte pas de tomaison.

et de 1767 reprennent les feuilles de 1754, en ajoutant tout simplement une nouvelle page de titre: procédé classique. En effet, on signale: 2(b), 2(c) *Discours politiques*, 1761, 1767. Traduction d'Eléazar Mauvillon.

1761: +Arsenal 8° S.6210[1].

1767: +Leeds A–F 3.

1761: Page de titre: la disposition typographique est la même; mais la gravure, une imitation de celle de 1754, est signée: «G. Sibelius fecit». La date: MDCCLXI.

1767: (1) Page de titre:
DISCOURS/[R] POLITIQUES/DE/[R] M^R. *DAVID HUME*, / TRADUITS DE L'ANGLOIS / *PAR* M^R. *DE M***** / [Gravure, sans signature, présentant les symboles de l'invention, surmontés de l'inscription «Invenit et perfecit»] / [R] *A AMSTERDAM* / Chez JEAN SCHREUDER, / [R] MDCCLXVII. //

(2) La signature de la 2e f., non-chiffrée: *2; la page 144 est numérotée 44.

Ces deux volumes, sortis des mêmes presses, ont été pourtant recomposés, ligne par ligne (sauf exception) et page par page. En plus les ornements ont été remplacés ou intervertis; les signatures ne sont plus au même endroit; d'autres changements, p. ex., en 1761, p. 112, correction à la note: le renvoi (* *) est restitué pour la référence à Pline; et en 1767, p. 327, les lignes 4–7 du «Discours XII» ne suivent plus l'arrangement de 1754.

Barbier, I. 1024, et Quérard, *Supercheries*, II (1870), 1018, proposent une éd. intitulée: «Discours politiques de M. D. Hume, traduits de l'anglois de M. de M ... (de Mauvillon). Amsterdam, Schreuder, 1761, 5 vol. in-8.»[16] La bibliothèque de l'Arsenal, d'autre part, possède, comme on a vu, le volume de Hume, daté de 1761, mais d'après le «registre» de l'Arsenal il y aurait eu erreur typographique, MDCCLXI pour MDCCLVI! Ces indications sont à corriger. Il y a une éd. de 1761, mais seulement des *Discours* de Hume. Les autre vol. de la série (II à VI) retrouvés jusqu'ici, portent d'autres dates, et ne font aucune mention de Hume. Le vol. qui comporte les *Discours* de Hume est devenu, après coup, une tête de collection, mais il n'y a pas de «tome I» désigné comme tel.

Le catalogue Kress (no. 6627) fait croire à une édition en 6 vol. de 1769; Harvard ne possède pourtant qu'un tome II isolé. Ce tome II est le seul des 6 volumes retrouvés jusqu'ici qui porte la date de 1769.

3(a) *Essais sur le commerce*, 1766. Hors-commerce. Traducteur inconnu. Edition (ou seulement tirage à part?) vue par A.-A. Barbier, *Dict. des ouvrages anonymes*, II (1874), 281:

Essais sur le commerce, le luxe, l'argent, etc., par David Hume, traduction nouvelle (dédiée à madame d'Arconville par le traducteur, ou plutôt par la traductrice, son amie intime, probablement mademoiselle de La Chaux). Amsterdam, 1766, in-12. Les exemplaires de cette

[16] Cette note erronée de Barbier, alléguant une éd. de Hume en 5 vol., de 1761, provient d'un catalogue de l'An XIII: *Catalogue des livres de la bibliothèque de S.E.M. le comte de Boutourlin* (Paris, An XIII, no. 631). Ce catalogue est de A.-A. Barbier et Ch. Pougens. Il arrive à J.-M. Quérard d'y ajouter du sien (*France littéraire*, t. IV et V, 1830, 1833): on y compte jusqu'à cinq erreurs pour la traduction Mauvillon.

traduction répandus dans le commerce n'ont pas d'épître dédicatoire, et ils contiennent des réflexions du traducteur, avec l'adresse de *Paris et Lyon*, 1767. Ces «Réflexions» n'étaient pas dans l'exemplaire de Mme d'Arconville.

L'ex. décrit par Barbier n'a pas été retrouvé.

Sur l'attribution à Mlle de La Chaux, voir ci-dessus.

3(b) *Essais sur le commerce*. Amsterdam, 1766. Traducteur inconnu.

ESSAIS / SUR / LE COMMERCE, LE LUXE, L'ARGENT, / □ L'INTÉRÊT DE L'ARGENT, LES IMPOTS, / □ LE CRÉDIT PUBLIC, ET LA BALANCE / □ DU COMMERCE; □ / *Par M. DAVID HUME*. / Traduction nouvelle, avec des Réflexions du / Traducteur; / *ET* / *LETTRE D'UN NEGOCIANT* / *DE LONDRES*, / A UN DE SES AMIS; / *CONTENANT des Réflexions ſur les Impôts auxquels* / □ *ſont aſſujetties les denrées de premiere néceſſité, &* / □ *ſur la conſéquence dont ils peuvent être relativement* / □ *à la main-d'œuvre dans les Manufactures d'Angleterre*; / Traduite ſur la ſeconde édition imprimée / à Londres en 1765. / [Ornement, 0·85 × 0·85] / *A AMSTERDAM*. / [Filet triple, maigre-gras-maigre 6.9] / M.DCC.LXVI. //

288. A⁸–S⁸. Niv signée Niij.

T; Essai sur le commerce [3]–29; Essai sur le luxe 30–53; Essai sur l'argent 54–78; Réflexions du traducteur 78–89; Extrait de l'Histoire de la Maison de Stuart, par M. Hume, tome I, page 117, 89–91; Essai sur l'intérêt de l'argent 92–115; Réflexions du traducteur 115–123; Essai sur les impôts 124–134; Réflexions du traducteur 135–148; Essai sur le crédit public 149–173; Réflexions du traducteur 173–187; Essai sur la balance du commerce 188–216; Lettre d'un négociant de Londres, à un de ses amis 217–288.

+Leeds A–F 3; Higgs '35, no. 3627.

La «Lettre . . .» est traduite d'une brochure anonyme: *Considerations on taxes, as they are supposed to affect the price of labour in our manufacturies . . . In a letter to a friend* (London, Johnson, 1765). On y commente un ouvrage anglais («*Apologie du commerce et des arts*») en faveur de l'exportation des grains, et l'article «Grains» du dictionnaire de Postlethwayt; il y a aussi des remarques sur la «jalousie du commerce».

Un compte rendu des *Essais sur le commerce* se trouve dans le *Journal de l'agriculture*, 1767.[17] Le *journaliste* résume, avec des extraits, les *Essais sur le commerce* et même la «Lettre d'un négociant». Il décrit à deux reprises l'ex. qu'il avait sous les yeux: (1) un «vol. in-8°, 1766» (*Journal* de février, 1767, p. 150), et (2) un «volume in-12, à Amsterdam. Il se trouve à Paris, chez Saillant,

[17] *Journal de l'agriculture, du commerce, et des finances*, 1767, févr. pp. 150–180; mars, pp. 136–157; avr., pp. 160–173; mai, pp. 148–171; juil., pp. 165–185.

Libraire; & à Lyon, chez Aimé de la Roche»(*Journal* de mars, 1767, p. 136). Les deux éditions retrouvées sont des in-8, identiques sauf pour les pages liminaires et le privilège; celle de 1767 n'est pas d'Amsterdam (voir 3(d), ci-dessous). Il est donc probable que le *journaliste* avait sous les yeux un ex. de 1766, mais qu'il attendait l'enregistrement de l'approbation (12 mars 1767) pour révéler aux lecteurs le nom du libraire de Paris.

3(c) *Essais sur le commerce.* Avignon, 1766.

Cette édition est citée sur la foi du *Catalogue des livres de la bibliothèque de feu M. l'abbé Morellet* (Paris, Verdière, 1819), no. 1528:
Essai sur le commerce, le luxe, l'argent, etc., par David Hume. *Avignon*, 1700 [*sic*]; in-12.
Elle n'a pas été retrouvée dans les catalogues compulsés, ni au Museum Calvet à Avignon (communication du Conservateur du Museum).

3(d) *Essais sur le commerce.* Paris, Lyon; 1767.

ESSAIS / SUR / LE COMMERCE; LE LUXE; / L'ARGENT; L'INTÉRÊT DE L'ARGENT; / LES IMPOTS; LE CRÉDIT PUBLIC, / ET LA BALANCE DU COMMERCE; / *Par M. DAVID HUME.* / TRADUCTION NOUVELLE, / avec des Réflexions du Traducteur. / *ET* / LETTRE / *D'UN NÉGOCIANT DE LONDRES,* / A UN DE SES AMIS; / *CONTENANT des Réflexions ʃur les Impôts* / *auxquels ʃont aʃʃuetties les denrées de premiere* / *néceʃʃité,* & *ʃur la conʃéquence dont ils peuvent* / *être relativement à la main-d'œuvre dans les* / *Manufactures d'Angleterre.* ☐ / TRADUITE SUR LA SECONDE ÉDITION, / imprimée à Londres en 1765. / [Ornement] / *A PARIS,* / Chez SAILLANT, Libraire, rue S. Jean-de-Beauvais. / *A LYON,* / Chez AIMÉ DELAROCHE, aux Halles de la Grenette. / [Filet orné 6.3] / M.DCC.LXVII. / *Avec Approbation,* & *Privilége du Roi.* //
[Au titre: les mots ESSAIS et LETTRE sont en caractères «historiés».]

[2], [292]. [ ]¹ A⁸–S⁸ [ ]². Niv signée Niij.

+BM 8205. aa. 14; +Goldsmiths' 1767 (imparfait: les pp. [289–292] manquent); +Arsenal 8° S.5560 et 8° S.5561; +Dijon 16706; Barbier; Quérard.

Probablement aussi: BN. F. 24973; Bordeaux 19887; Grenoble 11544; Nîmes 2112; Higgs '35, no. 3971 — bien qu'ils n'indiquent que «Paris, Saillant» ou seulement «Paris».

Ft; T; Texte (identique en tous points à celui de 1766), [3]–288; Approbation; Privilége du Roi, 3 p. non-chiffrées; Errata 4ᵉ page non-chiffrée.

L'approbation est du 31 oct. 1766; le privilège est du 31 déc. 1766, «registré 12 mars 1767». L. L. Bongie (*French Studies*, XII, p. 244, n. 3) rapporte qu'une permission tacite avait été donnée pour trois ans à partir du 4 déc. 1766, et que le censeur s'appelait Pulignieu.

3(e) *Essais sur le commerce*. Tome VII des *Œuvres philosophiques de M. D. Hume*, 1788.

[R] ŒUVRES / PHILOSOPHIQUES / [R] DE M. D. HUME, / TRADUITES DE L'*ANGLOIS*. / TOME SEPTIEME, / [R] CON- TENANT / Lɪs Essais sur le Commerce, &c. / [R] NOUVELLE ÉDITION. / [Fleuron: Bâtiment, une porte, deux arbres. 4.0 de large × 1.65] / A LONDRES, / [Filet double, 5.4] / 1788.

[4], [269]. [ ]² A⁸ B⁸–Q⁸ R⁷.

Ft; T; Essai sur le commerce [1]–34; Essai sur le luxe [35]–64; Essai sur l'argent [65]–95; Réflexions du traducteur 95–109; Extrait de l'His- toire de la Maison de Stuart, par M. Hume, t.1, p. 117, 109–112; Essai sur l'intérêt de l'argent [113]–141; Réflexions du traducteur 142–152; Essai sur les impôts [153]–166; Réflexions du traducteur 167–184; Essai sur le crédit public [185]–215; Réflexions du traducteur 215–233; Essai sur la balance du commerce [234]–268; Table [269]. (La «Lettre d'un négociant», et le «Privilège du Roi» disparaissent).

+BM 528. c. 29 (la table du t. VII est reliée avec le t. VI, 528. c. 28); BN Z. 34124; Grenoble 10464; Lyon, catalogue sur fiches 308996; Cat. de la bibl. de . . . Morellet, 1819, no. 708; Quérard; Jessop, p. 11.

Les *Œuvres philosophiques de M. D. Hume*, Londres, 1788, édition bien imprimée, paraissent provenir de Londres (en dépit de l'indication «Londres (Paris)» donnée par Quérard, et par divers catalogues: BM, Lyon, Nîmes). Pour les six premiers vol., c'est une reproduction, recomposée, plus aérée, et ornée de fleurons, bandeaux, fleurettes, de l'éd. de 1764: «. . . / A LONDRES, / [R] Chez *DAVID WILSON*, / M.D.CC.LXIV.» D. Wilson est mort en 1777 (H. R. Plomer, etc., *A Dictionary of the printers and booksellers . . . 1726 to 1775*, Oxford, 1932, p. 267).
    Dans l'édition de 1764 la pagination des t. III et IV est continue: VIII, 134 pp.; [4], [135]–226 pp.). Les ex. à +Besançon, 228.344-6, et à la BN, Z.34109–14, possèdent une page de titre pour chaque vol., celui de l'+Arsenal, 8° S.888 n'en a pas pour le T. IV.
    La pagination des six volumes permettra de distinguer ces deux éditions d'un certain nombre d'éditions hollandaises:
    1764: [4], XL, [152]; [4], [159]; VIII, 134; [4], [135]–226; [6], 222; [2], ii, 288.
    1788: [4], [263]; [4], [230]; [4], [200]; [4], [136]; [4], 319; [4], [416].
    Le tome VII, de 1788, conforme par la typographie et les ornements aux t. I–VI, reproduit le texte de l'édition de 1766, avec de légers changements. Les typographes de 1788 ne tiennent pas compte des *errata* de l'édition Paris-Lyon (1767); d'autre part ils sont avares de majuscules et prodigues de virgules.

4(a) *Le génie de M. Hume*. 1770. Composé par Auguste-Pierre Damiens de Gomicourt.

LE GÉNIE / DE M. HUME, / OU / ANALYSE / DE SES OUVRAGES, / *Dans laquelle on pourra prendre une idée* / □ *exacte des Mœurs, des U∫ages, des Cou-* / □ *tumes, des Loix, & du Gouvernement du* / □ *Peuple Anglois.*

☐ / [Fleuron, 3·6 × 2·4] / A LONDRES; / & *fe trouve* / A PARIS, / Chez VINCENT, Imprimeur-Libraire, / rue S. Severin. / [Filet gras-maigre 5.2] / M DCC LXX. //

viij, 472. a⁴ A¹²–T¹² V⁸. Liv et Qvj signées Liij et Qv; p. 89, l. 16, «à» pour «a»; p. 90, l.16 «avantages» pour «désavantages»; p. 444, dern. l., «oi» pour «roi».

T; Avertissement [iii]–viij; Le génie de M. Hume [1]–465; Table [466]–468; Catalogue des livres qui se trouvent chez Vincent 469–472.

+Leeds A–F 3; +BM 716. a. 25 (incomplet des pp. 469–72); +Besançon 246.704; Bordeaux 78; Dole 4268; Higgs '35, no. 5361.

Sur 56 chapitres non-numérotés, 8 se rapportent au commerce. C'est un précis, semé de morceaux tirés de la traduction Le Blanc. Les discours utilisés sont indiqués ci-dessous dans la Concordance.

C'est encore à L. L. Bongie que nous devons la découverte, dans les *Registres des permissions tacites* (BN, fonds fr. 21981, 21993) que Damiens de Gomicourt était responsable de ce travail, et que c'est Crébillon qui a accordé la permission tacite.

4(b) *Le génie de M. Hume.* 1771.

Il y aurait, d'après H. Higgs, *Bibliog. of economics*, 1935, no. 5361, une édition ou réimpression de 1771:

Le génie de M. Hume, ou analyse de ses ouvrages. Londres. 1771, 12°.

5. *Traductions partielles*

Certains des *Political discourses* ont été publiés en traduction française: 1°. *Journal œconomique*, 1754: «Of the balance of trade», sept., 176–184; nov. 167–176. (P. H. Meyer, *Hume in eighteenth century France*, 186).

2°. *Journal étranger*, 1760: «Of the jealousy of trade»: août, 85–97. Traduction attribuée à Turgot. (Meyer, 200–1).

Dugald Stewart, *Biographical memoirs of Adam Smith* ..., Edinburgh, Ramsay, 1811, 98, assure que Turgot avait entrepris la traduction de cet essai «with some other of his Political discourses».

3°. *Journal de l'agriculture* ..., 1767: fév. 150–180; mars 136–157; avr. 160–173; mai 148–171; juil. 165–185. (BN. S.19440; +New College, Edinburgh, ex. ayant appartenu à Adam Smith).

Ce compte rendu contient un certain nombre de citations des *Essais sur le commerce*, 1766 ou 1767.

4°. [W. Knox et] G. Grenville, *Tableau de l'Angleterre* (Londres; Paris, Desaint, 1769): extrait de l'essai «Of public credit», pp. 16–18. Voir aussi pp. 139–40.

Le traducteur, selon Barbier, serait Guyard, de Troyes. La traduction est fautive.

5°. R. Wallace, *Dissertation historique et politique sur la population* (Amsterdam; Paris, Rozet, 1769): les pp. [189]–380, «Examen critique du discours de M. Hume», portent sur l'essai «Of the populousness of ancient nations».

6°. I. Pinto, *Traité de la circulation* … (Amsterdam, 1771): extraits pp. 18–20 et 121–124, des essais «Of money» et «Of public credit».

Pinto raconte ses discussions avec Hume. Comme le traducteur de Grenville et le compilateur du *Génie de M. Hume*, Pinto ne peut pas s'empêcher de citer le dicton de Hume: «ou la Nation détruira son crédit public, ou le crédit public détruira la Nation».

7°. (a) *Journal de l'agriculture*, …, 1778. Traduction de l'essai «Of the populousness of ancient nations», dans les nos. d'avr., 107–135; mai, 99–130; juin, 77–107; juil., 102–131; août, 96–116; et sept., 101–119. (P. H. Meyer, 148–9).

(b) P. H. Meyer signale aussi que cette traduction fut publiée séparément avec une épître dédicatoire à sa fille, Madame de Crosne:

Essai sur la population des nations de l'antiquité, traduit de l'anglois de M. David Hume par M. de la Michodière, intendant de Rouen, 1778.

Les catalogues ne font aucune mention de cette traduction. On aimerait savoir, d'ailleurs, où se trouve l'ex. signalé par M. Meyer.

Un ouvrage qui peut avoir son intérêt par rapport à cette traduction par «M. de La Michodière», parut en 1766:

Recherches sur la population des généralités d'Auvergne, de Lyon, de Rouen et de quelques provinces et villes du royaume, avec des réflexions sur la valeur du bled tant en France qu'en Angleterre, depuis 1674 jusqu'en 1764, par M. Messance (Paris, Durand, 1766, in-4°).

Cet ouvrage est attribué à «M. de La Michaudière» par Grimm (*Correspondance littéraire*, VIII, 130, 1 oct. 1766) — et aussi à l'abbé Joseph Audra, par F.-J. Noel, dans la *Biographie universelle* (Michaud), iii (1811), 27–8. La page de titre ne signifie pas, comme on a cru, que «M. Messance» réclame autre chose que les «réflexions». Quérard, s.n. Messance, verse dans le débat, pour sa part, une référence de 1775 ou 1780, qui fait intervenir «un magistrat» comme auteur des *Recherches*. L'affaire en reste là.

8°. [N. Baudeau, éd.]. *Encyclopédie méthodique: commerce* (Paris, Panckoucke; Liége, Plomteux, 3 vol., 1783 '83 '84). I. 170–175, traduction Le Blanc du discours «Of the balance of trade».

9°. Un ouvrage de 1769, maintenant perdu (encore un!), et dont la trace a été relevée par L. L. Bongie (*French Studies*, XII, 1958, 238, et 245, n. 24) contenait peut-être des textes d'interêt économique. «Par jugement du 5 juillet 1770» — d'après les *Resgistres des syndics* (BN. fonds fr., 21932), deux exemplaires des *Œuvres posthumes de M. Hume*, 1769, saisis le 24 avril 1770 furent envoyés au pilon, à la Bastille. Même si les syndics s'étaient trompés de titre — «posthumes» pour «philosophiques» — la date de 1769 ne correspond à aucune autre édition connue.

Concordance

Les essais des *Political discourses* se trouvent répartis dans les différentes traductions comme suit:

Titre	Le Blanc 1754 I	Le Blanc 1755 I	Mauvillon 1754	Essais 1766,67	Génie 1770 (extraits)	Œ. phil. VII 1788
Of commerce	1–47	1–32	1–25	3–29	71–81	1–34
Of luxury	48–93	33–64	26–46	30–53	83–89	35–64
Of money	94–136	65–92	46–69	54–78	89–96	65–95
Of interest	137–176	93–119	70–91	92–115	97–100	113–141
Of the balance of trade	177–234	120–158	91–117	188–216	—	234–268
Of the balance of power	235–262	159–176	117–132	—	—	—
Of taxes	263–282	177–189	133–142	124–134	105–7	153–166
Of public credit	283–330	190–220	142–165	148–173	101–4	185–215
	II	II				
Of some remarkable customs	1–31	1–21	165–179	—	—	—
Of the populousness of ancient nations	32–279	22–181	180–307	—	9–14	—
Of the Protestant succession	280–325	182–212	308–327	—	—	—
Idea of a perfect commonwealth	326–382	213–249	327–355	—	—	—

Sources principales

J. H. Burton, *Life and correspondence of David Hume* (Edinburgh, 1846, 2 vol.)

R. Mertz, «Les amitiés françaises de Hume et le mouvement des idées», in: *Revue de littérature comparée*, IX, 1929, no. 4, 644–713.

D. Hume, *Letters*, ed. J. Y. T. Greig (Oxford, 1932, 2 vol.).

T. E. Jessop, *A bibliography of David Hume* ... (Brown, 1938).

Hélène Monod-Cassidy, *Un voyageur-philosophe au XVIIIe siècle, l'abbé Jean-Bernard Le Blanc* (Harvard, 1941).

L. L. Bongie, *Hume en France au 18e siècle* (Thèse, Université de Paris, 1952). Typescript.

— «David Hume and the official censorship of the *ancien régime*» in: *French Studies*, XII, 234–45, avr. 1958.

— «Hume, *philosophe* and philosopher in 18th century France», in: *French Studies*, XV, 213–227, juil. 1961.

P. H. Meyer, *Hume in eighteenth century France* (Thèse, Columbia, 1954) Typescript; microfilm 8734; voir *Dissertation abstracts*, XIV, p. 1414.

Diderot, *Contes*, edited with an introduction by H. Dieckmann (University of London Press, 1963).

Diderot, *Quatre contes, édition critique* (Droz, 1964).

En plus des bibliographies générales, plus de 30 catalogues imprimés de bibliothèques ont été compulsés, y compris le catalogue Kress. Parmi les bibliographies spécialisées il faut signaler celles de Mirabeau, 1791; Musset-Pathay, 1810; Morellet, 1819; Blanqui, 1842; Higgs, 1935; Hollander, 1937; et *Economie et population*, 1956, publié par l'Institut national d'études démographiques.

15

E. G. TAYLOR

Rousseau's Debt to Hobbes

I.

IN his article *Hobbisme* in the *Encyclopédie* Diderot sums up the relationship between Rousseau and Hobbes in the following manner:

La philosophie de M. Rousseau, de Genève, est presque l'inverse de celle de Hobbes. L'un croit l'homme de la nature bon, et l'autre le croit méchant. Selon le philosophe de Genève, l'état de nature est un état de paix; selon le philosophe de Malmesbury, c'est un état de guerre. Ce sont les lois et la formation de la société qui ont rendu l'homme meilleur si l'on en croit Hobbes; et qui l'ont dépravé, si l'on en croit M. Rousseau. L'un était né au milieu du tumulte et des factions; l'autre vivait dans le monde et parmi les savants. Autre temps, autres circonstances, autre philosophie.

M. Derathé, who quotes this passage in his book *Jean-Jacques Rousseau et la Science Politique de son temps*,[1] points out that this article was written before the publication of the *Contrat Social*, yet it is surprising how many people still continue to think of Hobbes and Rousseau in Diderot's terms. Rousseau himself must be held largely responsible, since whenever he mentions Hobbes in his writings it is almost always to speak disparagingly of him. For example, in the essay *État de Guerre*, which he wrote at about the same time as the *Discours sur l'Inégalité*, and which he intended as an attack on Grotius and Hobbes, he refers to Hobbes as 'notre sophiste', exclaims against the 'odieux tableau' which he painted of the state of nature, and denounces the 'fureur d'établir le despotisme et l'obéissance passive' which, according to Rousseau, inspired the whole of his political thinking.

Our aim in this article will be to correct the impression which Rousseau and others have left us of his attitude to Hobbes, and in so doing assess the debt which we feel Rousseau, in the *Contrat Social*, owes to his much maligned predecessor. In this way we hope to see justice done to Hobbes

---

[1] Robert Derathé, *Jean-Jacques Rousseau et la Science politique de son temps* (Paris, 1950) pp. 104–5.

and at the same time to arrive at a better understanding of Rousseau himself.

In the *Discours sur l'Inégalité*, Rousseau describes man in the first state of nature as a creature of instinct, isolated, innocent and amoral, but at the same time a free agent and 'perfectible' (i.e. capable of developing into a sociable, rational and moral being), and then goes on to show how he becomes corrupted by living in the society of his fellows.[2] Men, he says, in this corrupt condition vie and contend with each other for supremacy and a state of war ensues which is a transference to the social state of what Hobbes, wrongly, in Rousseau's estimation, inferred to be true of man's natural state. The causes and character of this state of war are otherwise the same in both cases. In the *De Cive* Hobbes tells us:

> All men in the state of nature have a desire and will to hurt, but not proceeding from the same cause, neither equally to be condemned. For one man, according to that natural equality which is among us, permits as much to others, as he assumes to himself [. . .] Another, supposing himself above others, will have a license to do what he lists, and challenges respect and honour, as due to him before others [. . .] This man's will to hurt ariseth from vain glory, and the false esteem he hath of his own strength; the other's, from the necessity of defending himself, his liberty, and his goods, against this man's violence.[3]

And Hobbes continues a few pages further on:

> If now to this natural proclivity of men, to hurt each other, which they derive from their passions, but chiefly from a vain esteem of themselves, you add, the right of all to all, wherewith one by right invades, the other by right resists, and whence arise perpetual jealousies and suspicions on all hands [. . .] it cannot be denied but

---

[2] A society which he requires if he is to realize the possibilities of his 'perfectibility', for as Rousseau asks himself in the first part of the *Discours*, 'quel progrès pourrait faire le genre humain, épars dans les bois parmi les animaux?' Unfortunately it is this same society which excites his passions and stifles his emerging moral sense.

This social state is still, technically, a 'state of nature', in the sense that it pre-exists the actual foundation of any society, but it is not man's natural state, because men now live socially and no longer in isolation. A. O. Lovejoy, in his essay, 'The Supposed Primitivism of Rousseau's "Discours sur l'Inégalité" ' (*Modern Philology*, Vol. XXI, 1927, pp. 165–186, and *Essays in the History of Ideas*, Johns Hopkins, 1948, pp. 14–37), distinguishes no less than four states of nature in this *Discours*, but for the sake of simplicity I will, in this article, distinguish only two: the primitive state, in which men lived in isolation, as creatures of instinct, and the state which preceded any organized society, but in which men nevertheless lived social lives.

[3] *De Cive or the Citizen*, edited by S. P. Lamprecht (New York, 1949) pp. 25–26. To appear as *D.C.* in all future references.

that the natural state of men, before they entered into society, was a mere war, and that not simply, but a war of all men against all men (p. 29).

To these passages corresponds a section in the *Discours sur l'Inégalité* in which Rousseau speaks of men developing 'un noir penchant à se nuire mutuellement', when those who have acquired power and possessions use these to acquire even greater power and possessions, while those without are obliged to wrest the wherewithal to live from those who have:

> C'est ainsi que, les plus puissants ou les plus misérables se faisant de leurs forces ou de leurs besoins une sorte de droit au bien d'autrui, équivalent, selon eux, à celui de propriété, l'égalité rompue fut suivie du plus affreux désordre; c'est ainsi que les usurpations des riches, les brigandages des pauvres, les passions effrénées de tous, étouffant la pitié naturelle et la voix encore faible de la justice, rendirent les hommes avares, ambitieux et méchants. Il s'élevait entre le droit du plus fort et le droit du premier occupant un conflit perpétuel qui ne se terminait que par des combats et des meurtres. La société naissante fit place au plus horrible état de guerre.[4]

In Rousseau as in Hobbes we have the same psychological insight into the way men are motivated when living in groups, when 'competition of riches, honour, command, or other power, inclineth to contention, enmity, and war',[5] Hobbes's only fault, in Rousseau's view, being to have supposed this state of war to be natural to man, whereas he arrived at it only gradually, once he had emerged from the authentic state of nature:

> L'erreur de Hobbes [says Rousseau in the *Manuscrit de Genève*] n'est donc pas d'avoir établi l'état de guerre entre les hommes indépendants et devenus sociables; mais d'avoir supposé cet état naturel à l'espèce, et de l'avoir donné pour cause aux vices dont il est l'effet (*V*. I. p. 453).

While the difference is critical and conditions the whole political thinking of the two men, setting them off in opposing directions, the immediately operative point is that in Rousseau as in Hobbes men, when they live

---

[4] *Discours sur l'Inégalité*, in *The Political Writings of Jean-Jacques Rousseau* edited by C. E. Vaughan (Cambridge U.P., 1915), pp. 179–180. This edition will appear as *V* in all future references. In the case of major quotations from the *Contrat Social* chapter references will be added.

[5] *Leviathan*, edited by Michael Oakeshott (Oxford, 1955), p. 64. To appear as *L* in all future references.

together, find themselves in perpetual conflict with one another, and it is in order to escape from this conflict that they agree to observe certain rules and thereby call society into being.

In the *Discours* Rousseau sees man not so much 'founding' society as being tricked into accepting it by consenting to a pact proposed by the rich with the object of perpetuating their domination of the poor, what Rousseau calls 'le projet le plus réfléchi qui soit jamais entré dans l'esprit humain',[6] turning thereby the 'property'[7] they had usurped into a supposedly legitimate right.[8] This is the first stage in the formation of society as Rousseau sees it in the *Discours sur l'Inégalité*. As yet there is no political society, for no political authority has been set up. Instead, society is made up of 'quelques conventions générales que tous les particuliers s'engageaient à observer, et dont la communauté se rendait garante envers chacun d'eux'.[9] Political society comes later when the passions of men prove too

[6] *Discours, V.* I, p. 181.

[7] In the state of nature, for both Rousseau and Hobbes, there are no specific rights, but only a natural independence which allows each individual to judge for himself what he requires for his own self-preservation. Property then is, as Hobbes put it in the *Leviathan*, 'only that to be every man's, that he can get: and for so long, as he can keep it' (p. 83). Rousseau says the same; what one person takes to himself another can as legitimately take away from him: 'Dans l'état de nature, où tout est commun, je ne dois rien à ceux à qui je n'ai rien promis; je ne reconnais pour être à autrui que ce qui m'est inutile' (*MS. de Genève, V.* I, p. 491). At one point in the *Discours sur l'Inégalité*, Rousseau does give the impression of accepting a form of right to property in the second state of nature when he accepts Locke's criterion of property being based on a person's needs and commensurate with the labour he has put into it: 'C'est le seul travail qui, donnant droit au cultivateur sur le produit de la terre qu'il a labourée, lui en donne par conséquent sur le fonds, au moins jusqu'à la récolte, et ainsi d'année en année: ce qui, faisant une possession continue, se transforme aisément en propriété (*V.* I, p. 177). But it is clear from the way he continues that this is not a natural right but an acquired right, and even then not a right properly speaking but rather the basis on which a right to property can be accorded to the individual by society, once society has been formed by the free consent of men. Even those who had genuinely won their property by the work they had put into it could not escape the accusation of having appropriated it to themselves: 'Ils avaient beau dire: "C'est moi qui ai bâti ce mur; j'ai gagné ce terrain par mon travail." — "Qui vous a donné les alignements, leur pouvait-on répondre, et en vertu de quoi prétendez-vous être payés à nos dépens d'un travail que nous ne vous avons pas imposé? Ignorez-vous qu'une multitude de vos frères périt ou souffre du besoin de ce que vous avez de trop, et qu'il vous fallait un consentement exprès et unanime du genre humain pour vous approprier sur la subsistance commune tout ce qui allait au delà de la vôtre?" ' (*V.* I, p. 180).

[8] Like all contractual thinkers, Rousseau accepts that society can only be founded on consent: 'tout homme étant né libre et maître de lui-même, nul ne peut, sous quelque prétexte que ce puisse être, l'assujettir sans son aveu' (*Contrat Social, V.* II, p. 105). But clearly, as in this case, all consent does not necessarily constitute the basis of a legitimate society. Any society founded on a consent that has been obtained by a piece of trickery is an illegitimate society, and the consent given is void. Contracts are made by people who expect to derive some advantage from them; all were agreed about this. It cannot be a person's intention to be worse off by his free consent than he was before. Yet one does find oneself worse off after concluding the sort of pact described here by Rousseau.

[9] *V.* I, p. 183.

strong for these general conventions and they are abused. This is what
Hobbes could very well have told these would-be citizens, that 'the bonds
of words are too weak to bridle men's ambition'.[10] It is indeed the realization of this truth that lies at the basis of his own theory of absolutism:

> It is not enough [he says in the *De Cive*] to obtain this security,
> that every one of those who are now growing up into a city, do
> covenant with the rest, either by words or writing, not to steal, not
> to kill, and to observe the like laws; for the pravity of human
> disposition is manifest to all, and by experience too well known how
> little (removing the punishment) men are kept to their duties, through
> conscience of their promises (p. 72).

Because of the 'pravity' of man, then, Rousseau found himself faced with
the necessity of imagining a form of political society which would set up
an authority capable of enforcing the observance of society's laws. So in
the *Discours* Rousseau shows himself to be a disciple of Pufendorf in
adopting the principle of two contracts, a contract of association, which
first brings men together in a loose form of society, and then later, a
contract of submission, which provides for a government. He is far
removed from the theory of Hobbes which allows for one contract only
which creates the sovereign at the same time as it forms the society.

At this point Rousseau's historical account becomes confused with the
question of right. For even supposing, for the sake of argument, that
certain societies came into being after the manner described by some of
the theorists of absolutism — by conquest, or by a voluntary transference
of certain of men's natural rights to the person of a sovereign, as the
jurisconsults Grotius and Pufendorf maintained, or, were it conceivable,
by a total renunciation of one's liberty, as Hobbes would have it[11] — for
Rousseau it was illegitimate for a man to give up his liberty because
liberty is the condition of his moral existence:

> Renoncer à sa liberté, c'est renoncer à sa qualité d'homme, aux
> droits de l'humanité, même à ses devoirs. Il n'y a nul dédommage-

---

[10] *L*, p. 89.

[11] Hobbes misleadingly speaks of a 'transference' of powers in the *Leviathan*, but he uses the
term simply in order to distinguish between those cases where men renounce their rights
without naming a sovereign, and those where they renounce their rights in favour of a
sovereign, in which latter case, Hobbes says, they 'transfer' them. The sovereign does not in
fact receive any rights over and above those which he already possessed, for in the state of
nature all men had a right to all things. What he 'receives' by this 'transference' is simply the
full enjoyment of his natural rights, as they no longer meet with the resistance of those of
other people: 'To *lay down* a man's *right* to any thing, is to *divest* himself of the *liberty*, of
hindering another of the benefit of his own right to the same' (*L*, p. 85).

ment possible pour quiconque renonce à tout. Une telle renonciation est incompatible avec la nature de l'homme; et c'est ôter toute moralité à ses actions que d'ôter toute liberté à sa volonté (*Contrat Social*, I, 4/*V*. II. p. 28).

So the question which Rousseau put himself in the *Discours* was, paraphrased: what, in the course of the evolution of society, must have been the legitimate form of government which men agreed upon by their free consent? And for want of a better one he accepted the only theory then current which appeared to him to preserve man's freedom, that is to say the liberal idea of a constitutional authority set up by the people and circumscribed in its functions by fundamental laws defined by the people at the time when the contract was made. Within these laws the magistrates were free to act, but beyond them they could not go without dissolving the state and releasing the subjects from their obedience:

... contrat par lequel les deux parties s'obligent à l'observation des lois qui y sont stipulées et qui forment les liens de leur union. Le peuple ayant, au sujet des relations sociales, réuni toutes ses volontés en une seule, tous les articles sur lesquels cette volonté s'explique deviennent autant de lois fondamentales qui obligent tous les membres de l'État sans exception, et l'une desquelles règle le choix et le pouvoir des magistrats chargés de veiller à l'exécution des autres. Ce pouvoir s'étend à tout ce qui peut maintenir la constitution, sans aller jusqu'à la changer (*Discours*, *V*. I. p. 188).

In the *Discours*, therefore, the legitimate society was defined, as in Locke, by the laws that set limits to the political authority it embraced, that is to say, by the constitution which laid restrictions on the legislative and executive powers of the magistrates. This Rousseau called 'un vrai contrat entre le peuple et les chefs qu'il se choisit'.[12] But at the same time this 'vrai contrat' clearly left him dissatisfied, for he said that in adopting this formula he was merely following 'l'opinion commune' (i.e. that of the *Encyclopédistes*) and this, 'sans entrer aujourd'hui dans les recherches qui sont encore à faire sur la nature du pacte fondamental de tout Gouvernement'.[13] In other words, the type of legitimate society which Rousseau accepted in the *Discours* was the only one which at that time he could clearly define, and the unrelieved pessimism which marked the end of the *Discours* was the result of his realization that this second contract was as ineffective as the first. For the liberal idea of sovereignty is self-contra-

[12] *V*. I, p. 188.
[13] *Ibid.*

dictory, if once one accepts the social nature of man as Rousseau described it in the *Discours*. It seeks to set up a force distinct from the members of the community, whose job it is to contain men and compel them to respect the laws of society, while at the same time ensure them a certain degree of independence vis-à-vis this force. Such a society would only be viable, says Rousseau, if men were morally good. If they were, Hobbes and Rousseau both agree, there would, however, be no real need for a political society in the first place:

> For if we could suppose a great multitude of men to consent in the observation of justice, and other laws of nature, without a common power to keep them all in awe; we might as well suppose all mankind to do the same; and then there neither would be, nor need to be any civil government, or commonwealth at all; because there would be peace without subjection (*L*. p. 110).

Words which Rousseau echoes when he says in the *Discours:*

> ... il serait aisé de prouver que tout Gouvernement qui, sans se corrompre ni s'altérer, marcherait toujours exactement selon la fin de son institution, aurait été institué sans nécessité; et qu'un pays, où personne n'éluderait les lois et n'abuserait de la magistrature, n'aurait besoin ni de magistrats ni de lois (*V*. I. p. 191).

But where men are moved by their passions, where they are 'avares, ambitieux et méchants' and have 'un noir penchant à se nuire mutuellement', this partial, divided sovereignty is ineffective. The 'pravity' of man proves too strong for the laws, or as Rousseau put it, 'les vices qui rendent nécessaires les institutions sociales sont les mêmes qui en rendent l'abus inévitable'.[14]

To some extent this is not just the fault of the citizens, but the fault of the laws. Society is established, according to Rousseau, for the same reasons as it is in Locke. Men give themselves rulers so that they will 'protéger leurs biens, leurs libertés et leurs vies, qui sont, pour ainsi dire, les éléments constitutifs de leur être'.[15] The contract which creates this form of society is conceived of in purely juridical terms. The laws it establishes 'contiennent les hommes sans les changer';[16] they have no moral function, they do not seek to instil principles of virtue into the citizen. It follows that so long as men remain what they have become in society, so long as their amour-propre has not been neutralized and the

[14] *Ibid*, p. 190.
[15] *Ibid*, p. 184.
[16] *Ibid*, p. 190.

laws are purely coercive, the only really effective laws are those which contain men completely, that is to say the laws of Hobbes, under which the subjects owe total obedience to a sovereign ruler, the Leviathan, whom the book of Job appropriately describes as 'king of all the children of pride'. Such a formula was perfectly acceptable to Hobbes because he sought only to provide men with security and so fulfil what, for him, was the first law of nature, 'that every man, ought to endeavour peace, as far as he has hope of obtaining it'.[17] For Rousseau it could never be acceptable, for there is no authority that is absolute where men do not first give up their right to judge of right and wrong.

Illegitimate as it might be for men to give up this right, Rousseau shows at the end of the *Discours* how men effectively 'progress' to the point where, if they do not voluntarily surrender this right, they nevertheless lose it. Because when conflict arises again within the community, there is no superior authority to arbitrate between magistrates and subjects on the basis of the constitution. The only way to overcome this conflict, therefore, is for the government to strengthen its powers by progressively concentrating them, until one day a despot emerges who, 'élevant par degrés sa tête hideuse et dévorant tout ce qu'il aurait aperçu de bon et de sain dans toutes les parties de l'État, parviendrait enfin à fouler aux pieds les lois et le peuple, et à s'établir sur les ruines de la République'.[18] As in Hobbes, but this time through the breaking of a contract and not the making of a contract, men have lost all right to act according to the dictates of their conscience. For the despot 'ne souffre aucun autre maître; sitôt qu'il parle, il n'y a ni probité ni devoir à consulter; et la plus aveugle obéissance est la seule vertu qui reste aux esclaves'.[19]

Since there can be no question of man's returning to the state of nature, Rousseau's problem is either to leave him as he is and establish the Leviathan along with Hobbes, accepting it as man's privilege to be born free, but his destiny to live in chains,[20] or else find some form of society which

[17] *L*, p. 85.
[18] *V*. I, p. 193.
[19] *Ibid*, p. 194.
[20] Where society has arrived at such a state of corruption that it has lost all love and care of liberty, then Rousseau agrees that the only way to avoid conflict in society is to establish a Leviathan. This is the conclusion he comes to in his celebrated letter to the Marquis de Mirabeau, dated 26th July, 1767:

Voici, dans mes vieilles idées, le grand problème en politique, que je compare à celui de la quadrature du cercle en géométrie, et à celui des longitudes en astronomie: 'Trouver une forme de gouvernement qui mette la loi au-dessus de l'homme.'

Si cette forme est trouvable, cherchons-la et tâchons de l'établir . . .

Si malheureusement cette forme n'est pas trouvable, et j'avoue ingénument que je crois qu'elle ne l'est pas, mon avis est qu'il faut passer à l'autre extrémité, et mettre tout d'un coup l'homme autant au-dessus de la loi qu'il peut l'être, par conséquent établir le despotisme

will both subject men to its laws and yet at the same time guarantee their freedom. Rousseau would appear to have set himself to square the circle. How was he to go about it?

II.

If we have so far discussed Rousseau's ideas in the *Discours sur l'Inégalité* with reference to those of Hobbes, it has been to point the contrast between them. What we now propose to do is to look at the logic which led Rousseau from his *Discours* to the *Contrat Social*. For it is not the least paradox of a man who took pleasure in calling himself an 'homme à paradoxes' that in the latter he should abandon the recognized liberal ideas concerning the nature of political society and seek in Hobbes a solution to his problem.

In reflecting on human society as he had described it in the *Discours* Rousseau realized, as Hobbes had realized before him, that where men are not totally subject to the law, society cannot endure. In planning his new contract, therefore, he will align himself with Hobbes in insisting that men surrender 'such rights, as being retained, hinder the peace of mankind'.[21] This in effect means all his rights (i.e. all his natural liberty), for as Rousseau says in the chapter of the *Contrat Social* in which he describes the pact:

... s'il restait quelques droits aux particuliers, comme il n'y aurait aucun supérieur commun qui pût prononcer entre eux et le public, chacun, étant en quelque point son propre juge, prétendrait bientôt l'être en tous; l'état de nature subsisterait, et l'association deviendrait nécessairement tyrannique ou vaine (*V*. I. p. 33).

The pact therefore stipulates, 'l'aliénation totale de chaque associé avec tous ses droits à toute la communauté'.[22] Rousseau has become an absolutist. Along with Hobbes, and quite contrary to his liberal contemporaries, Rousseau considers the precondition of a viable political society

arbitraire et le plus arbitraire qu'il est possible: je voudrais que le despote pût être Dieu. En un mot, je ne vois point de milieu supportable entre la plus austère démocratie et le hobbisme le plus parfait: car le conflit des hommes et des lois, qui met dans l'État une guerre intestine continuelle, est le pire de tous les États politiques.

This is a solution of despair and nothing can ever make it legitimate for Rousseau. It fills him with horror: 'Mais les Caligula, les Néron, les Tibère! ... Mon Dieu! ... je me roule par terre, et je gémis d'être homme.' And he exclaims to his correspondent: 'ne me parlez plus de votre *despotisme légal*. Je ne saurais le goûter ni même l'entendre; et je ne vois là que deux mots contradictoires, qui réunis ne signifient rien pour moi.' (*Oeuvres complètes*, Hachette, XII, p. 25).

[21] *L*, p. 93.
[22] *V*. II, p. 33.

to be the complete surrender of one's independence, for independence is the opposite of freedom, properly understood. Harmless in the first state of nature when men lived isolated lives, it is harmful in society where every man seeks his private advantage at the expense of his neighbour:

> On a beau vouloir confondre l'indépendance et la liberté [writes Rousseau in the *Lettres écrites de la Montagne*]. Ces deux choses sont si différentes que même elles s'excluent mutuellement. Quand chacun fait ce qu'il lui plaît, on fait souvent ce qui déplaît à d'autres; et cela ne s'appelle pas un état libre (*V*. II. p. 234).

No man therefore must be independent vis-à-vis his fellow citizens. As a necessary corollary to this it follows that no man may be allowed to remain in any way independent vis-à-vis the sovereign. Only where these conditions have been secured is it possible for men to live at peace together. Only when men are at peace can they live moral lives and in their actions obey the commands of God. For it is only in such a society that they enjoy the conditions in which they may safely do so.

Rousseau and Hobbes both rejected the notion of the natural sociability of man, and the contention that men obeyed the dictates of natural law without first being obliged to do so by the civil law. This did not mean that Rousseau and Hobbes denied that there were moral laws existing outside society, but simply that their application was frustrated because there was no authority to see that they were applied. Men were always under a theoretical obligation to obey the laws of nature, but they were not always obliged in fact to practise them when this might put their own self-preservation in jeopardy, that is to say, when any man had reason to believe (and he alone could be the judge) that others would not do to him as the moral laws would have him do to them:

> For he that first performs [said Hobbes in the *De Cive*], by reason of the wicked disposition of the greatest part of men studying their own advantage, either by right or wrong, exposeth himself to the perverse will of him with whom he hath contracted. For it suits not with reason, that any man should perform first, if it be not likely that the other will make good his promise after; which, whether it be probable or not, he that doubts it, must be judge of . . . (p. 36).

Exactly the same point is made by Rousseau in the second chapter of the *Manuscrit de Genève*, 'De la Société générale du genre humain', which he wrote as a reply to Diderot's article *Droit naturel* in the *Encyclopédie*:

> 'Je sens que je porte l'épouvante et le trouble au milieu de l'espèce

humaine,' dit l'homme indépendant que le sage étouffe; 'mais il faut que je sois malheureux, ou que je fasse le malheur des autres, et personne ne m'est plus cher que moi. C'est vainement,' pourra-t-il ajouter, 'que je voudrais concilier mon intérêt avec celui d'autrui; tout ce que vous me dites des avantages de la loi sociale pourrait être bon, si, tandis que je l'observerais scrupuleusement envers les autres, j'étais sûr qu'ils l'observeraient tous envers moi. Mais quelle *sûreté* pouvez-vous me donner là-dessus? et ma situation peut-elle être pire que de me voir exposé à tous les maux que les plus forts voudront me faire, sans oser me dédommager sur les faibles? Ou donnez-moi des *garants* contre toute entreprise injuste, ou n'espérez pas que je m'en abstienne à mon tour (*V.* I. p. 450) [italics mine].

Security then for both Hobbes and Rousseau is the first and indispensable condition for making the moral laws effective. Justice, which the Lockian school considered an attribute of nature, exists for them only as a virtuality outside civil society:

A considérer humainement les choses, faute de sanction naturelle, les lois de la justice sont vaines parmi les hommes; elles ne font que le bien du méchant et le mal du juste, quand celui-ci les observe avec tout le monde sans que personne les observe avec lui (*Contrat Social*, II, 6/*V.* II. p. 48).

Or as Hobbes puts it rather more bluntly:

Where there is no common power, there is no law: where no law, no injustice. Force, and fraud, are in war the two cardinal virtues (*L.* p. 83).

It is the sovereign's first function, therefore, to provide that security without which the moral laws are inoperative. By his power he shall remove the fear which any of his subjects might harbour concerning the behaviour of others consequent on his performing his duty. He will contain these other subjects with respect to the one, just as he will contain the one with respect to the others. This he can do only if all the members of the state agree to reduce their wills to one will by subjecting themselves totally to the sovereign. Sovereignty is absolute or it is nothing, 'la limiter, c'est la détruire'.[23]

Since the sovereign ceases to be absolute once restrictions are placed upon him, and thereby ceases to be sovereign, it follows that there can be no law in the state that can bind him. The sovereign's will is above the

[23] *Contrat Social, V.* II, p. 99.

law: it makes the law and can change the law, it cannot therefore be subject to it:

> The sovereign of a commonwealth, be it an assembly, or one man, is not subject to the civil laws. For having power to make, and repeal laws, he may when he pleaseth, free himself from that subjection, by repealing those laws that trouble him, and making of new; and consequently he was free before. For he is free, that can be free when he will: nor is it possible for any person to be bound to himself; because he that can bind, can release; and therefore he that is bound to himself only, is not bound (*L.* p. 173).

Rousseau endorses this view:

> ... il est contre la nature du Corps politique que le souverain s'impose une loi qu'il ne puisse enfreindre (*Contrat Social*, I, 7/*V.* II. p. 34).

To limit the will of the sovereign by what he had already willed would clearly be absurd. One cannot will today not to will something else tomorrow: 'il est contre la nature de la volonté, qui n'a point d'empire sur elle-même, de s'engager pour l'avenir'.[24] This does not mean to say that the state does not have its fundamental laws. It does. They are what provide it with form and outline. But they are not limitations laid upon the sovereign; they are willed by the sovereign in the first place, and however long such laws may have stood, it is not to the authority of tradition that they owe their existence, but to the silence of the legislator, 'for silence is sometimes an argument of consent; and it is no longer law, than the sovereign shall be silent therein'.[25] Rousseau makes the same point in the *Manuscrit de Genève* where he says: 'Mais c'est toujours en vertu d'un consentement présent et tacite que l'acte antérieur peut continuer d'avoir son effet',[26] for the law speaks 'au nom du peuple d'à présent, et non de celui d'autrefois'.[27] So both Rousseau and Hobbes would hold the belief that 'he that hath the sovereign power is subject to the civil laws'[28] to be a contradiction in the nature of civil society. While the laws may define the appearance of the state at any given time, what now constitutes the essence of the state for Rousseau, as it did for Hobbes, is not the laws, or constitution, but the will of the legislator:

> Ce n'est point par les lois que l'État subsiste, c'est par le pouvoir législatif (*Contrat Social*, V. II. p. 91).

[24] *MS. de Genève*, *V.* I, p. 480.
[25] *L*, p. 174.
[26] *V.* I, p. 461.
[27] *Ibid*, p. 481.
[28] *L*, p. 212.

There can therefore be no further question of a contract of government as there was in the *Discours sur l'Inégalité*, for the sovereign will cannot limit itself by making a contract with any other body in the state: the will either is sovereign or it is not. So what Rousseau considered in the *Discours* as 'un vrai contrat entre le peuple et les chefs qu'il se choisit' is 'un vrai contrat' no longer, and Rousseau has come round to Hobbes's way of thinking that there can only be one contract, that which creates a sovereign authority at the same time as it forms the society:

> Plusieurs ont prétendu que l'acte de cet établissement était un contrat entre le peuple et les chefs qu'il se donne: contrat par lequel on stipulait entre les deux parties les conditions sous lesquelles l'une s'obligeait à commander, et l'autre à obéir. On conviendra, je m'assure, que voilà une étrange manière de contracter. ... Il est absurde et contradictoire que le souverain se donne un supérieur; s'obliger d'obéir à un maître, c'est se remettre en pleine liberté (*Contrat Social*, III, 16/*V*. II. p. 99).

And Rousseau concludes:

> Il n'y a qu'un contrat dans l'État, c'est celui de l'association: et celui-là seul en exclut tout autre. On ne saurait imaginer aucun contrat public qui ne fût une violation du premier (*Ibid*).

Once Rousseau has accepted this view, a number of consequences follow. In the first place Rousseau allies himself with Hobbes in maintaining that the citizen does not come into the state with rights already his own, but receives any rights he holds from the sovereign. What the citizen might presume to be his rights are in fact what the sovereign accords him, and he retains them at the pleasure of the sovereign. Were this not so the sovereign could not be absolute and would not therefore be in a position to oblige his subjects to respect his laws. Property, for example, is not, as we have seen,[29] a natural right which civil society is brought into being to defend, as it is in Locke. Locke said that 'the Prince or Senate, however it may have power to make Laws for the regulating of Property between the Subjects one amongst another, yet can never have a Power to take to themselves the whole or any part of the Subjects Property, *without their own consent*. For this would be in effect to leave them no Property at all'[30] [italics mine]. For if men set up a political society it was 'with this express or tacit Trust, That it shall be imployed for their good, and the preservation of their Property'.[31] Hobbes and Rousseau would agree

---

[29] v. sup. p. 280, n. 7.
[30] *Two Treatises of Government*, edited by Peter Laslett (Cambridge U.P., 1960), p. 379.
[31] *Ibid*, p. 399.

with Locke that society was designed for the good of its subjects, but they would disagree with him as to who in point of fact decided what that good was. This does not mean to say that they admitted no private property, just as the fact that the sovereign was not to be limited by any fundamental laws did not mean that there were no fundamental laws. Private property does exist, but the right to it is something that is granted by the sovereign, who wills that it shall exist and who can withdraw the right whenever he likes. Whereas in the state of nature property was divided on the basis of 'only that to be every man's, that he can get: and for so long, as he can keep it',[32] in civil society the extent of one's property is 'just so much as he [the sovereign] will, and shall last so long as he [the sovereign] pleases'.[33] 'Car l'État, à l'égard de ses membres [observes Rousseau], est maître de tous leurs biens par le Contrat social, qui, dans l'État, sert de base à tous les droits'.[34]

If Hobbes and Rousseau agree that the sovereign is the source of all the citizens' rights, they diverge, however, in their attitude to the important moral problem which this principle raises. It is here that their relationship is most interesting. For they are both confronted by the same difficulty: if all men are totally subject to the will of the sovereign, does this not necessarily lead to the destruction of the moral autonomy of the individual? We have seen that the sovereign, being absolute, inherits the subjects' right to judge of right and wrong, good and evil, otherwise the subjects would be able to oppose the sovereign on the basis of an objection of conscience. They would represent a second will in a state the condition for whose existence is that there should be one will only. So in those things which concern the state (and we have seen that the sovereign is alone judge of what these things are), it is what the sovereign commands that is good and what he forbids that is evil:

> ... it belongs to the same chief power to make some common rules for all men, and to declare them publicly, by which every man may know what may be called his, what another's, what just, what unjust, what honest, what dishonest, what good, what evil, that is summarily, what is to be done, what to be avoided in our common course of life (*D.C.* p. 74).

The Book of Genesis says: 'Ye shall be as gods, knowing good and evil'.[35] In Hobbes the sovereign alone knows good and evil in the public domain,

---

[32] *L*, p. 83.
[33] *D.C.*, p. 134.
[34] *Contrat Social*, *V*. II, p. 37.
[35] Quoted by Hobbes in both the *De Cive* (p. 129) and the *Leviathan* (p. 135).

he is 'that *mortal god*, to which we owe under the *immortal God*, our peace and defence'.[36] Outside the public sphere, in those things 'which in regulating their actions, the sovereign hath praetermitted',[37] the citizen does, however, enjoy a liberty 'which is harmless to civil government'.[38] In this sphere he is his own moral judge; it is for him to interpret the natural law for himself in the silence of the civil law, and assume responsibility for his intentions and his actions in the court of his own conscience and before God. The natural law is, of course, superior to the civil law. It presides at the first compact establishing civil society, for it is a law of nature that men honour the covenants they have made, and it is the sovereign's duty to interpret the natural law for his subjects where the affairs of the state are concerned. The sovereign does not therefore create values out of nothing. So it would certainly be untrue to say that Hobbes's state could not be a moral one, for it is designed to provide conditions in which the natural laws can become operative, and a duty is laid upon the sovereign to rule according to his honest interpretation of these laws:

> The laws of nature are immutable and eternal: what they forbid, can never be lawful; what they command, can never be unlawful (*D.C.* p. 56).

Once the sovereign has interpreted the natural law, the citizen must obey him whatever his private opinion of this interpretation might be. He must, for the purposes of his actions, regard the sovereign's interpretation as a moral interpretation, whether or not it would have been his own. Men must perform the actions they are called upon to perform as if the law were morally valid; they have no right of remonstrance:

> ... the commands of them that have the right to command, are not by their subjects to be censured, nor disputed (*L.* p. 135).

Rousseau having opted for an absolute sovereign must accept Hobbes's logic, that it is the sovereign who says what is just and what unjust, and that there must be no power of resistance to what the sovereign decrees. For where there are no laws or no effective enforcement of laws, there is no effective concept of justice, 'car la Loi est antérieure à la justice, et non pas la justice à la Loi'.[39] And equally, as in Hobbes, the sovereign has a duty to govern according to the natural law. As Rousseau says in the *Lettres écrites de la Montagne*:

> ... il n'est pas plus permis d'enfreindre les lois naturelles par le

[36] *L*, p. 112.
[37] *Ibid*, p. 139.
[38] *D.C.*, p. 152.
[39] *MS. de Genève, V.* I, p. 494.

Contrat social, qu'il n'est permis d'enfreindre les lois positives par les contrats des particuliers; et ce n'est que par ces lois mêmes qu'existe la liberté qui donne force à l'engagement (*V*. II. p. 200).

Hobbes and Rousseau agree then that the natural laws are superior to civil laws, but that for the purposes of determining men's actions it is the civil law that counts.

But in that case, it will be objected, what of the moral identity of the individual in those things which are decided by the sovereign? So far we have assumed that where the sovereign is absolute men lose their moral identity. It is time now that we looked a little more closely into the matter. Hobbes, for example, rejects the contention. He answers the charge by exonerating the individual subject in advance from any sense of sin for the crimes he may be called upon to commit on the command of the sovereign. Since it is the sovereign who interprets God's commands in those things which concern the state, and since the sovereign is answerable for this interpretation not to his subjects but only to his conscience and to God, should he command that which in the eyes of any of his subjects is a sin, that sin is not the subject's, but the sin of the sovereign himself:

> Whatsoever any man doth against his conscience is a sin; for he who doth so, contemns the law. But we must distinguish. That is my sin indeed, which committing I do believe to be my sin; but what I believe to be another man's sin, I may sometimes do that without any sin of mine. For if I be commanded to do that which is a sin in him who commands me, if I do it, and he that commands me be by right lord over me, I sin not (*D.C.* pp. 129–130).

The contrary belief, 'that whatsoever a man does against his conscience, is sin', Hobbes calls a 'doctrine repugnant to civil society'.[40] This assertion Rousseau explicitly rejects towards the end of the *Discours sur l'Inégalité*, where he objects: 'il m'importe qu'on n'abuse point de ma liberté, et je ne puis, *sans me rendre coupable du mal qu'on me forcera de faire*, m'exposer à devenir l'instrument du crime'[41] [italics mine].

We are now left to discover how it is that Rousseau can both share Hobbes's view concerning the relationship between the sovereign authority and the moral laws, and yet escape the consequence of the destruction of the moral autonomy of the individual. It is here that we see Rousseau forsake Hobbes and construct his own highly individual idea of the nature

[40] *L*, p. 211.
[41] *V*. I, p. 187.

of sovereignty. In Hobbes the will of the sovereign is the will of an individual or of a group of individuals, and what makes the will of an individual are ultimately his own interests. Of course, Hobbes will say, it is in the sovereign's interest to encourage a just and flourishing society in which the citizens can live securely and enjoy 'all other contentments of life, which every man by lawful industry, without danger, or hurt to the commonwealth, shall acquire to himself'.[42] For as no man gives up his independence except in the expectation of bettering his lot, the sovereign has an obligation to ensure that 'he which giveth it, have no reasonable cause to repent him of his good will',[43] 'for the city was not instituted for its own, but for the subjects' sake'.[44] In other words, while the sovereign is the beneficiary of the pact which men make among themselves, the subjects are the beneficiaries of the civil society over which he presides. This is the reason why Hobbes preferred monarchy to all other forms of power, because:

... whosoever beareth the person of the people, or is one of that assembly that bears it, beareth also his own natural person. And though he be careful in his politic person to procure the common interest; yet he is more, or no less careful to procure the private good of himself, his family, kindred, and friends; and for the most part, if the public interest chance to cross the private, he prefers the private: for the passions of men, are commonly more potent than their reason. From whence it follows, that where the public and private interest are most closely united, there is the public good most advanced. Now in monarchy, the private interest is the same with the public. The riches, power, and honour of a monarch arise only from the riches, strength, and reputation of his subjects. For no king can be rich, nor glorious, nor secure, whose subjects are either poor, or contemptible, or too weak through want or dissention, to maintain a war against their enemies: whereas in a democracy, or aristocracy, the public prosperity confers not so much to the private fortune of one that is corrupt, or ambitious, as doth many times a perfidious advice, a treacherous action, or a civil war (*L*. pp. 122–123).

This, reflects Rousseau, would be all very well, but it still requires reason to show the monarch that his true interests are commensurate with the interests of the community as a whole. It is not, however, reason but will

[42] *L*, p. 219.
[43] *Ibid*, p. 99.
[44] *D.C.*, p. 142.

20

which is the mark of sovereignty and the will, as Hobbes himself admits, is not always reasonable. In Book III, chapter 6, of the *Contrat Social* Rousseau replies to Hobbes's argument as follows:

> Les rois veulent être absolus; et de loin on leur crie que le meilleur moyen de l'être est de se faire aimer de leurs peuples. Cette maxime est très belle, et même très vraie à certains égards. Malheureusement, on s'en moquera toujours dans les cours. La puissance qui vient de l'amour des peuples est sans doute la plus grande; mais elle est précaire et conditionnelle; jamais les princes ne s'en contenteront. Les meilleurs rois veulent pouvoir être méchants s'il leur plaît, sans cesser d'être les maîtres. Un sermonneur politique aura beau leur dire que, la force du peuple étant la leur, leur plus grand intérêt est que le peuple soit florissant, nombreux, redoutable; ils savent très bien que cela n'est pas vrai. Leur intérêt personnel est premièrement que le peuple soit faible, misérable, et qu'il ne puisse jamais leur résister (*V*. II. p. 77).

Hobbes's mistake was to conceive of the sovereign as someone standing outside the laws, making the law for his subjects. In this way he failed to provide any guarantee against the sovereign's damaging his subjects. For although he cannot do them an injustice, having no part in the compact and therefore no obligation to them for which they can hold him accountable, he can damage his subjects by procuring his own material well-being and that of his favourites at their expense. This is the fatal flaw. For Hobbes the state is an aggregrate of individuals, held in place by the sovereign. He regards it as the *sine qua non* of political society that the sovereign be apart from his subjects, necessarily standing outside the framework of the laws he makes. Subject and sovereign belong to different orders of relationship. The subject is in the civil state vis-à-vis the sovereign, but the sovereign is in the state of nature vis-à-vis the subject, enjoying an unrestricted right to all things. Whatever recommendations may be made to him to govern for the good of his subjects, nothing can change this relationship and place an actual and effective obligation on him to do so. That is why Rousseau conceived it to be his great task to bring every member of the state *without exception* back into the framework of the laws. But how was he to contrive that those people who were sovereign be subject to the laws, when the sovereign makes the laws and is superior to them? that those who command the laws should at the same time be commanded by them, and that the interests of the sovereign and the subject coincide? How was he to arrange for men to remain responsible for their actions and yet for the sovereign alone to be the one to judge of right and wrong? Clearly these things could not be done 'à moins que le peuple et le souverain ne soient une même personne'.[45]

It is in this way that Rousseau is brought to his great discovery of the sovereignty of the people. Not, of course, that he was the first to think of the idea. Far from it. That the people were sovereign was an assumption made by all contractual thinkers, since it was the sovereign will of the people as a whole which in the first place established civil society. The absolutists Grotius, Hobbes and Pufendorf all agreed about this, but however interesting their theories might claim to be as theories of power, they could be of little interest as theories of the sovereignty of the people when this sovereignty remained with the people only for so long as it took them to give it up. Rousseau's claim to originality is that his contract is founded on the *inalienable* sovereignty of the people, so that after the pact the people, still retaining sovereignty, remain a people, because there is no separate authority in the state equal or superior to theirs.

At this point a further problem arises. How can the people as a whole be sovereign if to be sovereign means to rule as well as to legislate, as it did for Hobbes and indeed all thinkers before Rousseau? For the sovereign would then be the government, and if this were so it would be impossible for the people to will morally, as their private interests would constantly interfere with their judgement concerning the public good. It is here that Rousseau parts company most radically with Hobbes over the issue of what constitutes the matter of sovereignty. For despite the originality of Hobbes's pact which sets him aside from all other political thinkers, his conception of what constitutes the matter of sovereignty is conventional. In the *Leviathan* Hobbes lists what he considers to be the attributes of the sovereign and then reduces these to a number of essential powers on which, he says, sovereignty wholly depends. Some powers there are which the sovereign may delegate without thereby ceasing to be sovereign, but among his powers there are a limited number of which, should he lose even one, it were as if he had lost them all, for without that one there can be no sovereignty. It is these fundamental rights of the sovereign which Hobbes calls fundamental laws:

> For a fundamental law in every commonwealth is that, which being taken away, the commonwealth faileth, and is utterly dissolved; as a building whose foundation is destroyed. And therefore a fundamental law is that, by which subjects are bound to uphold whatsoever power is given to the sovereign, whether monarch, or a sovereign assembly, without which the commonwealth cannot stand; such as is

[45] *Discours*, Dédicace, *V*. I, p. 126.

the power of war and peace, of judicature, of election of officers, and of doing whatsoever he shall think necessary for the public good (*L.* p. 188).

These rights, Hobbes declares, 'are the rights, which make the essence of the sovereignty; and which are the marks, whereby a man may discern in what man, or assembly of men, the sovereign power is placed, and resideth'.[46] Hobbes then is at one with all the thinkers of his time, and of the eighteenth century too, in conceiving of sovereignty as an amalgam of powers necessarily embracing both the legislative will and the power that executes it. As M. Derathé has pointed out,[47] on this absolutists and liberals alike concurred. What distinguished them was, broadly, whether they thought that these powers, or parts of sovereignty, formed a divisible or an indivisible whole. For the liberals these powers could, and should, be divided in order to act as a brake on power; for the absolutists they were indivisible, they were to be held in one pair of hands only. The sovereign was the Prince. To say that the supreme authority may be divided, says Hobbes in the *De Cive*, is 'a most fatal opinion to all commonweals',[48] and in the *Leviathan*, 'a kingdom divided in itself cannot stand'.[49]

In the *Contrat Social* Rousseau accepts Hobbes's thesis that sovereignty is indivisible, and that 'a kingdom divided in itself cannot stand'; but he does not accept the assumption that sovereignty can be identified with government, or that it is the Prince who represents the people. Government and sovereign must be kept strictly apart. The sovereign is not the ruler in the usually accepted sense of the term, but the lawmaker, the law being the expression of the legislative will, and it is this, and this alone, which is sovereign. That sovereignty is indivisible Rousseau readily agrees with Hobbes, but this is not because it is made up of parts which together constitute an indivisible whole, but because it is something single in itself. That is why in Rousseau's view neither the absolutist nor the liberal schools of thought could ever give rise to a viable political society, because they elevated to the dignity of sovereign certain things which in fact were no part of the sovereign. In this way either the subject was divested of all effective means of protection against the sovereign,[50]

[46] *L*, p. 118.
[47] Derathé, p. 290 et seq.
[48] *D.C.*, p. 132.
[49] *L*, p. 119.
[50] 'La perfection de l'ordre social consiste, il est vrai, dans le concours de la force et de la Loi. Mais il faut pour cela que la Loi dirige la force; au lieu que, dans les idées de l'indépendance absolue des princes, la seule force, parlant aux citoyens sous le nom de Loi et aux étrangers sous le nom de raison d'État, ôte à ceux-ci le pouvoir, et aux autres la volonté, de résister; en sorte que le vain nom de justice ne sert partout que de sauvegarde à la violence (*État de Guerre*, *V.* I, p. 304).

or a number of conflicting wills were set up within the state. What Hobbes and others took to be parts of sovereignty were, on the other hand, for Rousseau but emanations from the sovereign. As such they serve the sovereign but are of a different order from the sovereign:

> Mais nos politiques, ne pouvant diviser la souveraineté dans son principe, la divisent dans son objet. Ils la divisent en force et en volonté; en puissance législative et en puissance exécutive; en droits d'impôt, de justice, et de guerre; en administration intérieure, et en pouvoir de traiter avec l'étranger: tantôt ils confondent toutes ces parties, et tantôt ils les séparent [. . .] Cette erreur vient de ne s'être pas fait des notions exactes de l'autorité souveraine, et d'avoir pris pour des parties de cette autorité ce qui n'en était que des émanations (*Contrat Social*, II, 2/*V*. II. p. 41).

It is on the basis of this discovery, that sovereignty is limited to will, that Rousseau can now construct a political system which allows of an absolute sovereign and yet preserves the moral autonomy of the individual, because he can make the people sovereign while not at the same time being obliged to make them the government. Being the sovereign and retaining the power to judge of good and evil, the people remain a people, even though their obedience as subjects is as total as it is in Hobbes. So Rousseau's pact, while necessarily involving 'l'aliénation totale de chaque associé avec tous ses droits', constitutes not a sovereign ruler, but a sovereign community, since these alienated rights do not disappear, as they do with Hobbes, but are accumulated in the community which is brought into being as a result. Whereas in Hobbes the future citizens 'transfer' their rights (i.e. renounce their liberty) in favour of a sovereign of their choice, in Rousseau the future citizens make a real transfer of their independent rights from themselves as individuals to themselves as a community in the making.[51] As for the government, it is a separate body having no share in the sovereignty; it is 'une commission',[52] and the ministers are merely the officials of the sovereign charged with applying

---

[51] Rousseau formulates his pact as follows: 'Chacun de nous met en commun sa personne et toute sa puissance sous la suprême direction de la volonté générale; et nous recevons en corps chaque membre comme partie indivisible du tout' (*Contrat Social*, I, 6/*V*. II, p. 33).
  By contrast the terms of Hobbes's pact are: 'I authorize and give up my right of governing myself, to this man, or to this assembly of men, on this condition, that thou give up thy right to him, and authorize all his actions in like manner' (*L*, p. 112).
[52] *Contrat Social*, *V*. II, p. 65.

its will to the members of the state in detail and they are freely revocable
by the sovereign. The government's decrees are not 'du ressort de la
Loi'.[53] It is the sovereign who makes the law and the government is but
'la force appliquée à la Loi'.[54] It is the channel by which the people as
sovereign communicate with themselves as subjects, 'un corps intermédiaire établi entre les sujets et le souverain pour leur mutuelle correspondance'.[55] The will of the sovereign is no longer then the will of a
ruler, but the will of the community as a whole. It is the General Will,
an entity greater than the sum of its parts.

There is already in Hobbes a hint of a theory of a general will of the
community, but it pales by comparison with Rousseau's and seems indeed
to contradict his earlier assertions respecting the individual's freedom from
moral responsibility for those actions which he undertakes on the
command of the sovereign. For repeatedly Hobbes asserts that the subject,
by entering into a pact with his potential fellow citizens, renouncing his
liberty of action in favour of a commonly approved sovereign, thereby
wills all the future acts of that sovereign; for whatever the sovereign
might will cannot conceivably be worse than the state of war that is the
state of nature, from which all men must wish to escape. In the *De Cive*
Hobbes writes:

> ... a city is defined to be one person made out of many men, whose
> will by their own contracts is to be esteemed as the wills of them all,
> insomuch as he may use the strength and faculties of each single
> person for the public peace and safety (p. 117).

Elsewhere he speaks of the subject as being the 'author of whatsoever he
that beareth their person, shall act, or cause to be acted, in those things
which concern the common peace and safety'.[56] The multitude are said to
'own' all the actions of the representer and the representer is said to
'carry' their person. The clear implication of these often repeated statements must be that the actions of the sovereign are willed by the subjects,
so that what he does is the expression of their own will, i.e. of the general
will of the community. This is difficult to square with his saying that
those who commit what in their own consciences would be a sin do not
thereby sin if they act on the command of their legitimate sovereign, for
the sovereign's command is now not to be distinguished from their

---

[53] *Ibid*, p. 64.
[54] *Ibid*, p. 97.
[55] *Ibid*, p. 65.
[56] *L*, p. 112.

own.[57] Whether or not Hobbes contradicts himself here it is not our concern to determine. What is clear, however, is that his theory of the general will is no more than an embryonic one, inadequate in so far as in it the will only expresses itself the once. This is the negation of will, for will is continuous creation: it cannot be made to embrace a future it cannot foresee.[58] In Rousseau the general will is quite different, for the will of the people is the will of the sovereign and therefore inalienable. The general will expresses itself afresh each time the sovereign body expresses itself. It is something vital, living, ever re-created. For when the individual is called upon to determine the law, he must think of himself as part of the sovereign, that is, as an indivisible part of a greater whole, and not as an individual whose immediate material interests are at issue. The question he must ask himself is not, do I want, or do I not want such and such a law, but does the proposed law correspond to the good of the community. He must interrogate his conscience, 'rentrer en soi-même, et écouter la voix de sa conscience dans le silence des passions'. No-one can do that for him; that is why sovereignty is inalienable and cannot be represented. There can be no 'representer' of the general will as there is in Hobbes: 'la volonté ne se représente point: elle est la même, ou elle est autre'.[59]

Moreover the general will is infallible, whereas in Hobbes it is all too humanly fallible: 'la volonté générale est toujours droite et tend toujours à l'utilité publique'.[60] For the will which is indivisible in its essence is also indivisible in its object. Were the sovereign will to apply itself to a section of the community only, it could no longer be the general will but would be two things; the will of those legislating for the particular section of the community, and the will of that section of the community which would be the object of the legislation:

> Or, à l'instant qu'un peuple considère un objet particulier, fût-ce un de ses propres membres, il se forme entre le tout et sa partie une relation qui en fait deux êtres séparés, dont la partie est l'un, et le tout, moins cette même partie, est l'autre. Mais le tout, moins une

---

[57] 'For he that doth anything by authority from another, doth therein no injury to him by whose authority he acteth: but by this institution of a commonwealth, every particular man is author of all the sovereign doth: and consequently he that complaineth of injury from his sovereign, complaineth of that whereof he himself is author; and therefore ought not to accuse any man but himself' (*L*, pp. 115–16).

[58] Rousseau takes Hobbes up on this point in the *Manuscrit de Genève*: 'Si l'on dit que, tout le peuple s'étant une fois soumis volontairement, solennellement et sans contrainte à un homme, toutes les volontés de cet homme doivent, en vertu de cette soumission, être censées autant d'actes de la volonté générale, on dit un sophisme auquel j'ai déjà répondu (*V*. I, p. 479).

[59] *Contrat Social, V.* II, p. 96.

[60] *Ibid*, p. 42.

partie, n'est point le tout; et tant que ce rapport subsiste, il n'y a plus de tout, mais deux parties inégales (*MS. de Genève, V.* I. p. 492).[61]

Only when it applies to the community as a whole can the will be general. It must 'partir de tous pour s'appliquer à tous'.[62] In this way it is impersonal and therefore just for all the citizens. Each man in voting the law for himself votes the law that will apply to the community as a whole, and in voting the law for the community as a whole, he votes the law that will apply to himself. This is the only way of ensuring that man's passions do not interfere with his moral judgement and that he does not seek his own personal advantage at the expense of his neighbour, as did Rousseau's 'homme indépendant':

> Pourquoi la volonté générale est-elle toujours droite, et pourquoi tous veulent-ils constamment le bonheur de chacun d'eux, si ce n'est parce qu'il n'y a personne qui ne s'approprie ce mot *chacun*, et qui ne songe à lui-même en votant pour tous? Ce qui prouve que l'égalité de droit et la notion de justice qu'elle produit dérive de la préférence que chacun se donne, et par conséquent de la nature de l'homme (*Contrat Social, V.* II. p. 44).

'Personne ne m'est plus cher que moi', the independent man had said. Exactly the same is true of the citizen, but it is precisely this which, because he must identify himself with his brother, makes him automatically his brother's keeper. Where in Hobbes the sovereign may make laws which are bad, in Rousseau, 'le souverain, par cela seul qu'il est, est toujours ce qu'il doit être'.[63]

Rousseau's genius, by comparison with that of Hobbes, was to have imagined a single contract which established an absolute sovereign and yet at the same time limited that sovereign, not by any fundamental laws (for this would be a contradiction in terms), but by the very nature of sovereignty. Apart from one or two exceptions which need not concern us here, the powers of Hobbes's sovereign were unlimited. He could legislate for the community as a whole or for any member or group of members of it, and if, technically, he could do none of them an injustice in that he had made no contract with them, he could do them damage. In Rousseau the sovereign, willing for all, will always will what is good for the community; not because the law is founded on justice, 'ce qui pourrait n'être pas toujours vrai; mais parce qu'il est contre la nature

---

[61] cf. *Contrat Social*, II, 2/*V.* II, p. 40.
[62] *Ibid*, p. 44.
[63] *Ibid*, p. 35.

qu'on veuille se nuire à soi-même, *ce qui est sans exception*[64] [italics mine]. It was Rousseau's hope that in this way men would one day grow so accustomed to thinking in terms of the good of the community, and learn so to love the law, that there would be no further need to contain them. For as he said in the *Contrat Social:* 'quoique la Loi ne règle pas les moeurs, c'est la législation qui les fait naître'.[65]

III.

From the foregoing discussion it is evident that Rousseau had aspirations for men that were quite foreign to Hobbes. Yet it is no less evident, from a comparison of their thinking, that between the time Rousseau wrote the *Discours sur l'Inégalité* and the time he wrote the *Contrat Social*, he had taken a second and closer look at Hobbes, and had arrived at a new and deeper appreciation of a number of his most important ideas. Once Rousseau had painted the same 'odieux tableau' of the state of things which preceded the foundation of society by its future citizens, he was led by the same logic to establish a single sovereign authority that was absolute.[66] It was this sovereign authority which, as in Hobbes, was superior to the laws that it made, from which all rights were held, which decided issues of right and wrong, good and evil, and which, by the security it afforded, provided a framework within which men could safely obey the commands of natural law, commands which, in the public domain, they received in the form of the civil laws. But Hobbes's only concern was that men should obey the decrees of the sovereign. He was interested in the performance of the sovereign's laws, not in the moral intentions of the subject, whereas it was precisely man's intentions which interested Rousseau, for they alone are the measure of his morals. Paradoxically then one might say that in borrowing from Hobbes, one of Rousseau's principal aims was to do away with the need for a Leviathan, by neutralizing men's

[64] *MS. de Genève, V.* I, p. 494.

[65] *V.* II, p. 122.

[66] This sovereign was absolute to the extent that even the spiritual power was made subordinate to the temporal power. Both Rousseau and Hobbes agreed that were this not so the spiritual power would constitute a second will in the state, or, if each were free to interpret the Scriptures for himself, there would be a multiplicity of differing wills which would distract the people and prevent the sovereign from exercising his prerogatives to the full. Sooner or later this would necessarily lead to the dissolution of the state. In his chapter on the 'Civil Religion' in the *Contrat Social*, Rousseau for once praises Hobbes when he says: 'De tous les auteurs chrétiens, le philosophe Hobbes est le seul qui ait bien vu le mal et le remède, qui ait osé proposer de réunir les deux têtes de l'aigle, et de tout ramener à l'unité politique, sans laquelle jamais État ni gouvernement ne sera bien constitué. Mais il a dû voir que l'esprit dominateur du Christianisme était incompatible avec son système, et que l'intérêt du prêtre serait toujours plus fort que celui de l'État. Ce n'est pas tant ce qu'il y a d'horrible et de faux dans sa politique, que ce qu'il y a de juste et de vrai, qui l'a rendue odieuse' (*V.* II, p. 127).

self-destructive passions and thus paving the way for the fulfilment of their perfectibility. For Rousseau realized early on that perfectibility, though he had described it in the *Discours* as a natural faculty of man, was not something which, once released on man's emergence from the first state of nature, carried on on its own. Moral progress was not written into the historical process. On the contrary, beyond a certain point 'progress' was regressive. What was needed then was a conscious intervention in the historical process by the will of man that would correct this tendency and set perfectibility on the right road again. Hobbes on the other hand was not concerned with effecting any moral change in man, with educating the citizen to seek the good, for he believed that man's nature, as he had described it as existing in the state of nature, was permanent and ineradicable. 'I put for a general inclination of all mankind [he said in the *Leviathan*], a perpetual and restless desire of power after power, that ceaseth only in death'.[67] Rousseau's conviction was just the opposite. His belief was that if one could change society for the better, one could change man for the better. The problem, a moral one, was, in the first instance, a political one. As he put it in the early draft of the *Contrat Social:* 'Nous ne commençons proprement à devenir hommes qu'après avoir été citoyens'.[68]

In laying down the structure of a state which would bring these citizens into being, Rousseau drew inspiration from the very man whom earlier he had denounced as a sophist. It is our hope that in attempting to acknowledge on Rousseau's behalf a debt which, for reasons best known to himself, he neglected to acknowledge, we have been able not only to do justice to the genius of Hobbes, but to set in a clearer perspective the genius — we would say the greater genius — of Rousseau himself.

[67] *L*, p. 64.
[68] *MS. de Genève, V.* I, p. 453.

16

R. J. NORTH

Alexandre Weill

THE name of Alexandre Weill occurs frequently in the work of critics dealing with mid-nineteenth century writers. Denis Saurat in his *La Religion de Victor Hugo*[1] suggested that Weill played an important part in forming Hugo's ideas, introducing him to the doctrines of the Jewish Cabbala. P. Berret in his introduction to *La Légende des Siècles*[2] also discusses this point and in a subsequent article[3] suggests a reciprocal influence of Hugo on Weill. Biographers of Heine refer to the same man as Heine's friend in Paris and his intermediary with the German press during the 1840s; using Weill's *Souvenirs intimes de Henri Heine*[4] as a source, they are divided in their attitude to the author. Nerval scholars mention Weill as his friend and correspondent.[5] In *Le Socialisme et le Romantisme en France*,[6] H. J. Hunt quotes Weill's articles in *La Démocratie pacifique* to illustrate the attitude and aesthetic doctrines of Fourierist critics and further suggests that Weill may have been the agent of a reconciliation between Hugo and the Fourierists.[7] Nor is it only in these contexts that Weill's name appears; he figures in Nadar's *Panthéon*; he was known in the literary circles which met at Le Divan Lepelletier, the café Tabourey (Baudelaire, Babou, Banville, Poulet-Malassis, Leconte de Lisle, etc.), and the Brasserie des Martyrs (Monselet, Champfleury, Bouilhet, etc.);[8] newspapers, memoirs and correspondence of the period show that his biting pamphlets, his preaching of a new religion from 1855 to his death in 1899, and his denunciation of contemporary 'immorality' brought him notoriety, criticism and friends, though few converts.

When Weill's career is examined more closely and attention is paid to

---

[1] Paris, Hachette, 1929, 19 et seq.
[2] Éd. des Grands Écrivains Français, Paris, 1925; cf. also *La Philosophie de Victor Hugo*, Paris, Paulin, 1910, 47–48.
[3] *Revue Juive de Genève*, jan.–fév., 1934.
[4] Paris, 1883.
[5] Cf. correspondence in G. de Nerval: *Œuvres*, I, Pléiade, Paris, 1952.
[6] Oxford, 1935.
[7] Op. cit., 253.
[8] A. Delvau, *Histoire anecdotique des cafés et cabarets de Paris*, Paris, 1862, 97 et seq., 187 et seq.

him as a man rather than as a witness living in the shadow of the great, as a writer with views of his own rather than as a source of information about others, he emerges as a prolific though repetitious writer whose output included stories, plays and verse, political and philosophical treatises as well as articles in the French and German press. Journalism apart, his published works number over a hundred and fifty titles. While it cannot be claimed that he was a major artist or thinker, his development and ideas are of some general interest and, in this article, I propose to give a brief account of the man and his writings, as well as some information concerning his relations with Hugo.

Born on 10th May, 1811, in the village of Schirhofen, near Strasbourg, Alexandre Weill was the eldest son in a large Jewish peasant family. His father, Leopold, had been born in the same village but, on the Prussian invasion of Alsace in 1792 in which the grandfather was killed, he had fled into the Duchy of Baden, first working as a farm hand, later becoming a cattle dealer. After some ten years of exile, Leopold returned to his village and in 1805 married Gidel, the daughter of Rabbi Abraham Keller-meister of Bischeim. He soon became known and respected as an honest and hardworking dealer though he never seems to have known real prosperity. The family was devout and it was early decided that Alexandre should become a rabbi; his training began at the age of nine at a school in Hatten; later he studied in the newly opened school at Schirhofen. When he was just thirteen and had already begun to read the lessons and sing in the synagogue services, he one day had a vision and heard a voice telling him to go forth into the world. Leaving home for Metz, he sought a teacher who would inspire him, but in vain. He went to Nancy and from there to Marmoutier, where he stayed to study for a year. Then his father called him home to help with his trade but the hard life and his father's bullying drove him to rebellion. With his mother's connivance, he left home again to continue his studies, this time at Frankfurt, which for the major part of the next ten years was to be his home.

He kept himself by giving lessons and by singing in the synagogue to supplement the organized charity by which the Jewish community sup-ported its rabbinical students. His interests began to broaden and he started to read widely, literature and philosophy, in French and in German. As a result his respect for the dogmatic instruction of his teachers and for the Talmud began to diminish. An unhappy love affair and a serious illness that affected his singing voice seem also to have played some part in changing the pattern of his life. In 1832 he returned home for a time, but, though he played his part in the synagogue and in family rites, he found village life and the marriage proposed for him distasteful. The father, realising that he was unlikely now to become a rabbi, grew impatient with his son, who seemed to him idle and useless. So Weill returned to Frankfurt:

> Décidé plus que jamais à ne jamais me marier avec une juive orthodoxe, sentant vaguement que me faire rabbin, ce serait accepter une vie de tartufferies et de duperies, je ne songeai, dès le lendemain de mon retour à Frankfurt, qu'à gagner assez d'argent pour donner un démenti aux prédictions de mon père, et prouver à ma mère qu'elle n'avait pas fait en vain tant de sacrifices pour son fils.[9]

Continuing to study and to give lessons, he began to write: poems, plays, stories, sometimes in French, sometimes in German. Family and village life, Jewish customs, childhood love affairs, his early schooling and the occasional outbursts of hostility from Jew-baiting Christians provided him with material for his *Contes* as well as for the *Mémoires* he was to write in old age. His way of life became less austere, more 'bohemian', and led his teachers to reprimand him for lack of seriousness and religious zeal. He fell ill again, and again in love; his religious doubts grew and at last he abandoned all thought of becoming a rabbi. For a time he seriously considered becoming an opera singer — a possibility that was to tempt him on more than one occasion during his early struggles. He gave up the idea at this time, he says, on realizing that the singer is but an instrument in the hands of others. University studies, more liberal than his Talmudic instruction, tempted him and he went off to Heidelberg, only to find no more satisfaction in the lectures there than in the teaching of the rabbis.

From about 1835, he had been in touch with Charles Durand, the editor of the *Journal de Francfort* to which he had contributed news and gossip as well as items from the German press. He had even circulated his own Sunday journal, *Iris*, for some six months. During the same period he was becoming known as a correspondent and a contributor of translations to a number of German papers, including the *Allgemeine Zeitung* of Augsburg, the *Deutsche Courier* of Stuttgart, the *Elegante Welt* of Leipzig, as well as Gutzkow's *Telegraph* which published Weill's story *Stasi* in 1838. In November 1837 Gutzkow invited him to become his assistant and to move from Frankfurt to Hamburg with the *Telegraph*,[10] but Weill refused, though he was to remain in touch with Gutzkow for the next

---

[9] *Ma Jeunesse*, Paris, 1888, 321.
[10] Cf. letter in Weill, *Briefe hervorragender verstorbener Männer Deutschlands*, Zürich, 1889, 16–17.

twenty-five years.[11] He became friendly with Laube and others of the Young German movement and after writing an article in praise of *Robert le Diable* also met Meyerbeer, an acquaintanceship that was to endure until the 1860s.

He was therefore well connected in German literary circles and had a modest reputation when in 1838 he met Dumas and Nerval who stayed in Frankfurt for some weeks. (According to Weill, Dumas laid successful siege to Madame Durand.[12]) It was Nerval who encouraged the young Alsacian to go to Paris and when, in the winter of 1838-9, the Durands moved there, Weill willingly accepted an offer to accompany them as Charles Durand's secretary.

Writing his memoirs some forty years later, Weill says he arrived in Paris in 1836 and Saurat and Hunt have both accepted this date. Unfortunately, Weill's memory was defective and his dates are often inaccurate. It is clear from the Nerval correspondence[13] that it was in September 1838 that Nerval met Dumas and the Durands in Frankfurt. Since Weill says that he first went to Paris with Durand who suggested the move some three months after the Nerval visit[14] it seems clear that Weill did not in fact arrive in Paris until late in the winter of 1838-9, a date which fits certain other facts.

Soon after reaching Paris, Weill wrote to Heine presenting himself and asking for advice about his writings; Hirth dates this letter 16 March 1839.[15] Further, Weill tells us[16] that he wrote similarly to Hugo and the undated letter No. 1 printed below seems to be Hugo's reply; it was probably written in the spring of 1839 for Weill says that when, in reply to the invitation, he first visited Hugo, the other guests included Spontini and Gautier. We know[17] that these two had not met by 22 April 1839, the date of Spontini's letter thanking Hugo for finding him a librettist (Gautier), and asking him to arrange a meeting. Consequently the first meeting of Hugo and Weill may be assumed to have taken place in the late spring of 1839.

This is not the place for a renewed discussion of Hugo's debt to Weill but it seems worth while printing in appendix the known correspondence between them and commenting on their relationship. The second letter

---

[11] Cf. op. cit. and J. Dresch, 'Une correspondance inédite de Karl Gutzkow, de Madame d'Agoult et d'Alexandre Weill,' *Revue germanique*, jan.-fév., 1906.
[12] *Mes Années de Bohème*, Paris, 1888, 611-12.
[13] Op. cit., 769-75.
[14] *Mes Années de Bohème*, 616.
[15] Heine, *Briefe*, ed. F. E. Hirth, Mainz, 1950, II, 293.
[16] Weill, *Introduction à mes Mémoires*, Paris, 1890, 101 et seq.
[17] C. Daubray, *Victor Hugo et ses correspondants*, Paris, 1947, 258-9.

of 16 May 1840 shows Hugo willing to enlist support in an effort to ensure the success of *Les Rayons et les Ombres*, the others thank Weill for letters or works he sent: for example, the letter of 1856 is almost certainly an acknowledgement of the receipt of Weill's *Mystères de la création* (1855), a work which figured in Hugo's library and which is an important piece of evidence in the Saurat argument.

While it is clear that Weill remained in touch with Hugo until the 1860s, the paucity of correspondence and its tone suggest no great intimacy. Weill himself says 'Hugo était un dispensateur d'éloges universels, ne laissant pas le moindre témoignage sans réponse' but his irony deserts him when, speaking of the 'dozen' letters he had from Hugo he refers to the letter of 22 January as 'une exception à ses nombreux autographes. Le grand poète, en très peu de lignes, sort de la banalité et daigne, contre son habitude, par un trait d'esprit concis, me dire une amabilité qui témoigne de sa sincérité.'[18] It is highly probable that Weill would have given much more space to Hugo in his memoirs had the relationship involved more than occasional encounters. His friendship with Heine drew from him a volume of *Souvenirs*; of Hugo personally he says little more than of Balzac whom he admits meeting only occasionally. Moreover, Hugo's last letter, and Weill's references to his work after 1852 show a common recognition of deep differences of opinion. In 1837, before he met Weill, we find Hugo already writing lines that foreshadow the system set out in *Ce que dit la Bouche d'Ombre*:

> Le végétal devient animal sans qu'il y ait un seul anneau rompu dans la chaîne qui commence à la pierre, dont l'homme est le milieu mystérieux, et dont les derniers chaînons, invisibles et palpables pour nous remontent jusqu'à Dieu.[19]

Moreover, there is little hint of the Cabbala or of a Mosaic system in the writings of Weill during his early years in Paris when he was still in revolt against Rabbinical lore. The only two references I have found to such ideas as metempsychosis occur in later articles; in the first,[20] the tone is mocking: 'La transmigration des âmes produit des effets moins tristes mais beaucoup plus ridicules. Rien de plus fréquent, à en croire M. Cassou, que de voir des bonzes chinois courir après des canards et les soigner eux-mêmes, durant de longues années comme les dépositaires des âmes de leurs pères.' The second reference is more serious in tone: 'Je crois qu'il y a dans la création une échelle de gradation qui conduit

---

[18] *Mémoires*, 95.
[19] *En Voyage*, ed. Imprimerie nationale, Paris, 1910, II, 131.
[20] Review of C. Cassou: *Histoire des Religions de la Chine*, in *Corsaire-Satan*, 1 Oct. 1845.

directement à la divinité. On n'est jamais assez bon pour ne pas devenir meilleur; on n'a jamais assez d'esprit pour pouvoir se passer de celui des autres: et à moins d'être Dieu, on n'est jamais assez haut pour ne pouvoir plus monter. Il y a donc, ce me semble, un système de transformation permanente dans le monde. D'après moi, le minéral peut devenir planète, la planète peut devenir animal, l'animal, oui, l'animal, peut arriver jusqu'à l'homme, l'homme à son tour se transforme en ange, et l'ange se concentre en Dieu.'[21] How important to Weill was this view, expressed in 1847, is not clear, but it seems that he had not adopted the idea of punishment through descent in the scale of beings, as he was to do in 1855, in *Mystères de la Création*.

It may be, as Saurat argues, that during their conversation in Brussels in 1852,[22] Hugo learnt from Weill the central principle of the Cabbalist view of creation which somewhat modified his own earlier ideas and influenced him in the writing of *Les Contemplations*, but there is little evidence that Weill's influence was continuous from 1839 onwards or that it was at all considerable.

During the winter of 1839–40 Weill was away from Paris accompanying the violinist Bériot on his tour. He stayed some time in Vienna with Gérard de Nerval and claims to have helped him with translations.[23] (J. Richer suggests that Weill's mistress Rosa may have been the original of Vahby.)[24] He then went on to Prague and to Budapest, still presumably with Bériot. His writing was clearly not remunerative and he was seeking his living in any way that offered. Nerval's letter[25] informing Alphonse Karr, the editor of *Le Figaro*, that Weill would be calling on him suggests that in March 1840 Weill was still trying to establish himself as a German press correspondent in Paris. He was again away from Paris from mid-1841 to the end of 1842, travelling in Germany: visiting Carlsruhe and Berlin, taking the cure at Wiesbaden to recover from an attack of measles which damaged his eyesight, and staying some time in Frankfurt.

From 1838 to 1847 he divided his energies between travelling, journalism, history and writing stories. Journalism gave him a meagre living; he contributed to *La France musicale* edited by the Escudier brothers, translated some Dürer memoirs for Eugène Piot, exercised his wit and reviewed books in *Le Corsaire Satan* and he also campaigned in *La Démocratie pacifique* in favour of Fourierist principles. To its pages, as well as to *La*

[21] *A propos de la Guerre des Paysans*, in *Démocratie pacifique*, 13 fév., 1847.
[22] Cf. *Mémoires*, 124, and D. Saurat, loc. cit.
[23] Weill, *Gérard de Nerval, souvenirs intimes*, in *L'Evénement*, 16 avril, 1881.
[24] J. Richer, *G. de Nerval*, Coll. Seghers, Paris, 1950, 43.
[25] Nerval, op. cit., 816.

Phalange and to *La Revue indépendante*, he contributed accounts of events in Germany while in the German press he wrote of Paris and served the cause of Heine. In the mid-1840s he was becoming better known and was on good terms with such different figures as Nerval, Eugène Sue, Victor Considérant (a witness with M. Ancelot at his wedding on 15 April 1847), Hippolyte Babou, Nadar and others.

However, the writing of stories seemed his chief hope of literary celebrity. The first had been published in German, as we have seen, in 1838; *Le Corsaire* published *Selmel* in 1845 and in 1847 a collected edition in German was honoured by a preface from Heine (his wedding present to Weill, so he said). Rather loftily, but with considerable penetration, he wrote:

M. Alexandre Weill, l'auteur *des Idylles alsaciennes*, auxquelles nous vouons quelques lignes d'introduction, prétend avoir été le premier créateur de ce genre. Cette prétention est parfaitement justifiée, au dire d'un grand nombre de mes amis, qui ajoutent que l'auteur en question, non seulement a écrit les premières Nouvelles de village mais encore les meilleures. Devenu étranger aux chefs d'œuvre de la littérature actuelle d'outre-Rhin, il m'est impossible de décider en dernier ressort par mon propre jugement. Nous ne pensons pas pouvoir assigner un haut rang à ce genre de littérature de village, et, quant à la priorité de la production, nous n'aurons garde d'en surestimer la valeur. L'essentiel, c'est que le produit littéraire devant nous est bon, extrêmement réussi, et pour ce, nous lui donnons notre approbation élogieuse et sincère, accompagnée de notre témoignage.

M. Alexandre Weill n'appartient pas à cette catégorie de poètes, avec le don inné de créer une œuvre plastique par leur imagination d'harmonie intime et réflective; mais il possède, par contre, en débordante plénitude, une rare originalité de pensées et de sentiments, un cœur enthousiaste, facile à émouvoir et une vivacité d'esprit qui, dans ses contes, font merveille, et qui donnent à toutes ses productions littéraires la saveur d'un fruit naturel. Il saisit la vie réelle dans chacune de ses manifestations momentanées, il la surprend sur le fait, et lui-même est pour ainsi dire, un daguéréotype passionné, reproduisant les phénomènes du monde extérieur avec plus ou moins de bonheur, et parfois dans une forme poétique, selon les caprices de l'inspiration.[26]

To the end of his days Weill maintained that he had invented the

---

[26] Translated by Weill, *Mes Romans*, Paris, 1886, I, iii–iv.

'Village-tale' genre and that it was Gutzkow's insistence on using the cumbrous title *Sittengemälde aus dem Elsässichen Volksleben* instead of the simpler *Dorfgeschichte* which robbed him of success and delayed his recognition as a writer. A recent historian of the 'roman rustique', R. Zellweger, agrees that Weill's work has not received the attention it merits and suggests that he should share with Auerbach some of the credit for the new trend, though the literary merits of his tales are slighter: 'C'est lui l'inventeur du petit tableau de genre champêtre. Ce qu'on trouve chez Auerbach: réalisme descriptif, silhouettes villageoises originales, Weill l'a eu avant lui. Lorsqu'en 1853 il se traduit en français, il fait encore à Paris figure de novateur.'[27] Though they may have had the merit of novelty in their day, these idyllic stories of country loves and customs are not major works of literature; they lack psychological depth and verbal felicity; their charm is that of simple emotion and naïve realism. Nor was Weill any more successful with his plays. Extracts of an *Alexandre le grand*, written in 1837, had appeared in print, but the play, like all the others that he wrote, failed to achieve performance. His verse, of which he wrote a great deal, much of it dogmatic or narrative, similarly fails to rise above the pedestrian, as this example illustrates:

> Quand l'amour est entré dans un cœur solitaire,
> Dieu descend et se dresse un autel sur la terre.
> Un ange y vient poser de l'ambre et de l'encens,
> Et le feu qu'il allume embrase tous les sens,
> Et porte au créateur, sous les traits d'une femme,
> Tous les bouillons du sang, tous les parfums de l'âme!
> Une part d'infini, dans l'amour reflété,
> S'incarne alors dans l'homme et devient vérité.[28]

Weill said himself 'La pensée seule me dicte et m'impose parfois des vers';[29] it is to the reason that he appeals, not to the imagination. Certainly to a post-Romantic audience his verse never seems poetic. Heine's assessment is accurate: Weill lacked creative imagination though he never lacked ideas and enthusiasm.

However, in a very different genre, he achieved some success in 1845 with the publication of *La Guerre des Paysans*, shortly followed by *La Guerre des Anabaptistes*. Eugène Sue, he says, offered him 1,000 francs towards the cost of publication but in fact *La Phalange* published both

---

[27] *Les Débuts du roman rustique*, Paris, 1941, 40. The first of Weill's stories appeared in French in 1845, not 1853.

[28] *Amours et blasphèmes*, Brussels, 1862, 44.

[29] Op. cit. Preface.

works in instalments between 1845 and 1847. Armand Marrast, editor of *Le National* had encouraged Weill to write an account of this German political and social revolution since it was little known in France. The work proved something of a revelation and Weill cites Balzac in particular as having declared himself deeply impressed.[30] Weill interprets the Peasant's Revolt as an anticipation of the principles of 1789 and a demonstration of the power of thinkers and artists to shape events in spite of politicians.

Between 1845 and the second edition in 1860 there occurred a marked change in his views; in the 1860 preface he admits that the excesses of the peasants aroused in him some disgust with 'les rêves ultra-socialistes' though he protests his loyalty to the 'Sainte Cause' of all honest men which he had been accused of deserting. This change is not a simple reaction against revolution and republicanism but the outcome of a revaluation of principles and it led to a series of personal statements on politics, religion and morals.

His publishing success, marriage in 1847 to Mlle Agathina Marx whose thriving 'commerce de modes' kept both in comfort thereafter, and the 1848 revolution with its aftermath brought a change not only in Weill's life but also in his attitude. After marriage, his somewhat bohemian way of life gave way to a more settled existence. His friendship with Heine cooled, for Mme Weill was unimpressed by Heine and his wife Mathilde. Weill's visits to the household grew rarer; in October 1850 Heine told Laube he no longer saw Weill,[31] though he mentioned him in later letters until, in May 1853, he wrote to his mother that Weill no longer crossed his threshold, 'thank God!'[32] A squabble with Mathilde and differences of opinion with the sick and querulous poet seem to have led to this final breach. Weill's enthusiasm for the Young Germans as well as for Fourierism with its call for the emancipation of the flesh also waned with time and with the experience of love and companionship in marriage. Mme Weill indeed seems to have given him constant support and encouragement in his writing and thinking while moderating the intemperance of his sallies and his impetuosity.

Though before the 1848 revolution, Weill had thought of becoming a député, enrolled in the Fourierist ranks along with Considérant and others, he now modified his opinions. '[Cela] a été pour moi un coup de foudre ... dès le lendemain de leur victoire violente je les ai quittés.'[33] A

[30] *Mémoires*, 139.
[31] Heine, *Briefe*, no. 1047, vol. III, 232.
[32] Op. cit., no. 1196, vol. III, 470.
[33] *Au Président*, Paris, 1849, 14.

series of lively pamphlets on political affairs issued from his pen. On the appearance of Ledru-Rollin's circular, in an open letter which Girardin published prominently in *La Presse* under the headline *Une question de vie ou de mort*, he protested vigorously that liberty seemed to be the first casualty of the revolution:

> J'ai toujours été républicain, plutôt trop que trop peu. J'ai usé mon esprit et ma plume en faveur des travailleurs, alors que le *National* les traitait du bas de son talon, mais je commence à croire qu'il était plus facile d'être républicain sous Louis-Philippe, que n'importe quoi sous la République. En un mot, il paraît que rien n'est moins libre que le règne de la liberté ... Mais, souverains nouveau-nés, votre république n'est même pas sanctionnée par la majorité de peuple français.
>
> Elle le sera, mais jusqu'à présent elle n'existe que par la raison du plus fort, c'est-à-dire par le hasard des armes et de la violence. OR, fût-elle même reconnue par la majorité, ce dont je ne doute pas, la minorité a le droit absolu de penser ce qu'elle veut.[34]

In the May elections, Weill stood as an independent candidate, campaigning vaguely for freedom and justice but he was not elected. Later he was to declare that the incompetence, selfishness and pusillanimity of the provisional government and of the Assembly led directly to the success of Louis Bonaparte and so to the Second Empire. In 1849, he addressed a warning to the President: while government must replace anarchy, power must be used in the service of Justice and of the people:

> Malheur à vous si vous avez la vaine gloriole de la popularité. Justice, devoir et sévérité, c'est là l'unique devise d'un chef du pouvoir. ... Quand vous aurez appelé autour de vous tous les hommes de talent et de caractère, ... quand l'ordre sera rétabli, la paix assurée et le travail revenu, vous finirez par où la révolution de février aurait dû commencer. En vous adressant à la France, et avec la ferme volonté de lui obéir, vous lui demanderez et elle vous dira par la nouvelle Assemblée nationale *ce que tout le monde pense*.[35]

The political ferment of these years was followed by general disillusion as the Republic was swallowed up by the Empire. The government of men of talent did not materialize nor did the enlightened paternalism which would ensure order and liberty for all. Socialism and Fourierism seemed defeated: Considérant retired from public life in 1852; Louis Blanc and others were in exile, painfully maintaining their ideals and attacking tyranny from afar. Weill, turning against the Empire, turned also against

[34] *La Presse*, 12 mars, 1848.
[35] *Au Président*, 66.

the writers and thinkers of the early nineteenth century whose precept and example had, in his view, corrupted France. For four years he wrote little, devoting himself to rethinking the problems of politics and religion and re-examining the teachings of his youth.

> Après la révolution de 1848 et ses journées d'anarchie, j'avais cru un instant à une royauté légitime compatible avec les principes de '89 . . . Rêves et illusions! . . . La réalité, la lugubre réalité détruisit et mit à néant du coup, non seulement ces rêves mais toute ma science, toute mon expérience, tout mon avenir! toute ma foi, tout mon culte pour le génie! . . . Le désespoir dans l'âme, la révolte dans l'esprit, je me mis à scruter, à analyser, à juger, à critiquer.[36]

Once he had formulated his system, Weill devoted the remainder of his life to its promulgation and to denunciation of contemporary abuses. He continued to correspond with a wide circle of acquaintances (including Louis Veuillot, Emile Ollivier, Jules Simon, Ludovic Halévy, John Lemoine, Francis Magnard) and to the Weill salon came many friends. Juliette Adam wrote:

> J'aimais Alexandre Weill, c'est chez lui que je suis allée à mes premières mondanités à Paris.[37]

An earlier friend, Madame Ancelot, had described him thus:

> . . . Vous remarquez des yeux d'une vivacité et d'une profondeur qui vous attirent, un accent légèrement étranger donne quelque chose de singulier à des paroles déjà par elles-mêmes fort originales; de quoi que vous parliez, il émet une idée nouvelle à chaque phrase en vous répondant . . . Il a écrit un nombre infini d'ouvrages pleins d'idées ingénieuses sans compter ce qu'il a semé de ces idées-là dans les salons et les journaux.[38]

Among the few outstanding events of his later life was his stay in Brussels in the winter of 1864–5. Having spoken indiscreetly of Napoleon III, he left Paris to work in Brussels on his books. While there he gave some lectures which attracted satirical comment in the Parisian press[39] and a caustic caricature from Baudelaire of 'Alexandre Weill . . . proférant des phrases incongrues'.[40] He also made the acquaintance of Arthur Stevens, the art-critic, and of the Collart family. (Marie Collart's 'realist'

---

[36] *Mémoires*, 134.
[37] Unpublished letter to M. Paul Biquard, 2 nov. 1926.
[38] V. Ancelot, *Un Salon de Paris, 1824–1864*, Paris, 1866, 190.
[39] *La Petite Revue*, 21 janv., 1865.
[40] Cf. *Baudelaire, Documents iconographiques*, ed. C. Pichois et F. Ruchon, Geneva, 1960, plate 194; *v.* also the recent article of G. Blin, 'Baudelaire et Alexandre Weill,' *RHLF*, 63e année, no. 1, janv.–mars, 1963, pp. 28–45.

painting provoked him to violent criticism.) During the 'année terrible', he sent his wife to England, later joining her there and though he intended to return to France, he was compelled to stay by an accident which kept him three months in bed. His wife's death on 20 October 1878 was a grievous blow. He mourned her deeply and publicly, publishing as an example to others his verses to her and the letters they had exchanged. Thereafter, he turned to writing his memoirs, and to reissuing his works while still castigating his times. Often ill but still zealous, he corrected his proofs with the help of friends and towards the end, when he was bedridden and almost blind, dictated articles and insisted on having the newspapers read to him to keep in touch with events. His death on 18 April 1899 was announced in newspapers throughout Europe and in America.

★   ★   ★

His new ideas, first adumbrated in Les Mystères de la Création and L'Idéal of 1855, were expanded with illustration and commentary in a series of subsequent volumes and fervently proclaimed in La Parole nouvelle of 1866 — 'le livre de ma vie. C'est pour l'écrire que j'ai été créé . . . C'est la seule Parole nouvelle, à la fois Nouvelle et Vraie qui ait été dite à l'humanité depuis le Décalogue de Sinaï.'[41]

In 1847 Weill had thought that God was not external to creation, that all was in a perpetual process of becoming, that America, for example, had been created after Europe and that progress was, if not automatic, at least continuous. 'Jésus est plus près de Dieu que Moïse, Spinoza complétant Jésus, découvre une vérité de plus, et Fourier poussant la loi de Jésus et de Spinoza jusqu'à ses conséquences les plus éloignées, est plus hardi et par cela même un plus grand prophète. Il en est de même du mouvement des idées.'[42] In this interpretation evil was still something of a mystery, related perhaps to the creation's distance from the Creator with whom it sought reunion. The contradiction between a creation coextensive with God and a creation seeking reunion with God is obvious and now on re-examination Weill found this and his ideas on progress less easy to accept.

On other grounds Fourier had proved unsatisfactory: 'Il y a de grandes vérités sociales en Fourier, pas une d'elles n'a été mise en œuvre. Mais il y avait dans sa doctrine un vice rédhibitoire sur les relations entre les sexes et les familles; c'est ce vice que la France littéraire et politique a adopté en le poussant jusqu'au crime.'[43] After 1848 Weill rarely refers to Fourier; he quotes Spinoza and Voltaire but relies mainly on the authentic

[41] Preface to 4th ed., 1872.
[42] Cf. article nov. 1847 in La Phalange VI, juill.–dec., 1847, 391–9.
[43] Mémoires, 50, note.

doctrine of Moses as he himself rediscovered and reinterpreted it: '. . . en relisant la Bible comme une œuvre humaine, j'avais à ma grande surprise et à ma grande satisfaction, trouvé que tous ces récits miraculaires du Pentateuque actuel, que tous les miracles, tout le surnaturel de ce livre sont la création d'Esra, qui . . . a créé toute une nouvelle religion . . . d'où plus tard est sorti le christianisme; qui a créé le jour du grand pardon . . .'[44] Removing these accretions, Weill restores the 'pure' Mosaic teaching.

The first sketch appears in the fragmentary *Mystères de la Création*, published as the translation of a Hebrew manuscript, given to Weill in his youth by Rabbi Lazarus ben Aaron but for many years neglected. He offers it in 1855 without comment: 'il me suffit, en exposant ces principes, d'ajouter: "S'ils sont vrais, ils resteront; s'ils sont faux, ils passeront".' Saurat has identified the central principle as Cabbalistic but there is a problem of authorship. In 1896, Weill published *Lois et Mystères de la Création*, referring to the 1855 *Mystères* text as the first edition and as the source of all his subsequent thinking. However, the two texts differ markedly: the basic ideas, though the same, are quite differently expressed and ordered; there is amplification of some points and the lacunae of 1855 have been filled in. In the 1896 Preface, Weill says rather strangely: 'Si je n'ai pas publié plus tôt ce livre, petit par apparence, mais grand par ses vérités, c'est que je voulais d'abord rétablir avec les textes irréfragables, traduits de l'hébreu, les principes fondamentaux, religieux et philoso-phiques de Moïse.' It seems likely that, as Saurat suspected,[45] the 'transla-tion' is an original work by Weill, based on principles he had heard his teachers discuss and which he had rediscovered. By publishing it in fragmentary form as a translation, he may have hoped to give it authority and command attention. A later remark is relevant here: '. . . jamais feuille française n'a publié un compte rendu sérieux sur aucun de mes nombreux livres, que j'ai écrits avec le sang de mon âme, dans lesquels il ne se trouve pas une ligne d'autrui sans que j'aie cité le nom. Souvent même, honteux de la source toujours ruisselante de mes idées, je les ai attribuées à d'autres, bien qu'elles aient jailli de moi.'[46] Certainty is almost unattainable but whatever the status of the *Mystères*, Weill was to remain faithful to its ideas.

According to this doctrine[47] *God ens causa sui* did not exist before the creation; he is coexistent but not identical with it. 'Tout n'est pas Dieu mais Dieu est en tout.' Infinite Force, he is obedient to his own unyielding

[44] *Souvenirs intimes de Henri Heine*, Paris, 1883, 22.
[45] Op. cit., 28.
[46] *Le Nouveau Sinaï*, Paris, 1880, 7.
[47] The summary which follows is based, except where otherwise stated, on *Lois et Mystères de la Création*, 1896.

laws, and may be imagined as 'centre universel dont la circonférence n'est nulle part' or as 'axe central dont tous les rayons sont droits . . . infinis, divergents d'un bout dans la création, convergeant tous vers l'axe central qui est partout'. The act of creation is for Weill the Cabbalist 'withdrawal' in which the primal pure substance that is God brought into existence inferior beings of impure composition. For no Force can create another which is equal to itself. 'Dieu lui-même ne serait pas Dieu, la force toute-puissante ne serait pas infinie s'il n'y avait pas des Forces inférieures. Dieu se connaît et se juge puisqu'il se fait des lois. Mais pour se connaître et se juger, il a fallu établir une hiérarchie des comparaisons. CAR TOUTE RAISON N'EST QUE COMPARAISON.'[48] It follows that light has darkness as its contrary, goodness evil, beauty ugliness. These contraries, which are the absence of light, goodness and so on, do not exist for themselves, but 'pour servir de contraste à connaître et admirer le beau et le bien'. 'Pour juger la lumière bonne, il faut les ténèbres.' The existence of these contraries ensures the freedom of the creation and in particular of man to choose, for example, good rather than evil.

Man, the highest of earthly created beings, partakes of the nature of God in so far as he is soul, 'étincelle de la grande lumière centrale,' but he is also body which is matter and mortal. He bears witness to God, seeks reunion with God and has something of God's power to inform matter with soul. 'Il peut spiritualiser la matière et rentrer dans le cercle divin autonome plus grand qu'il n'en est sorti.' Weill goes so far as to say: 'L'homme en mangeant la bête, s'en assimile la chair et la transforme en substance pure. Autrement ce serait une cruauté que de tuer un animal. Mais ces existences n'ont pas d'autre but: vivre et mourir pour autrui. Elles gagnent par l'assimilation et la transformation.'[49] The contrary is also true, for the simple pure substance can be contaminated, corrupted and made more material: 'La substance intellectuelle autonome peut être sinon tout à fait éteinte, du moins tachée, rayée, amoindrie par les souillures de la matière.'[50] 'Il n'y a pas d'autre vrai mal sur la terre que l'esprit que l'homme maté-rialise.'[51]

The economy of the creation requires that the quantity of soul should not diminish but that God the source should be ever replenished. 'Si les hommes ne mouraient pas, Dieu mourrait.' 'A la mort, il fait nuit entière pour le corps qui retombe en poudre, c'est-à-dire en matière chaotique prête à être transformée, car cette matière première n'a jamais augmenté,

[48] *Mystères de la Création*, Paris, 1855, 45.
[49] *La Parole Nouvelle*, Paris, 1892, 92.
[50] Op. cit., 85.
[51] Op. cit., 189.

elle ne peut qu'être repétrie et métamorphosée. Mais l'âme, l'esprit, la
lumière, qui lui a donné la vie et la raison ne meurt pas, ne saurait mourir.
Elle va dès lors éclairer, animer un autre corps.'[52]
There is a scale of beings (and Weill does not exclude the possibility of
beings higher than man) whose ranking is determined by the quantity of
'pure substance' in the individual: 'La différence entre ces êtres et l'homme
ne serait pas dans la *qualité* de la substance, mais dans la *quantité*, l'un
contenant une plus grande dose d'essence simple et divine que l'autre,
absolument comme la différence entre l'homme et l'animal, entre l'animal
et la plante, entre la plante et le minéral.'[53] Since man can transform
matter, he can, it might seem, rise in the scale of beings. But Weill is
undecided about reincarnation. He has no firm belief in individual immortality, maintaining the views expressed in 1845 (*v. supra*) and declaring
that the dogma of immortality causes men to adore animals and to submit
to injustice.[54] None the less on occasion he admits the possibility of personal reincarnation: 'Tu pourras une fois née, refuser de vivre; mais, morte,
tu ne sais pas si tu resteras morte ou si tu renaîtras ange, homme, femme,
cheval, arbre ou caillou.'[55] In fact, his insistence on Justice almost compels
him to the view that the next state of being is determined by merit in
the present state: 'Le progrès de l'âme humaine, après la mort du corps,
ne serait autre chose . . . qu'une ascension vers la vie de l'éther céleste, ou
une chute vers les degrés inférieurs de la vie animale.'[56]
    In general, however, he sees punishment as falling on all men not upon
the evil-doer alone. Evil-doing harms both God and humanity nor can it
be wiped out by forgiveness, a false concept invented by Esra, nor by
Redemption through Christ, an equally erroneous belief. God, subject to
his own laws, does not intervene in creation either to punish or to pardon.
'Ce mal fait tombe quelque part. Nul pouvoir ne saurait l'arrêter.'[57] Not
only does it bring misfortune to mankind but it creates vermin, disease
and other so-called 'natural' ills. 'Si l'homme persévère dans le vice, la
terre produit des animaux venimeux et des végétaux vénéneux.'[58] These
'maux vivants', like the hereditary diseases of matter, represent the
working out in time of the inevitable punishment that follows all infrac-
tions of the divine law.
    Since all suffer from the evil-doing of the individual, society is justified

[52] Op. cit., 81–82.
[53] Op. cit., 36.
[54] Cf. *Moïse, le Talmud et l'Evangile*, Paris, 1864, 74.
[55] *Si j'avais une fille à marier*, Paris, 1860, 60.
[56] Op. cit., 102.
[57] *Ma Jeunesse*, 84.
[58] *Vérités absolues* in *La Parole nouvelle*, 5th ed., 1892, 239.

in taking severe measures to eradicate crime and drive out the criminal. Weill affirms thus the solidarity of all men and the importance both of Justice and Virtue. He goes further, claiming that the strong have a duty towards the weak: the manifest inequality of beings results from differences in *quantity* of the divine substance in each, nonetheless all are equal in rights and duties: '. . . tout être sent sa mission divine, tout être a ses droits de développement et d'expansion par la liberté de son travail . . . tous les êtres sont solidaires . . . le plus puissant ne peut jouir de sa puissance si le plus faible est opprimé . . . Tous, en effet, sortent de la même force et travaillent en vertu de la même loi . . . Leur bonheur est égal en qualité mais non en quantité.'[59]

This conviction explains why Weill is in reaction against the philanthropists, why he is fierce in his denunciation of evil, an advocate of stern repression, and almost of the Mosaic law. He preaches duties rather than rights and seeks to protect society rather than to reclaim the criminal. 'Les hommes ne sont malheureux que parce qu'ils sont injustes.'[60] 'La première chose à faire, c'est d'empêcher qu'il y ait des méchants, d'empêcher par tous les moyens qu'il puisse y avoir des hommes injustes pouvant impunément commettre des injustices.'[61]

He believes in the possibility of peace and happiness and of progress, but progress is not automatic, it is the work of man, and in particular of great men, those who are superior in soul and intellect to their fellows and who, therefore, seeing God's law more fully and more clearly, have the duty of educating and leading mankind. Though Weill shares the Romantic and Fourierist view of the thinker and the artist, he requires of them different teaching. 'Le progrès social, la civilisation, le règne de la Justice, et celui plus élevé de l'amour, en un mot, la marche de l'humanité est subordonnée à la somme accumulée . . . de cette force créatrice de l'art depuis que l'humanité existe.'[62] Art is a religion and the artist is a priest, but a heavy burden is laid upon the artist. His task is to guide and educate men as well as to humanize and spiritualize matter, so adding to the sum of 'essence divine' in the universe: '. . . l'artiste, plein d'essence divine lui-même, et pénétrant jusqu'à l'âme de chaque chose, s'y identifie, la vivifie, et fait refléter au dehors sa vie intérieure. L'artist en cela, non seulement transforme la matière sous sa main, mais encore fait œuvre de Dieu.'[63] Moreover, he must set an example in his life as well as by his works. '. . . les peuples ne règlent pas leur vie sur celle de leurs rois et

[59] *La Parole nouvelle*, 98.
[60] *Si j'avais un fils à élever*, Paris, 1891, 164.
[61] *La Parole nouvelle*, 12.
[62] *L'Art est une religion*, Paris, 1892, 17.
[63] *La Parole nouvelle*, 162.

empereurs, mais sur celle des hommes et poètes de génie. Et si les faits et gestes de ces hommes, dans leurs écrits, et *surtout dans leur vie publique et privée*,[64] ne sont pas conformes à la Justice et à la Vertu, la grande masse, se prévalant de ces exemples, s'affranchit bien vite de tout devoir, de toute vertu, de tout patriotisme, qui est le sacrifice de l'intérêt et de la passion au profit de la nation.'[65]

From 1855 onwards Weill spared no one who sinned against his doctrines. He denounced the financiers and speculators who exploited the poor and the weak;[66] he campaigned against Jesuits and against the Catholic church for its doctrine of forgiveness of sins and for its social attitude;[67] he fought for women's rights, against prostitution and in favour of marriage;[68] he fulminated against atheism and racial intolerance;[69] in particular, he attacked the great who failed in their duty and the artists who taught sentimentality instead of love and virtue, who emphasized the material and sordid instead of the ideal and the spiritual, who were responsible for the moral bankruptcy of France made manifest in 1870 and thereafter.[70]

This is why Weill judges Hugo as a great poet who failed the people. The success of *Hernani* is a national calamity;[71] only in *Les Châtiments* does Hugo serve the ideal. *Les Misérables* lacks social insight and is but a '*Banditenroman*'.[72] 'Moi, qui attaque Hugo, je le mets plus haut que tous ces hurleurs de bravos. Je prétends et maintiens que ce sont les œuvres de ce poète qui ont créé l'état social actual. C'est lui, c'est son génie puissant mais démoralisateur qui a affolé toutes les raisons, corrompu toutes les consciences . . .' Hugo is 'un grand enfant qui, de sa vie, n'a eu une notion, ni d'un principe, ni d'une idée, qui n'a jamais su ce que c'est qu'un devoir, que la raison, que la logique, qui s'est toujours cru au-dessus de la nature et de la loi, qui, j'en suis certain, s'admire lui-même, se croyant son propre créateur.'[73] Balzac fares little better, 'Un immense talent, un honnête homme, mais stérile comme poète, corrupteur comme penseur.'[74] Flaubert fares much worse: *Madame Bovary* extols vice, corrupts morals and so

[64] Weill's italics.
[65] *Souvenirs intimes de Henri Heine*, 10.
[66] *Les croquants financiers*, Paris, 1861.
[67] Cf. *Hommes noirs, qui êtes-vous?* Paris, 1869; *A nous deux. Défi à M. Dupanloup*, Paris 1868; *Ni Papisme ni Athéisme*, Paris, 1872.
[68] Cf. *Si j'avais une fille à marier*.
[69] *La France catholique et athée, réponse à 'La France juive'*, Paris, 1886. *Epîtres cinglantes à M. Drumont*, Paris, 1888.
[70] Cf. *Mes Contemporains*, Paris, 1864. *Mon Syllabus contre le XIXe siècle*, Paris, 1865.
[71] *La Méprise d'Hernani*, Paris, 1867, i.
[72] Cf. letter to Gutzkow, July 1863, cit. Dresch, op. cit.
[73] *Méprise d'Hernani*, iv.
[74] *Mon Syllabus*, II, ii.

destroys France. Dumas' *Dame aux Camélias* glamorizes prostitution and gives false ideas of love and marriage. Zola is poisonous: 'Si l'Allemagne nous a alcoolisés de son verjus de Wagner, nous l'avons bel et bien éborgné de notre vitriol de Zola qui heureusement y est aussi populaire qu'en France.'[75] Baudelaire and Gautier together do not add up to a real poet. Villiers de l'Isle Adam is a 'Tartuffe du néant.'[76] Among the few who escape Weill's censure is Lamartine for though he judges *Jocelyn* philosophically erroneous and Lamartine's presidency lacking in principle, *La Chute d'un Ange* is a brave attempt, 'le livre le plus sublime du XIXe siècle'.[77] It is evident that this application to art of moral criticism continues the strictures of the Saint Simonians and the Fourierists which Hunt has examined but the principles on which it is based have changed and the tone is fiercer. Well might Robert Dreyfus call Weill 'le prophète du Faubourg Saint Honoré'.[78]

It is remarkable that this 'Justicier du XIXe siècle', as he called himself, remained so well-liked, though understandable that posterity should have neglected him. Charles Monselet wrote of him: ' "Je ne prends pas la parole, c'est la parole qui me prend," a dit un jour M. Weill; et depuis ce temps la parole ne l'a point laissé tranquille. Cette imagination et ce tempérament me surprennent au dernier point, . . . j'ai lu [ses œuvres], j'ai toujours été ou charmé, ou intéressé, ou choqué, mais je n'ai jamais été ennuyé.'[79] Comments of this kind and the number of his correspondents suggest that Weill's evident sincerity robbed his criticism of its personal sting. There seems no reason to doubt the general accuracy of the accounts he gives of his arguments with Hugo, Balzac, Heine and others; they listened to his objections and disagreed radically with his criteria and his opinions but they acknowledged his good faith and the honesty of his intentions. However mistaken his principles, he was a man of integrity and without malice. For these reasons, Weill is to be distinguished from the waspish and venal journalists of his day and to be likened more to Saint-Simon, Fourier, Leroux and other men greater than he, but perhaps no less wayward and muddled, men in whom reforming zeal and mystical fervour were not matched by equal sensitivity and intellectual coherence.

I am much indebted to M. Paul Biquard and to M. Charles Lehmann, relatives of Alexandre Weill, as well as to the Curator of the Maison Victor Hugo in Paris for making documents available to me.

[75] *Julie Verrier* . . . Paris, 1890, ix et seq.
[76] 'Le Pessimisme, une blague ou une folie,' in *Les Petites Nouvelles*, 28 oct. 1889.
[77] *L'Art est une religion*, 98.
[78] R. Dreyfus, *Alexandre Weill ou le Prophète du Faubourg Saint Honoré*, Conférence du 23 mars 1907, Paris, 1907.
[79] *La Lorgnette littéraire*, Paris, 1857, 124.

APPENDIX

Correspondence between Weill and Hugo

1. From Hugo to Weill, probably in answer to Weill's first letter written soon after arriving in Paris and to be dated, as argued above, May, 1839. Text communicated by M. Paul Biquard.

Samedi 16 [mai 1839]

Je connais, Monsieur, et j'apprécie depuis longtemps votre vif et excellent esprit. Je l'aime, parce qu'il est profond et vrai sous sa forme originale. Vous m'envoyez un article plein d'idées et de hautes vues, je le lis avec bonheur. Venez donc me voir un dimanche soir, demain, par example. Madame Victor Hugo sera charmée d'avoir l'honneur de vous recevoir, et ce sera une joie pour moi de vous serrer la main.

Victor Hugo.

2. From Hugo, addressed to 'Monsieur A. Weill, 3 rue du Croissant'. Postmark 17 mai 1840. Text communicated by M. Paul Biquard.

Croyez, Monsieur, que je suis bien sensible à votre cordiale et sympathique lettre. Il y a dans votre esprit ce sens profond et sincère qui caractérise le génie de votre belle nation allemande. Je l'ai déjà dit il y a longtemps: Si je n'étais français, je voudrais être allemand.

Tout ce que vous voulez bien faire pour ce livre[1] me touche vivement. Recevez-en ici tous mes remerciements avec l'assurance nouvelle de ma considération très distinguée.

16 mai 1840   Victor Hugo.
Paris.

3. Hugo to Weill. Published in facsimile in Weill, *Introduction à mes mémoires*, p. 96.

Excellent, excellent, excellent. J'aurais à faire, Monsieur, quelques objections de détail. Si vous avez une minute, jeudi soir (8h. $\frac{1}{2}$), je serai charmé d'en causer avec vous.

Vous savez comme j'aime votre personne et votre talent. Avec vous on peut être à la fois ami de Platon et de la vérité.

Tuus,

Victor Hugo.

22 janvier.

[1] Probably a reference to *Les Rayons et les Ombres*, published in May 1840.

4. Weill to Hugo. Text communicated by Musée Victor Hugo.

Mon cher poète,

   Je me réveille d'un long rêve de volupté et en me réveillant
je sens seulement mon bonheur, car l'amour chez moi c'est la
volupté de l'amitié et celle-ci est infinie comme la poésie, comme
Dieu. Je vous remercie de votre petit billet, nous vous avons
répondu, ma femme et moi en lisant vos beaux vers, en com-
muniant avec votre pensée, en nous incarnant dans votre âme,
car la poésie c'est le sang de l'âme, sang blanc, le lait de la mère
dont elle nourrit ses enfants. Je suis fier de votre amitié, et je
tâcherai de m'en rendre digne soit par mes pensées, soit par mes
actes. Tout en moi me porte vers le beau et le haut, et souvent
si mes forces m'abandonnent, je me pose sur les ailes vigoureuses de
votre poésie qui avec un doux bruissement me porte vers les
régions supérieurs [sic] d'où je contemple l'homme. C'est une des
raisons pourquoi les hommes me paraissent si petits. Je les observe
de trop haut, de votre hauteur. J'ai épousé une femme qui serait
digne d'être l'ami d'un grand homme si c'était un homme, à
plus forte raison elle est digne d'être l'amie d'un homme de bien,
il est vrai, mais qui n'a de grand que la volonté de bien faire
et de bien aimer. Cette femme me met au-dessus du besoin, non
par sa fortune, mais par son travail, par son intelligence, elle veut
que je m'abandonne à mes rêves sans aucun souci. Mon dieu, mon
rêve unique, c'est de la rendre heureuse et de la faire aimer par
mes amis. Je sais que le bonheur d'une femme est uniquement
dans le sentiment d'amour. Un homme a besoin d'amour, une
femme a besoin d'être aimée. Nous sommes très heureux, et nous
avons assez de raison pour l'être toujours, car je crois que l'homme
doit employer son esprit pour donner le bonheur à tout ce qui
l'entoure. La grandeur du poète ne consiste que dans le sentiment
de faire frissonner d'aise des millions d'âmes. Un mari peut rendre
heureuse une femme, le poète est le mari de toutes les femmes qui
le lisent et l'écoutent.

                         A vous de cœur et d'âme.
                         A. Weill.

11 fbg St Honoré
le 3 juin. [1847][1]

---

[1] Weill married on 15th April 1847. This letter seems to have been written shortly after-
wards.

5. Hugo to Weill. Probably a reply to No. 4 and so to be dated 1847.
    Text communicated by M. Paul Biquard.

    C'est vous, Monsieur, qui êtes le poëte! c'est vous qui êtes l'esprit!
    je vous remercie de votre belle et noble lettre et de tant de choses
    élevées et charmantes où je suis fier de trouver quelquefois mon
    nom. Croyez, Monsieur, à mes souvenirs les plus vifs et les plus
    distingués.

                            Victor Hugo.
    16 juin [1847]

6. Hugo to Weill, addressed to 'Monsieur Alexandre Weill.' Text com-
    municated by M. Paul Biquard.

    Guernesey — Hauteville House.

                                            28 7bre 1856
    Je reçois, Monsieur, votre envoi et vos magnifiques vers.[1] Je ne
    veux pas tarder un instant à vous remercier. Je viens de lire déjà
    dans les livres d'un si grand intérêt bien des pages où j'ai retrouvé
    avec bonheur toute la hauteur et toute l'originalité de votre esprit.
    Vous êtes comme moi penché sur l'inconnu, et il y a, sur ce qu'on
    pourrait appeler la face de votre talent, le reflet des choses mystéri-
    euses. Je suis bien touché de votre souvenir et je vous envoie mon
    plus cordial serrement de main.
                            Victor Hugo.

7. Weill to Hugo. Autograph letter displayed in Exhibition 'Victor
    Hugo raconté par l'image', No. 933. From Collection Jean Hugo.
    The catalogue describes it as 'Lettre d'Alexandre Weill à Victor
    Hugo présentant quelques critiques sur *Les Misérables*'. Unfortun-
    ately, neither M. Jean Hugo nor the Musée Victor Hugo can now
    trace this letter and no copy exists to my knowledge.

8. Hugo to Weill, possibly a reply to No. 7. A defective reading was
    published in Maurice Bloch, *Alexandre Weill: sa vie, ses œuvres*
    (text of a lecture given on 20 October 1904), Vincennes, 1905, p. 39.
    Text communicated by M. Paul Biquard.

                                        Hauteville House
                                                6 mars
    Vous me gardez, monsieur, un peu de souvenir et j'en suis touché;
    je vous remercie de me faire lire les choses toujours substantielles

    ---
    [1] Weill's *Mystères de la Création* (but none of his poems) figured in the Guernesey library.

et fortes qui sortent de votre esprit. Nous sommes à la fois, vous et moi, en désaccord profond et en accord mystérieux; il y a en dehors de la terre et de l'homme des horizons où nos esprits pénètrent et se rencontrent. Je suis comme vous de ceux qui 'croyant en Dieu, se considèrent comme œuvre créée uniquement pour glorifier le Créateur'. La solitude sévère où je vis et où je sens que je mourrai n'admet pas d'autres pensées. Je suis composé d'un Hélas et d'un Hosanna. Hélas, quand je regarde la terre, Hosanna quand je songe au delà de l'homme, et que je sens dans mon cerveau, à travers mon crâne, la splendide pénétration du ciel.

En Dieu, donc, c'est à dire en fraternité, je vous serre la main.

Victor Hugo.

17

IAN W. ALEXANDER

The Phenomenological Philosophy in France. An Analysis of its Themes, Significance and Implications

A LL familiar with the development of philosophy in France during the present century are aware of the dominant role of phenomenology in this development. Indeed, it would not be too much to say that the influence of Husserl in reorientating philosophical speculation in France has been as powerful as that of Wittgenstein in Britain during the same period, and that the result in both cases has been to revolutionize the philosophical perspective.

The year 1930 may be considered a starting-point, for that year saw the publication of Levinas's *La Théorie de l'intuition dans la phénoménologie de Husserl* and Gurvitch's *Les Tendances actuelles de la philosophie allemande*. The resultant interest in German phenomenology was canalized, and the first applications centred, in the journal *Recherches philosophiques*, five numbers of which appeared from 1931, although it must be noted that one French thinker antedates this period, namely Gabriel Marcel, France's first phenomenologist in his own right. His article, *Existence et Objectivité*, published in the *Revue de métaphysique et de morale* in 1925, might well be classed as the first application, quite independent of Husserlian influence, of that phenomenological method which he brought to perfection later.

It was, however, in the immediate post-war years that phenomenology invaded the whole field of philosophical thought, leaving not one of its disciplines untouched, permeating literature itself and moulding a certain *style* which we have come to recognize and even to take for granted as a mode of thinking characteristically French.

Any study of the later issues raised by phenomenology must of necessity go back to Edmund Husserl, the founder of the 'phenomenological philosophy'. The development of Husserl's thought is highly complex and critics are by no means unanimous in their interpretations of it.[1] The

---

[1] For two interesting treatments of this problem see A. de Waelhens, *De la phénoménologie à l'existentialisme*, in *Le Choix, le Monde, l'Existence*, Arthaud, 1947; M. Farber, *The Foundation of Phenomenology*, Harvard, 1943, pp. 15 ff.

account of experience that he offers in his earlier period, from the *Logische Untersuchungen* (1900-1) to the *Ideen zu einer reiner Phänomenologie* (1913), would seem to preserve strong traces of both Cartesian and Kantian idealism, accounted for largely by the particular use made at that stage of the *epoche* or 'bracketing' of existence. The *epoche* or 'phenomenological reduction' is said to have for object to transcend all actual experience and to place us before the activity of a pure, transcendental ego. And there is a distinct reminiscence of the Cartesian *cogito* in that attention would seem to be concentrated on 'internal experience'. Much the same strain is continued in the middle period — the period of the 'constitutive' phenomenology — where, in Kantian manner, Husserl treats of phenomenology as a transcendental theory of knowledge, the object of which is said to be to bring to light the sense-giving operations of consciousness that lead to the constitution of a possible world and whose synthesis is the transcendental ego.

It would seem that we are still somewhat embedded in a cognitive idealism or a philosophy of pure consciousness.[2] The true, revolutionary nature of Husserl's thought becomes apparent, however, in the light of his later works. Already in the *Ideen* he made it clear (and decisively so in the *Méditations Cartésiennes* of 1931) that the bracketing of existence or 'suspension of the thesis' is a purely methodological device:

> *Ce que nous mettons hors de jeu, c'est la thèse générale qui tient à l'essence de l'attitude naturelle;* nous mettons entre parenthèses absolument tout ce qu'elle embrasse dans l'ordre ontique: *par conséquent tout ce monde naturel* qui est constamment 'là pour nous', '*présent*', et ne cesse de rester là à titre de 'réalité' pour la conscience, lors même qu'il nous plaît de le mettre entre parenthèses.
>
> Quand je procède ainsi, comme il est pleinement au pouvoir de ma liberté, je ne *nie* donc *pas* ce 'monde', comme si j'étais sophiste; *je ne mets pas son existence en doute,* comme si j'étais sceptique; mais

---

[2] Farber notes the 'pitfalls' involved in Husserl's use of the phenomenological method: 'Husserl's very language betrays his predisposition to treat the transcendent realm of existence, in which belief was suspended as a matter of method, as something reducible to pure consciousness' (op. cit., p. 520). But he claims, we believe rightly, that Husserl overcame this leaning and that a proper understanding of the nature and function of the phenomenological reduction, as Husserl came to see it, exculpates him on this score. Jean Wahl does, however, suggest that the resemblances between Husserl and both Descartes and Kant are greater than the former imagined (*L'Ouvrage posthume de Husserl: La Krisis*, Cours de Sorbonne, 1957, p. 123). There is, indeed, a latent ambiguity in Husserl's thought as a whole that lays it open to both an 'idealist' and a 'realist' interpretation according to the emphasis of the interpreter. (Cf. H. Kuhn, *The Phenomenological Concept of 'Horizon'*, in *Philosophical Essays in Memory of Edmund Husserl*, Harvard, 1940; R. Ingarden, *L'Idéalisme transcendantal de Husserl*, in *Husserl et la pensée moderne*, The Hague, Martinus Nijhoff, 1959).

j'opère l'ἐποχή 'phénoménologique' *qui m'interdit absolument tout jugement portant sur l'existence spatio-temporelle.*[3]

What Husserl indeed is seeking is an absolute foundation, which will 'make clear the presuppositions of experience', in short, reveal itself as both the logical ground of meaning and the ontic root of experience, to which all particular modes of experience and all particular meanings must be referred and which determines their sense radically and absolutely. Phenomenology is the science of meanings: it is not concerned with a mere realistic description of the world, but with making explicit the fundamental structures whereby the world is constituted as meaningful for consciousness. The *epoche* and transcendental reduction do not deny the existence of the world. What they do is to suspend the 'natural' attitude with all particular modes of intentional experience so as to leave visible within the 'transcendental *cogito*' a residual *a priori* — the intentional relation between consciousness and the world *in se*, now revealed in its essentiality as a *vécu* of which the subjective and the objective poles are correlates:

> La suspension phénoménologique fait apparaître immédiatement la corrélation à priori de la constitution et du constitué, de la noèse et du noème, de la conscience et du monde. Elle manifeste immédiatement la bilatéralité de la recherche transcendantale. Il s'agit d'une bilatéralité *à l'intérieur* de la réduction transcendantale, car la recherche transcendantale est à la fois noématique et noétique.[4]

The transcendental reduction works *within* the *vécu*, and its purpose is not to retreat from the world into a pure consciousness but to exhibit the fundamental relation between consciousness and the world as the permanent, universal structure underlying all particular experiences actual or possible. It suspends all judgements about the world, or indeed about the self, so as to concentrate on the structure which makes any reference to a world or to a self possible at all, that is the intentional self-world relation of compresence itself.

[3] *Idées directrices pour une phénoménologie*, Gallimard, 1950, p. 102. Cf. Farber: 'It is essential that the phenomenological reduction be viewed as a purely methodological device. . . . It is radical in the sense of helping us to make clear the ultimate presuppositions of experience . . . . But it must never forget its own 'mother-earth', its own actual ('naturalistic') genetic foundation, if it is to constitute a world which will satisfy experience. To do so, and to go the way of cognitive idealism, would mean that the phenomenological quest would have to rest content with the pale shadow of reality, depending upon a hypostatized *logos* in an ethereal absolute consciousness' (op. cit., p. 536).

[4] A. de Muralt, *L'Idée de la phénoménologie: l'Exemplarisme husserlien*, Presses Univ., 1958, p. 251. Cf. A. de Waelhens, *Existence et Signification*, Louvain and Paris, Nauwelaerts, 1958, p. 107; G. Berger, *Le Cogito dans la philosophie de Husserl*, Aubier, 1941, pp. 49–50.

Secondly, there comes to the fore the notion of *intersubjectivity*, according to which the self's experience involves an 'experience of others', who, although not presented directly to the self, are 'appresented'[5] by virtue of the intertwining of conscious activities or what Husserl calls 'intentional transgression'. That being so, I am, and know myself, as 'situated' and we are brought back to the concrete existent, and reflection on the plane of a universal thinker or absolute consciousness is excluded.

It is finally excluded with the clarification of the even more fundamental concept of the *Lebenswelt* in *Erfahrung und Urteil*, published in Prague in 1939. This concept places the self firmly 'in the world', the two constituting an indissoluble nexus and entertaining relations of complementarity rooted in 'la coexistence première avec les choses et avec autrui'.[6]

Here is the field of 'l'expérience originaire', now identified beyond doubt with the field of existence.[7] And it is the structure of this experiential, existential ground that phenomenology has to uncover and describe. The phenomenological reflection becomes a 'réflexion sur un irréfléchi':[8]

C'est une philosophie transcendantale qui met en suspens pour les comprendre les affirmations de l'attitude naturelle, mais c'est aussi une philosophie pour laquelle le monde est toujours 'déjà là' avant la réflexion, comme une présence inaliénable, et dont tout l'effort est de retrouver ce contact naïf avec le monde pour lui donner enfin un statut philosophique. C'est l'ambition d'une philosophie qui soit une 'science exacte', mais c'est aussi un compte rendu de l'espace, du temps, du monde 'vécus'.[9]

Husserl's philosophy may be viewed as an attack on two dominant currents of thought: the Kantian and the positivist. At the root of both of these is a similar dualistic fiction. Both ask us to picture a world on the one side duplicated by a mind on the other. The Kantian will explain their coming together in terms of synthetic acts of mind imposing its categories on sense-experience. The positivist will claim that external stimuli produce 'states' in the mind (psychological determinism); then, having got the object into the mind in the form of sense-data, will account

---

[5] *Méditations cartésiennes*, Vrin, 1947, pp. 126–7.
[6] A. de Waelhens, *L'Idée phénoménologique d'intentionnalité*, in *Husserl et la pensée moderne*, p. 128.
[7] 'Der Rückgang auf die Welt der Erfahrung ist Rückgang auf die "Lebenswelt", d.i. die Welt, in der wir immer schon leben, und die den Boden für alle Erkenntnisleistung abgibt und für alle wissenschaftliche Bestimmung' (*Erfahrung und Urteil*, Hamburg, Claassen u. Goverts, 1948, p. 38).
[8] M. Merleau-Ponty, *Phénoménologie de la perception*, Gallimard, 1945, p. iv.
[9] Ibid., p. i.

for the complexity and structuring of experience in terms of their combination (psychological atomism and associationism).

None of this, however, argues Husserl, corresponds to the reality of experience. We are encouraged in this dualistic fallacy by scientific psychology, taking its abstract concepts — states, sense-data, etc. — for concrete fact, and confirmed therein by linguistic usage, notably the subject-predicate form of grammatical discourse. What Husserl does is to direct attention back to concrete, 'ante-predicative' experience and to attempt the faithful description of the phenomena of consciousness as these are displayed in its operations at the level prior to conceptual elaboration. Such is the force of Husserl's slogan: 'to the thing itself'.[10]

According to Husserl, consciousness, as so revealed in its fundamental structure, is *intentional*, directed towards the object as the *telos* of an inner impetus to self-transcendence. The *cogito* of Descartes must be replaced by a *cogito cogitatum*: 'consciousness is always consciousness of something'. The world is presented to it immediately by virtue of what Husserl calls the 'noematic' structure of experience. At the same time, the world is apprehended in and through the intentions of consciousness (by way of the 'noetic' structure of experience), which grasp it in a certain way, give it or rather allow it to appear with a certain pattern, a certain sense, meaning or value. These two structures (noematic and noetic) are correlated structures of a *same* intentional structure of experience, the one being its objective and the other its subjective side, the mode of 'being given' and the mode of 'sense-giving', the presentation and the presentative act.[11]

There are various types of the basic intentional structure — perceptual, imaginative, mnemonic, emotive, cognitive.[12] These types are the Husserlian 'essences' revealed by the 'eidetic reduction' or 'intuition of essences'. Phenomenology is concerned with the description and clarification of those essences, the various modes of intentional sense-giving which are also the modes in which the world (Being) is apprehended and reveals its meanings.

All these structures or essences, however, refer back to, and are determinations of, the primary and 'most general formal structure' of ex-

---

[10] The appeal from constructions to what is directly given is the emphasis in the second volume of the *Logische Untersuchungen*.

[11] '. . . Ces concepts de noèse et de noème ne renvoient pas à des *composantes* du vécu, mais à deux structures corrélatives du même vécu. La noèse est le vécu comme intentionnel, l'accent portant sur ses composantes subjectives (noétiques). Le noème est la structure intentionnelle du vécu, regardé du côté objectif . . .' (Q. Lauer, *Phénoménologie de Husserl: Essai sur la genèse de l'intentionnalité*, Presses Univ., 1955, p. 200).

[12] *Méditations cartésiennes*, p. 43.

perience 'designated by the schema *ego-cogito-cogitatum*',[13] that initial compresence of self and world which lies at the root of the 'objective sense', defined by Lauer as 'le mode de présence de l'objet dans la conscience'[14] and which guarantees that the intentional structures of consciousness embody revelations of Being and of its meanings.

It has to be noted that we are not here dealing with mere psychological phenomena, but with the permanent, universal structures of consciousness.[15] For that very reason they are grasped as such, not by process of abstraction or comparison of instances, but as concrete operations directly visible to intuition.[16] And this in turn because the 'reduction' is a 'radical reflection' within the framework of existence, the object of which is to return to the root of thinking and which 'découvre finalement derrière elle l'irréfléchi comme sa condition de possibilité, sans laquelle cette réflexion n'aurait aucun sens'.[17]

Any treatment of phenomenology with reference to its developments in France must begin by emphasizing those realist implications so strongly urged by Husserl in the later stages of his thought, for it is they, in a country where the dominant currents have been either idealist or positivist, which have revolutionized its philosophical 'style'. Phenomenology, indeed, cuts beneath the predicative subject-object dualism by designating an antepredicative experience of the world as the ground and condition of the revelation and constitution of meaning:

> Sous toutes les acceptions du mot sens, nous retrouvons la même notion fondamentale d'un être orienté ou polarisé vers ce qu'il n'est pas, et nous sommes ainsi toujours amenés à une conception du sujet comme ek-stase et à un rapport de transcendance active entre le sujet et le monde. Le monde est inséparable du sujet, mais d'un sujet qui n'est rien que projet du monde, et le sujet est inséparable du monde, mais d'un monde qu'il projette lui-même.[18]

---

[13] 'La structure la plus générale qui, en tant que forme, embrasse tous les cas particuliers, est désignée par notre schéma général *ego-cogito-cogitatum*' (ibid.).

[14] Lauer, op. cit., p. 217.

[15] 'Car la Wesenschau, en tant qu'elle est expérience, en tant que l'essence est à saisir à travers l'expérience vécue, sera une expérience concrète; mais d'un autre côté, en tant qu'à travers mes expériences concrètes je saisis plus qu'un fait contingent, une structure intelligible qui s'impose à moi chaque fois que je pense à l'objet intentionnel dont il s'agit, j'obtiens par elle une connaissance, je ne suis pas enfermé dans quelque particularité de ma vie individuelle, j'accède à un savoir qui est valable pour tous.' (Merleau-Ponty, *Les Sciences de l'homme et la phénoménologie*, Introd. et 1ᵉ partie, *Le Problème des sciences de l'homme selon Husserl*, Cours de Sorbonne, n.d., p. 14.)

[16] Berger, op. cit., p. 51.

[17] Merleau-Ponty, op. cit., p. 53. Cf. *Phénoménologie de la perception*, p. ix.

[18] Idem, *Phénoménologie de la perception*, p. 491.

This is Heidegger's 'ontic truth', described by Marcel as a 'confused and global experience of the world',[19] the field of compresence and inter-subjectivity containing the self and, *in relation with it*, the world and other selves as, to quote Merleau-Ponty, 'l'horizon permanent de toutes mes *cogitationes* et comme une dimension par rapport à laquelle je ne cesse de me situer'.[20] Consciousness and the world are complementary, consciousness 'intending' the object, and the object being 'for' a consciousness. In experience, however, we may distinguish a subjective and an objective pole. Taking the first, phenomenology rejects the positivist, determinist explanation of conscious phenomena as the effects of external factors. These phenomena are less phenomena *in* consciousness than phenomena *of* consciousness. The subject is implicated therein since it is for and by my consciousness that the world appears in a certain perspective and with a certain sense, that from 'a' world it becomes 'the' world 'for me', 'my world'.

My consciousness is 'la source absolue', 'par laquelle d'abord un monde se dispose autour de moi et commence à exister pour moi'.[21] And this by virtue of my intention whereby I select certain rather than other possible senses that the world offers. A house in my immediate experience of it may be a fine piece of architecture, a subject of hope or fear: all these are one house, but its 'being' or 'meaning' is constituted on each occasion by the particular intention in which it is embodied. In visual perception itself the being or sense of the object is the result of an intention that makes *explicit* certain of its potential aspects. Similarly with emotional experience. If I am afraid to climb a precipice, it is not it that 'produces' my fear. It is I, says Sartre, who 'choose' to view it as terrifying, that is to make explicit that particular meaning: it is in that particular way that it comes to 'ex-sist' 'for me'. But not only does my intention determine the being of the precipice, it also determines the being of my self. I am 'choosing myself' as terrified. The precipice is the occasion for me to be 'for myself' in a particular mode.[22] Thus Sartre, like Heidegger, can assert that consciousness is 'nothing', being without content.[23] It is wholly definable in terms of the self's sense-giving relationship with the world. Emotion is such a 'total act' of consciousness. So too is imagination. Sartre's two works on imagination are designed to show that the image,

[19] See *The Mystery of Being, I: Reflection and Mystery*, Harvill Press, 1950, pp. 51–2.
[20] Op. cit., pp. vii–viii.
[21] Ibid., p. iii.
[22] F. Jeanson defines consciousness as 'un être dont l'être est en question pour lui-même, un être dont l'être n'est pas fait mais qui a à faire son être; un être, enfin, qui dépend de lui-même dans sa manière d'être'. (*La Phénoménologie*, Téqui, 1951, p. 70.)
[23] Sartre, *L'Etre et le néant*, Gallimard, 1943, pp. 71–2.

far from being a content of consciousness, is the result of an act of the whole of consciousness whereby an absent reality is evoked as present. In Merleau-Ponty's words, 'imaginer, c'est former un certain mode de relation avec l'objet absent'.[24]

Turning to the objective pole, the phenomenologist rejects the idealist account. Consciousness is a 'project towards the world': the latter is immediately present; it is 'there', as the primary situation which determines all senses.[25] We do not rejoin the world in the Kantian manner by some express act of synthesis. The mind-world unity is given. Hence the rejection of the traditional French 'reflexive analysis' which claims, as does the Cartesian *cogito*, to provide awareness of the thinking self independently of the world.

Thus Sartre argues that 'toute conscience est positionnelle, en ce qu'elle se transcende pour atteindre un objet', and that 'toute conscience positionnelle d'objet est en même temps conscience non positionnelle d'elle-même'. From which he infers that the reflective consciousness, far from being primary, has for condition a pre-reflexive *cogito*: 'il y a un cogito préréflexif qui est la condition du cogito cartésien'.[26] There is no consciousness of the self independent of the intentional consciousness directed towards the object. Not that Sartre denies 'self-consciousness'; what he argues is that there is no consciousness *of* the self (the 'of' is dictated by syntactical requirements and he proposes to bracket it). Self-consciousness is not another, additional consciousness, but one with the intentional consciousness, 'un avec la conscience dont elle est conscience'; 'cette conscience (de) soi, nous ne devons pas la considérer comme une nouvelle conscience, mais comme le seul mode d'existence qui soit possible pour une conscience de quelque chose'.[27]

Marcel equally strongly rejects the Cartesian *cogito* as secondary and refers it back to a pre-reflexive *ego sum* or *j'existe* expressive of the ante-predicative unity: 'une philosophie qui part du *cogito*, c'est-à-dire du non-inséré, ou même de la non-insertion en tant qu'acte, risque de ne pouvoir jamais rejoindre l'être'.[28] The subject is given 'in relation' as a self-transcending consciousness, intending a world which it renders meaning-

---

[24] Merleau-Ponty, *Sciences de l'homme*, p. 20.
[25] 'Cette certitude du monde général est toujours opération (ou accomplissement, *Verzug*) et elle précède tout, non pas comme énonciation et prémisse au sens propre, elle détermine le sens, elle fonctionne comme sol de dévaluation: étant signifie étant dans le monde.' (Husserl, quoted by Wahl, *La Krisis*, p. 123.)
[26] Op. cit., pp. 18–20.
[27] Ibid., p. 20. Cf. A. de Waelhens: 'La présence de soi à soi n'est pas une possession de soi significative en elle-même, mais une évidence *récupérée sur l'évidence de la présence à l'autre*.' (*Existence et Signification*, p. 114.)
[28] *Du Refus à l'invocation*, Gallimard, 1940, p. 90. Cf. *Etre et Avoir*, Aubier, 1935, p. 249.

ful by its presentative and constitutive acts, but never itself localizable, since it can never become a simple object of contemplation for itself.

Experience thus presents a nexus wherein consciousness and the world are mutually implicated, the latter as the 'permanent horizon of all my *cogitationes*'. In perception the conscious intention renders explicit some aspect or meaning of the object, so bringing it to be 'for' consciousness. But the other possible aspects remain implicitly as the 'horizon' and are an integral part of the perception.[29] In my perception of a chair, I 'intend' the chair and may secure an explicit vision of the front, but I also have an implicit vision of the back and sides. They are the implicit themes of my actual perception. And these in turn are fringed by other elements drawn from the object's wider environment:

> Ainsi chaque objet est le miroir de tous les autres. Quand je regarde la lampe posée sur ma table, je lui attribue non seulement les qualités visibles de ma place, mais encore celles que la cheminée, que les murs, que la table peuvent 'voir', le dos de ma lampe n'est rien d'autre que la face qu'elle 'montre' à la cheminée. Je peux donc voir un objet en tant que les objets forment un système ou un monde et que chacun d'eux dispose des autres autour de lui comme spectateurs de ses aspects cachés et garantie de leur permanence. Toute vision d'un objet par moi se réitère instantanément entre tous les objets du monde qui sont saisis comme coexistants parce que chacun d'eux est tout ce que les autres 'voient' de lui.[30]

Temporally, too, as well as spatially, the object of perception is seen in its relatedness and is bordered by a fringe of retrospection and prospection:

> . . . Chaque présent fonde définitivement un point du temps qui sollicite la reconnaissance de tous les autres, l'objet est donc vu de tous temps comme il est vu de toutes parts et par le même moyen, qui est la structure d'horizon.[31]

The present contains the immediate past and the imminent future and, implicated and enveloped in them, their immediate past and future.

All experience exhibits this seemingly limitless spatial and temporal *emboîtement*. And, as there is in addition an intersubjectivity of minds whereby my perceptual intentions are intertwined with those of others,

---

[29] See Husserl, *Méditations cartésiennes*, pp. 38-9.

[30] Merleau-Ponty, *Phénoménologie de la perception*, pp. 82-3. Cf. Kuhn, *Concept of Horizon*, loc. cit.

[31] Merleau-Ponty, ibid., p. 83. Cf. Kuhn: 'The present perception of the object before me is a link in a chain of successive perceptions each of which either had or will have a presence of its own.' (Op. cit., p. 113.)

my perceptual field takes in the whole world. My experience appears as a single field for the display and constitution of senses and values of the world, in which all possible senses and values are involved:

> Le réel est un tissu solide, il n'attend pas nos jugements pour s'annexer les phénomènes les plus surprenants ni pour rejeter nos imaginations les plus vraisemblables. La perception n'est pas une science du monde, ce n'est pas même un acte, une prise de position délibérée, elle est le fond sur lequel tous les actes se détachent et elle est présupposée par eux.[32]

The real of my experience is not a mass of discrete parts, but an organized whole of which the parts are enveloped. We do not, as psychological atomism would have it, build up the world out of isolated sense-data, any more than, as Bergson says, in reading we pass from the letter to the word. Being itself is a whole already instinct with meanings, and consciousnesses are in the world as the *media* through which those meanings, by their embodiment in the intentional structures of consciousness, are actualized and made explicit against the background of the whole, from which they emerge but without ever losing their relatedness to it.

At the centre of the process is what Merleau-Ponty calls 'le perspectivisme de mon expérience'. What is given is a whole, but a whole seen in perspective, its parts 'enveloped' in such a way that the moment or object of experience contains, as it were telescoped within each other, a limitless series of implicit 'horizons'. Pure objectivity — which is a conceptualisation of concrete experience — comes about precisely by an abstractive process whereby the enveloped, perspectival elements are disjoined and spread out as on a map. Such is the abstract, scientific notion of a 'universe', 'c'est-à-dire d'une totalité achevée, explicite, où les rapports soient de détermination réciproque', in place of what is given in experience, namely a 'world', 'c'est-à-dire d'une multiplicité ouverte et indéfinie où les rapports sont d'implication réciproque'.[33]

The relation then between self and world is one of compresence, as between a consciousness which 'pro-jects' towards the world and a world which seeks to become 'for' a consciousness. This being so, the phenomenologist argues, conscious phenomena are not susceptible of treatment by the scientific method of 'explanation'. Scientific or causal explanation works by way of analysis of a situation, which is resolved into its elements, one of the latter being then designated as cause of the event. The scientific

---

[32] Merleau-Ponty, ibid., p. v.
[33] Ibid., p. 85.

investigator will analyse a conscious event, such as my fear, into elements (states of mind, bodily states, external conditions, etc.), and will then designate one or other of these elements, as required, as the cause of my fearing. But, it is argued, this is simply to do away with the phenomenon, to dissolve the bond between the subject and his world in terms of which alone his phenomena have meaning. The causal explanation will have told us nothing. At the most it will have correlated series of data, established a constant relation or law. That may well suffice for the sciences where, as causality is now used, all that is required is the establishing of a permanence or equivalence. But in studying conscious phenomena what is sought is meanings, not mere legal connections.

These phenomena do not offer material for problems, or are problems of a special sort, problems, as Marcel puts it, 'that encroach upon their own data'.[34] For the 'data' here are not objective in the sense of their being dissociable from the self-world intention. They are in fact incorporated in this intention as the embodiment of a meaning which the intention realises, of a mode of being of the self and of the world which it constitutes. My fear is myself fearing, 'signifying' and constituting both the world and myself in a certain way; it is the revealing through the medium of my fearing intention of a particular meaning that Being offers.

My fear is therefore a single, total event in which situation, states, behaviour, image and act are indissoluble moments. All are part of one sense-revealing intention, one 'phenomenon', which simply vanishes when subjected to analysis. Phenomenology therefore proposes a method not of causal explanation but of description and clarification, what Husserl calls 'noematic reflection', as opposed to analysis, in that it works within the subject–object unity. Its task is to describe the meanings or senses of Being as they are revealed and actualized in intentional experience: as they represent modes of comprehending the world on the one hand, and modes of being of the world and modes of being of the self on the other. The phenomenologist describes the *total* event, both the sort of world that is so constituted, the way it 'appears' for a particular intention in terms of sensations and images, and the sort of intention that lies behind it in terms of the subject's particular situation. Marcel defines the method as 'the clarification of two unknowns',[35] thus emphasizing both the descriptive and clarificatory nature of the method and the fact that what is described takes place at the ante-predicative level of compresence, implication and obscure relatedness before conceptualization, where alone analysis functions legitimately. Phenomenology, declares Merleau-Ponty, 'c'est

[34] *The Philosophy of Existence*, Harvill Press, 1948, p. 8. Cf. *Etre et Avoir*, p. 145.
[35] *The Mystery of Being*, I, p. 13.

l'essai d'une description directe de notre expérience telle qu'elle est, et sans aucun égard à sa genèse psychologique et aux explications causales que le savant, l'historien ou le sociologue peuvent en fournir'.[36]

It is at this point that the phenomenological concept of 'negativity' emerges. In traditional logic negation at the predicative level is a function of exclusion purely and simply. It is Hegel who first considers negation in its relation to consciousness, and not merely with reference to negative propositions. For him negativity is what conditions the dialectical structure of consciousness, which advances by constant affirmations and negations, no sooner positing an idea than it posits its contrary.

Phenomenology develops this view and in particular the implication that negativity is constitutive of consciousness.[37] Conscious experience is both a way of being and of not-being, there is both identification with the object and differentiation from it, amounting to a negation of what is. Sartre points to emotional experience: when one is conscious of being sad, one *is* one's sadness, but at the same time one *is not* one's sadness (or, as he says, one is 'playing at being sad'). It is in this sense that it may be said that 'man is what he is not, and is not what he is'.[38]

All experience, however, exhibits this negativity within positivity characteristic of consciousness, whose 'structure d'être . . . consiste à être l'autre sur le mode du non-être'.[39] Involved in all conscious activities is a 'distancing' with respect to what is given immediately. Conscious appropriation of the object, it will be recalled, consists in endowing it with a certain sense by viewing it in a certain perspective. For the *en-soi* to become a *pour-soi* there must be selection and determination and therefore a transcending of the brute immediacy of fusion with the object, where all senses and all perspectives exist, but as mere possibilities because undetermined and undifferentiated:

Nous n'avons pas d'autre manière de savoir ce que c'est qu'un

[36] Merleau-Ponty, op. cit., p. i.

[37] Cf. J. Hyppolite, *Genèse et Structure de la Phénoménologie de l'Esprit de Hegel*, Aubier, 1946, p. 184; J. Wahl, *Le Malheur de la conscience dans la philosophie de Hegel*, Presses Univ., 1951, p. 2.

[38] Sartre goes on to an arbitrary hypostatization of 'le néant' and argues that, since 'la conscience ne peut produire une négation sinon sous forme de conscience de négation, . . . la condition nécessaire pour qu'il soit possible de dire *non*, c'est que le non-être soit une présence perpétuelle, en nous et en dehors de nous, c'est que le néant *hante* l'être'. (Op. cit., pp. 46–7.) In short, in all experience giving rise to negative judgements there is an intentional relationship with a 'néant' as an entity. The assertion 'Pierre is not in the café' is grounded in the *vision* of 'Pierre s'enlevant comme néant sur le fond de néantisation du café.' (Ibid., p. 45.) For an interesting critique of the 'négativisme philosophique' of Sartre and Heidegger, see E. Morot-Sir, *La Pensée négative*, Aubier, 1947, pp. 294 ff.

[39] A. de Waelhens, op. cit., p. 117.

tableau ou une chose que de les regarder et leur *signification* ne se révèle que si nous les regardons d'un certain point de vue, d'une certaine distance et dans un certain *sens*. . . .

Dans le monde en soi, toutes les directions comme tous les mouvements sont relatifs, ce qui revient à dire qu'il n'y en a pas.[40]

Negativity has its place in Marcel's phenomenology too. His 'participation' is not identification, but a reciprocal determining and constituting of subject and world that allows the terms of the relation to participate and yet preserve their distinctiveness. Experience itself, says Marcel, is no mere passive 'reception', but has active and 'dialectical aspects', all the more so the 'ontological reflection' that rises upon it. And Marcel stresses the importance of 'distance':

> What we are concerned with is a kind of borderland which thought must keep in existence between itself and its object; or, to express this more dynamically, we are concerned with the act through which thought is stiffened to resist the temptation to engulf itself in its own object and become merged with that object.[41]

At no point, however, is there radical disjunction between subject and world. This distance is purely 'internal': it is a sort of room which consciousness makes for itself within the world in order to bring the meanings of the world to light. But these views are only understandable when related to the phenomenological theory of truth which underlies its claim to be an ontology. Phenomenology returns to Greek, and primarily pre-Socratic sources by defining truth as a 'revelation of Being'; as 'the revealedness and revelation of what is', according to Heidegger, or as the 'sudden access to some reality's revelation of itself to us' according to Marcel.[42] The basis of true assertions lies in an 'ante-predicative evidence' by virtue of the initial compresence. 'Nous sommes dans la vérité et l'évidence est "l'expérience de la vérité".'[43]

But this revelation of Being is possible only through the sense-determining intentions of consciousness. If truth is a property of Being (the property of revealing itself as it is), it is also a quality 'conferred on the object by the mind that grasps it'.[44] And this determining of a particular

[40] Merleau-Ponty, op. cit., p. 491.

[41] Op. cit., p. 147.

[42] Heidegger, *On the Essence of Truth*, in *Existence and Being*, Vision Press, 1949, p. 334; Cf. *Being and Time*, SCM Press, 1926, p. 263. Marcel, op. cit., p. 53.

[43] Merleau-Ponty, op. cit., p. xi.

[44] Marcel, op. cit., p. 64. Cf. Merleau-Ponty: 'Un rocher infranchissable, un rocher grand ou petit, vertical ou oblique, cela n'a de sens que pour quelqu'un qui se propose de le franchir, pour un sujet dont les projets découpent ces déterminations dans la masse uniforme de l'en-soi et font surgir un monde orienté, un sens des choses.' (Op. cit., p. 498.)

sense or truth (out of the infinity of potential senses or truths offered) is made possible only by the negative structure of consciousness, which allows it both to be and not to be the object presented to it, since consciousness both possesses the object and, by distancing itself from the object, constitutes it as other than it is, as an object 'for itself', in short, as a particular, limited determination of the object, corresponding to its own particular intention or project. So that Being reveals its truth because it is appropriated by a consciousness which, by an act of withdrawal and limitation, determines a 'being' of Being, that is, a manifestation of Being in one of its modes, in one of the *particular, limited* senses or values implicit within it.

This distance, which allows for the determination and limitation that are the condition for Being to reveal itself, Heidegger calls 'openness'. It is the light which allows us to see Being manifested, but always within the limits of its determination in consciousness.[45] Moreover, paradoxically, it is this very distance, negativity and limitation which founds phenomenology as a positive ontology. For if I am, in so far as I intend it, one with Being, and at the same time distinct from it, since I grasp it as constituted by me, I hold it in its 'being-for-me', that is, I 'comprehend' it in the most fully positive mode of knowledge.[46] So that the negativity of consciousness that appeared to deny positive knowledge of Being is precisely what assures it:

> Car cette vie signifiante, cette certaine signification de la nature et de l'histoire que je suis, ne limite pas mon accès au monde, elle est au contraire mon moyen de communiquer avec lui.[47]

The notion of internal distance has other important implications. The self-world compresence is seen to possess a spatio-temporal volume. And the study of this qualitative structure leads to a reassessment of the classical concepts of space, time and the body.

Distinct from the *corps-objet*, the body as idea, is the body as experienced immediately at the ante-predicative level, the *corps-sujet*, 'ce corps que je

---

[45] 'L'Ouverture, lorsque nous y accédons (et nous y accédons par cela même que nous sommes homme) ne nous dissout donc pas dans une totalité sans limites: elle établit, au contraire, comme une sorte de champ clos, de lice, où l'étant selon *ses* limites, va se manifester pour que nous le dévoilions, pour que, selon ses diverses dimensions, nous le *disions*.' (A. de Waelhens, *Phénoménologie et Vérité*, Presses Univ., 1953, pp. 79–80). Cf. Marcel, op. cit., pp. 63–5.

[46] 'En effet, que je puisse être (pour les viser) les choses que je connais ou que je fais sans les être (puisque je ne me confonds pas effectivement avec elles), cela revient à admettre que je les saisis dans ce qu'elles sont sans pourtant m'identifier à elles comme étants, c'est-à-dire que je comprends leur être.' (A. de Waelhens, *Existence et Signification*, p. 117.)

[47] Merleau-Ponty, op. cit., p. 519.

suis sans pouvoir m'identifier logiquement à lui'.[48] 'Je ne suis pas devant mon corps, je suis dans mon corps, ou plutôt je suis mon corps.'[49] This experience of the body is a spatial experience. 'Le corps,' says Merleau-Ponty 'est éminemment un espace expressif.' But this 'spatialité du corps propre' differs from the abstract space of the physicist composed of points external to one another, being structured not upon the point but upon 'le point horizon', that is the parts enveloped so as to form a perspective. It is a 'spatialité de situation' and not 'de position'.[50]

The particular perspectival system is constituted in terms of a particular sense-giving intention or way of acting in the world. 'Mon corps m'apparaît comme posture en vue d'une certaine tâche actuelle ou possible.' The *espace vécu* is an 'espace orienté'.[51] The body is at the centre as the organ whereby the subject constitutes a meaningful world for itself, giving it form in its dynamic schemas, which represent not so much objective spatial determinations as 'qualified situations', in that they are the qualitative expression of the subject's active relation to the world.[52]

Similarly, there is a temporal structure of the body, the *temps vécu* of concrete experience, it too characterized by the envelopment of its parts, as distinct from conceptual time with its past, present and future external to each other. The present of real time is a 'champs de présence' containing past and imminent future as indistinct horizons (Husserl's retentions and protensions), and exhibiting what Marcel calls a 'triangulation' or 'rapport entre l'immédiat, l'anticipé, et aussi le remémoré'.[53]

Together concrete space and time form what Marcel terms the category of 'depth',[54] the spatio-temporal dimension centred on the full, volume-laden spatio-temporal present of 'being-in-the-world' — 'l'épaisseur du présent pré-objectif, où nous trouvons notre corporéité, notre socialité, la préexistence du monde'.[55] For phenomenology space and time have to be understood neither as subjective categories nor as empirical features of the world, but in terms of the ontological relation between subject and world, that is of the world-directed projects of the self:

. . . Je ne suis pas dans l'espace et dans le temps, je ne pense pas

[48] Marcel, *Du Refus à l'invocation*, p. 39. Cf. *Journal métaphysique*, Gallimard, 1935, p. 323.
[49] Merleau-Ponty, op. cit., p. 175.
[50] Ibid., pp. 171, 116–9.
[51] Ibid., pp. 116, 118.
[52] 'C'est seulement au prix d'une abstraction vicieuse que nous dissocions ce vivant, le fait qu'il vit, et les schèmes dynamiques par lesquels s'exprime sa situation.' (Marcel, *Du Refus à l'invocation*, p. 115. Cf. p. 117.)
[53] Marcel, *Homo Viator*, Aubier, 1944, p. 58. Cf. Merleau-Ponty, op. cit., pp. 475–6.
[54] Marcel, *The Mystery of Being*, I, pp. 192, 194.
[55] Merleau-Ponty, op. cit., p. 495.

l'espace et le temps; je suis à l'espace et au temps, mon corps s'applique à eux et les embrasse.[56]

In this sense, space and time are 'objective', and are found 'in the world'.[57] If this is so, it is by virtue of the self-body-world compresence, and this involves the attribution to the body of a new status. The body acts as what Marcel calls the 'médiateur absolu' and Merleau-Ponty the 'véhicule de l'être au monde'.[58] Experienced as 'une masse gestuelle disponible', 'mon corps est spatialisant et m'insère dans les choses'.[59] By it the self acts in the world and constitutes the spatio-temporal *ekstases* which give it shape and meaning. On the one hand, the body is continuous with the self, as the organ whereby the self selects its perspective and endows the world with a particular sense. On the other, the body is continuous with the world, and this in two ways: first, it is through the body and its situation that the world offers a particular possibility of sense to the presentative and constitutive act of the subject; secondly, it is through the body that the particular sense offered and absorbed into the intentional act is expressed in significant behaviour—action, gesture, language. There is not a self, plus a body, plus a world, but a single sense-formulating event with three moments: the taking up into consciousness of a sense from the world, its organisation within the bodily mechanism, its projection back into the world in the form of behaviour — an event, in short, of which 'thinking' is the subjective and behaviour the objective side.[60]

Essential to this account is the view that bodily activity is already a form of reflection. 'Déjà la motricité, prise à l'état pur,' writes Grünbaum, 'possède le pouvoir élémentaire de donner un sens.'[61] There is a 'rationalité du corps propre' inasmuch as the latter in its dynamic schemas is a selective and organizing activity. The dualism established between 'thinking' and 'experience' is the corollary of the mind-body dualism and

---

[56] Ibid., p. 164.

[57] 'Le temps universel vient au monde par le Pour-soi. L'En-soi ne dispose pas de temporalité précisément parce qu'il est en-soi et que la temporalité est le mode d'être d'un être qui est perpétuellement à distance de soi pour soi. Le Pour-soi, au contraire, est temporalité, mais il n'est pas conscience *de* temporalité, sauf lorsqu'il se produit lui-même dans le rapport "réflexif-réfléchi". Sur le mode irréfléchi il découvre la temporalité *sur* l'être, c'est-à-dire dehors. La temporalité universelle est *objective*.' (Sartre, op. cit., p. 255.)

[58] Merleau-Ponty, op. cit., p. 97.

[59] G. Madinier, *Conscience et mouvement*, Alcan, 1938, p. 448.

[60] One may note the close similarity between these views and those developed by Bergson in *Matière et Mémoire*. For a full analysis of the latter's theory of perception and its relationship with phenomenology, see my *Bergson, Philosopher of Reflection*, Bowes and Bowes, 1957, in particular chap. IV, *Mind as Act*, and chap. VI, *Meanings and Intentions*. Cf. also Merleau-Ponty, *Éloge de la philosophie*, Gallimard, 1953.

[61] Grünbaum, *Aphasie und Motorik*, Zeitschrift f. d. ges. Neurologie und Psychiatrie, 1930, quoted by Merleau-Ponty, *Phénoménologie de la perception*, p. 166.

is refutable on similar grounds. Relations are not imposed by mind in the Kantian manner on an inert matter of experience, nor are they, in the empirical manner, derived inductively or inferentially from experience. They are given in experience and constitutive of it:

La rationalité est exactement mesurée aux expériences dans lesquelles elle se révèle. Il y a de la rationalité, c'est-à-dire: les perspectives se recoupent, les perceptions se confirment, un sens apparaît. Mais il ne doit pas être posé à part, transformé en Esprit absolu ou en monde au sens réaliste. . . .

La rationalité n'est pas un problème, il n'y a pas derrière elle une inconnue que nous ayons à déterminer déductivement ou à prouver inductivement à partir d'elle: nous assistons à chaque instant à ce prodige de la connexion des expériences, et personne ne sait mieux que nous comment il se fait puisque nous sommes ce nœud de relations.[62]

The very generality that we associate with pattern, sense and meaning has its concrete source before ever conceptualisation proper develops, in experience, in the acquisition, that is, of motor habits. It is the body, says Merleau-Ponty, 'qui donne à notre vie la forme de la généralité et qui prolonge en dispositions stables nos actes personnels'. Such stable dispositions or habits are a form of understanding: 'on dit que le corps a compris et l'habitude est acquise lorsqu'il s'est laissé pénétrer par une signification nouvelle, lorsqu'il s'est assimilé un nouveau noyau significatif'.[63] For Marcel too experience is no mere passivity, but made up of acts constitutive of senses which come into being in and through the network of reciprocal relations of self and world. It is not a subjective but an intramundane and intersubjective event and, as such, contains the grounds of universality and generality, a generality that has its primary location in the body as the agent of 'permanence ontologique'.[64]

In short, sensations, images, all that is so often considered mere material to be worked up into 'thought', are already thought, comprehension taken at their concrete cognitive root and 'in process'. But, if there is rationality at the ante-predicative level, it is one that bears the mark of ambiguity, for it is the product of a fluid and variable relation between the self and the world, and it expresses itself only partially in the explicit act, image or word, which trail behind them an indeterminate and shifting background

[62] Merleau-Ponty, ibid., pp. xv–xvi.
[63] Ibid., p. 171.
[64] Marcel, op. cit., p. 83; *Etre et Avoir*, p. 138. One may compare Bergson's theory of the origin of the concept in action. Cf. my *Bergson*, pp. 79–80.

23

of implicit meanings and overtones — Being itself as the inexhaustible reservoir of sense, transcending all particular determinations of sense as their ultimate and ultimately undefinable ground and source. 'Le monde et la raison,' declares Merleau-Ponty, 'sont mystérieux, mais ce mystère les définit . . . la phénoménologie a pour tâche de révéler le mystère du monde et le mystère de la raison';[65] or, in short, to use Marcel's expression, 'le mystère de l'être'.

It would no doubt be hazardous to attempt any close parallel between contemporary French and British philosophical trends. Yet phenomenology, as it has evolved in France, is not without its bearing upon the most recent developments in analytical philosophy.

One will recall how the starting-point in Britain was the logical positivism associated with Russell, Carnap and the early Wittgenstein of the *Tractatus Logico-Philosophicus* and developed by Ayer and others. It led to the assertion that all meaningful statements fall into either of two classes: logical propositions, analytic, formal, tautological and irrelevant to factual experience; empirical, descriptive statements about matters of fact, susceptible of objective verification and therefore of being designated true or false. The application of this 'Occam's razor' excluded from meaningful utterance all statements not falling into those categories, such as moral, metaphysical and theological statements.

Even at this stage it might be noted however that phenomenology and analysis met on one point: the clear cut distinction between logic and fact. Both reject the old-fashioned ontologizing which claims to account for the universe by *a priori* reasoning. Both assert the impossibility of proving assertions about existence from logical premises. Both agree that the real cannot be accounted for, only described. Hume's distinction between the 'is' and the 'ought', which looms so large in current ethical discussions in Britain — such as the distinction Nowell-Smith makes in his *Ethics* between the theoretical and the imperative — has its parallel in much phenomenological thinking.

Phenomenology, of course, particularly in its French enlargements, differed from the outset in envisaging a new type of ontology. It affirms that the world is given *as it is* and that the structures that 'appear' to consciousness are the very structures of Being. The Kantian distinction between phenomenon and noumenon and the conception of substance as a substratum underlying what appears fall to the ground.

Relatif, le phénomène le demeure car le 'paraître' suppose par

---

[65] Merleau-Ponty, op. cit., p. xvi.

essence quelqu'un à qui paraître. Mais il n'a pas la double relativité de l'*Erscheinung* kantienne. Il n'indique pas, par-dessus son épaule, un être véritable qui serait, lui, l'absolu. Ce qu'il est, il l'est absolument, car il se dévoile *comme il est*. Le phénomène peut être étudié et décrit en tant que tel, car il est *absolument indicatif de lui-meme*.[66]

Phenomenology thus envisages an experiential or positive ontology consisting of the description of the typical structures of Being (or patterns of meaning) as they appear directly to consciousness in its typical modes or structures of intentional experience — religious, moral, cognitive, emotive, etc.

Returning to later developments in analysis, one may recall that doubts arose about the first statement of its position — about the verification principle (is it not metaphysical?) — above all, about the reasonableness of classing moral, metaphysical or religious statements as simply 'meaningless'. The result is seen in the recent work of Wisdom, Ryle, Nowell-Smith and the Wittgenstein of the *Philosophical Investigations*. The upshot has been to add a new class of statements, whose meaning is understood by the way the statement is used (the 'use principle').[67] Thus, according to Braithwaite, the use (i.e. the meaning) of moral and religious assertions is to express an intention to act in a particular way.[68]

But this is to recognize that such statements are relative to some way of acting in the world, some mode of sense-giving and of evaluating. To say 'I ought to be (or must be) courageous' has meaning only for one who seeks to 'choose himself' as courageous and to 'choose' the world as a place where courage may exist.[69] And it has meaning because he intends the world in this way and constitutes this particular sense which it contains.[70] Both phenomenology and recent analysis call back from

[66] Sartre, op. cit., p. 12.

[67] Cf. J. O. Urmson, *Philosophical Analysis*, Clarendon Press, 1956, p. 179: G. J. Warnock, *Analysis and Imagination*, in *The Revolution in Philosophy*, Macmillan, 1956, pp. 112–5: Wittgenstein, *Philosophical Investigations*, Blackwell, 1953, §109, 117, 340; cf. G. Ryle, *The Theory of Meaning*, in *British Philosophy in the Mid-Century*, Allen and Unwin, 1957, pp. 239 ff.

[68] 'Just as the meaning of a moral assertion is given by its use in expressing the asserter's intention to act, so far as in him lies, in accordance with the moral principle involved, so the meaning of a religious assertion is given by its use in expressing the asserter's intention to follow a specified policy of behaviour.' (R. B. Braithwaite, *An Empiricist's View of the Nature of Religious Belief*, Cambridge Univ. Press, pp. 15–6.)

[69] P. H. Nowell-Smith argues that 'I ought' is merely a special case of 'I shall' and expresses a decision purely and simply (*Ethics*, Penguin Books, 1954, pp. 267–8.) Cf. Braithwaite: 'To say that it is belief in the dogmas of religion which is the cause of the believer's intending to behave as he does is to put the cart before the horse: it is the intention to behave which constitutes what is known as religious conviction.' (Op. cit., p. 16.)

[70] Wittgenstein comes near to recognizing this in passages such as the following: 'You say to me: "You understand this expression, don't you? Well then — I am using it in the sense

abstract, generalized thinking to doing, and ultimately locate the source
of thinking in 'being-in-the-world'.[71]

These new conceptions, moreover, have raised doubts about empirical
statements themselves. A scientific theory does certainly more than
translate a state of affairs: it is operational in intent, a policy for action,
originating from activity in the world and implying an evaluation of the
world.[72] The phenomenologist would go further and assert that even a
simple empirical statement such as 'the table is round' is the expression of
a particular sense-giving intention.[73]

Both phenomenology and analysis indeed represent a reaction against
abstraction and a recall to the concrete, to the subject acting in the world
and expressing itself in meaningful behaviour. If the phenomenologist
might not accept all the implications of Ryle's definition of the self as
'the sum of its acts', he would agree that it is only in its acts and its
behaviour policies and patterns, linguistic included, that the self can be
studied, since for him consciousness is nothing but this sense-giving and
expressive activity. And both currents belong to their age of philosophical
'insecurity'. Both reject the complacency of the system builder, seeing the
starting-point of philosophy in a state of 'unease' ('I don't know my way
about,' as Wittgenstein puts it), its procedure as tentative and clarificatory,
and its function as in large part therapeutic.

To trace the influence of phenomenology in literature would be a major
task. Perhaps the nature of its impact is best seen in literary criticism,
particularly in the works of Gaston Bachelard, Georges Poulet and Jean-
Pierre Richard.

These writers are concerned with describing essences, structures,

you are familiar with." — As if the sense were an atmosphere accompanying the word, which
it carried with it into every kind of application. If, for example, someone says that the
sentence "This is here" (saying which he points to an object in front of him) makes sense to
him, then he should ask himself in what special circumstances this sentence is actually used.
There it does make sense.' 'A main source of our failure to understand is that we do not
command a clear view of the use of our words — our grammar is lacking in this sort of per-
spicuity. A perspicuous representation produces just that understanding which consists in
"seeing connexions" . . . The concept of a perspicuous representation is of fundamental
significance for us. It earmarks the form of account we give, the way we look at things. (Is
this a "Weltanschauung"?).' (Op. cit., §117, 122.)

[71] Cf. H. H. Price's account of concepts as dispositions rather than entities (Thinking and
Experience, Hutchinson, 1953, pp. 314–5). Cf. G. Ryle, The Concept of Mind, Hutchinson,
1949, chap. II, and my Bergson, chap. VI.

[72] For F. Waismann a scientific theory is a construction that reflects our own activity.
(Verifiability, in Essays on Logic and Language, Blackwell, 1951, First Series, p. 140.)

[73] Waismann describes a fact as 'What we notice . . . it is our work . . . something that
emerges out from and takes shape against a background.' (Ibid.)

patterns of meaning. Underlying their descriptions is a phenomenological postulate: that literary creation is a sense-giving and sense-revealing activity whereby the writer constitutes his self and a world for himself. It is a world of sensation and image before conceptualisation, what Bachelard calls 'la zone des rêveries matérielles qui précèdent la contemplation'.[74] But it is a meaningful world: indeed it is the world as the writer comprehends it directly in terms of his particular sense-giving intention.

To deal with it the critic must eschew analysis, disruptive of the texture of the whole, which *is* its meaning, and confine himself to description. He must submit himself to the text so as to allow the patterns of meaning embodied in its structure to disclose themselves. A sort of intuitive vision must come into play, if only because the meanings are not fully located in the express content, which carries overtones and undertones that constitute, as in perception, a carefully graduated implicit background. The critic's success will depend largely on his ability to bring to light relations and patterns not immediately discernible.

Above all, he must penetrate below the level of ideas to that pre-conceptual plane where the writer operates in his choice of image, symbol and sound, in Richard's words 'au cœur de la sensation, du désir ou de la rencontre'.[75] The critic will concern himself, says Bachelard, with the 'départ de l'image dans une conscience individuelle', with the image as the union 'd'une subjectivité pure mais éphémère et d'une réalité qui ne va pas nécessairement jusqu'à sa complète constitution'.[76] For it is not a fully objectified world that the phenomenologist studies, but concrete modes of being or meanings of the world grasped within the dynamic process of their revelation and organization, at the moment when the writer 'anticipe la représentation du réel' just because he still remains 'lié au réel par la présence selon le corps'.[77]

At this level the work is seen to exist in its own space and time, structured in depth and volume. This structure the critic has to bring to light. He cannot follow out the mere chronological order of image or sensation, for the development of a poem is no causal sequence: he must be sensitive to relations that lie below the surface. Such a criticism discards the traditional techniques of sociological, biographical and mere psychological criticism. It takes the work as a fact, an existent, a 'world', that has no condition other than itself. As such it cannot be accounted for nor

[74] *L'Eau et les rêves*, Corti, 1947, p. 6.
[75] *Littérature et sensation*, Ed. du Seuil, 1954, p. 14.
[76] *La Poétique de l'espace*, Presses Univ., 1957, pp. 3, 4.
[77] M. Dufrenne, *Phénoménologie de l'expérience esthétique*, Presses Univ., 1953, vol. II, p. 658.

explained, for its explanation is itself. It is the embodiment of a set of meanings, and the critic's sole task is to uncover and describe them.

The significance of phenomenology lies in the return to the 'expérience originaire du monde' as the root of thinking. In France this involves something of a revolution, signifying a rupture with the Cartesian tradition of dualism on the one hand, of analysis on the other. It is not, however, unrelated to French tradition — the tradition of Diderot and Rousseau, of Maine de Biran and Valéry. Maine de Biran is particularly significant, as witnessed by the renewed interest in his thought since the 'thirties. Beneath his at first sight dualistic psychology lies a subtle appreciation of the organic link between consciousness and the body, and his *Anthropologie* anticipates the method and views of phenomenology in a remarkable way.[78]

Of French phenomenologists Marcel and Merleau-Ponty come closest to its essential aim. Sartre, while asserting that the self exists only in its relation to the world, is led into a position which seems to empty the assertion of its fundamental import. His statement that 'je suis celui que je serai sur le mode de ne l'être pas' is phenomenologically valid in so far as it formulates the negative structure of consciousness as described above. But he goes on to hypostatize this negative factor: there is for him an actual entity — 'le néant' — introduced by consciousness between itself and the given. Thus he argues that 'il n'y a jamais de motif *dans* la conscience: il n'en est que *pour* la conscience', and all phenomenologists would agree, since consciousness, taking the motive up into its intention, makes it other than it is. But Sartre goes on to assert that 'du fait même que le motif ne peut surgir que comme apparition, il se constitue lui-même comme

[78] What Maine de Biran's reflexive analysis distinguishes as 'le fait intime' of consciousness is causal effort experienced concretely as a relation between two terms, one the determination of the will, the other the bodily movement effected. These two terms are given together and simultaneously as 'un seul rapport à deux termes, dont l'un ne peut être isolé de l'autre sans changer de nature ou sans passer du concret à l'abstrait, du relatif à l'absolu'. (*Réponses à Stapfer*, in *Œuvres choisies*, Aubier, 1942, p. 236. Cf. p. 239.) It is this immediate relation, which through the body secures the insertion of the self in the world, that is the source of positive knowledge and the concrete origin of the concepts such as cause, self and time. Each of the two terms of the relation 'entre comme principe élémentaire dans toute connaissance réelle ou de fait, sans constituer par lui-même cette connaissance'. (*Rapports des sciences naturelles avec la psychologie*, Ibid., p. 188.) For it is only by their embodiment in the relation as inseparable and complementary terms that they together provide knowledge. Abstracted from it and considered as absolutes they are not the objects of positive knowledge but of 'indeterminate belief' (ibid.). Failure to see this leads to the rationalist and to the empiricist error respectively, the one starting from the subject, the other from the object as absolutes. And Biran observes in a manner that would be acceptable to any phenomenologist: 'Toutes les difficultés de la science viennent de ce que nous voulons toujours concevoir dans l'abstrait ce qui nous est donné primitivement et nécessairement en relation.' (Quoted by J. Wahl, *Tableau de la philosophie française*, Ed. Fontaine, 1946, p. 102.)

inefficace' and that there is a 'rien qui sépare le motif de la conscience', this rien being precisely man's freedom.[79]

Now Sartre can only make this inference because of his initial premise, namely that there is an absolute opposition between the en-soi and the pour-soi, as between what by definition is fully positive and fully coincident with itself, without any inherent possibility of discrimination, and what is characterized by negativity, relation and difference.[80] From the very outset, in fact, Sartre places a sense-originating self over against a world which is devoid of meaning and incapable of any effective contribution to the emergence of meaning. The world, other selves, the self's own past, are a wholly indeterminate and passive ground for the projects of the self's unconditioned freedom and for its choice of values 'ex nihilo'.[81]

For Marcel and Merleau-Ponty on the other hand the self is truly 'in the world'. The latter is already a reservoir of potential values and meanings: it is therefore already structured, although its structures are potentialities and await the sense-giving intention to be actualized.[82] Included in those potential values is all that is significant in the self's past; and although they do not determine, they constrain and solicit the self. So that its sense-giving activity is no mere unconditioned choice or negating of the past or of the world as given, but the product of 'call' and 'response', to employ Marcel's phrase. Self and world entertain a relation of complementarity and meanings emerge within this relation as between a sense-giving and a sense-revealing term. This is the process of recueillement described by Marcel whereby 'the reality, confronting which one ingathers oneself, itself becomes a factor in the ingathering' and where 'a man's given circumstances, when he becomes inwardly aware of them . . . become . . . constitutive of his new self'.[83] And it is in this light

---

[79] Op. cit., pp. 69, 71, 72.

[80] Sartre argues that the Néant being nothing cannot produce itself, nor can it come from the en-soi, which is wholly positive; it can therefore only come from consciousness (ibid., p. 129). But, if this is so, it is difficult to see how the en-soi can be even potentially structured or contain even a possibility of meaning.

[81] Op. cit., p. 70. Cf. p. 76.

[82] 'Le Dasein est lui-même spatial ou, plus exactement, spatialisant, mais il n'exerce cette spatialisation que parce que lui-même lié à un monde qui implique l'espace, non point l'espace organisé et structuré de notre vie courante, mais la possibilité d'une telle organisation.' (A. de Waelhens, La Philosophie de Martin Heidegger, Louvain, Ed. de l'Instit. Sup. de Phil., 1947, p. 63.)

[83] The Mystery of Being, I, pp. 126, 134. For Marcel's detailed criticism of Sartre's views, see Homo Viator, pp. 233 ff. Cf. also M. Farber, Aspects of Phenomenology and Existentialism from 1945–1948, in Philosophie, XIV, Psychologie, Phénoménologie et Existentialisme, Hermann, 1950, pp. 145–8. It may be added that Sartre's recent Critique de la raison dialectique (Gallimard, 1960) would appear to mark an effort to resolve his dilemma. 'Le lieu de notre expérience

that Merleau-Ponty criticizes Sartre in his *Les Aventures de la dialectique*, attributing his political errors and his rejection of the humanist tradition to the failure to recognize historicity or the organic structure of experience which links the self in a relation of reciprocity with the world, other selves and the past.

These criticisms are to the point. All that has been gained by phenomenology would be lost by the return to what might prove to be a subjectivism and dualism in a new guise. Phenomenology defines experience as a project towards the world, initiated from the world and emerging again into the world in the form of meaningful action, and so securing the persistence and renewal of pattern in time and history. If it puts the self at the centre as the agent of change, it recognizes that the self is at every moment actively informed by the world on the one hand and actively committed to it on the other. The subjective is the pole of a relation, in itself nothing:

> Le pôle subjectif n'est *rien*: c'est-à-dire qu'il n'"est' pas à la manière d'une chose, il n'est pas localisable, il n'est pas un être du monde. Il n'"est' que dans la mesure où il *existe*, et il n'existe ('ek-siste') qu'en se projetant vers: il n'est qu'en étant ailleurs, *hors-de-soi-dans-le-monde*; il est, si l'on veut, cette impossibilité d'être soi.[84]

Experience is no mere subjectivity. The phenomenon of consciousness is the embodiment of a sense which comes from the world, is actualized in the sense-giving intention and is projected back into the world as action. Everything significant takes place 'out of' the self, in a closely woven nexus of space and time which commits the self directly to the world and to other selves. Participation, intersubjectivity, organism, these are the key words of phenomenology. If the self can be defined, it is as a 'relation agissante'.[85] It can, says Marcel, be assigned no precise frontiers. It is the focal point of a transcendence, the unlocalizable medium for the revelation of meaning:

> L'univers est un ensemble de significations que tisse et retisse

critique n'est pas autre chose que l'identité fondamentale d'une vie singulière et de l'histoire humaine:' '... ma vie ... doit se découvrir elle-même au fond de son libre développement comme rigoureuse nécessité du processus historique pour se retrouver plus profondément encore comme la liberté de cette nécessité et enfin comme nécessité de la liberté.' (Ibid., pp. 156, 157.) But the development of the *Critique*, which takes the form of a marxist logic of history — 'une totalisation mouvante et dialectique qui n'est autre que l'histoire ou ... que le "devenir-monde-de-la-philosophie"' (pp. 29–30) — seems to bear little relation to the phenomenologically inspired content of *L'Etre et le néant*.

[84] Jeanson, *La Phénoménologie*, p. 75. Cf. G. Gusdorf, *La Découverte de soi*, Presses Univ., 1948, p. 503.

[85] J. Wahl, *Traité de métaphysique*, Payot, 1953, p. 256.

incessamment l'expérience humaine. Ce ne sont pas des significations que nous créerions en constituant le monde; le monde est avant nous. Quand notre conscience s'éveille, il est déjà là et nous sommes en lui. Mais il est inachevé et ambigu; et dans une interaction réciproque nous constituons avec lui un ensemble de significations, qui est la réalité et la rationalité mêmes.[86]

This is the key discovery of phenomenology. It requires us to go beyond the psychologism of traditional philosophy and to view the human product not as the product of the individual, solipsistic mind, but as an 'intramundane phenomenon', a 'manière d'être du monde', a mode of Being itself, brought into 'ex-sistence' through the self-world project.[87] It also asks us to view the product as a trans-subjective, preconceptual but already rational system of meanings which, by virtue of the play of intertwining intentions, the intersubjectivity of selves and the unitary ground, which is Being itself, contains generality and universality sufficient to establish valid and significant discourse. For the integration and embodiment of meanings offered by the world in the sense-giving intention is not only the typifying structure of all creative activity, it is the foundation of all comprehension or understanding, grasped at their cognitive root.[88]

Finally, phenomenology recognizes the fact of 'mystery'. Meanings and values are known only as embodied in the mediating intentions of selves and as modes of Being. Being itself, the source and ground, remains hidden. Yet this Being is present as the ultimate reference, the ultimate horizon of experience. Herein lies what Marcel calls 'the ontological mystery of knowledge'. Being is the 'opaque datum', what resists, in that it transcends all determinations of value and sense as their hidden but implicated source and ground. This is what renders the philosophy of values 'susceptible de se transcender elle-même et de pointer vers ce qui la dépasse infiniment' — towards the realm of 'silence' which lies beyond language in that 'la parole est issue de la plénitude du silence, et que celui-ci lui confère sa légitimation'.[89]

Hence phenomenology as ontology assumes the ambiguous form of both a descriptive science and a mystical search. A science in so far as it

[86] G. Madinier, *Conscience et signification*, Presses Univ., 1953, p. 34.
[87] Cf. A. de Waelhens, *La Philosophie de Martin Heidegger*, p. 50.
[88] 'On comprend l'être des choses lorsque celles-ci sont intégrées et pro-jetées à l'intérieur de nos possibilités propres. Les choses acquièrent un sens — le seul dont elles soient capables — en tant que matière de nos possibilités.' (Ibid., p. 269.)
[89] Marcel, *Les Hommes contre l'humain*, La Colombe, 1951, pp. 129-30; Idem, Preface to M. Picard, *Le Monde du silence*, Presses Univ., 1954, p. xii.

describes, without seeking to explain or justify, the structures of experience and the modes of Being therein embodied. A mystical search in that this science is never complete but points to an ultimate transcendence never possessed:

> Il s'agit de reconnaître la conscience elle-même comme projet du monde, destinée à un monde qu'elle n'embrasse ni ne possède, mais vers lequel elle ne cesse de se diriger.
>
> Que l'être soit toujours ce qui n'apparaît que par un étant et que nous ne puissions nous fixer directement sur lui, rend cet être exprimable seulement par un acte de visée capable lui-même de porter au-delà de ce qu'il désigne.[90]

There lie the limits of ontology as of language itself.[91]

Here again perhaps phenomenology comes close to certain contemporary analytical views inspired by Wittgenstein in recognizing that language comes up against certain opaque data.[92] Of such ultimates are values, inseparable from our experience of things. They are neither entities existing in an autonomous realm and open to some special intuition, nor observable properties of things, nor arbitrary creations of the subject. In a sense they seem to be all these — both in fact and independent of fact, as E. W. Hall has said.[93] All that we can truthfully assert is that they are a function of the structures incorporating subject and object in experience where — in the modes in which they appear — they are open to description. In themselves they remain ultimates.

This recognition of the 'unsayable' coupled with the assertion that philosophy is concerned with what can be said defines the ambiguous status of reflection as understood by phenomenology. It inspires the tension which underlies philosophical writing in France, torn between the description of existence or 'being-for-me' and the 'nostalgie de l'être,' of Being as ultimate ground, that inhabits all thinking.[94] Nor may it be

[90] Merleau-Ponty, op. cit., pp. xii–xiii; A. de Waelhens, *Existence et Signification*, p. 120.

[91] Cf. J. Wahl, *Vers la fin de l'ontologie: étude sur l'Introduction dans la métaphysique par Heidegger*, S.E.D.E.S., 1956, p. 257. Cf. also G. Madinier, *Vers une philosophie réflexive*, La Baconnière, 1960, pp. 65 ff.; E. Lévinas, *De l'existence à l'existant*, Ed. Fontaine, 1947, pp. 170–2.

[92] M. B. Foster notes that the initial cause of collision between religious philosophy and earlier analysis lay in 'the assumption that all thinking is an answer to our questions'. (*Mystery and Philosophy*, SCM Press, 1957, p. 27.)

[93] *What is Value?*, Routledge and Kegan Paul, 1952, pp. 247–9.

[94] 'Tout langage apparaît comme indépassable (et c'est en ce sens qu'il y a pour nous primat de la connaissance sur l'Etre) et pourtant comme, en soi, dépassé (et c'est en ce sens qu'il y a primat de l'Etre sur la connaissance).' (F. Alquié, *La Nostalgie de l'Etre*, Presses Univ., 1950, p. 136.)

too much to attribute in part to the pervasive influence of phenomenology a similar tension apparent in contemporary French literature, the *nouveau roman* and drama being cases in point. At the centre of both philosophy and literature is the awareness of the self's ante-predicative relationship with the world and of consciousness as an unending process of constituting meanings against a background from which they emerge and into which they retreat — like so many shifting presences, testifying to a reality that transcends language and discourse and yet legitimates them.

18

GEORGES POULET

Bachelard et la Critique Contemporaine

CE qui paraît le plus remarquable dans la critique contemporaine, c'est l'effort qu'elle fait pour se situer à l'intérieur de la conscience d'autrui, sans se laisser toutefois capturer par la fluide épaisseur d'images que secrète toute conscience et dont elle est difficilement séparable. Du Bos, Rivière, Raymond, Béguin sont semblables sur ce point. A n'en pas douter, pour eux, l'intériorisation critique ne s'accomplit dans les meilleures conditions possibles que si la pensée de l'auteur dont ils s'occupent n'est pas comme engloutie sous le flot des expériences sensibles, et que son contenu est réduit à un minimum. Non qu'aucun des critiques précédemment nommés aspire à atteindre, dans les régions raréfiées de l'intellectualité pure, cette perception de la conscience nue qui fut une des hantises de Valéry. Pour Du Bos, par exemple, la conscience à son point le plus haut s'ouvre d'elle-même à un influx de richesses spirituelles; et si Raymond rêve d'une conscience non intellectuelle, aussi rapprochée que possible de l'inconscient, c'est pour y trouver la plénitude d'un sentiment de soi qui ne remplit jamais si bien l'âme que lorsqu'elle s'est dépouillée de tout autre objet. En somme, pour la plupart des critiques de notre époque, la conscience d'autrui n'est jamais si saisissable et pénétrable, que lorsqu'elle est également éloignée de son vide originel et de l'encombrement que cause en elle la foule d'images et de perceptions qui y viennent tout obstruer. D'où, chez beaucoup de critiques, l'importance accordée à de certains moments privilégiés, extases, rêveries, surgissement du souvenir affectif, états paramnésiques, où la pensée se découvre non plongée dans le flot de ses expériences ordinaires, mais dans une demi-transparence qui la rend spacieuse et accueillante au regard, sans que d'autre part elle se trouve offusquée par un excès de clarté.

Seul peut-être, par chance et presque à tâtons, Jacques Rivière avait découvert dans la conscience d'autrui l'existence d'une zone périphérique mal définie, dont la matière, proprement sensuelle, se révélait aux attouchements. Mais, pour lui, cette région trouble et touffue, rencontrée

à la lisière de l'esprit, avait plutôt le caractère d'une barrière, d'un obstacle.
C'était ce à quoi la pensée critique se heurtait, ce en quoi elle risquait de
s'engluer, dans le mouvement quasi aveugle par lequel elle tentait d'atteindre, au delà, une zone de conscience moins impure.

Aussi est-ce le mérite exceptionnel de Gaston Bachelard d'avoir fondé
dans ces régions dont se détournaient plus ou moins tous les critiques, une
nouvelle prise de conscience et une nouvelle critique. Avant lui, au moins
pour toute la critique non psychanalytique (et non marxiste), la conscience
était la chose du monde la moins matérielle qui soit, et c'est dans cette
immatérialité qu'il fallait précisément la saisir. Mais à partir de Bachelard
il n'est plus possible de parler de l'immatérialité de la conscience, comme
il devient difficile de la percevoir autrement qu'à travers les couches
d'images qui s'y superposent. La révolution accomplie par Bachelard
est donc copernicienne. Après lui, le monde des consciences et, par
conséquent, celui de la poésie, de la littérature, ne sont plus les mêmes
qu'auparavant. Il est le plus grand explorateur de vie mentale depuis
Sigismond Freud. Mais le chemin qu'il a suivi est très différent de celui de
Freud.

Jamais un homme n'a commencé par tourner plus précisément le dos au
point où il a fini par aboutir. Bachelard commence en effet par l'intention
professée de 'renoncer à sa propre intellectualité'.[1] Entendez par là:
renoncer à ce qu'il y a de proprement subjectif dans l'intellectualité, faire
en sorte que celle-ci devienne radicalement objective. C'est le rêve d'un
homme de science, pour qui il importe avant tout de débarrasser les
vérités scientifiques de toutes les interprétations subjectivistes qui, malgré
la plus grande vigilance, viennent sans cesse en corrompre les significations.

Or, plus Bachelard analyse les propositions de la science, plus il y
découvre d'éléments subjectifs. Tout homme de science est incapable de
penser de façon rigoureusement scientifique. Sans cesse il introduit dans ses
conceptions abstraites quelque chose d'intime et de concret, qui est une
invention à lui. Aussi tout est-il ambigu dans la pensée. Et la grande affaire
c'est de démêler les deux éléments inextricablement fondus l'un dans
l'autre, qui sont la vérité scientifique et le mensonge humain.

L'entreprise de Bachelard se caractérise donc à ses débuts par une
intention essentiellement discriminative: séparons le vrai et le faux, l'objet
et le sujet, la science et la pseudo-science; et, pour cela, choisissons le seul
moyen possible: psychanalysons la connaissance objective, distinguons-en
les images obsédantes que subrepticement nous y avons glissées.

Bachelard distingue donc et sépare. Il le fait avec scrupule, avec génie.

[1] La formation de l'esprit scientifique, p. 248.

Or c'est ici qu'un événement inattendu survient. Par un mouvement de conversion qu'il a été sans doute le dernier à prévoir et contre lequel il lui est impossible de se prémunir, c'est le côté subjectif qui de plus en plus occupe Bachelard, absorbe son attention, et qui finalement le séduit. Et la raison en est simple. En séparant l'une de l'autre deux substances qui forment un composé quelconque, ce n'est pas seulement l'une que l'on isole, c'est toutes les deux. L'objectivité est épurée, mais la subjectivité l'est aussi. Voici que dépouillée de toutes les préoccupations scientifiques qui empêchaient d'en percevoir la splendeur, la vie subjective apparaît à celui même qui l'engendre, dans une profusion de richesses dont il se trouve ébloui :

> Toute l'Alchimie est traversée par une immense rêverie sexuelle, par une rêverie de richesse et de rajeunissement, par une rêverie de puissance [. . .][2]

Toute l'alchimie, toute la poésie, toute la vie imaginative des hommes ! Surprenons ici l'enthousiasme du savant conquis par sa conquête. Ce que Bachelard découvre, et découvre à l'intérieur de lui-même, c'est qu'il n'y a pas une activité mentale de l'homme qui ne se révèle comme le lieu d'une prodigieuse floraison d'images fondamentales, à travers lesquelles c'est l'homme, c'est le moi-sujet qui se réalise imaginativement.

Scientifiquement, objectivement, les images sont fausses, car elles subjectivisent le vrai. Subjectivement elles sont vraies, car elles révèlent le moi :

> [. . .] Les images sont, de notre point de vue des réalités psychiques. A sa naissance, en son essor, l'image est, en nous, le sujet du verbe imaginer. Elle n'est pas son complément. Le monde vient s'imaginer dans la rêverie humaine.[3]
>
> Toute substance intimement rêvée nous ramène à notre intimité inconsciente.[4]
>
> La manière dont nous *aimons* une substance, dont nous *vantons* sa qualité, décèle une réactivité de tout notre être. La qualité imaginée nous révèle nous-mêmes comme sujet qualifiant.[5]

Rêver le monde, c'est donc se rêver. Rêver le feu, l'eau, l'air, la terre, c'est rêveusement prendre conscience de soi dans l'identification que l'on fait de soi avec les grandes matérialités élémentaires. Ainsi, à travers la

---

[2] La psychanalyse du feu, p. 106.
[3] L'air et les songes, p. 22.
[4] La terre et les rêveries de la volonté, p. 333.
[5] La terre et les rêveries du repos, p. 81.

réinvention mythique de son univers, la pensée subjective se saisit elle-même, non dans quelque nudité initiale, mais dans toute la chaleur des images grâce auxquelles elle se donne vie, substance, et en qui elle se mire avec bonheur. L'acte de conscience bachelardien dépend donc des images, ou plutôt de la puissance imaginante qui les fait naître: 'Cogito du rêveur',[6] qui, à la différence du cogito du penseur (tel celui de Descartes), ne sépare pas irrémédiablement l'esprit de ses objets. Cogito allègrement optimiste, puisque se découvrir dans les images, c'est se découvrir dans un monde en quelque sorte créé par nous, à notre mesure, un monde qui nous enchante, parce que nous nous y reconnaissons et que nous nous y sentons à l'aise. Et l'acte critique par excellence est celui par lequel le critique rejoint l'auteur dans un mouvement d'admiration généreuse, où vibre un optimisme équivalent: 'lire en essayant de sympathiser avec la rêverie créatrice ...'[7] Comme le poète prend conscience de soi par la sympathie avec laquelle il s'adapte à son monde en l'imaginant, de même, par sa sympathie pour le poète, le critique réveille au fond de lui-même un monde d'images personnelles, grâce auxquelles il réalise son propre cogito: 'Nous communiquons avec l'écrivain parce que nous communiquons avec les images gardées au fond de nous-mêmes.'[8] Or, retrouver en soi, au fond de soi, grâce à l'intercession de l'écrivain, les images qui y sont ensevelies, ce n'est plus participer à la poésie d'autrui, c'est poétiser pour son propre compte. A son tour, la critique devient poésie. Bref, quand la pensée bachelardienne s'abandonne à son élan de sympathie, l'activité imaginative du critique vient se surajouter, pour s'y confondre, à l'activité imaginative du poète. Chez l'un et chez l'autre, c'est la même exaltation sympathisante, le même pouvoir de création des mythes. Le poète et le critique poursuivent parallèlement le même rêve.

Immense, foisonnante, gorgée des richesses qu'elle découvre, la critique de Bachelard n'a qu'un défaut, c'est que partout elle tend à retrouver la même abondance. Elle finit par attribuer à tout le monde un égal coefficient de génie poétique. Assez rapidement l'effort fait par Bachelard pour discriminer entre les imaginations et établir une classification de celles-ci selon les préférences personnelles qu'elles manifestent (préférences pour l'eau, le feu, l'air ou la terre), fait place chez lui à un effort inverse pour concevoir à l'aide de toutes les imaginations investigables une manière d'imaginer commune et qui constituerait un patrimoine de poésie générale. Chose frappante, l'objet de la recherche bachelardienne est si

---

[6] La poétique de la rêverie, chapitre II, passim.
[7] L'eau et les rêves, p. 70.
[8] La poétique de la rêverie, p. 168.

vaste et ses trouvailles si universelles, qu'il ne peut plus être question pour elle de se limiter à l'étude de cas particuliers, quelque originaux qu'ils puissent être. En un mot, cette critique, n'ayant plus qu'une fin qui est d'atteindre le fond poétique de toutes les existences, se révèle merveilleusement apte à atteindre *la* poésie, mais inapte à atteindre en leur spécificité *les* poésies.

INDEX

A., M(onsieur), 233, 236, 237
Adam, 3, 10
Adam, Antoine, 107
Æsop, 53, 55, 57–9, 62–3
Agravadain des Mares, 10
Air et les songes, L', 355
Alain, 51, 52, 58, 59, 65
Alembert, J. Le Rond d', 259
Alexander, I. W., 340, 341, 344
Allégret, Marc, 193 n. 12
Alquié, F., 350
Analytical Philosophy, 342, 343, 344
Anthony, A. W., 24 n.
Arbelet, Paul, 145
Arconville, Mme Thiroux d', 257, 263, 264, 269, 270
Aristotelianism, 18
Aristotle, 206
Arthur, King, 5, 8, 10, 12, 13, 14, 17, 18
Assézat, J., 254, 260, 260 n. 8, 263, 264, 265 n. 14
Audra, Abbé J., 274
Augustine, St., 3, 4
Austin, Lloyd J., 89
Aux Abonnés de l'Opéra (Beaumarchais), 122
Ayda, Adile, 89
Ayer, A. J., 342
Azur, Madame. *See* Rubempré

B., M(onsieur). *See* Trudaine, Daniel
Bach, J. S., 159
Bachelard, G., 344, 345, 353–7

Bähr, K., 167 n. 13
Baillot, A., 165, 166, 166 n. 7, 167, 167 n. 13, 174 n. 63, 175
Balzac, Honoré de, 112
Ban, King, 10, 11, 12
Bandy, W. T., 91
Banville, Théodore de, 94, 96, 104
Barbey d'Aurevilly, 91, 137
Barbier, A.-A., 254–8, 262, 266, 266 n. 15, 269, 269 n. 16
Barbier, Paul, fils, 253 n. 1
Bartholmess, C., 167, 168
Baudeau, Abbé N., 274
Baudelaire, Charles, 83, 84, 89–114, 216, 226
Baudouin IV, Count of Hainaut, 27
Bauër, Gérard, 118
Beaumarchais et ses Œuvres (Lintil-hac), 117
Beaumarchais par lui-même (Van Tieghem), 122
Béguin, A., 353
Beguines, writings of, 36, 38, 43, 46
Bénac, H., 264
Béranger, 146
Bereyter, Angelina, 149, 150
Berger, G., 327, 330
Bergson, H., 334, 340, 341, 344
Berlière, Dom Ursmer, 24, 29, 30 n.
Bernard, Jean-Marc, 192 n. 6
Bernard of Clairvaux, 24
Bernard, St., 34, 43, 47–8
Berthet, Antoine, 147
Berton, 151

359

LIST OF SUBSCRIBERS

Ahmad, Janet E.
Alexander, I. W.
Ashcroft, A. R.
Aspley, K. R.
Austin, J. L.
Bagley, Cynthia P.
Barbier, C. P.
Barr, C. Stuart
Barton, A. B.
Bate, Jane
Bax, P. M.
Bingham, E. D.
Bishop, Joan, M.
Bold, Elaine
Brebner, L.W.
Burton, G. N.
Calvert, F. Irene
Cammish, Nadine K.
Corbett, J. A.
Davison, Geneviève
Dixon, K.W.
Doyle, M.
Dryhurst, J.
Edwards, J. D.
Flannagan, Janet
Forster, D. J.
Fowler, K.
François, Nancy
Garratt, D. F.
Goddard, K. A.
Grenfell-Banks, H.
Gunson, R.
Hackett, C. A.
Hartley, Noreen
Harvey, Elisabeth A.
Hatfield, Mary E.
Hawley, Edith
Haworth, J.

Henderson, N. G.
Heslop, Harold William
Hiddleston, J. A.
Hine, Elizabeth
Hird, Joseph H.
Hodgson, J. M.
Hoyle, E.
Hurrell, David
Jackson, A. Basil
James, J.
Jarvis, M.
Jordan, Peter H.
Kelsey, E. M.
Keys, A. C.
Labroche, Christine
Laycock, B.
Lee, E. J.
Leeds Polyglot Society
Lees, Ellis C.
Longmuir, M.
Lough, J.
McClelland, Anne
McFarlane, I. D.
Mackay, C.
McKay, John
Modern Languages Faculty
   Library, Taylor Institution,
   Oxford
Morris, P. D.
Muir, Lynette R.
Nother, Zoë
Nuttall, Bernice
Otter, H. S.
Pamphilon, Janet M.
Reader, M.
Reid, T. B.W.
Robinson, Marjorie
Robinson, Mavis

St. David's College, Lampeter
Sayce, R. A.
Sewell, I. W.
Shackleton, Robert
Shaw, Marjorie
Shaw, Rosalind
Shearer, Ann M.
Short, J. P.
Smith, Jane Christine
Spence, N. C. W.
Stanley, Margaret A.
Stockwell, Joan
Sutcliffe, F. E.
Thody, Philip
University of Birmingham

University of Cape Town
University of Dundee
University of Leicester
University of Manchester
University of Nottingham
Ward, June
Wenninger, G.
Wetherill, P. M.
Whale, David F.
Williams, Alma
Williamson, Dr. and Mrs. M.
Wilson, Carolyn Kilday
Woledge, B.
Wood, Beryl K.
Wray, Hubert K.